SAINTS WHO MADE HISTORY

MAISIE WARD

SAINTS
WHO MADE HISTORY

The First Five Centuries

SHEED AND WARD, INC.
NEW YORK

INTRODUCTION

I N my schooldays, history was to me and most of my school-
fellows an immense weariness: kings of England, battles
and invasions, inventions and discoveries, meant chiefly
dates to be memorised. Geography, which should have been
"the eye of history", meant lists of exports and imports, rivers
and capital cities; like the dates, they had to be committed to
a memory which, gladly absorbing poetry, revolted bitterly
against these aridities. Church history meant lists too: of
heresies, this time, and general councils, the dates of the popes
and the barest outline of leading events.

Christopher Dawson once said that a people unaware of its
own past is like a man who has lost his memory. And this
applies as much to the Christian people as to any human
society. *1066 And All That* brilliantly satirizes the Englishman's
broken and confused knowledge of his country's story. The
picture most Christians have of Church history is as broken
and confused. Just as so many philosophers leap from Aristotle
to Descartes, Christians—Protestants and Catholics alike—tend
to leap from Pentecost to the Reformation and from the
Reformation to the present day. Believing in Christ and loving
Him is all that really matters to them: the history of the
Church, they feel, belongs to history, not to religion.

The position is changing. More people are realising that to
know the Faith we must study not only God but men too.
Church history is beginning to come into its own. Those who
want it "straight" are far better served today than when I
went to school at the beginning of the century. The period
that this book sketchily covers is dealt with brilliantly and
profoundly in the Church History edited by Fliche and Martin,
by Batiffol, most vividly of all in Duchesne's pioneer work,
more popularly by Mgr. Philip Hughes. If we want to look
at the Church from the outside, there are many valuable

books to widen perspectives. Some of the best of these are by no means new. Who would give Gibbon to a schoolgirl? Yet it was from this brilliant old cynic that I, in unconscious imitation of Newman, first glimpsed the wide sweep of history. It is a pity that Bury's corrective notes and Christopher Dawson's very useful introduction do not appear in the one edition.

But even with the most abundant supply of historical works, there remain people like myself to whom history becomes most alive, not only pictorially but in its depths, through the men who made it. This book tells of those who brought the early centuries of the Church to life for me.

To the first Christians it seemed that the coming of Christ, while it brought with it a new world, heralded also His return in glory not to be long delayed. They were in haste to convert mankind that all might be ready for His coming. They saw themselves as men upon whom "the ends of the earth are come". But God, says Newman, "works out gradually what He has determined absolutely", and "from the nature of the human mind *time is necessary* for the full comprehension and perfection of great ideas". Men's minds are God's instruments in this process: St. Paul is succeeded by St. Irenaeus, by St. Athanasius, and by St. Augustine; the meaning of each great doctrine is fought out in council after council; development is the law of life. Historical truth has been called "the daughter of time"; while this cannot be said of revealed truth, time is at least her nurse, in whose God-given care she grows and develops.

This is one side of Church history, but the Church is not only a system of ideas; she is a living organism. She must grow "to the measure of the age of the fulness of Christ", because she is Christ in the world. As He taught she teaches men, as He commanded she commands, as He prayed she prays, as He suffered she suffers, as He died and rose again so will she in her members, as He was lifted up on a cross so must she be. And in all her aspects, as truth-teller, ruler, ascetic, mystic, martyr, she acts—that is, Christ acts in her—through men. There must be a balance in her life: it makes no sense to set against religions of authority a religion of the spirit, for beneath

her authority the spirit works most mightily; no sense to seek
for truth where authority has been cast away, to look back, in
Newman's words, at a "fabulous early simplicity", when God
wants us to "repose in Catholic fulness". Time has done and
still is doing its office: God's Church is still working out
gradually the absolute and eternal decrees of God.

As Urs von Balthasar has shown in his study of the theology
of history, holiness through the Christ-life in the Church takes
more glorious forms than the world has ever seen; but sin
becomes far worse, far more horrifying. The closeness of God
to man, the distance of man from God, both reach their climax
in the Church: the conquest of Babylon *in us* is the supreme
task of grace.

This element of evil inside the Church—of the difficult and
necessary conquest of Babylon in each of us—was for long
almost ignored by the Catholic historian. The lessons of history
are of small value if the history itself is distorted. And my
generation was brought up on Church histories, French or
English, whose silences amounted to falsification. Fear of
giving scandal today excused suppression of scandals of the
past. But their suppression meant the absence of any teaching
as to how they could be reconciled with the continued presence
of Christ in the Church. It might be well to recall occasionally
the names of some of the most distinguished ex-pupils of
Catholic schools—Voltaire, Renan, James Joyce. Leo XIII
spoke magnificently on the duty of historical candour but, as
so often with papal pronouncements, many years passed before
his words prevailed widely. More than half a century has
given the Pope's words time to sink in; most Catholic historians
today are frank about the blots on the human face of God's
Church. But there is one field in which reticence is still observed.

Theologically we know that the saints fell in Adam as we did,
that many of them had fearful struggles on their path to sanctity
—did not, perhaps, reach their goal till near the end. But there
is a strong tendency to omit or soften in their story anything
that witnesses to this struggle, anything that is puzzling,
"disedifying", or even too colourful. I have a feeling that if
St. Augustine had not written the story of his own youth it
would have reached us in a much weakened version.

St. Ambrose's curious behaviour when—still unbaptised—

he was asked to be Bishop of Milan, although related by his own secretary, is omitted in most Catholic histories. We are told in detail the splendid story of Ambrose putting to penance the great Emperor Theodosius for the massacre at Thessalonica, but it is to the Protestant Kingsley that most of us owe a tardy realisation of St. Cyril's failure to condemn to penance his own *parabolani* who had murdered Hypatia. St. Cyprian's remarks about Pope St. Stephen's "arrogant claims, irrelevancies and inconsistencies", St. Jerome's abusiveness—he describes St. Ambrose as "an ugly crow" who had "decked himself out in peacock's feathers", Rufinus as a "hydra-headed monster"— the colourful details of the quarrel between St. Leo the Great and St. Hilary of Arles, are often played down. St. Bernard of Clairvaux said of William of York that he was "rotten from the crown of his head to the soles of his feet"—but William was canonised too.

It is more realistic as well as more encouraging to discover the real humanity of the saints. Like us they quarrelled, like us they made immense mistakes; but unlike ours, their lives were as a whole given to God's service, their energies directed rightly, love of God driving out the love of self. The approach of the edifying historian was too negative; he attempted the impossible task of painting human faces without shadows— which is what Queen Elizabeth demanded of her portrait painter. And when the paintings were finished nobody wanted to look at them. They were altogether too much like statuary manufactured by the gross.

When Christ was carrying His cross He did not look much like a King, He did not look like God—small wonder that heresy said first that the suffering and death were illusion, and next that the Godhead was not there. Having chosen a human nature, Christ, in suffering and in dying, followed the logic of His choice; having chosen a Church of men He has done the same. His was a perfect human nature, ours most imperfect; in His He must save the world through pain in body and soul —"My soul is sorrowful even unto death"; in ours He must save the world through men who not only suffer but who also sin.

This truth, that not the saints alone but we sinners too are Christ working in the world, seems, as we reflect on it, almost the most mysterious of the mysteries. It has needed much safe-

guarding: that a sinful priest can give God's life through sacraments, that a sinful pope can give His truth in infallible definitions, while a saint who is not a priest or a pope can do neither
—these truths have been attacked as fiercely as the true manhood of Christ. Yet also we are never allowed to let go the
importance of intellect in the Church, the far greater importance of sanctity. Very few popes have been Doctors of the
Church, none has been placed on a level with Augustine or
Aquinas. Only those popes who were also saints live on in their
feast days, have Masses celebrated in their honour.

That thinking described by Newman—"many minds working freely together"—has preceded all the Church's great
definitions. Origen, St. Cyprian, St. Basil, all made mistakes,
but the truth, when defined, would have been less rich, less
complete without their thinking. Men being men, fallible
thought must precede and prepare infallible definition and
must again go forward from it. And meanwhile this same
Church, thinking and defining, must be teaching the nations
as Christ bade her, must be healing as He healed, must be
clothing the naked, harbouring the homeless, visiting the sick
and opening prison doors. In all the greatest periods of her
history these works of mercy have been as visible as the ferment
of the divine leaven of thought in the minds of her thinkers.
And for the most part in thought and teaching as well as in
suffering and prayer, the saints are pre-eminent.

This book is not a Church history, but a handful of portraits
to illuminate it. From the death of St. John to the fall of the
Babylon seen by him in its hour of triumph, the growth in the
Mystical Body was immense, the development many-sided and
balanced. It is an intensely dramatic period; truth is fighting
error, goodness fighting evil, creation battling with chaos, the
Empire crumbling, the Church emerging as the new soul of
civilisation.

And whether it be in the development of doctrine, in the
service of sick humanity, in heroic suffering or even in splendour
of speech and the drama of human greatness, it is above all
through the saints that the work of Christ in the Church is
accomplished.

NOTE. For reading this book both in manuscript and proof, and for advice about my own reading, I wish to thank most warmly Christopher Dawson and Edward Watkin. Conversations with them have been most illuminating and the book would have been very different without their help. There can be no end to reading on this period and I am well aware how inadequate mine has been. The books I have found most useful will appear in the text as well as in the bibliography. Quotations from letters and sermons of the Fathers I have occasionally translated from Latin or from the excellent French versions now appearing, but when an English translation is available this is given in the bibliography. With quotations involving nothing controversial I have not always thought it necessary to give detailed references. For scholars these pages contain nothing new, but I hope they may be useful to amateurs like myself.

CONTENTS

xi

I: THE AGE OF THE MARTYRS

St. Ignatius and St. Polycarp

THE spirit of man created in God's image is, like Him, creative. But by how tenuous a thread this divine prerogative is held. Destruction lies around the little island of human effort; we visit today the cities of antiquity and all is ruins. In his *Footsteps of St. Paul* H. V. Morton draws a vivid picture of Philippi, "desolate in the plain, its white bones shining wherever ten feet of soil have been removed", Tarsus, its aqueducts destroyed, its river silted up, marshes where once a splendid port welcomed the traveller; Ephesus a big stagnant pool, little chips of white marble, and the waterlogged remains of a temple once greater than the Parthenon; Cenchrae, Antioch, Salamis, all destroyed.

Much of this has come from sheer neglect: water must be brought for man's drinking, it must be held back from man's undoing; roads and buildings must be repaired and rebuilt. Much of this irreparable loss came from sheer indifference when the Turks possessed, without appreciating them, the splendours of Greece and Rome. But war works destruction faster than neglect or time, and the destruction of Jerusalem, forty years after Christ's death, came suddenly while the great cities of classical culture still shone in all their splendour.

Most Jews then hated Christianity as one of the destructive forces threatening their very existence. In Palestine the small body of Jewish Christians had split into two. The Ebionites held that Our Lord was the child of Joseph, made the Christ by God because of His devotion to the Law. The Nazarenes were doctrinally orthodox, but, clinging to the observance of circumcision and other Jewish customs, were increasingly separated from the vast world the Church was conquering. The

Epistle to the Hebrews appears, in its references to Jewish worship, to have been written before the Temple was destroyed; but we gain from it a poignant realisation of the loneliness of the Christian Jew living in isolation among his own race, of whose conversion there was now but little hope, yet to whom he yearningly belonged.

Yet we must beware of thinking of the early Christian Church in the terms of our classical parents and grandparents. The Gospels first came to us in Greek but there is a strong Semitic basis to them all and Matthew was originally written in Aramaic. The majority of the first converts were Orientals; but Greek was the official language of the Empire: the first post-Bible Christian writings are chiefly in Greek because Arab and Copt, Jew, Syrian, African and Roman could all in some degree understand it. Translations were made of Scripture and liturgy for the sake of the unlettered, but Greek was basic for two hundred years in both East and West. No Christian writer of any importance wrote in Latin before Tertullian.

The Church's "first great leap" had carried her into the pagan world;[1] for many years one of the chief struggles would be against attempts to get rid of the Old Testament, either by plain repudiation or by carrying the idea of allegorical and mystical interpretation so far that the literal sense was entirely abandoned. Yet too Ignatius of Antioch complained of Judaisers among his flock, and the Jewish Ebionites—the first heretics to deny Christ's Godhead—were followed by many others. Christians had always to be reminded both of their Jewish origin, and that the Law brought nothing to perfection; as St. Paul had told them, it was the bringing in of a better hope, now fulfilled in Christ. The Church had made her leap just in time to be free from the shackles of the Synagogue, not too late to take with her an understanding of the Prophets.

Before the end of the first century, Peter's third successor Clement was established at the heart of the Roman Empire, and Rome had replaced Jerusalem as the centre of unity and the seat of authority. The last Apostle was dead, the last book of Scripture written. There would be no new Scriptures, and

---

[1] See *Jew and Greek*, by Dom Gregory Dix, and *Histoire de la littérature grecque chrétienne*, by Aimé Puech.

no attempt was ever made to create new Apostles: the Church
realised from the first that an Apostle was one who had known
Christ and had been a witness to His earthly life. The choice
of Matthias was governed by this condition. The risen Christ
Himself chose the one exception, Paul. The *episcopoi*, first
mentioned in the New Testament, were by now territorial and
not itinerant. The epistles of Ignatius may be called intensely
episcopal; reading them side by side with the letter to Corinth
from Clement of Rome gives us a real vision of the early Church
in all its elements.

The sub-apostolic age is also called especially the Age of
the Martyrs. This period is not the high point of persecution,
but martyrdom as an ideal is its primary note. By it Christ's
passion is made manifest to the world and always in the light
of His resurrection. He strengthens His witnesses and turns
the tragedy of death into triumph.

> And I heard as it were the voice of a great multitude, and
> as the voice of many waters, and as the voice of great
> thunders, saying: Alleluia; for the Lord our God the Al-
> mighty hath reigned. Let us be glad and rejoice and give
> glory to Him: for the marriage of the Lamb is come, and
> His wife hath prepared herself. And it is granted to her that
> she should clothe herself with fine linen glittering and white.
> For the fine linen is the good deeds of the saints.
> And he said to me: Write: Blessed are they that are called
> to the marriage supper of the Lamb. (Apoc. xix. 6–9.)

The *Bible de Jérusalem* gives us a fascinating picture of the
Apocalypse as history—prophetic and apocalyptic—reflecting
the era of persecution through which the Church was passing
against the background of the eternal judgements of God and
the glory of His heaven. Intensely Jewish in inspiration, it
uses the language of Isaiah, Ezechiel, Daniel, to depict both
triumph and catastrophe. "And the stars from heaven fell
upon the earth, as the fig-tree casteth its green figs when it is
shaken by a great wind. And the heaven departed as a book
folded up: and every mountain, and the islands were moved
out of their places." And the kings of the earth and the
princes cried to the mountains and rocks to fall upon them

and hide them "from the face of Him that sitteth upon the throne and from the wrath of the Lamb".

Part of our difficulty in understanding this tremendous book arises from its use of symbols well-known to St. John's readers, to which we have lost the clue, part from its quality at once cosmic and in the narrower sense historical. Written almost certainly during the persecution of Domitian, it applies to the torments and triumph of the Church through the ages—to Hitler or Stalin as well as to Nero or Domitian. Age after age, pagan empires are sent forth by Satan as a flood to overwhelm the Church of God. The multitude of those who have washed their robes in the blood of the Lamb and for Him have shed their own blood is the *ingens multitudo* of martyred Christians spoken of by Tacitus, who were led by Peter and Paul, and to whom are added a vaster multitude as the ages pass.

St. Ignatius

To the age of the Apostolic Fathers Our Lord's parable of the mustard seed must have appeared already wonderfully fulfilled. Clement writes from Rome to Corinth; Ignatius travels to Rome for his martyrdom, meeting Polycarp at Smyrna, receiving deputations from the Churches through which his route did not carry him; there is tremendous growth in organisation and stability as well as territorial expansion, there is the enthusiasm which made it an age of martyrs. Peter and Paul were so pre-eminently leaders and teachers that their martyrdom appeared far less important than their lives; but the earliest Apostolic Father of the East was first and foremost a martyr. Ignatius was for the growing Church what Stephen had been in its beginnings. His letter to the Christians of Rome, begging them not to save his life, became a kind of martyrs' manual, echoed later by Polycarp, by Felicity and Perpetua, and eagerly studied by men and women who, like the great Origen, made martyrdom the main romance of this early age in the Church's history. Later was to come enthusiasm for the ascetic life, for learning; even, at the time of the Crusades, for fighting; but in these first centuries martyrdom was primary. It was a sharing in Christ's passion and thereby in His redemptive work.

"The days of real faith," says Origen, "were the days when there were many martyrs, the days when we used to take the martyrs' bodies to the cemeteries and come back and hold our assemblies . . . Christians saw amazing sights and wonders then." And again: the martyr "despoils the principalities and powers with Christ and triumphs with Him, because he shares in His sufferings and in the victories springing from them. That is what crushed the devil's power . . . The evil spirits are well aware of the blessings martyrdom brings to Christians; they dread it so much that they strive to slow down persecution."

The martyrs were the first saints in the Church's calendar, their relics alone were set in the altars. And Ignatius was, for the East especially, the chief of martyrs. His letters have in them an enthusiasm which contrasts interestingly with St. Clement's. Bishop Lightfoot has spoken of Clement's "intensity of moderation" and Ignatius's "intensity of passion". Behind Clement we see the balance and power of Roman thought and civilisation, behind Ignatius the more complex world of Eastern Christianity.

It is strange that his name—Ignatius or Egnatius—should be an old Italian one rather than Syriac or Greek. We know nothing of his early life save slight indications that he was a convert. He speaks of himself three times as the last in the Church of Antioch, as unworthy to have a place among them; he uses St. Paul's expression concerning his spiritual birth, calling himself an "abortion". Even translated as this commonly is, "one born out of due time", it would seem, to quote Bishop Lightfoot again, to indicate "something violent, dangerous and unusual in his spiritual nativity".

Made Bishop of Antioch, he lived through the persecution of Domitian and the brief peace that followed it. The very earliest tradition speaks of him as "an Apostolic man", meaning a man ordained by an Apostle. Theodoret claims that he "received the grace of the high priesthood at the hands of the great Peter", whose successor at Antioch he was. Between their bishoprics, according to Eusebius, came that of Evodius, of whom we know nothing but the name. Another widespread tradition makes Ignatius a pupil, with Papias and Polycarp, of St. John. All of this is possible by dates; what is not possible is the later tradition that his second name Theophorus was given him as the child Our Lord set in the midst of His disciples, whom He embraced, saying: "Whosoever shall receive one such child in my name receiveth me." (Mark ix. 36.)

Ignatius must have been born not earlier than A.D. 40; most authorities think as late as 50 or 60. The date of his martyrdom was probably within a few years either way of 110. Trajan (98–117) was one of the "good" Roman emperors; his persecution of the Christians was based on his determination to protect the Empire. It was severe only in Bithynia, but outside that province two outstanding men were put to death— Simeon, Bishop of Jerusalem, and Ignatius. Simeon suffered on the double accusation of being descendant of David and a Christian bishop. He had led the Christians to Pella at the time of Titus, and had led them back to the ruins of Jerusalem. Fear of another insurrection was always present to Rome, and the Christian hope was often couched in terms of a kingdom. Add Jewish animosity, and we can almost see the pattern of Christ's condemnation repeated in His aged cousin.

The correspondence between Pliny and Trajan illuminates the Bithynian persecution—for we learn that what Trajan feared supremely was any sort of assembly. He refused Pliny's petition to form a fire brigade of 100 to 150 men. Even brought together for this useful purpose they might well, he said, form their assembling into something anti-imperial. And Christians did indeed, Pliny told him, meet early in the morning, though for no evil ends, and sing hymns to Christ as to a God.

Judaism and Christianity were by now clearly separated; Judaism was one of the countless religions permitted by Roman Law, Christianity was not. Trajan approved Pliny's method— not to seek Christians out, but, if they were denounced, to test them by asking them to offer incense to the Emperor, to abjure Christ. If they would not do this the law must take its course and they must die.

There are two accounts (both late) of the martyrdom of Ignatius, one setting the trial in Antioch, the other in Rome. But the seven letters recognised as authentic show that he was certainly taken to Rome and there died. We do not know how the journey started; probably by ship—for Ignatius speaks of travelling "by land and sea". (*Rom.*, v.) In the centre of

Asia Minor, near the junction of the Lycus and the Maeander, the road from East to West divides, the northern branch running through Philadelphia and Sardis to Smyrna. By this road Ignatius travelled, as we learn from his letter to the Church of Philadelphia. He does not mention Sardis, but at Smyrna he was cordially welcomed by Polycarp, the bishop, and received deputations from cities on the southern route. The Bishop of Ephesus came in person. "You heard," writes Ignatius to the community, "that I was on my way from Syria in bonds for the sake of the common Name and hope, and was hoping through your prayers to succeed in fighting with wild beasts at Rome... I have received your whole multitude in the person of Onesimus, whose love passes utterance ... Blessed is He that granted to you, according to your deserving, to have such a bishop."

From Magnesia too came its bishop. We are reminded of St. Paul and Timothy as we read the letter to the Magnesians: "It becomes you not to presume on the youth of your bishop, but according to the power of God the Father to render him all reverence, even as I learned that the holy presbyters also have not taken advantage of his outwardly youthful state, but give place to him as to one prudent in God; yet not to him but to the Father of Jesus Christ, even to the Bishop of all . . ."

Tralles was further away and from it came the bishop only, but "so greatly did he rejoice with me in my bonds in Jesus Christ, that in him I beheld the whole multitude of you".

If his relations with his fellow Christians remind us of St. Paul, it is far otherwise in the circumstances of Ignatius's journey. Both men were prisoners. But Paul was travelling as an appellant to Caesar, Ignatius as a condemned man; Paul was a Roman citizen, Ignatius was not, or he could not have been destined for wild beasts in the amphitheatre. Paul was treated courteously by the centurion in charge, but of the maniple of soldiers guarding him Ignatius says: "From Syria even unto Rome I fight with wild beasts, by land and sea, by night and day being bound amidst ten leopards, I mean a company of soldiers, who only grow worse when they are amiably treated." (*Rom.*, v.)

Not to complain does he write to Rome, but to entreat his brothers there that they will not try to save him from his

martyrdom. "I dread your very love lest it do me an injury. . . .
For if you are silent and let me alone I am a word of God;
but if you desire me in the flesh, then shall I be again a mere
cry. Grant me that I be poured out a libation to God, while
there is still an altar ready. . . . I am God's wheat and I am
ground by the teeth of the wild beasts that I may be found
pure bread."

They halted again at Troas. Here St. Paul had seen the
vision of a man beseeching him: "Pass over into Macedonia
and help us." Ignatius too was now passing from Asia into
Europe. He wrote from Troas to the Churches he had so
lately visited. He had not been entirely satisfied with Philadelphia—some were making divisions. "Be careful", he
exhorts them, "to observe one Eucharist (for there is one
flesh of Our Lord Jesus Christ and one cup unto union with
His blood; there is one altar as there is one bishop, together
with the presbytery and the deacons my fellow servants),
that whatsoever you do, you may do it after God." (*Phil.*, iv.)

In all his letters Ignatius stresses and summarises Christian
doctrine with the clarity of an Athanasius. The two immediate
dangers were Judaising and Docetism—a curious heresy which
denied the reality of Our Lord's manhood.

"The priests", Ignatius tells the Judaisers, "were good, but
better is the High Priest to whom is committed the Holy of
Holies; for to Him alone are committed the hidden things of
God; He Himself being the Door of the Father, through which
Abraham and Isaac and Jacob enter in, and the Prophets
and the Apostles and the whole Church; all these things
combine in the unity of God. But the Gospel has a singular
pre-eminence in the advent of the Saviour, even Our Lord
Jesus Christ, and His passion and resurrection. For the
beloved Prophets in their preachings pointed to Him; but the
Gospel is the completion of immortality." (*Phil.*, ix.)

And to the Docetists, who did not believe in the reality of
Christ's body, he cries: "He suffered all these things for
our sakes; and He suffered truly, as also He raised Himself
truly. . . . For I know and believe that He was in the flesh even
after the Resurrection and when He came to Peter and his
company He said to them: 'Lay hold and handle me, and see
that I am not a spirit without body.' And straightway they

touched Him and they believed, being joined unto His flesh and blood. Wherefore also they despised death, nay they were found superior to death. And after His resurrection He ate and drank with them as one in the flesh, though spiritually He was united to the Father . . . I endure all things seeing that He Himself enables me, who is perfect Man." (*Smyr.*, ii-iv.)

The Docetists, says Ignatius, "have no concern for love, none for the widow, the orphan, the afflicted, the prisoner, the hungry, the thirsty. They stay away from Eucharist and prayers because they do not admit that the Eucharist is the flesh of our Saviour Jesus Christ, that flesh which suffered for our sins and which the Father of His goodness has raised up. Thus those who deny the gift of God find death in their contending. Let them rather love that they may rise again". (*Smyr.*, vii.)

To the faithful he cries out, "You all break the one bread— the medicine of immortality, the antidote preserving us from death and making us certain of life everlasting in Jesus Christ." (*Eph.*, xx. 2.)

Again and again he calls Christ "Son of man and Son of God"; the Eucharist is "His flesh", "His passion invites us, who are His members. Now it cannot be that a head should be found without members, seeing that God promises union, and this union is Himself." (*Rom.*, ii.) "There is one only physician, of flesh and of spirit, generate and ingenerate, God in man, true life in death, Son of Mary and Son of God, first passible and then impassible, Jesus Christ Our Lord." (*Eph.*, vii.)

From Troas Ignatius wrote also to Polycarp: "In all things I am devoted to you—I and my bonds which you cherished."

At first sight this letter seems surprising: for, while praising and loving him, Ignatius also criticises or at least suggests, "Be more diligent than you are. Mark the seasons." "Let meetings be held more frequently." And then we realise—this is an older bishop writing to a younger one, a man on the verge of his passion advising one who has many years yet to prepare for his. Because Polycarp lived to be so old, we forget that he too had once been young.

The age known as sub-apostolic goes on longer in the East than in the West, because of the great age to which three men lived: St. John, Simeon and Polycarp. Polycarp especially, though not the oldest of the three, is the chief link with the Apostles. For he had been St. John's disciple.

With his letter to Polycarp Ignatius passes into silence. He had asked his friend to convey messages to various Churches since, by the will of God, the departure from Troas had been suddenly put forward. The Philippians asked Polycarp to send them copies of Ignatius's letters to the other Churches—and to this fact we owe perhaps their preservation, certainly their authentication. In his reply Polycarp begs them to let him know of any certain news of Ignatius. He was not even aware whether the passion of his friend had been consummated.

We know no details of this martyr's death, except that he, like countless others, was butchered to make a Roman holiday. At his journey's end, Ignatius was thrown to the wild beasts in the amphitheatre.

ST. POLYCARP

It is difficult to assess with any kind of certainty the degree of persecution under a given emperor. The Empire was so scattered, the communications so uncertain, that in one place Christians might be praising the name of an emperor while his proconsuls were persecuting vigorously in another. Nor was it always by his desire; laws existed and the man on the spot might, like Pliny, write to Rome for orders or might act on his own initiative. "By what a slender thread of accident", says Lightfoot, is the record of the persecution in Bithynia preserved—and he notes that while Vespasian is praised by almost all Christian writers, Hilary of Poitiers ranks him with Nero and Decius. On the other hand Melito exempts Trajan and Antoninus Pius, not knowing apparently of the Bithynian persecution under the one, or of that in Smyrna under the other. Earlier historians have often depicted the emperors according to very incomplete information, nor can we be certain that we have the full picture even today.

Yet it can, I think, be said that the scene in which the life of the Church was set shifted a little with the death of Trajan. Hadrian (117–38), who succeeded him, is an enigmatic and entertaining figure "half sceptic, half devotee, a scoffer and a mystic by turns"; Lightfoot describes him as "this paradox of humanity". And he quotes Spartian's *Hadrian*: "Idem severus, laetus, comis, gravis, lascivus, cunctator, tenax, liberalis, simulator, saevus, clemens, et semper in omnibus varius."[1] But Hadrian has spoken himself and we have only to open a school-book of our youth to read the address to his own soul of this surprising emperor, who stands in the midst of such very different men as Trajan, Antoninus Pius and Marcus Aurelius.

Animula vagula, blandula
Hospes comesque corporis,
Quae nunc abibis in loca
Pallidula, rigida, nudula;
Nec, ut soles, dabis jocos.[2]

Lightfoot surmises that Hadrian would have viewed Christianity "with mingled respect and amusement . . . he was just the man to have offered a place to Christ in his pantheon if there were any chance of his offer being accepted".[3] And, very significantly, it is in this reign that for the first time Christian apologists attempted to address arguments to the Emperor. There is only one recorded martyrdom—Pope Telesphorus'—and Hadrian did his best to mitigate the anti-Christian laws by introducing severe punishments for false informations. His reign of twenty-one years was a fairly long peace for the Church: nor was Antoninus Pius (138–61), who succeeded him, a persecuting emperor, compared with Marcus Aurelius (161–80), who came next.

Yet we hear of more martyrdoms under Antoninus than under Hadrian, and the difference arose partly from a change that was passing over the spirit of the people. The age of the

---

[1] One man—grim, gay and friendly, serious and playful, slow to move yet tenacious, liberal and deceitful, savage and merciful—always in all things incalculable.

[2] Little soul, restless, eager to please,
Guest of the body and comrade,
Soon to depart for other regions,
Dim, bleak, bare;
Even there will your jesting cease?
(But in English one cannot reproduce all the diminutives.)

[3] *The Apostolic Fathers*, pt. ii, vol. i, p. 441.

Antonines marked a real pagan revival with efforts at pro-
paganda running parallel with those of Christianity—and with
a success marked by the building of temples and the increase
of religious festivals. "The contrast between the elder and the
younger Pliny," says Lightfoot, "marks the transition. The
avowed disbelief of the uncle is replaced by the religious
activity of the nephew." The mood of scepticism which had
possessed the educated classes was changing, and the change
brought opportunity for the Church.

But a peril was arising too. Rome was friendly to the religions
of all her subject peoples, and Hadrian in his tours of the
Empire was to be found seeking initiation into mysteries and
building temples to this or that god, while also officiating as
Pontifex Maximus of the Roman rites. But the cultus of the
Emperor himself was growing rapidly. Augustus had been
proclaimed a god after his death, and this honour was not
for him alone. Nerva, Trajan, Hadrian, had all been thus
deified, and Antoninus, now reigning, would be a god in his
turn. Dead emperors mattered little. Unhappily the cultus of
the living Emperor was growing too, and was to become a
test of loyalty for Christians.

The growth was most notable in Asia. It was there that the
startling phrase had been used of Augustus in his lifetime:
"The birth of the god was for the world the beginning of the
good news."

By the time of the Antonines, emperor-worship had made
great headway—and the people of Smyrna were prominent
in it, mingling the Emperor with Rome itself in their worship.
Coins and inscriptions have been found to the God-Emperor
and the Goddess Rome. They had several temples of the
Augusti and boasted of being the first city to dedicate a shrine
to Rome. A corporation called the Commune Asiae had
charge of this cult, and its festivals were held with outstanding
splendour at Smyrna. Twice during Polycarp's bishopric
Rome bestowed new honours and privileges on Smyrna in
connection with this worship, and the great festival at which
his martyrdom took place was probably that of the Commune
Asiae.

Jewish hostility, of which Christians had been from the
beginning the object, was increased by one element in Hadrian's

policy. In the second great Jewish revolt, under Bar Cochba, the Christian Jews would take no part, and had in consequence been very savagely treated by their compatriots. Hadrian, erecting on the site of the Holy City a new Roman town, Aelia Capitolina, allowed Christians to reside there, but after the revolt forbade it utterly to Jews. Asia Minor already teemed with Jews from the older dispersions: the abortive revolts under Titus and Hadrian added greatly to their numbers— and the new arrivals were especially bitter. The Bishop of Smyrna was to experience Jewish hatred. Probably he helped to draw it upon himself by the vehemence of his speech. St. John had called the Jews of Smyrna the synagogue of Satan, and the disciple copied his master.

Polycarp's name is one of a series borne by slaves and legend relates that he received the Faith as a boy slave in a Christian family. But the light of history is thrown on Polycarp only at three points: in youth as disciple of St. John; in middle life as Bishop of Smyrna, host of Ignatius, and visitor to Rome; in old age as teacher of Irenaeus. Irenaeus links Polycarp's youth and his age in a letter to the heretical Florinus (quoted by Eusebius): "I can tell", he says, "the very place in which the blessed Polycarp used to sit when he discoursed, and his goings-out and his comings-in, and his manner of life and his personal appearance, and the discourses which he held before the people and how he would describe his intercourse with John and with the rest of those who had seen the Lord, and how he would relate their words."

Rebuking Florinus for the heresies into which he had fallen, Irenaeus reminds him of the great experience they had shared as disciples of Polycarp, and recalls their master's fashions of speech and gesture: "I can testify in the sight of God that if that blessed and apostolic elder had heard anything of this kind, he would have cried out, and stopped his ears, and would have said after his wont, 'O good God, for what times hast thou kept me, that I should endure these things', and would have fled from the very place where he was sitting or standing when he heard such words."

It is to Polycarp, via Irenaeus and Eusebius, that we owe the story of St. John leaving the baths when Cerinthus the heretic entered them, saying, "Let us flee, lest the roof should fall in, for Cerinthus the enemy of truth is in it." And when the arch-heretic Marcion claimed recognition from him, Polycarp answered: "I recognise the first-born of Satan." There was nothing mild in the reaction to heresy either of the beloved disciple or of Polycarp the Elder. Heresies were swarming around the cradle of Revelation and they had a sacred duty as its guardians. In the early Church the bishop was *the* teacher: as bishop, Polycarp would teach by pastoral sermons to his flock and by opposing all false teaching—the poisonous herb of heresy, as Ignatius called it. They were not anathematising men brought up in error but men who were fabricating and teaching it to others. "Polycarp saw teacher after teacher spring up, each introducing some fresh system, and each professing to teach the true Gospel. Menander, Cerinthus, Carpocrates, Basilides, Cerdon, Valentinus, Marcion—all these flourished during his lifetime, and all taught after he had grown up to manhood."[1]

In Rome, Polycarp was troubled by another question relatively unimportant, but destined to agitate the Church for many years—that of the date at which Easter should be kept. Polycarp had received one tradition from St. John, Pope Anicetus another from St. Peter. Neither of the two saints could persuade the other to change, but the Pope testified his love and veneration for Polycarp by yielding to him the celebration of the Eucharist in Rome, and, adds Eusebius, "they parted from each other in peace, for the peace of the whole Church was kept both by those who observed and by those who did not". (*Hist. Eccles.*, v, 24.)

The disciple of John, ordained bishop by him: we repeat these phrases glibly enough, but perhaps without realising all that they must have meant to Polycarp. How ardently he must have studied John's Gospel, and the letter to his own Church of Smyrna in the Apocalypse; he himself may well have been the "angel" of whom John speaks:

To the Angel of the Church of Smyrna write: These things saith the First and the Last, who was dead and is alive: I know thy tribulation and thy poverty, but thou art rich: and thou art blasphemed by them that say they are Jews

[1] Lightfoot, *Apostolic Fathers*, pt. ii, vol. i, p. 458.

and are not, but are the synagogue of Satan. Fear none of these things which thou shalt suffer. Behold the devil will cast some of you into prison that you may be tried: and you shall have tribulation ten days. Be thou faithful unto death and I will give thee the crown of life." (Apoc. ii. 8–10.)

In the year 155 a great festival was being held at Smyrna: persecution was on foot and victims for the wild beasts would add quite a feature to the celebrations. The proconsul was present but the Asiarch Philip presided in virtue of his office.

The story is told in a circular letter from the Church of Smyrna to the Church of Philomelium "and to all the brother-hoods of the holy and universal Church sojourning in every place". Concerned chiefly with Polycarp himself, it tells of other heroic martyrdoms, of "nobleness and patient endurance and loyalty to the Master". One man only "when he saw the wild beasts turned coward . . . He it was who had forced himself and some others to come forward of their own free will . . . That is why, brethren, we do not praise those who deliver themselves up, since the Gospel does not so teach us."

Another, Germanicus, encouraged his companions and "fought with the wild beasts in a signal way". Sometimes this would have roused the spectators' admiration; but today their mood was bad and we are told that "all the multitude, marvelling at the bravery of the God-beloved and God-fearing people of the Christians, raised a cry, 'Away with the atheists; let search be made for Polycarp.'"

The search was not a long one: he had consented to leave the city for a nearby farm where he stayed "doing nothing else night and day but praying for all men and for the Churches throughout the world; for this was his constant habit". Falling into a trance, he saw his pillow burning and "said to those that were with him: 'It must needs be that I shall be burned alive.'"

A member of his own household guided the police to his second hiding-place,

. . . and though he might have departed thence to another place, he would not, saying, "The will of God be done." So when he heard that they were come, he went down and

conversed with them, the bystanders marvelling at his age
and his constancy, and wondering how there should be so
much eagerness for the apprehension of an old man like him.
Thereupon forthwith he gave orders that a table should be
spread for them to eat and drink at that hour, as much as
they desired. And he persuaded them to grant him an
hour that he might pray unmolested; and on their consenting, he stood up and prayed, being so full of the grace of
God, that for two hours he could not hold his peace, and
those that heard were amazed, and many repented that they
had come against such a venerable old man.

But when at length he brought his prayer to an end, after
remembering all who at any time had come in his way,
small and great, high and low, and all the Catholic Church
throughout the world, the hour of departure being come,
they . . . brought him into the city, it being a high sabbath.
(*Smyr.*, vii, viii.)

There followed, twice, the misunderstanding inevitable
between the best sort of pagan and the Christian he is trying
to help. First, the head of the police, Herod, and his father
Nicetes, later the proconsul, tried to persuade Polycarp that
there *could* be no harm in casting a few grains of incense on a
flame in honour of the Emperor, and thereby saving his life.
For some of them it was the merest convention; and even
those for whom it had a meaning could not see for the life
of them why Christians need take it so seriously. A man's
spiritual integrity had no relation with this conventional
gesture. The often violent rejection of their well-meant intervention indicated nothing to the pagans but madness. So
Herod felt, and made the obstinate Polycarp get out of the
carriage so hurriedly that the old man bruised his shin.

The proconsul did his best, urging him to take the oath "by
the genius of Caesar", and to say "Away with the atheists"
(so Christians were called for rejecting the gods):

Then Polycarp, with solemn countenance, looked upon
the whole multitude of lawless heathen that were in the
stadium, and waved his hand to them; and groaning and
looking up to heaven he said, "Away with the atheists."

But when the magistrate pressed him hard and said, "Swear the oath, and I will release you; revile the Christ", Polycarp said, "Fourscore and six years have I been His servant, and He has done me no wrong. How then can I blaspheme my King who saved me?" (*Smyr.*, ix.)

The crowd was filled with the blood-lust of the amphitheatre: they had seen deaths enough to thirst for more. When the proconsul sent his herald to proclaim three times in the midst of the stadium "Polycarp is a Christian", "the whole multitude both of Gentiles and Jews which dwelt in Smyrna cried out with ungovernable wrath. There were loud shouts: 'This is the teacher of Asia, the Father of the Christians, the puller-down of our gods.'" With loud yells they demanded of the Asiarch Philip that he let loose a lion on Polycarp. Again the ruler was kinder than the multitude, for "he said it was not lawful for him since he had brought the sports to a close".

They then "with one accord" shouted a demand that Polycarp should be burnt. Proconsul and Asiarch both disappear from the story at this point, there remains only a raging mob who, "quicker than words can tell", gathered a pile of wood from the workshops and the public baths. They wanted to nail him to the stake but Polycarp said, "Leave me as I am; for He that hath granted me to endure the fire will grant me also to remain at the pyre unmoved."

The fire was lit—"a mighty flame", but those who stood by saw it part "like the sail of a vessel filled by the wind . . . round about the body of the martyr". Finally the executioner had to stab him with a dagger, and his own blood "extinguished the fire". The Christians tried to recover the body but the Jews prevented them, representing to the magistrate that they might begin to worship Polycarp instead of Christ. ". . . not knowing," says the narrator, "that it will be impossible for us either to forsake at any time the Christ who suffered for the salvation of the whole world of those that are saved—suffered though faultless for sinners—nor to worship any other. For Him, being the Son of God, we adore, but the martyrs as disciples and imitators of the Lord we cherish as they deserve for their matchless affection towards their own King and

Teacher. May it be our lot also to be found partakers and fellow-disciples with them."

The story ends on this note of exultation. The body was burnt indeed but "we afterwards took up his bones, more valuable than precious stones and finer than refined gold, and laid them in a suitable place". The brethren of Polycarp would joyfully keep his birthday near these holy bones, thus honouring all those who had triumphed in the contest, and preparing themselves, who would still have to endure.

Irenaeus in Rome, awaiting news from his friend, "on the very day and hour when Polycarp was martyred in Smyrna, heard a voice as of a trumpet saying 'Polycarp is martyred'."

Polycarp an old man, Felicity a young mother, Agnes a mere child, the long procession of youths and girls, men and women in the prime of life, priests, bishops, popes—as time went on every Church had its martyrology, and although the Middle Ages did some curious feats of multiplication (as with St. Ursula and her eleven thousand virgins) the multitude of witnesses was great enough to startle the pagan world. But to what were they witnessing?

St. Paul had long ago answered the question—the witness of Christianity was to Jesus Christ crucified and risen from the dead. Christianity is a knowledge of His life and teaching, from which is born love. Christ said to His Apostles, "Go ye and teach", and official teachers are mentioned in the earliest Christian documents—by Clement of Rome before the first century was ended, in the *Didache*, in the *Shepherd of Hermas*. These teachers were the clergy and more specifically the bishops. Before the Gospels were put into his hands the neophyte would have learnt a great part of them in the catechesis—that scheme of Christ's life and teaching underlying them, which Matthew and Peter had witnessed and heard, which Mark so often listened to as Peter repeated it. Perhaps he had never seen the Old Testament, but in the liturgy of the Church he learnt the Psalms, and heard how his Lord had "risen again according to the Scriptures". The Christian Church faithfully handed on those writings, and pointed to Christ found in them through type and prophecy.

As well as being martyrs, Ignatius and Polycarp were Apostolic Fathers, and their writings, together with those of

Clement, give us the best picture of the Church as yet hardly out of the Apostolic era. Clement, says Irenaeus, "not only had seen the blessed Apostles, but had also conferred with them and had their preaching still ringing in his ears, their tradition still before his eyes". Clement wrote before, Ignatius just after, St. John had written his Gospel. Polycarp had known John. With the Gospels, says Père Lebreton, we are in the Holy of Holies; with the Epistles, in the Temple; with these Fathers we are still standing on its steps.

LITURGY

To anyone living in a later age, one impression is overwhelmingly strong. The life of the Church and of her children is made up of many elements: Scripture, theology, liturgy, mysticism, social service. All these things have their specialists; we go to different books, we choose different teachers, not for the subjects only but often for sub-sections of them. Then, too, as a result of controversy and apologetic, we examine unity almost in terms of division: there is authority, there is obedience, there are spheres presbyteral, episcopal, papal.

Looking at the early Church one is reminded in contrast of the story of Creation. The light was made first: later came sun, moon and stars, the greater and the lesser lights each illuminating in its own order. Here in the early Church we seem to have almost undivided light: Scripture, liturgy, doctrine, prayer and life are intermingled. Sun, moon and stars are beautiful but it feels good to linger sometimes in the radiance of that light without trying to turn it even into stars. Streaming from the altar in heaven where John saw the Lamb standing as it were slain, it is reflected supremely at the altar on earth where His sacrifice is re-presented. Worship is the heart of Christian life.

The liturgy had from the first a definite shape, although its content varied. There were readings from the Old Testament, especially from the prophetical books where the coming of Christ is shadowed forth. There were readings from the books later to be called the New Testament—and from some later excluded from the Canon, such as the Epistle of Clement. The Psalms had become Christian prayers. There was improvised prayer, but improvised on traditional themes and within the

traditional framework. Besides the Psalms, the prayers of the
New Testament were there as models: supremely the *Our
Father*, but also the *Magnificat*, the *Benedictus*. The Eucharist
was instituted at a sacred feast and for a long time it remained
connected with, at first embedded in, the *agape* or love feast.
There was an immense amount of intercessory prayer.
"Christians," says the *Epistle to Diognetus*, "are in the world
what the soul is in the body. . . . This is the high rank to which
God has appointed them; and it is not permitted to seek
exemption." The Good Friday prayers in our missal today
remind us of this all-embracing intercessory prayer, daily Mass
with its mementoes of living and dead keeps it before us.
Clement, Ignatius, Polycarp, interceded not at the Altar only
but writing a letter, waiting to be arrested, bound to the stake.
All these prayers are intensely liturgical. Our Lord in His
supreme cry from the Cross used a psalm which foretold His
death, and which He had often spoken in His worship. His
followers also found on their lips, in life and in death, the words
with which they adored God, and prayed for men in the
liturgy. Life was wholly one to these early Christians. "We
do not speak great things; we act them," says Minucius Felix.
To "liturgize" meant, in Greek, to "do their service", and
this service was not for Sundays only but for every day and hour.
  Christians, Pliny told Trajan, came together early in the
morning and sang hymns to Christ as to a god. The *Gloria in
Excelsis*, in its primitive form, was the morning hymn. The
evening hymn, still used by the Greek Orthodox, begins,
"Blest Jesus Christ, Light of the heavenly Father's eternal
glory", and ends, "Son of God who givest us life: therefore
the world proclaims Thy glory." But although there was
prayer direct to Christ, more commonly it was directed
through Christ the High Priest to His Father. Baptism was the
initiation into Life—"Let none eat or drink of this Eucharist
of yours except those who have been baptised into the name
of the Lord." But this name was that of the Holy Trinity—
"baptise in the name of the Father and of the Son and of the
Holy Ghost". There was a threefold immersion; but if there
was not water enough it was to be poured "on the head thrice
in the name of the Father and the Son and the Holy Spirit".
(*Did.*, vii.)

The evening prayer says, "We sing the Father, the Son and the holy Spirit of God"; and St. Justin says, "For all that we receive, we bless the Maker of all things through His Son Jesus Christ and through the Holy Spirit." The earliest creeds are far shorter than those that follow, but in West and East baptismal creeds of the late second century open alike, "I believe in the Father Almighty and in Jesus Christ His only Son Our Lord, and in the Holy Spirit."

Later on questions arose which must be answered by the magnificent definitions of Athanasius and Leo. Later on, necessity would impose a long and searching catechumenate, reverence would introduce a discipline of the secret. But the earlier attitude, though no less intellectual than that of the great post-Nicene Fathers, was through circumstances less polemical, one might almost say, more contemplative. The words of Athenagoras belong to every age of the Church's life, and not least to these first centuries. "We who know that our present life is short . . . are absorbed by the one longing to know the true God and His Word . . . the Spirit, the Son and the Father."

II: THE AGE OF THE APOLOGISTS

St. Justin Martyr, Clement, Origen

PREACHERS of the Faith are apt either to proclaim its glory by bitter attacks on "man-made" religions in which they can see no good, or to find it even more glorious as the fulfilment of man's aspirations and the crown and completion of all true thinking and living. The Church had quite a struggle to save the Old Testament itself from minds of the former type, but there was of course a much stronger case when it came to denouncing the pagan world with its welter of gods and superstitions. "The gods of the heathens are devils" was often enough a statement literally true; and it has taken centuries for a close study of comparative religions to sort out the yearnings towards truth deep hidden under the darkest-seeming worship.

The Christian apologists' chief concern with paganism was with the philosophers. The first Christians were mostly simple men, but the Faith was also a profound philosophy. It could meet all the great schools of men, and, having defeated them where they were wrong, could, in Newman's language, "divide the spoils" after conquest, taking to itself the true elements, rejecting the false in every system.

There is no such thing, says Newman, as the blank mind which some men urge as the ideal state for the reception of truth. "The mind can never resemble a blank paper, in its freedom from impressions and prejudices . . . he who believes a little, but encompasses that little with the inventions of men, is undeniably in a better condition than he who blots out from his mind both the human inventions, and that portion of truth that was concealed in them."[1]

For there is truth in every system of religion and philosophy,

[1] *Arians of the Fourth Century*, p. 85.

and one teaching of the early Apologists was what Newman called the divinity of Traditionary Religion.

Revelation, properly speaking, is a universal, not a local gift; and the distinction between the state of the Israelites formerly and Christians now, and that of the heathen, is, not that we can, and they cannot, attain to future blessedness, but that the Church of God ever has had, and the rest of mankind never have had, authoritative documents of truth, and appointed channels of communication with Him. The Word and the Sacraments are the characteristic of the elect people of God; but all men have had more or less the guidance of Tradition, in addition to those internal notions of right and wrong which the Spirit has put into the heart of each individual.

This vague and uncertain family of religious truths, originally from God, but sojourning without the sanction of miracles, or a definite home, as pilgrims up and down the world, and discernible and separable from the corrupt legends with which they are mixed, by the spiritual mind alone, may be called the *Dispensation of Paganism*.[1]

St. Justin Martyr

The words "dispensation of paganism" are quoted from Clement of Alexandria, but the idea is found first in Justin Martyr, who defended the Faith in Rome and there died for it.

St. Justin was a Palestinian, born in Flavia Neapolis, now Nablus—the ancient Sichem—and he speaks of himself as uncircumcised. In his *Dialogue with the Jew Trypho* he tells of learning philosophy first from a Stoic, whom he left because the man could tell him nothing of God; next from a Peripatetic, who proved himself no philosopher by demanding a fee; then a Pythagorean, who insisted that his pupil should learn music, astronomy and geometry before he could enter upon philosophy. Justin's last master was a Platonist in whose teaching he took a keen delight. And then one day he met a mysterious old man who told him the soul could not attain divine knowledge by a merely human road but only from the prophets who

[1] Newman, *Arians*, pp. 80–1.

were inspired by the Holy Ghost. The scene in which the
Dialogue is placed is not Rome but Ephesus. "The literary
setting," says Lebreton, "lacks neither probability nor life,
the chance meetings under the porticoes, the groups of curious
onlookers who stop awhile and then disperse during the interviews, offer a vivid picture of such extemporary conferences."
But Puech calls it "a pale reflexion of the art of Plato".

The *Apology*, with its supplement known as the *Second
Apology*, is more concerned with the moral beauty of
Christianity, the *Dialogue* with its truth. Both these had won
Justin, and, even if his account of his various schoolmasters
is a little contrived so that he may develop in turn the inadequacy
of each pagan school, it is clear he had a grasp of their various
tenets. And again he shows anxiety to point to the ideas of
Stoic or Platonist which are true as far as they go, but can only
reach their completion in the full truth of Christianity. "Call
it folly if you will," he says of his faith, "but do not condemn
men to death as enemies, who have done no evil."

He believed that Greek philosophy owed much to the Bible—
that Plato and the others had borrowed from Moses. But
although, like all the Apologists, he sought a foothold in the
pagan or Jewish mind through the truths they already held, he
did not believe that philosophy was for the pagan a really
serious thing, affecting life and leading to action. Before his
conversion the old man had said to him, "Thou art a friend
of discourse but not of action or of truth."

Justin is far the best known in the earliest group of Apologists
—so called from the word *apologia*, which of course did not
mean an apology for, but a defence and explanation of, the
Christian faith. The Apologists mostly taught and argued at
the height of persecution: they were so excited about the good
news that they must spread it, even at the risk of failure and
death. And part of this news was that death itself had been
overcome by life.

The really surprising thing is the dedications of their writing.
Quadratus wrote an *Apologia* addressed to Hadrian, Aristides
one to Antoninus, Justin to Antoninus and his two adopted
sons; Athenagoras to Marcus Aurelius and Commodus. The
reasons for this were probably mixed. Although Christians
stood aloof from emperor-worship and refused the tribute of

incense that expressed it, they did sincerely believe the imperial power to be God-given. St. Peter had ordered obedience when the ruler was Nero. "We render worship to God alone," says Justin, "but in all other things we gladly obey you, acknowledge you as kings and rulers of the earth, and pray that in you the royal power may be found combined with wisdom and prudence." (*Apol. I*, xvii.)

All power was in the Emperor's hands—it was logical to appeal to him if there were the faintest hope that he would listen. This hope Justin at least seems certainly to have had, and it was not wholly unreasonable in the case of Antoninus Pius and Marcus Aurelius. They might have been open to the belief that Christians were not atheists but believers in one supreme God—above all, that Christians, as lovers of the whole world, were likely to be good citizens of the Roman Empire. What might be called this plea of character occurs again and again. It had played a part in Justin's own conversion; the author of the *Epistle to Diognetus* stresses it; so does Athenagoras. Later Minucius Felix wrote: *Non magna loquimur sed vivimus*. The *Shepherd of Hermas* gives us to understand that Christians did not always live up to their ideals, but by and large the stress laid on their charity, unselfish generosity and heroism was fully justified by the facts. Christian lives turned pagans into Christians and this all the more from reaction. For behind the emperors was a mass of uninformed opinion in which the wildest fables were current about this new sect: that they killed and ate a baby at their assemblies, that they indulged in incest and unnatural vices (their addressing one another as "Brother" and "Sister" was highly suspicious), that they worshipped the head of an ass. The sudden discovery of the reality of the Christian people excited the converts. We all know the saying, *Poeta nascitur non fit*. But Tertullian said, *Fiunt non nascuntur Christiani*—"Christians are made, not born".

Justin is a witness in a twofold sense, for it was the sight of the martyrs that first opened his own mind to the falsity of what he had heard concerning Christians. "When I was a disciple of Plato," he says, "hearing the accusations made against the Christians and seeing them intrepid in the face of death and of all that men fear, I said to myself that it was impossible that they should be living in evil and in the love of pleasure."

What man ever died for Socrates as they were dying for Christ? Pagans, in persecuting Christians, were persecuting a name only; neither atheists nor criminals, Christians led in fact lives of singular purity—their charity was wonderful, they practised forgiveness of enemies and endeavoured to help them. They worshipped the true God. The heroes of paganism— Perseus, Hermes, Aesculapius and the rest—paled in comparison with Christ, whom the Prophets had foretold and to whom philosophy witnessed. Philosophy was Christianity before Christ. It was for the pagans what the Law was for the Jews, a pedagogue to lead them to the true teacher: Stoics believed in a "seminal word", Christ was indeed the word of God.

"Christ is the First-Born of God . . . the Logos ["Word" or "Reason"], of whom all mankind have a share, and those who lived according to reason are Christians. . . . For example, among Greeks, Socrates and Heraclitus, among non-Greeks, Abraham, Ananias, Azarias, and Misael, and Elias and many others." (*Apol. I*, xlvi.)

Plato, the Stoics, the poets and prose authors, "each through his share in the divine generative Logos spoke well, seeing what was akin to it . . . Thus, whatever has been spoken aright by any men belongs to us Christians . . . For all those writers were able, through the seed of the Logos implanted in them, to see reality darkly". (*Apol. II*, xiii.)

More surprising than this appeal to philosophy is what has been called "the earliest example of Christian symbolism", whereby Justin makes another kind of appeal to the rulers of the world. The cross of the criminal, the cross of the Christian, is also a figure wrought into the very pattern of things.

Think for a moment, and ask yourself if the business of the world could be carried on without the figure of the cross. The sea cannot be crossed unless the sign of victory—the mast—remains unharmed. Without it there is no ploughing; neither diggers nor mechanics can do their work without tools of this shape. The human figure is distinguished from that of brute beasts solely by having an upright posture and the ability to extend the arms and also by the nose, through which the creature gets his breath, which is set at right angles to the brow, and displays just the shape of the cross. (*Apol. I*, lv.)

The very standards of the army, the ensigns and trophy-poles, are cruciform; emperors, after death, are depicted in "such a figure" and called gods in the inscription.

From the cross Justin takes his imperial masters into the sanctuary of the Christian mysteries. He tells how, after prayer and fasting for the forgiveness of their sins, the neophytes are brought "to a place where there is water where they are regenerated in the same way as we were . . . in the name of God the Father and Lord of all, and of Our Saviour Jesus Christ, and of the Holy Spirit".

There follows an account of the Eucharist of which only those can partake who believe in the teaching and "have received the washing for the remission of sins and for regeneration—we do not receive these gifts as ordinary food and drink. But as Jesus our Saviour was made flesh through the Word of God and took flesh and blood for our salvation, in the same way the food over which thanksgiving has been offered through the word of prayer which we have from Him—the food by which our blood and flesh are nourished through its transformation—is, we are taught, the flesh and blood of Jesus who was made flesh". (*Apol. I.*, lxvi.)

In Rome Justin opened a school of higher studies in Christian theology. He called himself a philosopher and as such argued with the philosophers of paganism, especially Crescens the Cynic. Eusebius says he dressed like (or perhaps the phrase means "stood like") a philosopher.

We learn one fact of great importance about Justin's school from the Acts of his martyrdom. With him died a group of his disciples, all slaves or poor men, several of whom had come to him, not as pagans to learn the beginnings of their faith, but as Christians to deepen and enlarge their understanding of it. "Was it Justin that made you Christians?" asked the prefect. Hierax replied, "I was already a Christian and I shall remain one"; Peon, "We received this noble profession of faith from our parents"; Evelpistus, "I listened with joy to Justin's teaching but I also learnt to be a Christian from my parents."

Although the school never reached the stature of the famous one at Alexandria, it was carried on after Justin's death by Tatian. Rhodon succeeded Tatian after he had become a Marcionite, and attacked his heretical ideas.

Justin taught and disputed with full consciousness of the end that almost certainly awaited him. "I, too," he wrote, "expect to be persecuted and to be crucified by some of those I have named or by Crescens, that friend of noise and ostentation." Eusebius, apparently on the evidence of these words, says that Crescens was indeed the cause of Justin's death. Ironically enough, this took place under the philosopher Marcus Aurelius. It may be that the Emperor felt he could not go counter to the law—but one wonders if he would have cared. Had he read the *Apology*, did he know of Justin's school? And would he have protected a philosopher who blazed out a message of divine hope while he himself was satisfied with the contemplation of his own excellence?

The prefect Rusticus tried and condemned Justin together with his pupils—Chariton, Charito (a woman), Evelpistus, Hierax, Peon, Liberianus—about the year 165, and the authentic account of the trial remains to us.

Justin was given a brief opportunity to declare his faith and made full use of it. "The true teaching", he said, "which we Christians devoutly follow is faith in the one God, Creator of all things visible and invisible, and in the Lord Jesus Christ, God's Son, foretold by the Prophets as the Messenger of salvation for the human race, and the Master of faithful disciples. I who am only a man cannot speak adequately of His infinite divinity: I should need prophetic power, but the Prophets have indeed proclaimed the coming of Him who is, as I have told you, the Son of God."

Rusticus, instead of answering Justin, continued to question him and the others. Finally, addressing Justin, he said: "Listen you, who are esteemed eloquent and whose claim it is to know the truth, suppose I have you flogged and then beheaded, do you believe that will get you to heaven?" "I hope", Justin answered, "to receive the reward if I suffer what you promise. For I know those who have so lived will win God's favour everlastingly." "You do imagine, then," said Rusticus, "that you will go up to heaven to receive rewards?" "I do not imagine it. I know it with fullest assurance."

RUSTICUS: "Approach and sacrifice, all of you, to the gods."

JUSTIN: "No one in his right mind gives up piety for impiety."

RUSTICUS: "If you do not obey you will be tortured without mercy."

JUSTIN: "That is our desire, to be tortured for Our Lord Jesus Christ and so to be saved, for that will give us salvation and firm confidence at the more terrible universal tribunal of Our Lord and Saviour."

ALL THE MARTYRS: "Do as you will, for we are Christians and do not sacrifice to idols."

The prefect Rusticus read the sentence: "Those who will not sacrifice to the gods and obey the Emperor will be scourged and beheaded according to the laws."

The holy martyrs, glorifying God, betook themselves to the customary place, where they were beheaded and consummated their martyrdom confessing their Saviour[1].

CLEMENT OF ALEXANDRIA

"When the Jewish Patriarch comes to Alexandria he finds himself obliged to adore Christ and Serapis; those who call themselves Christian bishops are at the same time devotees of Serapis."

Thus ironically did Hadrian describe the eclectic quality of this brilliant city. And it is not surprising that here, even more than in Rome, the Christian effort at penetrating the pagan mind should have issued in a Christian school, side by side with those of paganism and Judaism though far less richly endowed. St. Jerome claims that the school went back to St. Mark. This tradition is hardly to be relied upon, and it is only from the end of the second century that we begin to know the names of its heads: Pantaenus, Clement, Origen, Heraclas, Alexander, and the rest, covering the third century; in the fourth only Didymus the Blind, and Rhodon, who takes us to the beginning of the fifth. These heads were often the sole teachers in the school; yet the tradition of Alexandria, both pagan and Jewish, demanded an encyclopædic teaching, a "universal" knowledge —more nearly possible then than at a later date, but still

---

[1] Père Lebreton holds these *Acta* to be certainly authentic. See the *Catholic Encyclopaedia*, article "Justin".

improbable enough and perhaps only approached in the person
of Origen.

Clement is attractive for the non-specialist reader, interested
in people and their historical setting. He becomes in his books
so very much alive, with the pagan world that shaped him
and the transformation wrought by the Faith. Origen belongs
to the exegetes, the philosophers, the theologians, who have torn
him apart and put him together again over the centuries. There
have been no combative schools of thought claiming Clement,
or destroying men out of hate of him, as there have been with
Origen. Clement seems much more one of ourselves, yet able
to lead us into a deeper knowledge and love.

Alexandria was a town seething with intellectual activity,
where Jew and Greek did in fact come closer in mind than in
any other city. Here the Old Testament had been translated
into Greek, here Philo had tried to wed Jewish and Grecian
thought. "The wisdom of the Egyptians" can be traced in the
Sapiential Books of Scripture—called Apocrypha in the King
James Bible but received by the Catholic Church as part of
God's inspired word. Newman notes that at Alexandria,
though not in the neighbouring Church of Jerusalem, these
books were given to the catechumen as part of his instruction.
The introduction to Proverbs in the *Bible de Jérusalem* points
out how the wisdom of two Arabian sages and the maxims of
the Egyptian Amenemope have been mingled with the sayings
of Solomon so skilfully that the originality of the Jewish thinker
is in no way impaired.

So must it be with Christian thought. Nowhere more than
in Alexandria was it urgent that the Church should win
men capable of dealing with the strong intellectual forces
surrounding them. One of the earliest of her conquests was
Clement. Like Justin, he speaks of the teachers under whose
influence he successively came. Unlike Justin's, they were a
series of Christian teachers. Although known as "of Alexandria", Clement was probably born in Athens (date uncertain; he died about 215). He is a witness to the Church's
growing mark of Catholicity, as he journeyed from place to
place in search of deeper knowledge. His first instructor was a
Greek of Ionia, next came one of Magna Graecia, then one

of Coelo-Syria. After that he approached an Egyptian, next an Assyrian, and then a converted Jew of Palestine. Last of all, "concealed in Egypt", he "tracked out the first in power" and with him, he says, "found rest".

The schools of Christian philosophy in Rome and Alexandria are passionately interesting, and they show in the early ages of the Church a vigorous lay element, not discouraged by authority but not dominated by it. Some of these lay philosophers became priests, others, like Justin, remained laymen; of others, including Pantaenus, we know too little to be certain. Each Christian philosopher came to the work as a result of a conversion and with the conviction of a personal mission. The idea already existed in paganism of a conversion to philosophy. This meant to a life as well as to a manner of thinking. From Diognetus, says Marcus Aurelius, he had learnt to "become intimate with philosophy . . . and to have desired a plank bed and skin, and whatever else of the kind belongs to the Grecian discipline".

The Christian philosopher would have been ashamed to be outdone by the pagan—his was a severer discipline as well as a deeper philosophy. But he admired and yearned after his pagan friends: Clement, like Justin, believed that God had for them a "dispensation" manifested in certain true ideas. "As the proclamation [of Christianity] has come now at the fit time, so also at the fit time were the Law and the Prophets given to the barbarians, and philosophy to the Greeks to prepare their ears for the Gospel."

Greek philosophy was, Clement insisted, from God. "And should anyone say that it was through human understanding that philosophy was discovered by the Greeks, still I find the Scriptures saying that understanding is sent by God."

Again he writes—and this quotation was dear to Newman, who inserted the words printed in parentheses: "His are all men, some actually knowing Him, others not as yet: some as friends (Christians), others as faithful servants (Jews), others as simply servants (heathen) . . . He it is who gives to the Greeks their philosophy by His ministering Angels . . . for He is the Saviour not of these or those but of all . . . His precepts, both the former and the latter, are drawn forth from one fount . . . now at length by His own personal coming, He has closed the course of unbelief, which is henceforth inexcusable; Greek and barbarian being led forward by a separate process to that perfection which is through faith." And again: "The Hellenic. philosophy is like the torch of a wick which men kindle, artificially stealing the light from the sun. But on the proclamation of the Word all that holy light shone forth."

But to bring men to this light, to this perfection, men must use, not neglect, what God has already given them. Of his own work in this respect he says in a bold simile, "Few are those who have taken the spoils of the Egyptians and made of them the furniture of the Tabernacle."

Ordained priest at some period of his life (exactly when we do not know), Clement taught in Alexandria until the persecution of 202. He and his school became special objects of pursuit. He escaped to Caesarea in Cappadocia where the bishop, Alexander, was one of his former pupils. Here too he met the persecution and when, in 212 or 213, Alexander was thrown into prison, Clement took care of the Church in his stead, consoled the faithful and made converts. Alexander told this to the Church at Antioch, in a letter which Clement, being known to them, was charged to deliver. But, in a letter to Origen in 215, Alexander speaks of Clement as of one then dead. Did he die a martyr? Down to the seventeenth century his feast appeared in several martyrologies on December 4th. But when Clement VIII revised the calendar, the historian Baronius advised that Clement of Alexandria's name be dropped. Benedict XIV, in a letter to the King of Portugal, gave reasons for this: too little was known of his life, he had never obtained public cultus, and some of his opinions were suspect.

Newman, who had for Clement a very loving devotion, points out how hard is the path of a pioneer seeking the words in which to express transcendent truth, how careless were many of the copyists, how barbarous the translations in which the works of the early Apologists were transmitted to posterity. And he makes his own the words of St. Jerome:

> It may be that they erred in simplicity, or that they wrote in another sense, or that their writings were gradually

corrupted by unskilful transcribers; or certainly, before Arius, like "the sickness that destroyeth in the noonday", was born in Alexandria, they made statements innocently and incautiously, which are open to the misinterpretation of the perverse[1].

In places Clement appears, like the Gnostics, to be claiming an esoteric knowledge passed on secretly from one adept to another and not accessible to the ordinary Christian. But in other places he speaks, as Père Lebreton points out, like Irenaeus, showing the same veneration for the Church's hierarchy and speaking of the Tradition as a sacred treasure handed down orally lest it might be profaned by being set down on paper. Some writing, he agreed, there must be also; the risk must be taken of giving sacred knowledge to the unworthy but, as a magnet acts on steel, those only who are worthy will be attracted by its power.

Clement attacks the leading Gnostics, Basilides and Valentinian. But he will not allow that they are Gnostics. He claims that word for the Christian philosopher, who is also the complete and perfect Christian. "The unholy knowledge" (*gnosis*), he remarks near the end of the *Stromateis*, "of those falsely called [Gnostics] shall meet with confutation at a fitting time . . . the only really holy and pious man is he who is truly a Gnostic, according to the rule of the Church." "The *gnosis* itself is that which has descended by transmission to a few, having been imparted unwritten by the Apostles. Hence, then, knowledge and wisdom ought to be exercised up to the eternal and unchangeable habit of contemplation."

Greatly as he had praised the Hellenic philosophy, he points out that in relation to Revelation it had been called by St. Paul "the rudiments of this world". Men must "be saved by learning the truth through Christ, even if they attain philosophy". And "enquiry was obscure and dim, but the grace of knowledge is from Him by the Son".

"Nothing is incomprehensible to the Son of God, whence nothing is incapable of being taught. For He who suffered out of His love for us, would have suppressed no element of knowledge requisite for our instruction."

[1] *Arians of the Fourth Century*, p. 99.

Clement is writing essentially for people playing their part in the world, not withdrawn, like St. Anthony, into the desert or, like St. Benedict, into a monastery. "He, then, who faultlessly acts the drama of life which God has given him to play, knows both what is to be done and what is to be endured." He recognises that though "man is made principally for the knowledge of God . . . he also measures land, practises agriculture, and philosophises". "How irrational", he remarks in another place, "to regard philosophy as inferior to architecture and ship-building."

The danger of over-estimating intellectual values is rare enough at any period. Clement might have fallen into it had he remained a pagan, but as a Christian he knew that the life of the Christian must be fulfilled in love of God and service of his neighbour. "He impoverishes himself that he may never overlook a brother brought into affliction . . . he considers the other's pain his own grief . . . he prays in the society of angels . . . he is never out of their holy keeping; and although he pray alone he has the choir of the saints standing beside him." This life of prayer is "the royal road by which the royal race travel". "The service of God, then, in the case of the Gnostic, is his soul's continual study and occupation, bestowed on the Deity in ceaseless love."

Deeply concerned with the relation between *gnosis* and goodness, he writes, "Assuredly it is impossible to attain knowledge by bad conduct." And again: "Works follow knowledge as the shadow the body." "Above all this ought to be known, that by nature we are adapted for virtue; not so as to be possessed of it from our birth, but so as to be adapted for acquiring it." And: "What is the use of good that does not act and do good?"

They say in the traditions that Matthew the Apostle constantly said that: "If the neighbour of an elect man sin, the elect man has sinned. For had he conducted himself as the Word prescribes, his neighbour also would have been filled with such reverence for the life he led as not to sin."

These quotations are from the *Stromateis*, called usually in English *Miscellanies*, but by Newman a tapestry; described by the author himself as a plantation of fruit trees, as a variegated meadow, and as just a haphazard collection in which the reader may wander as he will, seeking out what pleases him. It is the delightful picture of a delightful man in the ripeness of his age, discursive, entertaining, profound.

An earlier book, *Exhortation to the Greeks*, shows the other face that Christianity turned to the pagan world. Clement's love for Greek philosophy was great, his hatred for the gods almost greater. An amusing little detail, when one thinks of the Christian hermits a very little later, is Clement's picture of the pagan priests: "Ruffians with filthy hair, in squalid and tattered garments, complete strangers to baths, with claws for nails like wild beasts." He adds, "Many are also deprived of their virility."

Clement had certainly made good use of the great library of Alexandria and also of his eyes and ears.

He has been likened to St. Francis de Sales, and this because he tried to penetrate with the Christian ideal every level of human life. He discusses eating and drinking, luxurious furniture, laughing and jesting, society life, perfumes and wreaths, sleep, family life and marriage, luxury shoes, jewels and gold ornaments, coquetry male and female, the use of baths and the practice of gymnastics!

Yet the comparison with St. Francis becomes almost comic when we look at the chapters in the *Miscellanies* printed by the Victorian editors in Latin, or the descriptions in the *Exhortation* for which the editor of the Loeb Classics almost apologises when translating them into English. The horrors of mythology concern Clement more than any beauties it may contain: adultery, fornication, pederasty, intercourse between humans and animals. He writes of "sacred initiations that are really profanities, solemn rites without sanctity . . . unspeakable symbols . . . manifest shamelessness." The night-worship of such deities is a foretaste of hell.

Quench the fire, you priest. Shrink from the flaming brands, torchbearer. The light convicts your Iacchus. Suffer night to hide the mysteries. Let the orgies be honoured in darkness. The fire is not acting a part: to convict and to punish is its duty.

Nature-worship is far less intolerable than all this; it is God who has created nature, but, "I long for the Lord of the Winds, the Lord of Fire, the Creator of the World, Him who gives light to the Sun. I seek for God Himself, not for the works of God." Plato had said, "'It is a hard task to find the Father and Maker of the universe, and when you have found Him, impossible to declare Him to all.' Why, pray, in God's name, why? 'Because He can in no way be described.' Well done Plato! you have hit the truth. But do not give up. Join me in the search for the good."

There is in this book an inexpressible fervour leading one to think it must have been written soon after Clement's own conversion. He breaks into exclamations: "Only, my child, do you thirst for the Father", "Seek after Him who created you ... you are a son, recognise your Father", "Trust, ye slaves, in the living God who was dead. Trust, all men, in Him who alone is God of men."

The last pages of this book can only, the editors say truly enough, be followed in all its allusions by one who has read the *Bacchae* of Euripides. But the idea is plain to anyone who reads the *Exhortation* itself and is accustomed to Clement's line of thought. "Come, frenzy-stricken one," he says to the pagan worshipper, begging him to throw aside the staff he leans on, to cast off his headdress and fawnskin, "Come to me, old man, come you too. Fling away your prophecy and Bacchic revelry and be led by the hand to truth. Behold, I give you the wood of the Cross to lean upon ... I will show you the Word, and the Word's Mysteries, describing them according to your own image of them."

Yes, it is unavoidable. Not philosophy only but even the hated mysteries have, in their elements of human craving and human framework, some shadow of the divine. The nocturnal worship of the pagan was darkened by vice, but it was still an attempt at worship. Away with false and evil mysteries— Christianity is the religion of the true and pure. But it is still mysterious.

> O truly sacred mysteries! O pure light! In the blaze of the torches I have a vision of heaven and of God. I become holy by initiation. The Lord reveals the Mysteries; he

marks the worshipper with His seal, gives light to guide his way. This Jesus, being eternal, the one great High Priest of one God who is also Father, prays for men and encourages men [saying] . . . I freely give you divine reason, the Knowledge of God; I give you Myself . . . this is the Son, this is Christ, this is the Word of God, the arm of the Lord, the might of the universe, the Father's will.

And Clement cries to his readers: "Let us hasten, let us run, we who are images of the Word, beloved of God and made in His likeness . . . let us love Christ, the noble Charioteer of men. He led the foal and its parent under the same yoke and now, having yoked together the team of mankind, He shapes the course of His chariot for the goal of immortality . . . He drove at first into Jerusalem, but now into heaven, a most noble spectacle for the Father, the eternal Son bringing the victory."

Whether Clement died a martyr or not, he was fully possessed by the heavenly nostalgia with which Christians viewed martyrdom as the likeliest road to an early vision of Christ. What makes this especially interesting in Clement is that he was not one of those ascetics, like Origen, who are felt by unheroic Christians to be cheating us a little in their views on life. By denying themselves food, sleep, recreation and the joys of marriage and the home, they make life hard to bear— and then they cry out against it as an unendurable vale of tears! Clement's longing for the life to come never seems to take its rise from distaste for the life that now is. "The body," he says, "as one sent on a distant pilgrimage, uses inns and dwellings on the way, having care of the things of the world, of the places where he halts, but . . . readily following Him that leads him away from life . . . giving thanks for his sojourn, and blessing [God] for his departure, embracing the mansion that is in heaven."

And ever mindful of his Greeks, Clement, after quoting St. Paul, goes on to quote Euripides: "I am shod with the winged sandals of the sirens, and I shall go aloft into the wide ether to hold converse with Zeus."

"But I", cries Clement, "shall pray the spirit of Christ to wing me to my Jerusalem. For the Stoics say that heaven is properly a city, but places here on earth are not cities . . . And

we know Plato's city set as a pattern in heaven." This world is
a pilgrimage but a happy one; the halting places are only
inns, but an inn can furnish good cheer to mind and body.
Only Clement teaches us never, in enjoying that good cheer,
to lose the nostalgia which literally means a longing for what
is ours: *patria nostra.* In the collect for the Third Sunday after
Pentecost we do not pray that we may learn to give up all the
good things of time; but that we may so pass through them as
not to lose those which are eternal.

ORIGEN

With the later Apologists we have reached a period at which
Christianity was becoming hereditary. Origen's father, thinking of the Holy Ghost dwelling in his small son's soul, would
kiss his breast as he lay asleep. Converts had to receive an
increasingly intensive Christian teaching, and we should
naturally expect convert schools to be matched by primary
and secondary schools for Christian children. The Jews had
theirs but, strange to say, the Christians made no attempt at
all at setting up separate schools. Throughout the Roman
Empire their children went to the ordinary pagan schools to
be taught to read and write, to study the great classics of
Greece and Rome. The stories told in their earliest textbooks,
though probably a little less crude than the actual plays and
poems, were of the gods and heroes of antiquity; they learned
to read by copying lists of their names. In these schools, it
seemed to Tertullian, no Christian should teach. These
classics, Jerome said, it was shameful for a Christian adult to
read. Yet neither of these two, the most severe of the Church
Fathers, ever suggested that Christian children should be withdrawn from the classical schools, or that Christian primary or
secondary schools should be established to take their place.

They must learn their letters to become educated men, with
a fullness of culture which seemed to the Church of considerable
importance. They could be shown easily enough that the
heathen gods were mere myths: like bat and ball, heathen
myths were the things of a child, to be thrown aside when
manhood came.

With peoples not already literate, the Church's attitude was entirely different, and the monastic schools created the cultures which shaped medieval Europe. But inside the Hellenist civilisation, even after the Church had triumphed, Christians kept in being the old classical schools and used them for their children until they were swept away by the barbarians.

The Jewish tradition had its share in creating the Christian outlook. Hellenist education was founded on the teacher and the school, Jewish on the home. The Jew made the school important but the home far more so; the Christian went further. Adult Christians had often passed through the catechumenate; they had a profound knowledge of what they were handing on. It was the parents' mission, St. John Chrysostom said, to develop their children's religious consciousness. But the Church was helping them all the time. Religious education did not end with the catechumenate—or with school days. All his life the Christian was learning from the liturgy, with Scripture readings, doctrinal prayers and sermons woven into its texture. We can see from St. Augustine, for example, how grand a structure was built by the greatest of the Church's teachers through sermons which taught the whole Christian scheme of revelation and life.

The child went fortified, his parents believed, to the schools in which they themselves had studied. Copy-books have been found with a little cross drawn by the Christian schoolboy at the head of the page; his parents would teach him to pray to be kept from evil. Courage to face martyrdom was often the answer to their prayers, the outcome of their teaching. Thus it was with Origen, who had learnt both Classics and Greek philosophy, as the Christian son of Christian parents in a pagan school.

When Clement left Alexandria for Cappadocia at the beginning of the persecution of 202, Origen was a boy of seventeen. His father died in that persecution: Origen never forgot that he was the son of a martyr and never ceased to hope that one day he himself would die for Christ. His mother had hidden his clothes to prevent his going to martyrdom with his father. She, poor woman, had younger children, and Origen was sole support of the family after his father's death. He began by opening a boys' school in which to teach the ordinary curriculum to pagan and Christian alike. He was most successful, and pupils flocked to him. A year later the bishop chose him for

a more important task. The persecution had thoroughly disorganised the catechetical school of Alexandria. Young as
Origen was, the bishop put him in charge of reorganising it.
This task he undertook with what has been called "tragic
earnestness". Converts came in such multitudes that Eusebius
says "they left him no time even to breathe".

The persecution was still fierce, and coming for instruction
meant offering oneself to death. To teach men faith meant to
prepare them for martyrdom. Origen prepared himself by
studying Scripture, often half through the night, by prayer,
and by ministering to the martyrs in their prison, thus daily
risking his own life. Often he came up to the martyrs and
kissed them on the way to death, and the pagan crowd would
rage and threaten. "He went from house to house," says
Eusebius, "changing his lodgings all the time and being turned
out of every place he went to, because such crowds came to
him to learn about the things of God . . . What made people
want to imitate him was supremely the divine power that
governed his actions."

When he began this work, Origen sold his books of philosophy
to devote himself totally to Scripture. But later he came to
feel that, for the conversion and stabilising of the faith of
thoughtful men, he must make use of philosophy as well as of
Revelation. He got an assistant to relieve him of the elementary teaching, and devoted himself to more advanced courses
of philosophy and exegesis. When mocking pagans said that
the Church addressed herself only to the simple and illiterate,
they stated a fact which must always be a profound truth—but
without the word "only". The Church's mark of universality
is shown no less in her appeal to learned and simple than in her
appeal to East and West. Faith is an act of the mind, to be prepared for and strengthened by the mind's faithful use. In this
great intellectual centre, Christians must be ready to bear their
part in discussions which might lead both to the conversion of
others and to their own martyrdom.

"Those blessed fathers who have gone before us," wrote
Alexander of Jerusalem to Origen, "in whose company we
shall soon be: Pantaenus our master truly blessed, the venerable
Clement who became my teacher . . . Through them I came to
know you, in all things excelling, my master and my brother."

Written about 215, this letter shows the high opinion Origen had already won. He was conscious that the vast work had barely begun of a full unfolding of the meaning of Revelation. He himself, we are told, wrote six thousand books. Books in those days were sometimes so short that we should call them only pamphlets—Père Prat thinks chapters may have been reckoned as books—but even so the number is astonishing. We get a glimpse of the way he worked and the equipment of the times when a rich friend, entreating him to write Scripture commentaries, supplied him with all material aid. "Seven or more shorthand writers," says Eusebius, "worked in relays and took down what he dictated, and there were as many copyists and girls trained in calligraphy."

St. Jerome later made much use of Origen's commentaries: his was the first systematic Christian work on Scripture. He learned Hebrew and discovered other Greek versions of the Old Testament besides the well-known Septuagint, copying them out in six parallel columns. This was known as the Hexapla. Of the Book of Psalms he copied eight versions. When we think of the amazing way manuscripts have come to light in modern days it is especially fascinating to read that he found one of these versions in a barrel at Jericho.

First at Alexandria, then at Caesarea, Origen led his laborious, ascetic, prayerful life. In the pulpit at Caesarea he preached daily, and towards the end of his life he had these sermons, says Eusebius, "taken down by fast writers, a thing he had never allowed before". Some of them remain and are the oldest collection of Christian sermons that we possess. He corresponded with Pope Fabian, with the Emperor Philip, who had been attracted by the Church, with Julius Africanus and other great men of the age.

Origen was a man of vast intellectual power, activity and curiosity: the Christian faith was the centre of his thinking and he wanted not only to probe into it as far as the human mind could go, but also to reconcile with it all valid human knowledge. Scripture, the nature and destiny of man, the nature of God, had not yet been searched into with this fierce energy, and Origen plunged deeper than the other Apologists into philosophy and theology. But his thinking was not always clear: St. Athanasius said of him that he was sometimes only giving opinions for and against some doctrine as an intellectual exercise; St. Jerome, that it is one thing to dogmatise, another to put out hypothetical opinions to be cleared up by discussion.

Origen declared most solemnly that he submitted wholly to the Church's judgement. In intent he was fully orthodox—yet after his death he was often called a heretic and the term "Origenism" was often used as of a heresy: St. Epiphanius defended him, St. Jerome first defended, later attacked. Athanasius, Basil, Ambrose, all drew from his books, yet Origen was condemned either at the second Council of Jerusalem or at a Synod which preceded it, and the Lateran Council named him among the heretics. We find the name of Origen cropping up again and again and then suddenly disappearing in some of the great contests of Church history. We must, I think, conclude with Père Prat that it was sometimes used as a weapon without any real relation to his teaching; yet, as his works have reached us, there are in them some strange sayings.

Origen far more than Clement made Alexandria the intellectual centre of the Christian East and partly for that reason it became also the storm centre. Arius, though himself educated at Antioch, claimed Origen as his precursor. A century and a half after Origen's death, Theophilus of Alexandria—St. Cyril's uncle—persecuted St. John Chrysostom as an Origenist; and much in Church history is incomprehensible without some idea of what Origen did in fact teach. But this is not altogether easy to discover.

The attacks began in his lifetime, and in one instance at least Origen reproached his friend Ambrose with publishing ideas which he had put out only as speculations for private discussion. In his most important book *Peri Archon*, or, *De Principiis*, he says at least six times, "We must not be supposed to put these things forward as settled doctrine, but as subjects for enquiry and discussion." And he tells his readers that he leaves it to their judgement to choose which opinion is the better.

Then, again, he frequently contradicts himself. Sometimes he says that at the end of the world "all will lay aside their bodies", yet one of the anathemas pronounced against him was for saying that bodies after the Resurrection would be "spherical". For in other places he discourses at immense length on the nature of the risen body, declaring that "to exist without material substance and apart from any association with a bodily element is a thing that belongs only to the nature of God". In places he calls God omnipotent, in others he puts limits to His power. Repeatedly he speaks of Christ as God, but in other places as created. He says that the Holy Spirit is only given to the saints, then again he says that the Holy Spirit is given to all men. On free will he is always clear and emphatic, and he teaches that man creates his own hell: "Of this fire the food and material are our sins." But while here (bk. ii, ch. 10) he speaks of "eternal" punishment, he says in several places "There is punishment, but not everlasting . . . For all wicked men, and for daemons too, punishment has an end." This is from fragments reconstructed by Koetschau in his edition of *De Principiis*. As Jerome put it bluntly, "It will be the same for Gabriel as for the devil, for Paul as for Caiphas, for virgins as for prostitutes."

Koetschau's text is translated with an excellent introduction by Dr. Butterworth, and it introduces us to the second difficulty in stating Origen's teaching in anything like its completeness. Rufinus, translating the book into Latin, toned down un-orthodox statements or even omitted them altogether; the original Greek is lost. Parts can be found in a collection of extracts made by St. Basil and St. Gregory Nazianzen, fragments in the works of other Fathers. There are also long quotations made by St. Jerome, and a collection of extracts sent by Justinian to the Patriarch of Constantinople in preparation for Origen's condemnation. Neither Koetschau nor Butterworth sees any reason to doubt the accuracy of these quotations —while Rufinus admitted that he had in places altered the Greek MS. he used. What man of genius, he asked, would contradict himself within a few pages?—the manuscript must have been tampered with by heretics.

Confusion is worse confounded by the fact that in France today Origen is very much the fashion and, as of old, his friends and foes are fighting about his meaning—they are sometimes at least as eclectic as Rufinus in their selection of material!

Obviously he was a giant of a man, but he was attempting to write a *Summa* for which the materials did not yet exist. By the nature of the human mind, ideas must, as Newman

reminds us, gradually grow and ripen. The Christian revelation
had been given in its fullness to the Apostles, but it had yet to
grow in the mind of the Church. Origen expressed most
earnestly his desire to be faithful to the Tradition—in intention
he was orthodox—but he was not trying, like Irenaeus, to go
deeper into theology so much as to widen its borders.

He believed that in Scripture "are thousands of passages that
provide, as if through a window, a narrow opening leading to
multitudes of the deepest thoughts". That these openings
might be "worthy of God", the literal meaning must often be
discarded for a spiritual one; but we must enquire always
"what are the methods of interpretation that appear right to
us, who keep to the rule of the heavenly Church of Jesus Christ
through the succession from the Apostles".

With a mind already full of Greek—especially Platonic—
ideas, he was trying to deal *as a Christian* with what he called
"the tragic tale of human miseries". Because God was loving,
he saw the answer to suffering in a theory of transmigration
whereby the sufferer in one life is expiating sins in a former one.
At the end will come restoration, when God is "all in all" and
man's expiation of sin is ended.

Reading *De Principiis*, I was haunted by a picture gradually
forming of Origen at work. Rufinus is not alone in finding
something odd in the numerous contradictions. Nor is it common to be so generous in entreaty to the reader to make up his
own mind. Then, too, the final remarks at the end of each
"book", or chapter, are a little unusual—"Let these remarks
suffice"; and twice, "Let these arguments which we have set
out to the best of our ability be sufficient"; again, "For our
part, we shall here bring the third book to a conclusion", and
"Let it be sufficient that we have spoken briefly on this
subject".

I wondered why he should thus often state his intention of
pausing—and then I remembered the seven stenographers.
There they sat with their hungry pens waiting for dictation.
Surely much contradiction and incoherence is explained if we
think of them "in relays", and of the need to keep them busy.
His other helpers—men and girls—were doing his copying:
Scripture and other books, fair copies of corrected manuscripts.
Each day employment must be found for the seven. It might

well have served Origen better if he had had to write like Irenaeus amid the stress of immense pastoral duties, had had with his own hand to put down what his mind had long ruminated. *His* stresses were different—and all intellectual: men flocking to be taught, begging for answers to the profoundest questions.

Whether Origen's writings always served their purpose, there is not the slightest doubt of his immense personal ascendancy, of the spiritual powers he poured out on his disciples. One of them, St. Gregory Thaumaturgus, has left an account of how for five years he and his brother studied in the school of Origen. He not only taught, but disciplined and purified his pupils, implanting in them the habit of reasoning. He taught them to examine all save the atheistic philosophers, but to cling to none of them—"only to God and His prophets". No one, Gregory goes on, can interpret a prophet unless he shares in the prophetic gift, and this God had bestowed on Origen. The school became for his pupils "a paradise, the image of God's great paradise. We needed not to cultivate the earth beneath or to feed our bodies to grossness; all our work was to develop fully and abundantly our soul's treasures: beautiful plants which we had planted ourselves or which the Cause of all had planted within us".

Origen's total gift of himself to God enabled him to bring his disciples with him, and if he was deeply hurt by the attacks upon him which began in his lifetime it is touching to note that he disliked also what he felt were the exaggerated praises of his admirers.

His love for Our Lord, his fears of his unworthiness, his sense of the immensity of the Christian hope, are revealed in a passage about the Incarnation in which, leaving aside all his hesitations, he takes on suddenly the dimensions of an Athanasius:

> When, therefore, we consider these great and marvellous truths about the nature of the Son of God, we are lost in the deepest amazement that such a Being, towering high above all, should have "emptied Himself" of His majestic condition and become Man and dwelt among men . . . how this mighty power of the divine majesty, the very Word of the Father,

and the very Wisdom of God, in which were created "all things visible and invisible", can be believed to have existed within the compass of that Man who appeared in Judea; yes, and how the Wisdom of God can have entered into a woman's womb and been born as a little child and uttered noises like those of crying children; and further, how it was that He was troubled, as we are told, in the hour of death, as He himself confesses when He says, "My soul is sorrowful even unto death"; and how at the last He was led to that death which is considered by men to be the most shameful of all—even though on the third day He rose again.

When, therefore, we see in Him some things so human that they appear in no way to differ from the common frailty of mortals, and some things so divine that they are appropriate to nothing else but the primal and ineffable nature of deity, the human understanding with its narrow limits is baffled; struck with amazement at so mighty a wonder, it knows not which way to turn, what to hold to, or whither to betake itself. If it thinks of God, it sees a man; if it thinks of a man, it beholds One returning from the dead with spoils after vanquishing the kingdom of death. For this reason we must pursue our contemplation with all fear and reverence, as we seek to prove how the reality of each nature exists in one and the same Person, in such a way that nothing unworthy or unfitting may be thought to reside in that divine and ineffable existence, nor on the other hand may the events of His life be supposed to be illusions caused by deceptive fantasies. But to utter these things in human ears, and to explain them by words, far exceeds the powers we possess either in our moral worth or in mind and speech. I think indeed that it transcends the capacity even of the holy Apostles; nay, more, perhaps the explanation of this mystery lies beyond the reach of the whole creation of heavenly beings.[1]

If a note so religiously resonant is rarely struck in *De Principiis*, it must be remembered that its name states just what this book is. In his sermons and his Scriptural commentaries Origen's deep piety appears more clearly. A passage must be

---

[1] *De Principiis*, bk. ii, ch. vi. I have used Butterworth's translation.

quoted from his commentary on St. John's Gospel in which he shows awareness of Our Lady's office in the Church, given to her by her Son—and sees it in terms of the Mystical Body:

> Of this Gospel none can receive the meaning except he has reclined on the breast of Jesus and except he has received Mary from Jesus so that she becomes his own mother also . . . For if there is no other son of Mary, according to those who entertain wholesome opinions about her, except Jesus, and Jesus says to His mother, "Behold this too [is] thy son", this is all the same as if He had said, "Behold this is Jesus whom thou didst bear." For indeed everyone that is initiated liveth no longer, but Christ liveth in him [Gal. ii. 20]; and since Christ liveth in him, it is said concerning Mary, "Behold thy Son, the Christ."

This is the Origen so much loved by Gregory Thaumaturgus. To Gregory, in his turn, it is related that Mary appeared with the Apostle John: she told John to instruct him concerning the Trinity. Gregory was still young. He had just been consecrated bishop, and in the midst of heresies was frightened by the task of instructing his people. St. John helped him gladly, and the Creed of St. Gregory is a statement, marvellously clear and perfect, not merely of the relation between Father and Son but of the equality, eternity and unity of three Persons in one God.

For some years Origen was able to work tranquilly during a peace of the Church, but his life ended, as it had begun, in a persecution—and that one of the fiercest. Christianity had spread widely enough to frighten Decius, who became Emperor in 249. All inhabitants of the Empire were ordered to burn incense in worship of the Emperor and to obtain certificates declaring they had done so. Newman's lovely story *Callista* is set in this period, and we learn how Christians often managed to buy certificates when they had not the courage for martyrdom yet would not actually forswear the Faith. Origen was tortured terribly, but he survived the tortures for two years and has therefore never ranked as a martyr.

Martyrdom was still the crown of a Christian life, and while Clement taught men the sanctification of daily human living,

Origen's emphasis was on the heroic. The thought of asceticism, not only as a preparation for martyrdom but as an alternative to keep the Christian community sound in times of peace, developed more fully in the next period, but Origen was already alive to it. In boyhood he had mutilated himself, taking literally Our Lord's counsel to become a eunuch for the Kingdom of Heaven. Later he recognised his mistake, but, short of flight into the desert, there was little of renunciation that he did not practise. He slept briefly and that usually on the ground, he ate sparingly, he prayed intensely.

Origen lived in a world of extremes—and indeed it is frightening to us ordinary Christians to think of an atmosphere so alien, yet which has of late come very near to us. What more glorious than the name of martyr, what more hideous than the name of apostate—and yet how narrow is the gap between them when weak humanity is threatened with torture and death. There were men who fell once and later died bravely. There were men who suffered torture and later fell. God knows the weakness of the beings He has made out of nothing. God alone gave strength to the brave. It seems sad that after all his courage, after living on in pain and weakness, Origen did not win the name of martyr—but I suppose he does not much care now.

In the year 251 the persecuting Emperor Decius met defeat and death at the hand of the Goths. It was the second of the three greatest disasters in Rome's conflicts with the barbarians—and it occurred almost two and a half centuries after the first: the battle of Teutoburg in A.D. 9, when the legions of Augustus were annihilated. With the death of Decius the Roman historian Ammianus Marcellinus finishes his history: it was perhaps the end of old Rome.

III: ST. IRENAEUS

THE FIRST THEOLOGIAN

If the order of these sketches were strictly chronological St.
Irenaeus should be placed earlier than Origen. The order
of time, however, is not always the same as that of ideas.
Clement is in thought very close to Justin; the two great
Alexandrians Clement and Origen could not be separated.
And in the order of theological development Irenaeus is
beyond them all, creator of the best in Tertullian, precursor of
the mightier Augustine.

IRENAEUS

The Mass of St. Irenaeus dwells on his love of truth and his
love of peace. The Introit is taken from the prophet Malachy:
"The law of truth was in his mouth . . . he walked with me in
peace and justice and turned many away from iniquity." The
Collect prays that, through him "who drove out heresies by
true teaching and most excellently strengthened the peace of
the Church", we, God's people, may be given "constancy in
our holy religion and peace in our days".

The first we hear of Irenaeus is that he was sent to Rome by
the Church of Lyons in 177, twelve years after Justin's martyrdom, carrying with him a letter from the confessors of that
Church. Pothinus, their bishop, aged ninety, had been
thrown into prison, where he died of ill treatment. More than
forty others, who were, their Church declared, "the indis-
pensable support of the Christian Churches in Gaul", had
been martyred. Worse than all these sufferings was the
threat to truth and unity. Montanism had begun in the East
whence Pothinus himself had come to Gaul, and was spreading
to the West. The Church of Lyons sent Irenaeus to Rome

49

with a statement of their ideas on the subject—"very pious and orthodox", says Eusebius. He does not quote the document, but he gives the words of praise introducing Irenaeus to Pope Eleutherius: "We have charged Irenaeus our brother, companion in our sufferings, to give you these letters and we beg you to welcome him as a man devoted to the message of Christ. If we thought of ecclesiastical rank as a guarantee of justice we should introduce him primarily as priest of the Church, for this he is."

"These letters" meant both the statement concerning Montanism and the story of the martyrs' sufferings given by Eusebius in painful detail. A fragment of Irenaeus' own writing refers to this persecution.

The Church of Lyons had written to Asia and Phrygia as well as to Rome. They wanted, they said, to be "ambassadors of peace between the Churches". (*Hist. Eccl.*, v. iii. 4.) The mission of ambassador of peace was always that of Irenaeus. It is the meaning of his name, from the same word comes the adjective "eirenical". In an amazing sentence he sees Christ as Peacemaker for the fulfilment of justice in fallen man: "The all-powerful Word of God, who never fails in justice, acted justly even in dealing with the spirit of rebellion. For it was by persuasion, not by force, that He redeemed His own property."

Born probably around 140, Irenaeus, himself an Eastern, probably a little older than Clement of Alexandria, had known and loved Polycarp, as he says, "in the first age of my life". All he had heard from him he had treasured, "not on paper but in my heart (for the things we learnt from our very childhood grow on with our soul and are a part of it)". The stories Polycarp had told were his own memories of John "and the other disciples who had seen the Lord". How close it brought Irenaeus to Christ Himself through the Beloved Disciple! And now he had come to Rome, meeting the successors and drinking in the traditions of Peter. It must have been on this visit that he learnt about the Western dating of the Easter feast, which he introduced in the Churches of Gaul. Later, again ambassador of peace, he would persuade Pope Victor not to excommunicate the Churches of Asia which refused to follow the Roman rule.

Irenaeus returned to Lyons and was elected successor to Pothinus. We know that he ruled this Church down to the reign of Septimius Severus, and Mgr. Duchesne attributes to his bishopric a sudden spread of the Faith. Southern Gaul had been slow to receive it. But now new Christian groups sprang up at Tours, Châlons and Autun. Dijon, Langres, Besançon were also probably reached at this time, and perhaps the Rhineland. Irenaeus speaks of Germans who have heard the words of Christ, and this means, in all probability, inhabitants of those provinces, cut out of the ancient Gallic territory, which bore the name of Germany. The Passions of several martyrs, too late to be of themselves conclusive but witnessing to an older tradition, represent them as in contact with Irenaeus. We know little with certainty of the external events of this tremendously important life, yet we know the man intimately as he is revealed in his writings.

Apologists and Heresiarchs

The effort to meet the philosophers on their own ground was not without its dangers. Even Justin, often so clear in his statement of Christ's divinity, appears sometimes to speak of Him as less than God: "Next to God we worship and love the Logos." In his use of the term *logos* he does not always make clear that the philosophers and he might be at cross-purposes— for Christians, the word had taken on a new meaning.

It would be still some time before the teaching of the New Testament on the divinity and humanity of Christ, on the relation of the three Persons of the Trinity, would be fully elaborated. Theology had begun; and it had begun with an attempt to explain to Greeks and Romans a religion even more new to them than to the Jewish world in which it had arisen.

"It was harder work", says St. Irenaeus, "for him who had received the Apostleship of the Gentiles, than for such as preached the Son of God to the Circumcision. For these were helped by the Scriptures, which the Lord confirmed and fulfilled, being, when He came, such as He was announced. But here it was a strange sort of teaching and a new doctrine, that the *gods of the nations*, so far from being gods, are rather *images of demons*; and that there is but one God who is *above all princedom and dominion and power and every name that is named*; and that His Word, a Person naturally invisible, had become such as to be touched and seen among men, and descended even *unto death*, and that the *death of the cross*; and that such as believe in Him shall be incorruptible and impassible, and receive the Kingdom of Heaven. And these things were preached to the Gentiles in discourse, without Scriptures: wherefore they did work harder who preached to the Gentiles. And again the faith of the Gentiles is shown to be more noble, in that they attain the word of God without instruction in letters."[1]

Irenaeus was writing about the same time as Clement: it is a pity that Origen could not have read him. His approach was very different from that of the Alexandrians, but he had set himself a very different task. They were trying to link up with Revelation the truth already known by the highest human reason; he chiefly to show that "the coming of the Son of God is made manifest in the last times, that is, in the end, being as it is the Beginning". He was even more excited than they over the newness of Christianity; he was more concerned to go deeper and deeper in his meditations on what the Church was already teaching than to try (like Origen) to widen its boundaries. Origen was by far the greater scholar, Irenaeus by far the deeper thinker. Both men were concerned with souls, but Origen's pupils were also scholars, those of Irenaeus the mixed multitude that any bishop rules. Here in Gaul, those skilled in Greek and even Roman letters must have been comparatively few, but ideas seep through also to the multitude of the unlearned. The Graeco-Roman world was amazingly unified despite the absence of radio, television or aeroplane; but most of its problems were not special to any world in particular: they rose from the depths of men's souls. It is fascinating to notice how often Irenaeus is answering the same questions as Origen. He answers them from Scripture and from Tradition, but also from the riches of a deep reflection upon the Revelation thus given.

One of their difficulties was language—both in a wide and a narrower sense. The Jewish convert brought with him the language of revelation with all its spiritual overtones. The pagan had it not. Also, the actual words in which Christ had

---

[1] *Adversus Haereses*, bk. iv, ch. xxiv (Keble's translation).

spoken must be translated—first into Greek, later into Latin. It has often been said that this passing from the Semitic to the Graeco-Roman world was providential, because Aramaic was a language much poorer in philosophical terms than either Latin or Greek. Semitic modes of thinking are poetic rather than philosophical. Perhaps the contrast, though valid, has been a little exaggerated. After all, Our Lord Himself chose to be born a Jew whose language was Aramaic.

Was Greek so innately apt for the expression of Christian theology, or did the Church have to make it so? A fascinating small book by William Barclay, *A New Testament Word Book*, traces many Greek words in the Classics, then in the *koiné*, or popular Greek speech, and lastly in the New Testament, showing their new meanings. Greek and Latin are indeed richer languages than Aramaic, but no language was rich enough for this new truth which had to be uttered. The Apostles were to teach all nations—the truth could be and has been told in all tongues, but God's angel touched with the burning coal of mystery the lips of His teachers.

A profound love and reverence safeguarded the greatest of the Apologists from any but verbal errors: in the effort to formulate Revelation these were inevitable. Except Irenaeus— and even he believed in the Millennium—there is no pre-Nicene theologian whose exposition is perfect in the light of later theology. But there was a far greater danger into which men fell, some of whom had begun as teachers of Revelation.

St. Paul and St. John and their earliest disciples were already warning their flocks of the danger of false teaching, but the voices were muted that tried to utter it while the Apostles still lived and taught. Hegesippus says that heresy grew far bolder after the Apostles and those who had known them were dead: until then the Church had been "a pure and stainless virgin". When heresies began, their authors claimed some sort of apostolic connection: the teacher of Basilides had, he declared, been Peter's interpreter; Valentinus had learnt from Theodas, a disciple of Paul. Both these men were Apologists gone astray. So, too, was Tatian, who had succeeded Justin. He is best known to us from his *Diatessaron*, a harmony of the Gospels long read liturgically in the East. He fell into heresy and is usually spoken of as a Marcionite. But Irenaeus shows that this is an over-simplification. He speaks of Tatian's "blasphemy" in denying the salvation of the first man, and goes on to says that "having been a hearer of Justin, as long as he was with him Tatian uttered nothing of the kind; but after his martyrdom elated and puffed up with the conceit of being a teacher, fell away from the Church, and, as one excelling all others, established for himself a school with a peculiar stamp: like Valentinus's people, making out a mythology of certain invisible aeons; like Marcion and Saturninus, denouncing marriage as corruption and fornication; but his denial of Adam's salvation he invented for himself".[1]

Two movements of recent years—Modernism and the left wing of the French priest-workmen—make it easier for us to understand what was happening when Basilides and Valentinus, or even Tatian, turned from Apologists of the faith into Gnostics or Marcionites. These modern movements were both directed towards the conversion of an élite—though the élites were very different ones; the first the world of the intellectuals, the second the world of the Communist workers. In each case Catholics set themselves not only to learn a new language, but to enter into a mode of thought far removed from that of Christ's revelation. In each case they did so with an ardent and sincere desire to bring Christ to the world they were entering. In each case the mode of thought, the *mystique*, of that world enveloped them so completely that instead of Christ being the Absolute, the Saviour needed by all mankind, the *mystique* of the élite became their Absolute. For them, the Church's teaching must henceforth abide the results of Scripture criticism or of Marxist ideas, and the men who had gone out to bring Christ, whether to intellectual or to worker, found themselves with empty hands. The teacher was sitting at his pupils' feet. The sick man had infected the doctor.

Neither teacher nor doctor discovers immediately what is happening to him. Confusion is an inevitable element in such a situation: the students too are convinced that they are still learning, the patients are calling for consultations. A clear mind was needed, then as now, and a means of testing between truth and error. That mind was given to the Church in the person of Irenaeus.

[1] *Adv. Haer.*, bk. i, ch. xxviii, § 1.

"Against the Heresies"

Irenaeus was writing not so much to win pagans as to refute heretics and enlighten Catholics. His great work *Adversus Haereses* has been preserved not in the Greek in which he wrote it, but in a Latin translation. He was concerned with all the heresies, but Gnosticism was by far the most dangerous and the most important.

Pre-Christian in its origin, this very confusing philosophy had two main tenets—that matter is evil, and that salvation comes not from love but from knowledge—a secret knowledge available only to a chosen few. Claiming to put upon them a deeper interpretation, it seized on the pagan mystery religions, Judaism, and ultimately Christianity; so that there was a pagan Gnosticism, a Jewish Gnosticism, and a Christian Gnosticism. We see hints of its beginnings before the death of St. Paul, in his condemnation both of vain talk about genealogies and of those who forbade marriage. We see it developed in the Manicheism that was its logical successor.

The Gnostics drew out of the Church some of the best minds of the century; they tried to reinterpret Christianity, turning it into Gnosticism. The Apologists welcomed truth wherever they found it—but for them Revelation was primary. They were, like St. Thomas or Newman, expressing Christianity in the language of their time. The Gnostics were changing it into something quite different. Thus development of doctrine and heresy are visibly in conflict from the very beginning.

Gnosticism was an attempt at an elaborately false development; the next outstanding heresy was an effort to get rid of the Old Testament and return, even so soon in the Church's history, to what Newman has called "a fabulous early simplicity". Marcion, born a Catholic, son of a bishop, came to Rome about the year 135 and taught there for twenty-five years, being however excommunicated in the year 144. His chief tenet was that there was total opposition between the Old and New Testaments. Christianity was not a development but a denial of Judaism. St. Paul was Marcion's great hero. "Our Lord came not", retorts Irenaeus, "to save Paul alone, nor was God so poor as to have one Apostle only who could know the 'economy' of His Son." Marcion exaggerated

St. Paul's attack on the Law and repudiated as interpolations all the elements in the Epistles which show St. Paul treating the Law as a preparation for the Gospel, as a revelation from the same God who later sent His Son to complete it. Of the Gospels he rejected all except St. Luke's—and even that he amended!

Marcion had a great following and built a rival Church which continued in existence for many centuries, with hierarchy and sacramental ritual. Marcionites, like Catholics, died rather than sacrifice to the gods.

Adversus Haereses begins like a personal letter. Charity urges Irenaeus "to make known to you and all who are with you" the secret teachings of heresy, which "now at length by the grace of God have found their way into the light".

"But you will not expect of me," he goes on, "dwelling among Celts and conversing for the most part in a foreign language, skill in discourse, which I have never learnt, nor power of composition, which I have not practised, nor eloquence of phrase, nor persuasiveness, of which I know nothing. Rather, in simplicity and truth and plainness, the things which are written to you lovingly you will lovingly accept . . . as a kind of seeds and principles," which "you will cause to bear much fruit in the wide field of your understanding, forcefully representing to those who are with you what I have but faintly outlined."

The first two books of the five are devoted to a lengthy account of the heresies. Reading about Irenaeus one often gets the impression that he relied solely on authority; but read instead his own words upon the Gnostics and all the heretics:

> Whoever would convert them must carefully acquaint himself with their rules or arguments: it being impossible for one to cure any sick persons, not knowing the ailment of the same.
>
> For which cause they who have been before us, yea, and much better men than we, were nevertheless unable to dispute against the Valentinians, as not knowing their system.[1]

---

[1] Bk. iv, preface, § 2.

Irenaeus declares that Simon Magus was the first and the father of all heretics. Whether there were once books, now lost, to substantiate this theory it is impossible to know, but it was held by all early Church writers. All we actually know about Simon comes from the Acts of the Apostles: that he was a magician of Samaria, of whom the Samaritans said, "This is the power of God that is called great." Baptised by Philip, ·he afterwards offered money to St. Peter for the power to call down the Holy Spirit (hence buying sacred things is called simony); after Peter had rebuked him, he repented and begged the Apostles to pray for him. To these few facts a great multitude of legends were added, in the Pseudo-Clementines and in the Acts of Peter, in which he turns up in Rome as Peter's great adversary. The two books then part company, one sending Simon back to Samaria, where he is buried alive, confidently promising (but failing) to rise on the third day, the other ascribing his death to a fall when he is magically flying through the air and the prayers of Peter and Paul bring him to the ground. Justin Martyr believed in his having been in Rome; and the sect of Simonians, claiming him as founder, continued the practice of magic arts learnt from him.

Simon, says Irenaeus, claimed himself to be "the most High Power, i.e., the Father who is over all". He had bought a slave called Helena, whom "he took about with him saying that she was the first conception of his mind, the mother of all". From her came angels, archangels, powers, through whom in turn the world was made. Her own creatures had shut her into a human body and from age to age, "transmigrating as it were from vessel to vessel", she had gone into other bodies. She was that Helen of Troy for whom war was waged, but, ending as a harlot in a brothel, it was she that was meant by the lost sheep. Simon had rescued her and had come to "give salvation to men by knowledge of himself . . . release to the world and deliverance of those who are his from the empire of those who made the world".

Menander, Saturninus, Basilides, Carpocrates, Marcellina, "who came to Rome under Anicetus", Cerinthus and the Ebionites, the Nicolaitans claiming one of the seven deacons as their founder, Cerdon who, "taking his beginning from Simon and his sect, sojourned in Rome", Marcion of Pontus—

all these, even if "they profess not their master's name", yet "are disciples and successors of Simon".

Gnostic myths usually had in common the assigning to the female principle of the conception of the Deity, her descent to the lower regions and inability to return, and the ignorance of the rulers of the world concerning the Supreme Power. The titles of the aeons or angels varied widely. Irenaeus speaks of the Quaternion, Mother of Aeons, of the sums, made up of Monad and Duad, and the resulting Ogdoad, mother of thirty Aeons—almost as many theories as there were heretics, but all pushing far away the Infinite God, creating causal chains of creation, believing in salvation as for the soul alone, disbelieving that Christ the Son of God took a real body, suffered a real passion, rose from the dead.

Every fresh heretic had his own special twist. Thus Valentinus, "who first adapted his principles from the heresy called Gnostic, to the peculiar principles of his own school, bore his dry fruit" in the invention of "a Duad which cannot be named, whereof the one part is called *Ineffable*, the other *Silence*". Ptolemy and his sect "devised and granted to the God who among them is called the Deep, two wives: and these also he called Dispositions, first Thought and then Will", and therefrom a long genealogy, which others reject, one saying that the first Ogdoad came, not from gradual descent, but "brought forth once for all by the Forefather and his thought: this he affirms as though he himself had assisted at the birth". This idea of the Gnostic's function evidently took Irenaeus' fancy, for he speaks later of such a man "doing a midwife's part in the production of Mind and of God".

Yet another Gnostic, "boasting to be a corrector of his own Teacher (and his name is Mark), most skilful in magical jugglery", would make the cup of the Eucharist appear purple and red, would prophesy himself and "cause women to prophesy"—all this ending in his receiving the goods of the worshipper and often her body also.

Yet, says Irenaeus, "Whether or no they practise among themselves such things as are godless and lawless and irreligious I cannot make up my mind, but so it is written down in their books."

They may not be immoral, but of the futility of their teaching he has no doubt. They are "falsely called Gnostics". Is it likely, he asks, that St. Paul "should have held back knowledge from St. Luke in order to entrust it to these men", whose boast it is to explain "the greatness of that Power which is truly unspeakable, and such vast economies of God, by their Alpha and Beta"? Their Silence is "full of babbling but uttering no kind of truth". She "names the unnamed and explains the unspeakable". Yet her worshippers can find no point of rest in an abiding truth: "They try to show that there is some Pleroma or God above the Framer of Heaven and Earth; by the same argument one can make out above the Pleroma another Pleroma, above the Deep another ocean of Godhead: and so their view will lose itself in infinity . . . nowhere at any time to stay themselves . . . there will be nothing stationary or fixed to limit our conception, but it will be forced to go forth among immense worlds and indefinite Gods."

And in another place—"If the Creation is an image of those other existences, what hinders one's saying that those are images of what is above them, and those above them again of others, and so cast ourselves into endless images of images."

Nor anywhere is unity of belief to be discovered: "So many diversities are there amongst them concerning one and the same thing, maintaining as they do different meanings for the same Scriptures; and at the reading of one and the same passage, they all contract their eyebrows and shake their heads, and say that they themselves indeed perfectly comprehend the passage, in its exceeding depth, but that all cannot receive the greatness of the meaning therein contained; and therefore that silence is a main point with the wise, it being meet that the *Sige* who is above should be delineated by the Silence which is among them. And so they go their ways, all of them; and whatever their number, so many opinions do they take with them on one and the same subject: they bear about with them unseen their own sharp thoughts."[1]

Despite his sojourn among the Celts, Irenaeus seems to have known as much as the Alexandrians of the Greek literature that was in men's minds and had seeped into all the heresies. "Much more naturally and more elegantly," he says, spoke Aristophanes when he said "that of Night and Silence Chaos

[1] *Adv. Haer.*, bk. iv, ch. xxv, § 4.

was produced, then from Chaos and Night, Desire, and from this Light", and so on to the rest of the minor gods. We are back into paganism, and not the poets alone, but the philosophers, are laid under contribution: "As to the Shadow and the Void they speak of, they took it from Democritus and Epicurus . . . As to their affirming that things here are images of real Beings"—again this is Democritus, and Plato, who "speaks of Matter and the Archetype and God".

The opinion that nothing can pollute them because of their high origin "they have inherited from the Cynics". The idea of translating the world into numbers they took from Pythagoras. "And frivolous talk, and subtlety of disputation, being of Aristotelian origin they try to bring into the Faith."

Adversus Haereses is not an orderly treatise refuting the heresies point by point: it is a book written, one would guess, in the scant intervals between pastoral duties, burning with love of God and of the souls this bishop desired to help. In so brief a sketch as this only a slight idea can be given of the power and beauty of his writing.

While Irenaeus is deeply intellectual, the note of love is even stronger in him, and he sees love growing as knowledge grows: "While we practise ourselves in enquiry concerning the mystery and ordinance of the Living God," we must, he says, "grow also in love of Him who does so great things for us." "For we never come to an end in our loving of God, but the more we shall have looked upon Him so much the more we love Him." It was not the following of the Law that Christ condemned in the Scribes and Pharisees: "He was blaming these men because while they uttered the words of the Law they were destitute of love." "And the more we love Him the more glory we shall receive of Him; since we are always in the Father's sight." Our witness before God and man must be "to assent to God and to follow His Word and to love Him above all things, and one's neighbour as oneself (and man is man's neighbour)".

"It being impossible without God to learn of God, He teaches men by His Word to know God." And "to such as believe and follow Him, He vouchsafes a fuller and larger illumination of mind".

The Christian God is not the God of the Gnostics. "He is

the Framer of Heaven and earth: not the pretended Father, invented by Marcion or Valentinus", etc. They announce an unknown God: "But Our Lord did not say that the Father and the Son could not be known at all, else were His advent superfluous. For why came He hither? To say to us, 'Think not of seeing God, for He is unknown, and ye shall not find Him'? as the Valentinians feign that Christ also said to their Aeons. But this is merely vain. Rather, the Lord instructed us, that no one can know God, except upon God's teaching: i.e., that without God, God is not known: and that for God to be known is itself the free-will of the Father. For *they shall know Him, to whom the Son will reveal Him*."[1]

In one of the fragments that remain besides *Adversus Haereses*, Irenaeus says, "The work of a Christian is nought else save to study and to die"; and in the fifth and last book of his great treatise he demands intense concentration as he pours out profound thought on his favourite theme—the recapitulation or summing-up of all in Christ, the second Adam. In the recognition of this stupendous fact he sees the destruction of all heresies.

First, those which deny the reality of Christ's manhood, "for He could not have had even flesh and blood in reality (whereby He redeemed us) except by gathering up into Himself that old creation of Adam".

Second, those which deny the Godhead, for they "reject the infusion of the Heavenly Wine and will have it to be earthly water alone, not receiving God into that which they mingle, but abiding in him who was overcome and cast out of Paradise, even in Adam".

PRECURSOR OF AUGUSTINE

It is tempting to quote long extracts, but books iv and v especially are so tremendous one would soon be copying the whole. Irenaeus is the precursor of Augustine in his mastery of phrase. I have tried therefore to sew together some of these phrases with a few longer quotations to give some idea of the line of his thought on Christ as the second Adam, and what results therefrom.

[1] *Adv. Haer.*, bk. iv, ch. vi, § 4.

In the former times it was said indeed that man was made
in the image of God, but it was not revealed. For the Word
was yet invisible after whose image man was made. But when
the Word of God became flesh He made both good. For
He both truly revealed the image, Himself having become
that very thing which the image of Him was; and He
firmly established the resemblance by causing man to partake
of His own complete likeness to the invisible Father through
the visible Word.

And,

Summing up in Himself that original man of whom the
formation of the woman took place, that as by a conquered
man our race went down into death, so by a conquering
Man again we might go up into life.

Christ healed "the disobedience which had been wrought
at the tree by the obedience which was also at the tree".
And in this "coming of the Lord to His own" His mother bore
her part. The Virgin Mary becomes "an advocate for the
Virgin Eve. And as mankind was bound unto death through
a virgin it is saved through a Virgin; by the obedience of a
Virgin the disobedience of a virgin is compensated".

Man's glorious destiny is not forced upon him. The prophet
Osee had, in taking a wife of whoredom, graphically prophesied
"that the earth should utterly go a-whoring from the Lord . . .
and of this sort of men shall God be pleased to take to Himself
a Church to be sanctified by partaking of His Son".

But "in that He saith, *How often would I have gathered thy
children and thou wouldst not*, He declared the ancient law of
man's liberty".

The idea of transmigration Irenaeus rejects utterly; for
"souls remember not at all any of what was before". If they
are to be tested by life, "they ought to remember the things
that were before in order to fulfil what was wanting, and not
toil in wretchedness, always wallowing in the same things
without intermission". Given that the soul even remembers
much of what happened in dreams, "I suppose she would
remember the things which she did before she came into the

body." Plato got out of the difficulty by supposing a Cup of
Oblivion, but if that be remembered why not all the rest? "And
how, being in the body, should she either learn divine things or
remember the same, were the body, as they say, itself oblivion?"

Such fancies are not, to his mind, needed to safeguard belief
in God's mercy. The terrible picture which grew up later of
a vengeful God is no part of Irenaeus' belief in the possibility
that man by his liberty can choose to "flee from God's light".
The darkness that becomes their prison "they have chosen for
themselves". God sent some to call men "to the marriage, but
those who did not obey Him *deprived themselves* of the King's
supper. It is not therefore God's skill that fails; for He is able
of these stones to raise up sons to Abraham; but he who doth not
follow it up, causes himself his own imperfection".

God is light but man may choose to blind himself. "So they
who fly from the eternal Light of God, which contains in itself all
good, are themselves the cause of their so abiding."

Later on would come the psychology that makes it easier to
see how men who hate God cannot be forced into that heaven
where God is all in all; Irenaeus sees them as "justly shut up"
in the darkness they have chosen—but he sees clearly that the
choice is wholly theirs. He reminds us how Elias was "taught to
deal more gently" with a sinful people, how in Our Lord's
coming "He neither brake bruised reed nor quenched smoking
flax"; after the earthquake and fire come the times of His
Kingdom, "wherein with all gentleness the Spirit of God gives
life and increase unto men".. And he cries out, pleadingly,
"Do thou yield thy heart to Him soft and tractable, and keep
well the shape in which the Workmaster hath shaped thee . . .
lest thou be hardened and so lose the print of His fingers . . .
For to make is proper to God's kindness and to be made
is proper to man's nature." "All things, moreover, which
were made, He made by His unweariable word."

Irenaeus is as preoccupied as St. Paul with the question of
the Resurrection—he quotes St. Paul largely and himself
dwells on the fact that "if one take away the substance of the
flesh, i.e., of God's formation, and consider the spirit barely
alone, that which results is no longer . . . man". "To say that
the temples of God, in which the Spirit of the Father dwells,
and the members of Christ, do not partake of salvation, is the

greatest blasphemy." No; as Christ rose, so shall we—and the pledge of Resurrection is the Holy Eucharist. In mere material life a sponge can be filled with water, a lamp lit from a fire: "Why may not the life of more energy—eternal life—why may not it quicken the flesh, practised already as it is and accustomed to carry about Life in itself?"

Irenaeus sees the Eucharist as the culminating point on earth of one great cosmic cycle:—God's creation of man and of creatures for His service, then God's coming to man, for "the Son of God hath not then His beginning, who is for ever with the Father". Then our redemption and the building of men into the mystical body of the God-Man for all eternity: "For we gave Him nothing before, nor does He desire aught of us, as one in need, but we are in need of communion with Him: and therefore He mercifully poured Himself out, that He might gather us into the Bosom of the Father. . . . Since, therefore, both the cup which is mingled and the bread which is made receives the Word of God, and the Eucharist becomes the Body of Christ, and of these the substance of our flesh grows and subsists:—how say they that the flesh is not capable of the gift of God, which is eternal life?—that flesh which is nourished by the Body and Blood of the Lord, and is a member of Him: as blessed Paul says in his Epistle to the Ephesians, *We are members of His body, of His flesh, and of His bones.*"[1]

What evidence can be found, Irenaeus asks, that what he is teaching is indeed the Revelation received from God, and that the heretics are building a baseless fabric? Two things they themselves profess to receive: Scripture and the Tradition of the Apostles. But it is not actually possible to meet them on either ground, for ". . . when they are convicted out of the Scriptures, they betake themselves to accusation of the Scriptures", claiming that the truth cannot be found in them "by persons ignorant of Tradition". The wisdom of the Apostles each heretic claims for himself, but when faced with the Tradition "guarded by the succession of presbyters in the Churches, they oppose Tradition", claiming to be wiser not only than the presbyters but than the very Apostles themselves, who had, they declared, "mingled with the words of the Saviour the things of the Law".

[1] *Adv. Haer.*, bk. v, ch. ii, §§ 1, 2, 3.

Behind all this wrangling, Irenaeus invites us to go to the true Tradition and the Scriptures kept safe by it.

It would take too long, he says, to enumerate the succession in all the Churches, so he will take one "very great and most ancient and known to all, the Church founded and established at Rome by the two most glorious Apostles Peter and Paul". To this Church he points for the confounding of all who set up Churches of their own. "For with this Church, *propter potentiorem principalitatem*, the whole Church (I mean the faithful everywhere) must needs agree. For here the Tradition of the Apostles has ever been kept."

Clement of Rome "had both seen the blessed Apostles and conferred with them and had the doctrine of the Apostles yet sounding in his ears and their Tradition before his eyes . . ." This living Tradition he had reiterated to the Church at Corinth in "a most effective letter . . . Those who will may learn from the letter itself and discern the apostolical Tradition of the Church, the letter being more ancient than our present false teachers and devisers of another god above the Artificer and Creator of all things that exist".

He enumerates the Roman succession from Clement down to Eleutherius: "By the same order and in the same succession both the Tradition from the Apostles in the Church and the preaching of the truth have come down to us. And this is a very full demonstration of the unity and sameness of the life-giving Faith, which from the Apostles even until now has been preserved in the Church and passed onward in the truth."

What Irenaeus had to say of the origin of the Gospels has been told so often I will not linger on it here. Besides his book against the heretics we have another work of his, *The Demonstration of the Apostolic Teaching*. It seemed to him that "now the times of the Church are verging towards the Middle Age". In his earlier book he had shown his belief in the Millennium, but in the later he is no longer looking for the immediate return of Christ upon earth; he interprets the Apocalypse more allegorically. He was getting near to his own meeting with his Lord, through, as tradition avers, the gate of a violent death. We cannot do better than leave him with the words of Père Lebreton which so beautifully sum up the width of his vision and the beauty of his character.

If we seek the source of Irenaeus' wide understanding of the great dogmas, we shall find it in his respect and love for Tradition in its totality. There is nothing of the partisan in him; he is not a man of one school. His only school is the Church, his only party is Christ's. He holds in veneration St. Polycarp and Papias, the presbyters of Asia, and along with them St. Justin, the philosopher and Apologist. The whole of the Bible is sacred to him and intimately known to him—the history of the patriarchs, the prophetical books, the Psalms, the wisdom literature; the teaching of St. Paul, so much in eclipse in most of the second-century writers, stands out in bold relief in Irenaeus; so also does the Gospel of St. John, which occupies no large place with the Apologists.

The wideness of mind, the comprehensive formation so evident in his writings, are evident in his life too. He is at once a man of Asia, a man of Rome, a bishop of the Gauls— all were united in the embracing charity of a truly Catholic soul.[1]

---

[1] "Saint Irenée", in Fliche and Martin, *Histoire de l' Église*, vol. ii, pp. 64–5.

IV: ST. ANTHONY

The Age of the Hermits

JUSTIN and Clement were teachers, Irenaeus a teacher and a bishop. In all the men we have studied, prayer was the mainspring of action. In Anthony we meet for the first time an unmixed contemplative.

With him we move from the cities into the solitude of wide empty spaces. Christian art has depicted him chiefly in combat against the devil. The world of the eighteenth century, not believing in the devil, treated him as a half-crazed being, anti-social, unwashed, illiterate, leading with him a crowd of fanatics, giving up home, family and all the joys of life to get in return nothing but a dream. "Gloom" and "vacancy" are the words chosen by Gibbon to describe the hermit's life.

The modern world, still not believing in the devil, has begun slowly to perceive the profound social significance of Anthony and his monks. Other men have stood in the midst of the stream of history and, so standing, have succeeded in diverting it. But this man, standing right outside it, and not even trying to affect it, diverted it powerfully. The world is interested and perplexed by this strange fact, and questions how it came about.

Anthony would certainly have answered that Christian art had been right all along—that it was by combat with the devil, "the prince of this world", that he changed the world.

Newman, when writing the lives of the Saxon saints, doubted if his compatriots could endure them, they were so full of "miracles and monkery". So too with Anthony. He is the first Christian hermit whose story we really know. He wrought many miracles. But even more is his life one tissue of events and agencies alien to our common experience. Of course, the Church does not vouch for every supernatural story. But the life makes no sense unless the main outline of it is true and is reasonable. The Life of Anthony was first written by "Athanasius the Bishop", that great saint who twice joined him in his desert exile and returned to Alexandria strengthened to fight against the Arian heresy.[1]

THE FIRST HALF-CENTURY

Born in Egypt of Christian parents in the year 251—the year Origen died, to say nothing of the Emperor Decius— Anthony passed most of his youth in a period of peace for the Church. There was persecution in his early childhood and again in his middle life, but not as he was growing up. Yet all those years Christians were something of a people set apart; persecution at all times threatened, and they were excluded from the full rights of citizens. They often showed their profound patriotism for Rome, especially in time of war, and they suffered from this exclusion.

But another kind of separation was theirs from choice. As the gods of the East were more and more accepted in the Roman system, as the framework of life was fitted to the ideals that they represented, it became less and less possible for Christians to breathe the air and live in the climate of their fellow citizens. Ritual prostitution was a part of worship, symbols inciting to sexual vice were prominent in every street, every house and garden. Promiscuity between boys and girls was taken practically for granted. Homosexuality, idealised in Greece, was now accepted by Rome and throughout her empire. Short of human sacrifice, there was nothing in Carthage or in Asia to which the Roman Empire did not give the hospitality of its altars and its homes. The air of early Rome had been far purer; now the odours of decadence—sweet odours, some of them—were breathed on all sides, while the many altars reminded men to pay their customary unconsidered tribute of incense to the *genius* of the Emperor.

Literacy was not universal in the Roman Empire and it seems unlikely that Anthony went to school. Living in the country, his parents would be less likely than townsmen to

---

[1] This study is based on the Life by Athanasius, and all quotations are from it unless otherwise indicated.

think culture important. Newman has given us in *Callista* a grim picture of the African countryside at about the same date. And it may well be that Anthony's parents had a greater fear of pagan influence than urban Christians, because of the crude forms it took among half-educated villagers. However this may be, the great hermit became a potent influence in that stream of Eastern monasticism which, unlike the Western, thought learning unimportant and valued only piety and asceticism.

Anthony's parents died when he was eighteen or twenty, leaving him the guardian of an only sister. St. Athanasius describes how, walking one day to church, he was turning over in his mind the calling of the Apostles and the way in which the early Christians had all things in common. And entering the church, he heard the words of Our Lord being read: "If thou wilt be perfect sell all thou hast and give to the poor and come, follow Me."

Forthwith Anthony gave away to the village the three hundred acres of fertile land that were his, sold all he had and gave most of it to the poor, keeping back only a little for his sister. But on his next visit to the church he heard the words, "Be not solicitous for the morrow", so, parting with the rest of his patrimony, he put his sister in a convent to be educated for the religious life (the editor of the *Library of the Fathers* tells us this is the first use of the word *parthenon* for a convent).

He himself now began to practise the ascetic life in front of his own house, "for monasteries were not yet numerous in Egypt, nor did any monk yet know the wide desert". Anthony came almost at the beginning of the vast movement that was to fill the Church with monks, but there were already men living a life of solitude, prayer, labour with their hands, and alms-giving in their own neighbourhoods. Anthony visited them, and in all humility studied the special excellence of each: ". . . how gracious was one, how intensely prayerful another . . . of one he observed the long vigils, of another the eager love of reading . . . and in all he saw the same reverent love for Christ and mutual affection for one another."

Anthony tried to carry out in his own life all that he had seen. He worked steadily, giving most of what he earned to the poor; he prayed much "He listened so closely to what was read that he forgot none of it, and his memory later served him in place of books." And always he "kept his mind steadily away from his inheritance and would not think about his relatives".

Good reason as there was to escape the temptations of that strange, luxurious, crumbling civilisation, we certainly never catch in anything said by Anthony the most distant note of escapism. He speaks not as one fleeing from danger, but as one advancing to meet it. So his enemy the devil perceived, and soon began in his turn to advance upon Anthony. "At first he tried to tempt him away from the ascetic life by bringing before him thoughts of his property, of anxiety about his sister, the companionship of his kind, greed for money and fame, the pleasure of rich and varied foods and the other delights of a luxurious life. How harsh, he reminded him, was virtue, how steep the winning of it, how weak the body, how slowly time would pass." Anthony did not know how long his life was to be, but all these thoughts filled his mind "like a cloud of dust", bewildering and confusing his judgement. The devil pressed on, disturbing him by night and day. "The devil threw filthy thoughts in his way: Anthony drove them away by prayer; the devil stirred his senses and Anthony, hot with shame, fortified his body by faith, prayers and fastings. By night the fiend vilely tempted Anthony, taking the form and using the gestures of a woman. But thinking on Christ, the nobility that is ours through Him, and the spirituality of the soul, he put out the flame of temptation."

St. Athanasius takes delight in the devil's discomfiture, which was such that "he who fancied himself like God was now mocked by a mere youth". The devil, appearing again as a black boy, admitted his own defeat at Anthony's hands. But he retired only to re-furbish his weapons and prepare a new attack. Nor did Anthony grow careless through victory but decided "to get himself used to harder ways". He watched and prayed longer, often through the whole night. His meal of bread, salt and water was taken only once a day after sunset, and he would sometimes fast for one, two and even four days. Such sleep as he took was on a mat or, more often, on the bare ground.

After some years spent in this fashion, Anthony, preparing

for the supreme combat with Satan, left the village and went
away to the tombs which lay at some distance.

Having asked a close friend to bring him bread at intervals
of many days he went into the tombs, shut himself in and
stayed there alone. This his enemy could not bear, for he
feared that Anthony would soon fill the desert with the power
of his asceticism. Coming one night with a crowd of demons,
he scourged him so fiercely that Anthony lay on the ground
speechless from the intensity of his torments. By God's
providing . . . his friend came back the next day, opened the
door and saw him lying on the ground as though dead; he
carried him into the church in the village near by and there
laid him down. Many of his friends and the people of the
neighbourhood took their station around Anthony as though
he were a corpse. But about midnight Anthony came to,
and, rousing himself, perceived that they were all asleep
except his friend, who was still watching; he nodded to him
to approach and asked him, without waking anyone, to take
him back to the tombs.

The man carried him back; again the door was shut,
again he was there alone. He was too battered to stand but
he prayed flat on the ground. And when he had prayed he
cried out with a mighty shout, "Here am I, Anthony. I am
not going to run away from your blows, for even if you beat
me again nothing can separate me from the love of Christ."
And then he intoned the psalm *Si consistant adversum me
castra, non timebit cor meum.*

There followed a fearful noise and crashing as though the
place were shaken by an earthquake, and then an onslaught:

. . . demons taking the forms of different beasts and reptiles.
The place was one mass of spectral lions, bears, leopards,
bulls, serpents, asps, scorpions and wolves, each one moving
in the manner of the shape it wore. The lion roared crouching for the spring, the bull made to toss him, the serpent
coiled but could not reach him, the wolf was held back as it
leaped. The noise of the demon animals was hideous and
their rage terrible. Scourged and goaded by the demons,

Anthony's pain grew even greater. He lay groaning in body, but watchful and fearless of soul.

He spoke to them, we are told, "jokingly" and "gaily". But his pain was extreme, the tumult excessive and he appeared utterly alone. Then suddenly,

> ... looking upwards he saw the roof open and a ray of light shone through it. The demons vanished in a flash, his bodily anguish ceased and his dwelling was whole again ... he drew a deep breath and, freed from pain, he challenged the vision that appeared to him: "Where were You? Why were You not there sooner to lighten my torment?" "I was here, Anthony," came a voice in answer, "waiting and watching your struggle. Because you have endured and conquered I will always be your Helper and I will make your name renowned throughout the world."
>
> Hearing this he rose up and prayed, and so much power was given him that he felt stronger in body than before. His age was now about thirty-five.

After his first combats with Satan, Anthony had intensified the severity of his life. After this supreme fight, he intensified his solitude, deciding to make his way into the desert. The devil still tried to turn him back, dropping gold in the path of a man who had already shown his sheer contempt for it, and, after he had found his abode, clamouring to him to leave it. Friends seeking Anthony heard "a tumultuous crowd ... uttering piteous cries, shrieking, 'Stand off from our domain; what have you to do with the desert?'"

Athanasius describes to us the spot chosen by Anthony in which he dwelt *for the next twenty years*:

> He found beyond the river a fort long unused and full of reptiles: he crossed over to it and there dwelt. The reptiles left at once, as if someone were chasing them. He closed up the entrance and laid in bread for six months (the Thebans do this and the bread will keep unspoilt for a full year). There was water inside. Anthony went down as though into

a shrine and there abode alone. He never went out nor would he see those who came to him. There for a long time he worked at asceticism, twice a year only receiving bread that was lowered to him from above.

Many came seeking Anthony in his solitude, but he would seldom see them. When they were terrified by the noise the demons made, he would call out to them to make the sign of the cross and "go away, trusting God, and leave the demons looking silly". His friends kept returning thinking to find him dead, only to hear him singing the most triumphant of the psalms.

Meanwhile monasteries were growing up in the desert. The monks required the help of Anthony, and his friends would no longer be gainsaid. After all, twenty years is quite a period. Small wonder the world became impatient for the sight of this solitary. He had shut himself up a young man of thirty-five; he was now fifty-five. Few could have guessed he had another half-century of life before him.

When they had smashed in the doors and removed them Anthony came forth, like one initiated in the Mysteries and breathed upon by the Godhead, coming from the shrine. Now for the first time he was seen outside the fort by those who sought him. And when they looked upon him they marvelled at how unchanged he was in body: neither grown fat through want of exercise nor gaunt from fasting and battling with devils. In fact he looked exactly the same as before his retirement. His clarity of soul shone through his conduct. Grief had not narrowed or joy dissipated his mind. His look was neither over-merry nor gloomy. He was not excited to see all these people acclaiming him. Utterly tranquil, he seemed a man ruled by reason and shaped as nature had designed him. Through him God healed many who were sick and set others free from devils.

Often when he refused to open his door "a great many in need of help remained outside the monastery and even slept there, eager in trust and in prayer—and they were healed".

THE SECOND HALF-CENTURY

Soon after Anthony came forth from his solitude, persecution broke once more upon the Church and he was seized with a great longing for martyrdom. "He burned with the desire," says Athanasius, "but as he did not think it right actually to give himself up, he ministered to the confessors in the mines and prisons. He made a point of being in court to exhort to joyfulness those under arrest and examination. He accompanied those condemned to martyrdom and upheld them until the end. The judge, seeing not only Anthony but also his companions so full of courage, ordered that no monks should be present in court or even stay in the city. The others all thought it best to keep hidden that day, but Anthony paid so much heed to the order as to wash his tunic, take his stand in a conspicuous position next day, and let the judge see him looking his best."

The whole picture is a pleasant one—especially that of Anthony washing his tunic. For it was a part of his asceticism that he never bathed or even put his feet into a bath. But at first sight it is puzzling that the judge should have banished the monks from the court and not arrested them as Christians. Roman law, however, was very orderly. Christians were under condemnation only if they were denounced. Few would think it worth while to fill the prisons with this horde of ragged, starving fanatics. So Anthony returned reluctantly to his desert. But he took back with him many who had, by seeing and hearing him, become inspired with the wish to lead the same life as his.

> The monasteries in the mountains seemed like tabernacles filled with men singing the praises of God, eager in study and fasting and prayer; rejoicing in the hope of eternity, labouring that they might distribute alms, all united in love and peace. It seemed indeed like a land apart, full of justice and the love of God. No one did injury there, no one suffered it; there was no tax-gatherer with his demands; only a populace of ascetics whose one concern was the pursuit of virtue.

That ancient world was not so unlike ours, when it occurred
to a saint and a bishop to mention the absence of taxes as one
of the advantages of the monastic life.

This period of Anthony's life was spent (comparatively
speaking) in the eyes of the world. He dwelt in a monastery,
visited other monasteries and was himself visited by great
numbers. He was "guide and father" to the other monks and
induced many to take up a solitary life. His sayings are of
great simplicity and depth. St. Athanasius devotes almost a
third of his book to a sermon of Anthony's to his fellow hermits.
He begs them to bring what they know "and tell it like
children to your father; while I, as your elder, share with you
the things I know and those I have learnt by experience".
Discussing the vocation of a hermit he stirs up their zeal,
reminding them of their reward.

Short indeed is man's life if set beside the ages to come,
and nothing is all our time compared with life eternal. In
the world everything is sold for what it is worth, and a thing
is exchanged for another of equal value. But the promise
of eternal life is cheaply bought.

. . . Let us not look back upon the world and fancy we
have given up great things. For the whole of earth is a very
little thing compared with the whole of heaven.

. . . What is the use of gaining things that we cannot take
with us? Why not rather gather those that we *can* take with
us: prudence, justice, temperance, fortitude, understanding,
charity, love of the poor, faith in Christ, graciousness,
hospitality? If we gain these we shall find them again in the
land of the meek.

. . . Our life is uncertain of its nature and is daily measured
out to us by Providence . . . living our life day by day we
shall not sin, either by grasping at anything, getting angry
with others, or piling up treasure on earth.

. . . For the soul to be upright the mind must be as it
was created: on the other hand, what is called evil in the
soul is a turning-away from, a desertion of, the natural. Nor
is the thing so difficult: if we stay as we were made we are
virtuous. . . . Let us guard our soul for the Lord, giving back
to Him what we received from Him: that He may recognise

His own work, since our soul is still as it came from His hand.

The rest of the sermon is mainly devoted to a study of the devil and his wiles. Anthony tells them how they are to distinguish the different kinds of spirit—the good from the evil, and the various kinds of evil from one another. Demons will pose as angels or will foretell the future, being able to do so merely as a man on a horse can outrun one on foot. Anthony spends some time on this point: devils cannot know what has not come to pass, for this knowledge belongs to God only, but they can see the waters rising in the hills and run to announce the flooding of the Nile which will follow. "Men also could announce it if they could run like these. . . . Thus the oracles of the pagans came to be, and thus of old men were deceived by demons."

Really powerless since the coming of Christ, the devil can only win through human weakness and fearfulness. Name but the name of Christ and he will vanish, "for he cannot endure the burning heat of it". If then we want to "despise the enemy, we must think at all times of the things of God and our souls must be joyful with hope". We shall have help from God's angels and saints. They too may appear to us and "with them is Our Lord, who is our joy and the might of God the Father".

To philosophers who mocked him because he had not learnt letters Anthony's reply cut deep. "Which is first, the mind or letters? And which caused the other, the mind letters, or letters the mind?" When they said that the mind was first and had invented letters, he answered: "Then one whose mind is sound, has no need of letters." The friend of the learned Athanasius meant no disrespect to learning. But a mind as close to God as Anthony's finds its own food.

What he says on faith might find a place in Newman's University Sermons: "How do we get our knowledge of things, and especially of God? Through proof from arguments or through the operation of faith; and which comes first, the operation of faith, or proof from arguments?" And when they answered that the operation of faith comes first, and that this is sure knowledge, Anthony said, "You are right; for faith comes from the very energy of the soul; but logic from the skill of its discoverers. So if you have faith, proof by argument is totally unnecessary. For what you are labouring to establish by proof, we already know by faith. In fact, you are often unable to find words for the things we know; so that the operation of faith is surer and more valuable than your academic arguments."

And then he challenged the sophists to cure some men possessed by demons—"or if you cannot, then give up your attacks on us, and see what power is in the Cross of Christ". And he invoked Christ and three times made the sign of the cross over the sufferers. And they stood up, healed, blessing God.

The victory was won without bitterness, for the philosophers departed, "embracing Anthony and admitting that he had taught them much".

All this time Anthony was longing for a deeper solitude, and finally he decided to go further into the desert, where he might once more be alone. He fell in with some "Saracens" (nomad Arabs) who welcomed him and took him with them a three-day and three-night journey until they reached a mountain. At its foot was water, very clear, fresh and exceedingly cold; beyond the mountain was level ground where a few wild palm trees grew.

Here Anthony decided to dwell. At first the Saracens brought him bread, later his brethren found him and ministered to him. But presently, anxious not to weary them with the journey, he asked the next who came to bring him a pronged hoe, an axe and some corn. He found a very small patch of land that could be tilled and he dug and sowed it, "having more than enough water for its cultivation". Later he added a few vegetables wherewith to refresh any visitors that might arrive weary with the journey. "The very sight of him inspired his visitors with faith; but he was on his knees wrestling with God in prayer."

Anthony was ninety years old when there came the meeting, so celebrated in medieval art, between him and the first hermit, Paul. We must always remember that, amazing as are some of the incidents related above, they are all vouched for by Athanasius, who knew Anthony well and had them at first hand from him and his monks. But the story of this meeting is not

told by St. Athanasius, and St. Jerome, who does tell it, is
clearly writing in poetic vein and not vouching for every part
of the legend.

Anthony, he tells us, inspired by a vision of a greater solitary
than himself, set out across the broad desert and travelled for
two days. At last, following a she-wolf, he made his way to the
cave where Paul dwelt. But Paul, hearing his visitor approach,
shut and bolted the door and only opened it after hours of
tearful and prayerful entreaty from Anthony: "Thou who
receivest beasts, why dost thou turn away men? If I prevail
not here I shall die before thy door."

> The two embraced each other and greeted one another
> by their names, and together returned thanks to God. And
> after the holy kiss, Paul sat down beside Anthony, and
> began to speak. "Behold him whom thou hast sought with
> so much labour, a shaggy white head and limbs worn out
> with age. Behold, thou lookest on a man that is soon to be
> dust. Yet because love endureth all things, tell me, I pray
> thee, how fares the human race; if new roofs be risen in the
> ancient cities; whose empire is it that now sways the world;
> and if any still survive, snared in the error of the demons?"
> And as they talked they perceived that a crow had
> settled on a branch of the tree, and softly flying down,
> deposited a whole loaf before their wondering eyes. And
> when he had withdrawn, "Behold," said Paul, "God hath
> sent us our dinner, God the merciful, God the compassionate.
> It is now sixty years since I have had each day a half loaf of
> bread: but at thy coming, Christ hath doubled His soldiers'
> rations." And when they had given thanks to God, they sat
> down beside the margin of the crystal spring.[1]

Anthony lived to the age of 105, seeing under Constantine
the beginning of Arianism, all but winning his coveted crown
of martyrdom as a Catholic under the Arian Constantius. An
officer had set out towards his dwelling to seize Anthony when
a horse turned on the man and tore his thigh. Taken back to the
city, he died in three days. And Anthony waited to be called
by God.

[1] I have used Helen Waddell's translation.

He had always strongly opposed the Egyptian habit of embalming. So when he knew he was dying he left his monastery and returned to the stronghold in the inner desert, where now in his old age two monks lived with him. He made them promise they would bury him in the ground and let no one know where they had laid him. He bade them farewell, again warning them against the demons and telling them: "With every breath you breathe draw in Christ . . . And now God be with you, my children; for Anthony departs and is with you no more."

When he had finished speaking and they had kissed him goodbye Anthony "as if gazing up at friends coming to meet him, and whose coming made him joyful—for his face was radiant as he lay—drew his last breath and was gathered to his fathers".

What It All Meant

St. Anthony and the solitaries have powerfully fired the Christian imagination. Medieval art delighted especially in picturing the more dramatic episodes: devils beating St. Anthony, offering him phantom gold, appearing in hideous or alluring aspects either to frighten or to tempt him.

The chroniclers of the desert paint word pictures of the quiet life of every day. We can see the scattered solitaries making their way to the church where they met every Sunday for Mass—and if any brother were absent they would go and seek him out, knowing he was sick. We can see them helping a newcomer to build his cell of wattle and thatch it with palm leaves. Those leaves had many uses. A pile of them in every cell furnished employment: they were woven into mats (the hermit would sleep on one and sell the rest; a mat was one day's work). Again, they could be woven into baskets for the market and even into rough garments. Of the money thus earned a very little was spent on bread; the rest went to the poor. (In harvest time many solitaries helped the farmers and gave away their wages.) A small vegetable garden near the cell supplemented the dry bread and salt which was their basic food (some hermits would have none other, but Anthony planted a garden and successfully begged the wild animals not to destroy it).

Inside the cell two stools and a sheepskin completed the furnishing. On the window ledge was sometimes a codex or two. In the corner a jar of water (it must have grown warm in the air of Egypt) and perhaps oil and wine for the visitor, a person always greatly considered. Among these visitors were the animals so often painted with the desert saints. (In St. Francis of Assisi we meet again this power of innocence taming wild nature.) The worst we are ever told of a desert lion is that "he took in very bad part" the suggestion of a solitary to share his cave "and departed roaring". Many hermits had wild beasts for pets and for their servants.

In all the lore and the legends surrounding the desert we are touching something much larger than at first we realise. During Anthony's lifetime and for a hundred years after his death men "were flocking for religion to the desert, as eight hundred years later they flocked for philosophy to Paris, and to Bologna for law. Pachomius, for his monastery of Tabenna on the Nile, had seven thousand men and women living in various congregations under his rule; there were five thousand monks on Mount Nitria; Serapion at Arsinoë ruled over ten thousand; and a traveller through Egypt and Palestine about 394 reports the dwellers in the desert as all but equal to the population of the towns".[1]

Multitudes of these men lived their whole lives in the desert. Others remained for some years. Yet others came to get advice from the solitaries. They learnt to drive away "all indecision and pettiness in business, all backwardness and pusillanimity in the domain of character, all resentment, worry, grief and irrational fear". Palladius, who tells us this in his *Lausiac History*, travelled from group to group, and he was not the only writer of books about this vast movement which so deeply influenced Christian civilisation. All the great men of the period were touched by it; St. Athanasius made retreats with Anthony as well as writing his life, St. Jerome spent years in the desert. So did St. John Chrysostom, St. Basil, and St. Gregory Nazianzen. St. Augustine was converted through the example of the solitaries.

The martyrs had witnessed in the sight of a hostile world to the reality of that which is not seen, "for the things which are

---

[1] *The Desert Fathers* by Helen Waddell, pp. 7–8.

seen are temporal, the things which are not seen are eternal ".
With the peace of the Church came the danger of a pagan world
seeping into it; another kind of witness was needed and this the
hermits gave. If man be made for eternity, the affirmation of
eternity is vital to his soul while he is yet in time. The
martyrs affirmed it by dying; the hermits by living in it. For
Boethius calls eternity "that which encloseth and possesseth
the whole fullness of the life everlasting, from which naught of
the future is absent, and naught of the past hath flowed away".

This is the air we breathe when we join them in the desert.
They pray, they labour, gaining enough by their toil to feed
the hungry on a vast scale (in time of famine one group sent
a shipload of grain to a distant port), going hungry themselves,
yet practising hospitality to all who came, gentle, courteous,
wise and full of love towards man as well as towards God,
sleeping as little as they ate, contemplating night and day.

Because they were human there were among them strange
men whose exaggerations were food for the scorn of Gibbon,
Lecky and other materialist historians. Every great movement has a camp-following of eccentrics. But the hermits
were proposing a new thing in human life: a reversal of normal
values; a community based on humility instead of pride,
simplicity instead of splendour, austerity instead of lust;
built out of labour, silence, charity, dependence upon God.
All this they called nature; but it was the nature the Fall had
spoilt, and therefore their lives were hard.

The doctrine of the Mystical Body means that the Church
is Christ. Therefore there well up within her in every age the
thoughts and the actions most needed by the world she is
saving. Into a world long debased by idolatry and immorality
came St. Anthony and his hermits.

V: ST. ATHANASIUS

MANY things are uncertain about the life of Athanasius, including the date of his birth. Probably he was born around the year 296; probably in Alexandria, probably of Christian parents. The historian Sozomen says, and the writings of Athanasius show, that he had what is still sometimes called "a liberal education"—grammar, rhetoric, philosophy. To this must be added the influence of Christian and pagan Alexandria. The city had two immense libraries which were also lecture halls. How far the work of Origen still continued in the higher studies available to young Christians it is hard to say, or whether Athanasius had any connection with the Catechetical School. But whatever the influence of the Classics and the pagan philosophies may have been on his growing mind, we know that the bishop Alexander enrolled Athanasius, still quite young, among his deacons, and presently chose him for his own personal secretary. A still stronger influence on that inner life, the direction of which so profoundly influences thought, may already have been intimacy with the monks and solitaries near Alexandria—"the swarms of monks", as Gibbon calls them, "who arose from the Nile, overspread and darkened the face of the Christian world". In his Life of St. Anthony we feel that Athanasius had long known the world of asceticism so bewildering to the unbeliever, and had breathed the air of the desert that was its natural home.

If 296 be the correct date of his birth, his first books, *Contra Gentes* and *Oratio de Incarnatione*, were written when he was still young—between 318 and 323.

Athanasius was to go further and deeper in his own thinking as time went on, but he retained always a fear which made him hesitate to write on "the highest and chief doctrines . . . lest what is imperfectly expressed through my inadequacy or the obscurity of language, do hurt to the reader". Thus he wrote to the monks in his story of the Arians, saying of the writings he was sending them, "I think they are defective in all respects." And he gives the reasons for his fear, which arises from the infinity of the truths he is approaching.

> For the more I desired to write, and endeavoured to force myself to understand the divinity of the Word, so much the more did the knowledge thereof withdraw itself from me; and in proportion as I thought that I apprehended it, in so much I perceived myself to fail of doing so. Moreover, I was unable to express in writing even what I seemed to myself to understand; and what I wrote was unequal to the imperfect shadow of the truth which existed in my thoughts.[1]

This fear of laying profane hands on the Ark of God's Covenant, or at the best uttering inadequate words of human wisdom, handicaps the reverent believer in his struggle with the blasphemy of the heresiarch. Already in 318 the adversary against whom Athanasius was preparing himself had begun the teaching which, in Carlyle's phrase, would, if triumphant, have reduced Christianity to a legend.

A few words must here be said about one problem the Church had to face in teaching the Trinity to the world. The doctrine is a mystery which the human mind can never fully comprehend, yet for what God has revealed about it the Church had to find words. She must give men creeds in which to state their faith in face of a Jewish world which accused them of polytheism, and a pagan world alternately bent on their destruction and ready to welcome Christ and his Apostles alike to a place among the gods. The pagans of Lystra, the Acts of the Apostles tells us, "called Barnabas Jupiter but Paul Mercury because he was chief speaker", and tried to offer sacrifice to both.

We have seen how, from the first, converts were baptised in the name of the Father, Son, and Holy Ghost, how the liturgy witnessed to their faith in the Trinity, how clearly a great bishop like Irenaeus taught it, how the Apologists were struggling to express it, how heresy about it was rejected as contrary to the Tradition—that is, to the Original Revelation.

---

[1] *Historical Tracts of S. Athanasius: Epistle to the Monks,* I, 1.

Words were in part the problem. Something totally new had to be taught, and all the words men had at their disposal bore well-worn meanings, none of them adequate to the weight of the revelation they had to carry. We shall see how much apparent heresy was really only apparent. St. Athanasius himself was one of the first to see that this was so.

Words alone never, of course, account for the great heresies; they arise from false thinking. But where a heresiarch was teaching a false doctrine his followers were sometimes innocently receiving a true one, as St. Hilary remarked during the Arian crisis. And again, as Newman has pointed out in the case of Origen and Arianism, a man perfectly orthodox in intention may use words that are later made instruments of heresy. Deeper than the problem of words and their meaning was that of expressing a doctrine at whose heart is mystery; the heresiarch always wants to simplify—to remove the mystery, which cannot be removed because it is the doctrine. It is easier to believe that Christ is God *or* is Man than that He is both, easier to believe that the three Persons are merely aspects of God than to accept Them as distinct Persons yet one God.

This last was the teaching of Sabellius, who immediately preceded Arius. He taught that there was no real distinction of Persons in the divine nature—God creating we call the Father, God suffering and redeeming we call the Son. The Church was still combating this heresy when Arianism arose, and a word or two must be said of the sources whence Arius drew a heresy which he claimed was an answer to the Sabellian identification of Father and Son.

THE ROOTS OF ARIANISM

Newman spends many pages in his *Arians of the Fourth Century* proving that this heresy hailed from Antioch, and that the Judaizing tendencies of the Antioch Church were partly responsible. It is a historical fact that not only Arius but nine out of the thirteen Arianizing bishops of Nicaea came from the school of Lucian of Antioch, who wrote a semi-Arian creed and was excommunicated for many years as a heretic. Ultimately he was reconciled with the Church, died a martyr, and is known to us today as St. Lucian.

Arius, native of Libya, educated at Antioch, priest of Alexandria, had a reputation for learning and sanctity. A man of middle age, he had a large following, especially among women. And he was fortunate in the time at which his novel ideas were launched—the backwash of the Sabellian heresy.

Almost invariably in the Church's history a heresy has been followed by another exactly opposite, which is at first not seen as heresy because it *is* opposite. Thus, at its beginnings, Arianism was tolerated because it was an attack on Sabellianism. Sabellianism had so obscured the distinction between the Persons of the Trinity as practically to abandon the doctrine, and Arius claimed to be reasserting it; and he did indeed distinguish the Son from the Father.

He began by calling Bishop Alexander a Sabellian—and anyone who has lived through a crisis of heresy can realise how terrifying such an accusation might be, even to a bishop; can see too, how a perfectly orthodox bishop, if he were not a highly intellectual man, might feel something wrong, yet find it difficult to put his finger on the exact spot of the new heresy. Newman, in his *Arians of the Fourth Century*, relates how the accusation was made at a public meeting of the clergy: ". . . an insult which Alexander, from deference to the talents and learning of the objector, sustained with somewhat too little of the dignity befitting the ruler of the people."

Arius was a public preacher of the city, possibly head of its Catechetical School. Alexander summoned another meeting of the clergy, at which he allowed Arius to defend his doctrine and at which, Sozomen says, he did not commit himself, "applauding sometimes one party, sometimes another".

Surely we can already see Athanasius, keener of mind than his primate, writhing at such a procedure. Yet it may be that the bishop's patience made his final action more effective; he tried private interviews with Arius; the clergy of Alexandria wrote the heretic a joint letter begging him to retract; finally Alexander summoned a synod of over one hundred bishops of Egypt and Libya at which Arius and his followers were deposed. The letter sent out by Alexander to the Churches, the words spoken by him later at the Council of Nicaea, read like the work of the young deacon who was to become leader in this more than life-long battle.

It is their doctrine, that "God was not always a Father", that "the Word of God has not always existed, but was made out of nothing; for the self-existing God made Him, who once was not, out of what once was not. Hence He is mutable and alterable by nature, as other rational beings; and He is foreign and external to God's substance, being excluded from it. He was made for our sakes, in order that God might create us by Him as by an instrument; and He would not have had subsistence, had not God willed our making". Someone asked them, if the Word of God could change as the devil changed? They scrupled not to answer, "Certainly He can."[1]

Arius, on his side, set his creed to music. His *Thalia*, a song for banquets and merrymakings, describes him as "the famous among men, the long-suffering for God's glory". "Taught of God," it continues, "I have gained wisdom and knowledge." He goes on to say clearly that "God made the Son the origin [or beginning] of creation, being Himself unoriginate, and adopted Him to be His Son; who, on the other hand, has no property of divinity in His own *hypostasis*, not being equal, or consubstantial with Him". There is much more; as that the Father is invisible to the Son, is infinitely more glorious . . . Various forms of this doctrine were also set to popular tunes, arranged for sailors, millers, travellers.

At Antioch two enthusiastic laymen, Flavian and Diodorus, retorted by bringing into the Cathedral large numbers of monks from the surrounding deserts who chanted in a mighty chorus, "Glory be to the Father *and* to the Son *and* to the Holy Ghost."

CONSTANTINE INTERVENES

Arius went to Nicomedia, where he was received by the bishop, Eusebius, an old schoolfellow of his at Antioch, who exerted his influence both to make Arius more cautious in his statements and to win other bishops to his support, hoping finally to persuade Alexander to reinstate him. In the first two aims he was highly successful. Arius agreed to use various evasions in his own statements—beginning what Athanasius

[1] Newman's translation in *Arians*, p. 218.

later complained of as common Arian usage: "They keep
back those particulars respecting which their heresy is accused
and merely bring forward passages out of the Scriptures."
Several synods of bishops acknowledged Arius and (vainly)
interceded for him with Alexander. Alexander stood firm.

With the triumph of Constantine at the battle of Chrysopolis
(323) a more brilliant possibility opened before the minds of
Arius and Eusebius; could not something be achieved by
imperial intervention?

Constantine and Licinius had in 313 decreed perfect freedom
and equality for all religions. As Gibbon has pointed out, this
was to elevate the persecuted and comparatively small body
of Christians to a position of relatively astonishing power. But
the medieval conception of Constantine as a sort of St. Louis
was an absurd one. He had at the Milvian Bridge conquered in
the sign of a cross—but it is doubtful whether at the time he
saw in this (as later he certainly did) the Cross of Christ. The
shape of it as usually depicted might equally have been the
emblem of the Sun God, and after the vision "he publicly
invoked the Deity" (says Newman) "as one and the same in
all forms of worship". In 321 he ordered *both* the observance
of Sunday and the consultation of the omens; he continued to
accept his imperial position as High Priest of paganism. "The
mind of Constantine", says Gibbon, "might fluctuate between
the pagan and Christian religions. According to the loose and
complying notions of polytheism, he might acknowledge the
God of the Christians as *one* of the *many* deities who compose the
hierarchy of heaven. Or perhaps he might embrace the
philosophic and pleasing idea that, notwithstanding the variety
of names, of rites, and of opinions, all the sects and all the
nations of mankind are united in the worship of the common
Father and Creator of the Universe."

Newman goes far deeper in his analysis of the character
of a man very much statesman, very little philosopher. Despite,
he says, the gratitude we owe him for the freedom he gave
to the Church, it was Constantine who "burdened it with
the bequest of a heresy which outlived his age by many
centuries and still exists in its effects in the divisions of the
East". Had the emperors stood aside, the Church would
herself have quickly cured the disease which they rendered

almost mortal, and Newman feels that this story of political
intervention "still has somewhat of a warning in it".

Constantine, says Newman,

> . . . found his empire distracted with civil and religious
> dissensions, which tended to the dissolution of society; at a
> time too, when the barbarians without were pressing upon
> it with a vigour, formidable in itself, but far more menacing
> in consequence of the decay of the ancient spirit of Rome.
> He perceived the powers of its old polytheism, from what-
> ever cause, exhausted; and a newly-risen philosophy vainly
> endeavouring to resuscitate a mythology which had done
> its work, and now, like all things of earth, was fast returning
> to the dust from which it was taken.
>
> . . . The Gospel seemed to be the fit instrument of a civil
> reformation, being but a new form of the old wisdom, which
> had existed in the world at large from the beginning. Rever-
> ing, nay, in one sense, honestly submitting to its faith, still he
> acknowledged it rather as a school than joined it as a polity;
> and by refraining from the sacrament of baptism till his
> last illness, he acted in the spirit of men of the world in every
> age, who dislike to pledge themselves to engagements
> which they still intend to fulfil, and to descend from the
> position of judges to that of disciples of the truth . . .

But Constantine was dismayed to find this religion which
he had relied upon to pacify and unite the Empire becoming
itself disunited as the development of its doctrines proceeded.
God alone was able, says Newman,

> to discern through what a succession of difficulties divine
> truth advances to its final victory; shallow minds anticipate
> the end apart from the course which leads to it. Especially
> they who receive scarcely more of His teaching than the
> instinct of civilization recognizes (and Constantine must,
> on the whole, be classed among such), view the religious
> dissensions of the Church as simply evil, and (as they would
> fain prove) contrary to His own precepts; whereas in fact
> they are but the history of truth in its first stage of trial,
> when it aims at being "pure" before it is "peaceable";

and are reprehensible only so far as baser passions mix themselves with that true loyalty towards God, which desires His glory in the first place, and only in the second place, the tranquillity and good order of society.[1]

Constantine sent Hosius of Cordova, a bishop in whom he had great trust, to Alexandria with a most revealing letter addressed to both the disputants, which another Eusebius (of Caesarea) has preserved. He wishes to bring the diverse judgements concerning the Deity to a settled conclusion, and to restore health to the world. He is dismayed to find in the East, where the holy religion originated, a controversy about questions *that ought not to have been discussed.* "Consider", he says, "whether it be right on the ground of *some trifling and foolish verbal difference* to assume the attitude of enemies and that an august meeting of the synod be rent asunder by *profane disunion,* because of you who are wrangling *on points so useless and altogether unessential.*"[2] Later he again speaks of the difference being "on so unimportant a matter". What matters to him is the disunion only —that is profane, and he entreats them to end it. But it did not dawn upon him that the real profanity lay on one side or other of the dispute. If the Son be God it is profane to call Him a creature. If he be a creature it is profane to call him God.

The idea of summoning all the bishops into universal council may have been suggested by Hosius. It had a strong appeal for Constantine. He made it possible, through the public travelling services, for all to come to Nicaea from both East and West. The Pope was an old man; he did not come, but sent two legates. Men were there who still had upon them scars from the tortures of persecution; one was blind, another lame. How strange it must have been, how thrilling, to be welcomed and feasted by the Emperor himself, robed with overwhelming splendour and showing in his very respect for the bishops an incredible condescension.

Hosius presided. The vast majority of bishops were from the East, but there was almost unanimity in their condemnation of Arius. Indeed, as he and his small group entered the hall chanting their hymn, most bishops stopped their ears and cried

---

[1] *Arians,* pp. 242–4. [2] Italics are mine.

out at the blasphemy. Arius spoke openly at the council, forgetting the advice of Eusebius. It was not easy for the bishops to find the perfect formula for their profession of faith, but in the end only two of them failed to sign the declaration that Jesus Christ was "the sole-begotten of the Father, that is to say, of the Father's substance, God of God, Light of Light, true God of true God; begotten not made, consubstantial with the Father [*homoousion to Patri*] . . . As for those who say, 'There was a time when He did not exist; before He was begotten He did not exist; He was made from nothing or from another substance or essence; the Son of God is a created being, changeable, capable of alteration', to such as these the Catholic Church says, *Anathema*".

The two bishops who refused to sign were sent into exile. Constantine was proud of his council. He loaded the bishops with gifts, he exhorted them to preserve the peace of the Church —but he understood not one word of what the definition really meant.

ATHANASIUS, BISHOP OF ALEXANDRIA

Alexander's deacon was the hero of Nicaea and returned to Alexandria in triumph. Within a year Alexander was dead. He had wanted Athanasius for successor and at about the age of thirty the deacon was chosen for bishop of the chief city of the East. .His enemies said later that he was under the canonical age, that the appointment had been made in hole-and-corner fashion by a couple of bishops and was quite irregular. But the Egyptian bishops replied in a letter "to the bishops of the Catholic Church everywhere", that the people, "assembled as with one mind and body, cried and shouted, that Athanasius should be bishop of their Church, made this the subject of their public prayers to Christ, and conjured us to grant it for many days and nights, neither departing themselves from the church nor suffering us to do so".

An emperor was chosen either by his predecessor or by the army; but in the Church the populace had a large share in the choice of their rulers. The bishops declared that Athanasius "was elected by a majority of our body in the sight and with the acclamation of all the people". How large the majority of

bishops we do not know, but there could have been no secrecy
in a choice made in response to this intense popular demand.
Thus it was with Ambrose, still a catechumen, thus with
Augustine. And none of the three ever lost the love of the
people who had chosen them.

The first few years of office were peaceful enough at Alexandria, but much was happening elsewhere. The Arian and
Eusebian bishops had yielded too easily at Nicaea; they had
not really accepted their defeat, they were only waiting. The
condemned heretics now had, what no heretics had ever had
before, a Christian Emperor to appeal to. And they had almost
from the start the perfect model of a figure to reappear again
and again—the court prelate, the bishop skilled at handling
monarchs. For Nicomedia was Constantine's capital, and
Eusebius, the friend of Arius, was ever at the Emperor's side.
He had had the sense to sign the decrees of Nicaea. But his
mind was not changed nor his tenacious will; for a short while
he too was sent into exile for political intrigue, but on his return
he began to work at undoing what Nicaea had done. It would
take too long to follow every move of this patient, subtle warfare. He did not attack the council directly; he worked on the
double policy—get rid of the bishops who supported the Nicene
decrees and find another formula to replace the Nicene—a
formula which should seem to mean the same, but which yet
should be subtly different, and different in such a way as to be
acceptable to the Arians.

The first part of the policy proved ridiculously easy for one
who had the Emperor behind him. In city after city there was
the same comedy. The Catholic bishop was accused of this or
that, a local council picked by Eusebius deposed him, there was
rioting among the people, so the Emperor exiled him. The
Emperor would then present the council with names of men
whose orthodoxy he personally could guarantee (for indeed
Eusebius had already guaranteed them to him), and the
council obediently and even gratefully chose the Emperor's
nominee. The details were not always the same, but that was
the general plan. And the result was that innumerable cities
were deprived of their Catholic bishops and ruled by Arians
or Eusebians, called by Newman "politicals". These cared
little about doctrine but had espoused the Arian cause and used

its more fanatical supporters to further their own worldly ambitions.

In the Arian and Eusebian ranks there would appear as time went on countless shades of opinion. The semi-Arians who accepted the word *homoiousios* (of like nature), while rejecting *homoousios* (of the same nature), were followed by Anomeans, Homeons and others. I shall not in this slight sketch differentiate between these sects, but shall speak of them all as Arians. Something, however, must be said about the difficulties some bishops felt about the word *homoousios*; for though it finally established itself as the best possible expression of so mighty a reality, it yet had to fight its way on account of its history.

The word *usia* was early chosen by Christians to express "being" or "substance". Tertullian was the first to speak of the Trinity as *unius substantiae* (of one substance), and St. Cyril later defined *usia* as meaning "That which has existence in itself independent of everything else to constitute it," i.e., an individual. But this was not the sense in which philosophers had been wont to use it; they meant by it "genus" or "species". And the gnostic Valentinian, bringing in the Eastern theory of Emanations and making these spirits or "aeons" more or less partakers of God's nature, applied to them the word *homoousios* (or consubstantial) in the sense it had originally borne philosophically. Then the Manicheans began to speak of the human soul as consubstantial with God—and thus gradually Catholics began to be afraid of the word.

"Why should I give up a word in a right sense", Tertullian asks, "because heresy uses it in a wrong one?" Tertullian was here referring to another disputed word—*probole*—but his remark applied even more strongly to *homoousios*. Paul of Samosata—himself later excommunicated, but at the time Bishop of Antioch—attacked the word as materialistic. Newman points out that *homoousios* was "a word long known in the Church, almost found in Scripture, less figurative and material than any which could be selected, objectionable only in the mouths of heretics", who "were gradually silencing the Church by a process which legitimately led to Pantheism, when the Alexandrians gave the alarm". Ideas or words favoured by Alexandrians became almost automatically suspect for the

theologians of the great rival school of Antioch. Despite the
almost unanimous vote at Nicaea, men even of good will
educated in the Antioch tradition continued to be chary of
using a word not actually to be found in Scripture.

Besides these intellectual problems there was that fresh element in Christian life, a new kind of imperial pressure. Why
was the Christian Emperor's power so readily accepted by men
who had been prepared to face torture and death from the
pagan emperors? The answer is not really difficult, if we grasp
the mentality of the age. There was the aura of divinity ever
belonging to the Roman Emperor; there was a kind of grateful
astonishment that so mighty a personage should be any kind of
Christian. From Constantine's point of view, the one essential
was to get the quarrel settled. Who stood in the way of settlement? Obviously the Catholics, with their unreasonableness,
their refusal to compromise! The Arians, Constantine found,
were reasonableness itself. They would sign creeds that to his
uninstructed eyes appeared just like that of Nicaea, they would
live at peace with the Catholics in the same Church—but the
Catholics would not live at peace with them.

Nor must Constantine's court be omitted from the picture.
We feel how amazing it was that Eusebius, whose banishment
had been the result of Constantine's discovery of his past intrigues with Licinius, so quickly won his ear again. And then
we remember Constantine's love for his sister Constantia—
who had been married to Licinius, and who worked steadily
both for Eusebius and Arius. At every date, court ladies and
hangers-on of all types have a large share in guiding the ruler's
policy. Constantia and her court were mostly Arian. She
wanted Eusebius back from exile; she got him. She wanted
Arius back; she got him also. And the supreme barrier between
these men and total success was Athanasius.

Arius, brought before the Emperor, offered an ambiguous
confession of faith which satisfied this amateur theologian—
and Eusebius persuaded Constantine to command Athanasius
to receive the heresiarch again at Alexandria.

"On being informed of my pleasure," wrote the Emperor,
"give free admission to all who are desirous of entering into
communion with the Church. For if I learn of your standing
in the way of any who were seeking it, or interdicting them, I

will send at once those who shall depose you instead, by my authority, and banish you from your see."

Athanasius refused, and in his circular letter to the bishops of Egypt and his *Apologia* against the Arians, he collects letters and documents which give a picture of the next few years. Among them perhaps the most interesting is the letter of the Egyptian bishops which they wrote "to all bishops and to Julius Bishop of Rome". One charge after another had been laid against Athanasius: clandestine consecration, helping plotters against the Emperor, sanctioning the overthrow of an altar and the breaking of a chalice. "Whence comes it", the Egyptian bishops ask, "that Christ's chalice is known to them who know not Christ?"—and they point out that there was no church and hence no altar at the supposed scene of sacrilege. The final accusation was that of murdering and dismembering Arsenius, a heretical bishop.

The Emperor's own letters are quoted by Athanasius. It seems amazing that as one accusation after another was proved false—the dead and dismembered bishop was actually produced alive and whole—Constantine could still be deceived by a new charge. But after letters of complete trust from Constantine, Athanasius next found himself called upon to stand trial at a council in Caesarea packed by Eusebius (334). He refused to go, but a year later Constantine forced him to attend another council at Tyre. "How can they have the boldness", exclaim the bishops of Egypt, "to call that a council, at which a single Count presided, which an executioner attended and where a chief jailer, instead of the deacons of the Church, introduced us into Court . . . the Count alone spoke . . . we were dragged about by soldiers."

Realising the futility of pleading under such circumstances, Athanasius determined on a bold step. He started off post-haste for the Emperor's new capital and suddenly appeared before him. In a letter to the bishops assembled at Tyre, the Emperor himself describes the scene:

As I was entering on a late occasion our all-happy home of Constantinople, which bears our name (I chanced at the time to be on horseback), on a sudden the Bishop Athanasius, with certain others whom he had with him, approached me in the middle of the road, so unexpectedly, as to occasion me much amazement . . . When he requested to be heard I refused, and all but gave orders for his removal, when with increasing boldness he claimed only this favour, that you should be summoned to appear, that he might have an opportunity of complaining before me in your presence of the ill-treatment which he has met with. As this appeared to me to be a reasonable request and suitable to the times, I willingly ordered this letter to be written to you, in order that all of you who constituted the council which was held at Tyre, might hasten without delay to the court of my clemency, so as to prove by facts that you had passed an impartial and uncorrupt judgement.[1]

Julian later described Athanasius as hardly a man—so small was he. We can imagine the tiny figure seizing perhaps the bridle of the Emperor's horse, compelling by the force of his personality the unwilling attention of his Lord. But at the interview he had demanded, the Arian bishops abandoned all their earlier charges and suddenly accused Athanasius of holding back the corn with which Alexandria should have supplied Constantinople, and of making his own profit out of imperial grants of corn for the poor. And Constantine, says Athanasius, "was immediately incensed, and instead of granting me a hearing, sent me away into Gaul".

Can this vacillating man be in truth the great Emperor? Eusebius, obsequious in his worship of the imperial divinity, Constantia and he pointing out unceasingly the growing power of Athanasius—a bishop too independent in his acts, too bold in his attitude—none of it seems enough to explain Constantine's behaviour. Clearly his conscience troubled him—for although he banished Athanasius, he appointed no one in his place: and as imperial exiles went, this was a mild one.

The first act of the Arian drama ended in 336 while Athanasius was at Trèves. He has told the story twice, although, as he wrote to Serapion, friend of Anthony, he had hesitated, "fearing lest anyone should suppose I was exulting".

Sent for by Constantine, Arius swore in his presence that his belief was fully Catholic. Constantine said, "If your faith is

[1] *Historical Tracts of S. Athanasius, Apology against the Arians,* vi, 32.

right you have done well to swear; but if your faith be impious and you have sworn, God judge you according to your oath."

As soon as Arius had satisfied the Emperor, the Eusebians clamoured for his reception back into the Church. Another Alexander was Bishop of Constantinople and he firmly refused to admit Arius. But the Emperor confirmed the threats of the Eusebians; if Alexander would not on the appointed day admit Arius to communion, he was to be thrown out of his see. For a week the Church in Constantinople prayed and fasted while its bishop tried vainly to change the Emperor's purpose. Athanasius relates of Alexander that on the final day, "entering into the church he stretched forth his hands to God and bewailed himself, and casting himself on his face in the chancel he prayed, lying upon the pavement".

A priest praying at his side heard Alexander beseech God that if Arius were to be received, he himself should die, "but if Thou wilt spare Thy Church . . . take off Arius lest, if he enter into the Church, the heresy may enter with him and piety henceforth may be counted for impiety".

As Alexander prayed, Arius, surrounded by his Eusebian supporters, paraded the town and "talked very wildly", all being confident of his restoration. And then Arius, "urged by the necessities of nature, withdrew, and suddenly, in the language of Scripture, *falling headlong he burst asunder in the midst,* and immediately expired as he lay, and was deprived both of communion and of his life together".[1]

All this while, the Emperor had not even asked for baptism. But not long after the death of Arius, Constantine himself fell ill. He went to pray at his mother's birthplace, re-christened by him Helenopolis, and then became aware that his sickness might be to death. He offered himself as a catechumen, confessed his sins kneeling on the pavement of the church, and received the imposition of hands which marked the beginning of the catechumenate. He sent for all the bishops to meet him on his re-entry into Nicomedia, and told them that he had hoped to go to the Holy Land and there be baptised in the Jordan "wherein our Saviour for our example is recorded to

---

[1] *Historical Tracts, Epistle to Serapion,* i, 3.

have been baptised". But now, since this was impossible, he desired baptism without hesitation or delay.

Clad in the white robe of the newly-baptised, Constantine died, sorrowing for his sins, begging God's mercy and promising, should his life be spared, to live it in closer accord with the faith he now professed. But it was no Catholic who baptised him. Eusebius of Nicomedia, the Arian, baptised Constantine in the name of the Father, Son and Holy Ghost. Doubtless the baptism was valid since he intended by it to do what the Church did, to give what the Church bestowed—sanctifying grace. But Eusebius did not believe that the Son, in whose name he had solemnly baptised the Emperor, was God.

AFTER CONSTANTINE

Constantine had accepted the teaching formula of Nicaea, says Newman, "as a formula of peace, not of belief". But when he died, discord already reigned and it grew far worse in the divided Empire. Of his three sons, Constans and Constantine were Catholics, Constantius was an Arian. Constantine II ruled Spain, Gaul and Britain; Constans, Africa, Italy, Rome, Dacia, Macedonia; Constantius, Thrace, Asia, Pontus, Egypt and the province called The East; four years later Constantine II was dead. Constans the Catholic then ruled the Western, Constantius the Arian the Eastern Empire.

Caesaro-Papism is a clumsy word, but it is the best we have to express the attitude to the Church inaugurated by Constantine, which became common form with his successors. The Middle Ages pictured Constantine in close relation with the Pope, but in fact he all but ignored him. And while Constantine meant less to decide what the Church should believe than to insist on peace and unity, his successors quickly went a great deal further. The saying *Cujus regio ejus religio* belongs to the Reformation period, but it was in action directly after Constantine's death.

A new kind of imperialism had come in: Christopher Dawson sees in the Christian Empire of Byzantium a close parallel with the Zoroastrian Kingdom of Sassanian Persia. The ruler of old Rome had been first Princeps, then Imperator; but the ruler of New Rome was "surrounded with all the oriental prestige and the ceremonial pomp of oriental despotism. The ruler is the Orthodox and Apostolic Emperor. His court is the Sacred Palace; his property is the Divine Household; his edicts are the 'celestial commands'; even the annual assessment of the taxes is known as 'the Divine Delegation'."[1]

But besides interference by bishops and theologians, another element manifests itself in occasional modification of this despotic "divine" authority—and that is the people. Modern historians have often failed to convey the atmosphere of a world in which the supernatural was not only as real as daily bread and taxes to the man in the street, but in which it was his chief interest. If, says St. Gregory of Nyssa, you go into a shop in Byzantium "the money-changer will talk about the Begotten and the Unbegotten instead of giving you your money, the baker, instead of telling you the price, will argue that the Father is greater than the Son, and if you want a bath the bath-keeper assures you that the Son surely proceeds from nothing". (*Oratio de Deitate Filii*, iv.)

As we read of the discussions of theologians and the encroachments of emperors we must always remember, especially in the Greek world, this passionately interested populace whose life "was lived in a world of religious hopes and fears . . . They all accepted the subordination of secular activities to the purely religious life. To them the real forces that ruled the world were not finance and war and politics but the powers of the spiritual world, the celestial hierarchy of angelic Virtues and Intelligences. And this invisible hierarchy had its counterpart and manifestation in the visible order of the ecclesiastical hierarchy and in the sacramental order of the Divine Mysteries".[2]

The younger Constantine knew and admired Athanasius and began his reign by a letter to the people of Alexandria (17 June, 338) dated from Trèves itself in which he stated firmly that his father had sent Athanasius away simply to save him "from his bloodthirsty and inveterate enemies". Constantine had fully intended to recall the exile and "I have thought proper to fulfil that intention of the Emperor of sacred memory". As Constans was in accord with his brother it was impossible for Constantius to resist, but the Arians were overwhelmingly strong in the East, and the Arian Emperor had only to wait awhile.

---

[1] Dawson, *The Making of Europe*, p. 83.   [2] ibid., p. 87.

Eusebius of Nicomedia had got himself installed in the new capital as Bishop of Constantinople and Athanasius had returned to Alexandria immediately after Constantine's death; the scene was set for a fresh struggle between Arian and Catholic. And curiously enough Eusebius and his followers, perhaps not at first sure of their ground with the new emperors, began by an appeal to Rome, although writing also to the rulers.

"The Eusebians themselves", says Athanasius, "wrote to Julius and, thinking to frighten me, requested him to call a council and to be himself the judge if he so pleased." At first the emperors held aloof, but before the appeal could be heard in Rome, Constantius suddenly intervened, banished St. Athanasius once more and set a prominent Arian in his place. Gregory, the new bishop, was escorted to Alexandria by a military guard and hideous scenes of rape and torture followed.

Athanasius, driven from Alexandria, repaired to Rome on the Pope's invitation for the council requested by the Arians. But now the Arians would have none of it. *Their* emperor was clearly on their side. *Their* bishop was safely installed at Alexandria, and they told the Pope that unless he would confirm this and the other depositions they had made they would have no further part with him. This letter, bitter and sarcastic, was drawn up by a council held at Antioch by a group of Arian bishops, and the whole thing set a new pattern. For it was the first time in the history of the Church that the primacy of Rome had been denied and schism threatened by a body of bishops. Also, until Arianism died out, these men would now match any council of the orthodox with a council of their own—and these councils were often quite nakedly assemblies governed by the imperial power. At Sirmium, for instance, Constantius set eight court officials to judge of the orthodoxy of a bishop.

The Arians refused to come to Rome, but Rome was filled with bishops deposed by them. All these bishops stated their case, which the council carefully considered. They had all been unjustly condemned and Pope Julius wrote very strongly demanding their reinstatement. In the case of Athanasius it was especially obvious that his see had been usurped, for "this Gregory" ordained at Antioch by the schismatic group had to be (the Pope reiterated) "escorted thence to Alexandria, not by priests and deacons of his Church but by soldiery".

Had there been real complaints against the exiled bishops, the rule should have been observed of the appeal to Rome. "Are you ignorant that the usual thing is to write first to us and then for a just sentence to be passed from this place? . . . Now they desire to obtain our concurrence though we never condemned him. Not so have the constitutions of Peter and Paul, not so have the traditions of the Fathers, directed; this is a new form of procedure, a novel practice . . . For what we have received from the blessed Peter, that I signify to you."[1]

The Pope's commands were powerless before the Emperor's arms. At Antioch, the doctrine of Nicaea was watered down by an Arian council; at Sardica it was reasserted by an orthodox one. But the bishops remained in exile. Athanasius was a tough fighter and around him the battle raged for many years. He was back in his see in 346 after seven years of exile; but, after the death of Constans in 350, which left Constantius as sole Emperor, the latter made another, and horribly successful, attempt to conquer the orthodox bishops. Pope Julius was dead and it might be easier to deal with Liberius. Constantius called a council at Arles (in 353) where he put forth a decree that every bishop who did not condemn Athanasius should himself be banished—and every bishop present except Paulinus of Trèves signed—including the legates of Liberius. Lack of communication was one great trouble. Some of the bishops present had not even heard of Nicaea. This did not excuse the papal legates—probably sheer brute fear was stirred. The East had already fallen before imperial power and prestige, now the West showed the same weakness.

That it was not easy to hold out was made even clearer when, in apparent response to a demand from Liberius, Constantius called another council at Milan in 355. For here the Arian bishops began by dragging the pen from the hands of the Bishop of Milan as he was about to sign the Nicene formula to manifest his orthodoxy. All save a handful again signed what the Emperor decreed. St. Athanasius himself has described the scene that followed:

---

[1] *Historical Tracts, Apology against the Arians*, ii, 26.

These the Emperor summoned before him, and commanded them to subscribe against Athanasius, and to hold communion with the heretics; and when they were astonished at this novel procedure, and said that there was no ecclesiastical canon to this effect, he immediately said, "Whatever I will, be that esteemed a canon; the bishops of Syria let me so speak. Either then obey, or go into banishment."

When the bishops heard this they were utterly amazed, and stretching forth their hands to God, they used great boldness of speech against him, teaching him that the Kingdom was not his, but God's who had given it to him, whom also they bade him fear, lest He should suddenly take it away from him. And they threatened him with the day of judgement, and warned him against infringing ecclesiastical order, and mingling Roman sovereignty with the constitution of the Church, not to introduce the Arian heresy into the Church of God.[1]

The bandy-legged dwarf Constantius brandished his sword at these bold men and in the deep voice that he affected, ordered their instant execution—a sentence which he immediately altered into banishment. But, says Athanasius, "as they passed along, bound as they were, they preached the Gospel, in every place and city proclaiming the orthodox faith, stigmatising the Arian heresy".

CONSTANTIUS, SOLE EMPEROR

Nothing that had happened under his father was comparable with the horrors opening upon the Church when Constantius became sole Emperor. Athanasius says in his *Apology against the Arians*, "This heresy has come forth upon the earth like some wild monster, which not only injures the innocent with its words, as with teeth, but has also hired external power to assist it." And again, "The truth is not preached with swords or darts, nor by means of soldiers; but by persuasion and counsel. But what persuasion is there when fear of the Emperor prevails? or what counsel is there, when he who withstands them receives at last banishment and death?"

[1] *Historical Tracts, History of the Arians*, iv. 8.

Constantius was a convinced Arian and the eunuchs of his court were so too. Although Athanasius speaks in passing of the influence of the court ladies, it seems that with this Emperor had begun the far more powerful influence of the eunuchs, which became such a bane in the eastern court. "Many of those who are about Constantius," he says, "or rather, the whole number of them, are eunuchs, and it is impossible to do anything there without them."

Athanasius adds a most curious comment. It was, he says, the eunuchs who instigated the persecution of the Catholics. "And the most remarkable circumstance in the matter is this; that the Arian heresy, which denies the Son of God, receives its support from eunuchs, who, as both their bodies are fruitless, and their souls barren of the seeds of virtue, cannot bear even to hear the name of Son. The eunuch of Ethiopia indeed . . . believed the words of Philip when he taught him concerning Our Saviour, but the eunuchs of Constantius . . . madly rage against those who say that the Son of God is His genuine Son, thus claiming as a heresy of eunuchs that there is no genuine and true offspring of the Father."[1]

While other bishops were going into exile, it was unlikely that Constantius and his advisers would leave Athanasius in peace at Alexandria. First came a fresh lot of accusations; he had spoken against Constantius to his brother Constans, he had intrigued with Magnentius, who had killed Constans, he had conducted worship in a church Constantius was building, without the Emperor's authorisation and before it had been consecrated. In a long and patient letter answering each of these charges Athanasius suddenly cries out despairingly, "I have passed sleepless nights contending against the charge, as if in the presence of my accusers; and suddenly breaking forth into a loud cry, I have immediately fallen to my prayers, desiring with groans and tears to obtain a favourable hearing from you."

Writing the story down must have stirred the feelings of the lonely exile. For Constantius had determined that this man should be left in a total solitude. Most of the bishops had given in or been exiled, imprisoned, tortured, and killed. One old bishop was dragged as far as Cucusus, the later scene of

[1] *Historical Tracts, History of the Arians*, v, 6.

Chrysostom's martyrdom, and there brutally put to death. But two leaders still remained in the defence of Athanasius and the maintaining of Nicaea—Liberius, Bishop of Rome, and the aged Hosius of Cordova. Constantius was determined to bend them to his will. "If we can persuade Liberius," Athanasius quotes the Arians, "we shall soon prevail over all."

Constantius sent a eunuch to Rome—yet another Eusebius —with gifts and letters—"to bribe Liberius with the presents, and to threaten him with the letters." Liberius refused the gifts; Eusebius carried them to "the martyry of the Apostle Peter" and laid them on the shrine. Liberius ordered them thrown into the street. There was great ferment in the court of Constantius; the other eunuchs, prompted by Eusebius, stirred the Emperor into further action. And after he "had frequently written to Rome, had threatened, sent commissioners, devised schemes . . . Liberius is dragged before him". This was at Milan, now the western capital.

The story is tragic enough of a courage that finally crumbled under a process analogous to what is today called brainwashing. For Liberius, at the Court, "used great boldness of speech" to the Emperor, and, when banished, sent back the money given him for his support, with the remark that Constantius and his eunuchs would need it to pay their soldiers and their bishops.

The Emperor wanted two things from Liberius: a condemnation of Athanasius and the signing of a formula which the Arians would accept in place of the Nicene. Newman relates the careful composition of a creed eventually signed by all parties, and indeed the Arian skill lay in using Scripture terms and omitting rather than contradicting definitions of their meaning laid down by the Church.

The mind of Liberius had been prepared no less carefully than the definitions. "Two years of exile," says Newman, "among the dreary solitudes of Thrace broke his spirit." The Bishop of Beroea, who had already conformed, watched his growing melancholy, and chose the moment to get other conforming bishops to work on him. They represented to him that he was not really suffering for the Church of which God had given him the government but merely for the obstinacy

of a private person named Athanasius, who had been condemned for various crimes both by the other bishops and earlier
by the great Constantine himself. Meanwhile his own see and
the whole Church were suffering from his absence, for Liberius
learnt from Rome of how three eunuchs had come from the
Emperor and had staged the election of another Pope. The
populace, who loved Liberius, paraded the streets crying out,
"One God, one Christ, one Bishop", thus calling upon themselves certain vengeance. Were he there, Liberius might save
them.

Physical and mental sufferings brought a surrender. We
do not fully know its extent, since no one is certain precisely
which formula Liberius did sign. But that he had violated his
conscience, he later made plain, and he certainly threw
Athanasius overboard. This at least Hosius would never do.
Like Liberius, he had stood firm when brought to the court of
Milan. He had even written to the Emperor in words which
seem to echo in advance the great St. Ambrose. "I was a
confessor," he tells him, for he was now 101 years old, "in the
time of your grandfather Maximinian."

He went on to assert the guilt of the Arians and the innocence of Athanasius, and then addressed Constantius in such
terms as prophets use: "Remember that you are a mortal man.
Be afraid of the day of judgement . . . meddle not with Church
matters, nor give commands to us concerning them, but rather
learn them from us. God has put into your hands the Kingdom,
to us He has entrusted the Church."

They tortured the old man, scourged him and stretched him
on the rack, till at last, broken in body and spirit, he signed a
formula "which", says Newman, "forbad the mention of the
Homoousion and thus virtually condemned the creed of
Nicaea". Two years later he died, abjuring the heresy which
dishonoured his Saviour's name and protesting against the
violence that had been used to him. Liberius, says Athanasius,
gave way "for fear of threatened death", Hosius, "broken by
suffering". And he judges them not, "for what men are forced
to do contrary to their first judgement, ought not to be considered the willing deed of those in fear, but rather of their
tormentors".

And as he tells the story Athanasius cries out in the words

of Scripture: "Wilt Thou make a full end of the remnant of Israel?"

Not Arianism alone but a bitter personal hatred moved Constantius in his pursuit of Athanasius. In his letter to the Alexandrians he calls him "impostor and cheat", "a man who had come forth from the lowest dens of infamy", "superior in nothing to the meanest of the people". He is sending them "the most venerable George", who will lead them on the path to heaven while "that pestilent fellow Athanasius is driven from place to place"—and ten deaths would be too good for him.

Fear was doubtless an element in this relentless hatred as it would not have been with the more courageous Constantine. Emperors were so often murdered and replaced that a powerful subject was a real menace. The historian Theodoret tells us that Constantius declared he was more eager to subdue Athanasius than he had been to conquer Magnentius or Sylvanus—the two armed rebels who had aspired to rule his empire. "The caution, the delay, the difficulty," says Gibbon, "with which he proceeded in the condemnation and punishment of a popular bishop, discovered to the world that the privileges of the Church had already revived a sense of order and freedom in the Roman government." It is an interesting acknowledgement from a historian, certainly not favourable to Christianity, of where freedom was maintained during those tyrannical centuries.

With Liberius and Hosius out of the way, Constantius did at last feel safe in directly attacking Athanasius. Gregory was dead, but the man whom he had now decided to intrude into the See of Alexandria, George of Cappadocia, was if possible even worse. He had been a purveyor of pork to the Army (not, Athanasius indicates, even an honest one), not a cleric of any kind. On a night of vigil the cathedral, filled with worshippers preparing for Mass and Communion when day should dawn, was surrounded by soldiers "having arms and drawn swords, bows, spears and clubs". Athanasius seated himself on his bishop's chair and, calming the people, ordered the deacon to read Psalm cxxxv (cxxxvi, A.V.) and the people to answer.

"Praise the Lord for He is good," the deacon began, and the people answered, "For His mercy endureth for ever."

The Psalm has twenty-seven verses, some of them singularly appropriate. We can imagine their power as the voices of thousands chanted them:

> Who made the heavens in understanding:
> For his mercy endureth for ever.
>
> .   .   .   .   .
>
> Who smote Egypt with their firstborn:
>
> .   .   .   .   .
>
> Who brought out Israel from among them:
> For His mercy endureth for ever.
>
> .   .   .   .   .
>
> Who smote great kings:
> For His mercy endureth for ever.
> And slew strong kings:
>
> .   .   .   .   .
>
> Sehon King of the Amorrhites:
>
> .   .   .   .   .
>
> And Og King of Basan:
> For His mercy endureth for ever.
>
> .   .   .   .   .
>
> Give glory to the God of heaven:
> For His mercy endureth for ever.
> Give glory to the Lord of lords:
> For His mercy endureth for ever.

The soldiers rushed in and the archbishop, "having bidden prayer", told the congregation to depart, saying that he would stay till all were gone. It was in a church almost empty of worshippers that his ministers seized Athanasius and dragged out the tiny figure through the very midst of the soldiers. Little wonder that in his *Apologia*, or explanation, for his flight, he later asked whether his critics would have wanted St. Peter to return to prison after an angel had opened the doors and led him through the armed guard. To every man a time is allotted and Our Lord Himself had set the example when "He neither suffered Himself to be taken before the time came, nor did He hide Himself when it was come".

The persecutors sought after the saints that there might be
no one to teach, as the Jews charged the Apostles; but for
this cause they endured all things that the Gospel might be
preached . . . they passed not the time of their flight un-
profitably, nor, while they were persecuted, did they forget
the welfare of others . . . when while they fled they preached
the Gospel, and gave warning of the wickedness of those who
conspired against them, and confirmed the faithful by their
exhortations.

Triumphant Exile

Gibbon sees in this exile of the Patriarch the final defeat of
the Emperor: "He received from an invisible hand a wound
he could neither heal nor revenge." And in the words quoted
from his *Apologia*, Athanasius has indicated the purpose of
his flight. He had, the Emperor sarcastically commented
to his flock, exiled himself. But it was an unusual sort of
exile.

Athanasius had disappeared—but where was he? The
details we shall never know in full, but there are interesting
stories and indications. In the surrounding deserts the monks
could hide him, passing him from one monastery to another,
and as one monk among many he was perfectly safe. But the
bishop had not abandoned his see; he had not abandoned the
Church in her need.

Both Newman and Gibbon are of opinion that in his allusion
to the Councils of Seleucia and Rimini Athanasius may be
indicating that he was secretly present at both. If so it can only
have been for a part of each. For they were held simultaneously—Seleucia for the eastern bishops, Rimini for the
western. At Seleucia not many were present and almost all
were the Emperor's men. But Rimini above all must have been
heartrending.

This council seemed full of promise, since of the four hundred
bishops present only about eighty were Arians. But the
Emperor was determined, and the Arians, as usual, patient and
subtle. Month after month the council dragged on. An
imperial prefect presided, with orders from Constantius that
the bishops should not stir from the city until they had agreed

on a formula to replace the Nicene. All attempts at an orthodox agreement were swiftly blocked by a combination of Arian skill and imperial threats. After almost a year the Arians finally declared they only wanted to avoid a *word* that was not in Scripture and their leader loudly pronounced anathemas on all who called the "Word of God, begotten of God before all time . . . a creature as other creatures".

It is inconceivable that Athanasius was then present; he would most certainly have risked both capture and death to avert the final catastrophe, for, says Newman, "the inexperienced Latins did not detect their insincerity. Satisfied and glad to be released they gave up the Homoousion, and signed the formula of the Homœon". The Arians were immediately able to boast that by the very phrase, "not as other creatures", they had declared the Son a creature.

"The whole world," St. Jerome commented, "groaned in astonishment to find itself Arian."

Another phrase in which this period has been summed up is "Athanasius against the world". But there was another less visible world that had not yielded to emperor or heresy, that was entrenched behind Athanasius. Speaking generally, "the Catholic people," says Newman, "in the length and breadth of Christendom, were the obstinate champions of Catholic truth and the bishops were not". But his own bishops of Egypt were behind Athanasius, and the bitterness of his return to Alexandria was sweetened by the love and loyalty of his people.

The days of Diocletian or Decius seemed to have come again and the salt-mines were filled with Catholic convicts. Enough still remained in the city to give their bishop food and sometimes shelter. There were strange places of concealment— one a dry cistern. The old hairbreadth escapes were renewed and Palladius tells a fascinating story of one asylum that served Athanasius. A girl, celebrated for her beauty and only twenty years old, was startled one night by his sudden appearance; he told her that he had been instructed in a vision to find safety under her roof. She hid him in the most remote room in the house, told nobody of his presence, borrowed books for him, brought him paper, handled his correspondence and waited on him like a maid or nurse, washing his feet and preparing his food. All this she told Palladius in her old age.[1] As Gibbon charmingly sums it up, "she dexterously concealed from the eye of suspicion this familiar and solitary intercourse between a saint whose character required the most unblemished chastity and a female whose charms might excite the most dangerous emotions". But it must be said in all fairness that it was from the neighbouring clerics and not from herself that Palladius learned the fame of her past beauty.

The time of hiding was also a time of much writing, and another thing pointing to Alexandria as the headquarters of Athanasius is the way he was able to collect documents for insertion in his narratives. The Emperor's letters to him and his to the Emperor naturally find their place, and one is startled by the obsequious note so long held by the saint towards the man he was defying. He calls him "Your Piety" and "most religious Augustus" again and again. Defending himself for not coming to Constantinople in response to an order from Constantius he asks, "O, Augustus, blessed and beloved of God, what would you have had me to do? To come to you, while my calumniators were inflamed with rage against me, and were seeking to kill me; or, as it is written, to hide myself a little, that in the meantime they might be condemned as heretics, and your goodness might be manifested to me?"

As long as possible, indeed one would say longer, the fiction was maintained of mischief made by interested parties. But there was something else in the attitude of Athanasius. Churchmen stood for the liberty of the subject, but they also saw the Emperor as the anointed of God. A divinity hedged the King and he must be reverenced. When his sins drove away the Holy Spirit the ruler still remained more than life-size; from the anointed of God he became the anointed of Satan! This at least is the sudden transition with Athanasius. In the *Apology against the Arians*, Constantius has become Emperor of Heresy, "this modern Ahab, this second Belshazzar". The "pretended" Arian bishops are actors who dance like the daughter of Herodias before Herod and "accomplish through false accusations the banishment and death of the true

---

[1] The value of Palladius as a historian having been questioned, Abbot Butler subjected him to the closest scrutiny. He emerged triumphant. A story told by him cannot be dismissed as mere gossip. But he certainly exaggerates the time spent in this particular hiding-place.

believers". Constantius is like Saul with David; he is bitterer
than Pilate. And after a long catalogue of his crimes Athanasius
concludes: "Who will any longer venture to call this Costylius
[a contemptuous diminutive] a Christian and not rather the
image of Antichrist?"

THE LAST YEARS

When Constantius died in 361 Athanasius was found, so the
story goes, seated in his episcopal chair in one of the churches
of Alexandria, ". . . a legend [says Newman] happily expres-
sive of the unwearied activity and almost ubiquity of that
extraordinary man." He had work enough to do still, not for
his own city alone, but for all Christendom.

Julian the Apostate, in the hope of fomenting divisions in the
Christian body, declared a general amnesty for the banished
bishops. Indeed, he invited to his palace leaders of various
hostile sects, that he might enjoy listening to their arguments.
But Athanasius soon heard that he was not included in the
amnesty. Newman thinks that Julian imagined Eusebius,
the time-serving prelate who had been his tutor, to be typical
of Christian bishops. And then he encountered Athanasius.
The only thing Constantius and Julian had in common was
hatred of the great bishop, and Julian expressed the highest
indignation that this criminal, condemned by both his predecessors, should dare, without awaiting a mandate from his
sovereign, to usurp the episcopal throne. Julian had, he said,
no doubt that his renewal of the decree of banishment would be
acceptable to the Alexandrians—but if he really believed this,
he was quickly undeceived. The clamorous entreaties of the
whole city showed him that most Alexandrians were Christians,
or at least that almost all the citizens devotedly loved the
bishop. They had better not have spoken: Julian, even more
enraged, extended the terms of banishment beyond the city to
the whole of Egypt.

But the prefect delayed in executing the Emperor's order—
perhaps on account of the great influx of bishops for the
Council of Alexandria. It was, indeed, mainly due to Athanasius that Julian's hopes went unfulfilled and a large measure
of peace returned to the Church. The matter of the bishops

who had given in during the persecution would have been
handled very differently had not he been there. The western
extremists, especially St. Hilary of Poitiers and Lucifer of
Cagliari, wanted a severe policy. But Athanasius, the greatest
confessor of them all, stood in the East, as firmly as Liberius
in the West, for moderation.

The conforming bishops were in possession of the Churches:
to expel them would have meant a fresh schism. Athanasius
was convinced not only that those who had yielded through
fear had sincerely repented and should be restored, but also
that there were others who (as Hilary himself admitted concerning the laity) had perfectly good wills and were merely
confused in mind. "Their own piety", Newman summarises,
"enabled them to interpret expressions religiously which were
originally invented as evasions of orthodox doctrine."

A decree was passed allowing those bishops who had communicated with the Arians "through weakness or surprise"
to retain their sees after signing the Nicene formula. Those
who had actually maintained the heresy publicly were reduced
to lay communion. Councils followed in Rome, Spain, Gaul
and Achaia, at all of which the same decision was adopted.
The part played by mental confusion was still further recog-
nized in the discussion which followed concerning a new
doctrinal problem which had arisen—and Newman both quotes
the synodal letter of the council and gives his own fascinating
summary. Greeks and Latins, he says, while agreeing on the
doctrine of the Trinity, had chosen different words to express
their faith. Human language being ever inadequate to the
divine reality, each side saw this inadequacy plainly in the
words chosen by the other. Besides the philosophical difficulty,
a common measure had to be created among three languages:
Greek, Syriac and Latin.

Hence arose differences both among the Greeks themselves
and between Greeks and Latins as to the proper use of the
words *persona, hypostasis, usia*, in relation to the divine Trinity
in Unity. The Council of Alexandria questioned separately
those who used *hypostasis* as meaning "substance" and those who
used it as meaning "person". Having satisfied themselves of the
orthodoxy of both parties and that alike they anathematised
Arianism, Sabellianism and all the other heresies, they decided

unanimously that the words of Nicaea should henceforward be used exclusively, since these other expressions "were not so desirable or accurate".

The Arians had chosen Meletius for Bishop of Antioch, thinking him a supporter, though a mild one, of their party. But Meletius, although most of his friends were at least semi-Arians and the danger was great of any opposition to them, boldly preached on his installation an orthodox sermon on the Trinity. His Catholic congregation applauded loudly. His Arian deacon rushed up and clapped a hand over his mouth. Meletius, unable to make himself heard, held up alternately three fingers and one to signify his belief. He was sent into exile and an Arian bishop appointed in his place.

Now Meletius was back, but despite the cause of his exile, was suspected by many of some degree of Arianism. The Council of Alexandria decided to send a commission to investigate the situation. But before they could get to Antioch, Lucifer of Cagliari had ordained another bishop for the Catholic party—Paulinus. That party had been throughout the object of the same persecution as Athanasius himself and, although he had hoped they would accept Meletius, there was enough doubt about the Meletian group in general to decide Athanasius in the end on supporting Paulinus.

Meanwhile Julian was growing angry. He wrote a furious letter to the prefect in which he threatened him with a heavy fine unless he heard before the end of the year of the departure of Athanasius from Egypt. In a postscript in his own handwriting he called Athanasius an infamous wretch. "The contempt shown for the gods fills me with grief and indignation . . . Under my reign the baptism of several Grecian ladies of the highest rank has been the effect of his persecutions." Gibbon comments: "The death of Athanasius was not expressly commanded", but the man who had declared his wish that the whole venom of the Nazarenes might be summed up in the single person of Athanasius would not have been likely to regret his demise. And one cannot but feel that a very powerful motive had arisen in the destruction by Athanasius of the Emperor's hopes of getting the Christians to fight one another.

Again Athanasius went into hiding—but he is said to have consoled his infuriated flock with the prophecy that this exile would be a short one. Within a year Julian was dead. Under Jovian, the bishop returned, his energy not at all diminished by sufferings or the weight of years. He summoned another council at which Nicaea was again reaffirmed, and carried its synodal letter to the Emperor at Antioch. Jovian has been described as "convivial and Christian". He received Athanasius cordially and would probably have continued to protect the Church. But he died after a reign of only eight months in an obscure town on the borders of Galatia and Bithynia. He had eaten an enormous supper and gone to sleep in a room filled with fumes from a charcoal fire—passing from heavy sleep into death.

Now the Empire was again divided, for Valentinian, the choice of the Western army, was urged, on being proclaimed in the East, to choose a second emperor. This proclamation was made, ironically enough, at Nicaea—for although himself a Catholic, Valentinian named his brother Valens, who was an Arian—and in October 364 Athanasius was again on the run. It was during this fifth and last exile, when approaching the age of seventy, that he is said to have hidden for a time in his father's tomb. To this exile also belongs the story of a police boat on the river. "Has Athanasius passed this way?" called out the officer through the darkness. "He is not far off", came the reply. On sped the boat, the police not knowing that the voice was the bishop's.

Valens had immediately issued an edict banishing all the bishops recalled by Jovian. But the Prefect of Alexandria, terrified by the vehement excitement of the people, begged him to make a special case of Athanasius and to reinstate him immediately, even the Arians of the city consenting to his return. It was on a vast wave of popular enthusiasm that Athanasius, against the will of princes, was carried through the storms of his forty-five years' episcopacy and finally brought back permanently to the throne in his cathedral. He worked to the end, toiling for purity both of faith and morals. With St. Basil's strong agreement, he excommunicated a governor of Libya for cruelty and vice; he carried on a vast correspondence with his fellow bishops; "Your concern for all the Churches", Basil wrote to him, "is no less than what you feel for the Church especially entrusted to you by the Lord of us all . . . ceaselessly you speak, exhort, write and send messengers to give advice in each crisis as it arises."

Athanasius had become a legend to the whole Christian world. Basil sees him as on a high tower watching the ships below battered by raging storms. "What capable pilot can be found? Who is worthy to rebuke the sea and waves?" This watcher is himself the pilot; in another metaphor he is the physician chosen by Our Lord to heal diseases in the Church. Basil longs "to be worthy to see you, to rejoice in your goodness, to add to my life's history a meeting with your truly great and apostolic soul".

They do not seem to have met, but when Athanasius died in 373, Basil above all took up in the East the burden he laid down. In the West that same year Ambrose was consecrated Bishop of Milan.

CONSTANTINE, Eusebius tells us, said to the Christian bishops, "You are the bishops of those inside the Church, I am the bishop of those outside". His earliest legislation accorded with this statement and he kept the title of Pontifex Maximus. Equal liberty was given to Christianity and to the ancient polytheism of Rome. Jewish worship was also expressly permitted. But as its High Priest, Constantine proceeded to "purify" paganism. He forbade black magic and private divining in 318 and 320. He shut in 330 certain temples in Syria where the worship was contrary to public morals; the books of Porphyry were burnt, like those of Arius, and Constantine interestingly called the "Porphyrians" Arian schismatics. It was all part of his policy of moderation and unification: the pagan Libanius states expressly, "Constantine changed nothing of the legal worship. It is true that the temples were poor but all the ceremonies of worship were carried out."

As De Labriolle has noted in his *Littérature latine chrétienne*, it is a little difficult to discover exactly what did happen—and when—in the various parts of the vast Empire. The Christians were eager to proclaim Constantine as destroyer of the gods and creator of a new era. Even in his lifetime Eusebius, in "one of the most successful examples known of fulsome flattery", after exalting him above Cyrus and Alexander, praises Constantine's piety, his generosity towards the Church, and his determination to abolish the darkness of paganism.

The pagans, as embittered as the Christians were joyful at the change in their respective positions, far from contradicting Eusebius, cried out that they were being persecuted long before they really were. And while the official documents might be supposed to settle the question beyond dispute, there is a curious ambiguity of language which sometimes makes them difficult to interpret. The word "superstition" was freely used and had many meanings. It covered every unauthorised cult, every magic incantation, every practice aimed at endangering a man's life or destroying his will-power. For long it had been the favourite pagan term for Christianity—and now many Christians were using it of their enemies. Cicero had said that "not philosophers alone but our ancestors distinguished between superstition and religion". But one man's religion is only too often the superstition of another. And it is by no means easy to be certain, even in an official proclamation, when *superstitio* is being used in a Roman sense and when in a Christian.

Constantine was not above robbing the temples of their treasures for the benefit of his new great city. Byzantium, now Constantinople, was to be the first glory of the world: in it no pagan temple was to be found. In this matter Constantine acted as a Christian who was making a Christian city. But he was by no means the iconoclast he is often represented as being, and while he forbade private divination, black magic and private sacrifice, he permitted the public traditional consultation of the *haruspices*, public sacrifice and beneficent magic—i.e., for personal health and the protection of the home.

With the sons of Constantine a change begins: Libanius complains bitterly of Constantius the Arian—"His father had robbed the gods of their wealth but *he* razed the temples to the ground, abolished all the holy rites . . . Philosophers, sophists, initiates in the mysteries of Hermes and the Muses, had no entry to the palace . . . His favourites . . . whose advice he accepted, were barbarians and wretched eunuchs."

Libanius, foremost rhetorician and classical scholar of the age, convinced pagan and close friend of Julian, was understandably bitter. But in fact there seem to have been few destructions of temples even in the East at this date, and those usually the result of inflamed local feeling rather than imperial commands.

JULIAN "THE APOSTATE"

When Julian first entered Antioch he found "the luxurious capital of the East plunged in mimic grief for the annual death of Adonis". But, as he approached the city, "he was received with public prayers as if he had been a god and he marvelled at the voices of a great multitude who cried that the Star of Salvation had dawned upon them in the East". Telling this story in *The Golden Bough*, Frazer sees in it either "a fulsome compliment paid by an obsequious Oriental crowd", or Julian's mistake in thinking that worship directed to the planet Venus, identified with "Astarte, the divine mistress of Adonis", was meant for himself.

It is surely not unlikely that paganism recognised in Julian the last hope of restoration. Cousin of Constantius, he had been educated as an Arian and all he had noted of Christianity was its warring sects. He had been baptised and even given minor clerical orders. But it is related that in mock disputes between him and his brother Gallus he always chose to maintain the pagan side, alleging that, being the more difficult, it would give greater scope to his talents. It is unlikely that he ever felt affection or respect for that very dubious character Eusebius of Nicomedia, under whose care Constantius had placed him. When at the age of sixteen he was released from the seclusion of his earlier years, he threw himself passionately into the study of philosophy. He had already imbibed strong literary tastes from his tutor Mardonius, and at Constantinople and Nicomedia, at Ephesus and later at Athens, he haunted the philosophers.

How far Julian had been a Christian by conviction it is hard to tell: most certainly he became passionately pagan. He had received "a call from the gods"; he did his best to wash away the waters of his baptism. In 351, at the age of twenty, he was ritually initiated into the mysteries of sun-worship, in 355 into those of Eleusis; later on, in Gaul, into those of Mithra. Gibbon describes his imperial letters as "pastorals", but if Constantine had been the bishop of the pagans, Julian was their Pope. Nay, he was more, for from the moment he became Emperor, he began to design a vast scheme of paganism that was in fact a new creation. It was to be a syncretism, not only of the ancient Greek and Roman worship with the various Eastern religions, but also with the tenets of all the leading philosophers save Epicurus, together with the practices of austerity and charity which he recognised in the priesthood of "the Galileans".

His own life was one of unremitting toil and austerity: he slept little, he ate little. He seems hardly to have washed at all;

in a sardonic speech he drew attention to his long black finger-nails and the insect inhabitants of his beard. He swept away the crowds of eunuchs and attendants in the imperial palace. The money thus saved he poured out on costly worship of the gods. Morning and evening Julian offered sacrifice in his palace grounds—or rather he waited on the priests, bringing the sacred fire or examining for omens the entrails of the animals. It was a curiosity that the man who designed this "new" religion should take so humble an attitude towards its hierophants—and also towards the philosophers from whom he believed himself to have learnt so much, many of whom grew rich at his expense.

Outside the palace, all through the East Julian laboured at the undoing of what Constantius had done—or at least had permitted. Treasures taken from the temples were to be restored, temples destroyed were to be rebuilt by the destroyers. These directives were carried out in some places—Arethusa, Ancyra, Alexandria and elsewhere—with considerable en-thusiasm, and resulted in the torturing or killing of several Christian priests, bishops and even laity—crimes rebuked but not punished by the Emperor.

Julian had begun his reign with a general decree of tolerance. From the experiences of his childhood and youth, he believed that freedom to quarrel would destroy Christianity much faster than any persecution. It was probably, as we have seen, the unifying power of Athanasius, even more than jealousy of his extraordinary ascendancy, that made Julian hate him so bitterly. Short as his reign was it was marked by a definite change of policy. He was determined against that shedding of Christian blood which had in the past proved "the seed of the Church", but he started a method of repression which might well have been more effective. He forbade those to teach who "despised the gods" who were honoured in the Classics, ex-pounded in the schools. It was, he said, a mere matter of honesty. Christians could no longer hold posts in provincial administration or the Imperial Guard "because their own law forbids them to use the sword". He must have smiled grimly as he wrote these words, knowing perfectly that there were no more loyal soldiers in the army than the Christians and that the philosophy of pacifism put forward by Tertullian and others had been repudiated by the Church's rulers. The policy had begun of squeezing Christians out of public life: the schools, the army, the forum.

Julian believed himself the mouthpiece of the gods, and it seems to have been the experience of speaking to deaf ears that inaugurated his change of policy. "It was in vain", writes Bidez, "that his acolytes threw open the temples, re-erected and regilded the statues . . . made the oracles speak again in the rustling of forest leaves and the murmuring of fountains, restored their power to the rays of Helios and to the stars and all her magic to nature. Vainly did they mount the pulpit and preach philanthropy quoting Homer, Hesiod and Plato."

As he turned to look upon the effect of his organisation, with all its pomp and splendour, Julian's eyes met only too often "the sneering gaze of an indifferent public or the desolating sight of an empty temple".[1]

Perhaps most miserable of all his experiences had been a visit to the beautiful groves of Daphne near Antioch. Probably his first welcome as a god had fed his hopes of Antioch's religion. His imagination pictured vast crowds and a worship worthy of Apollo, whose temple at Daphne was world-famous. He found a deserted shrine and an ancient priest who, for sole sacrifice, had ready a goose. Hard by stood a splendid Christian church, the shrine of the martyr St. Babylas. Julian ordered the martyr's remains removed, and they were carried to the city by a vast crowd of Christians in what became a triumphal march. That night the shrine of Apollo was burnt down and, although no proof was found, Julian asserted that the Christians were guilty and had their church stripped of its treasures and closed. Perhaps it was on this occasion that he ordered the public markets of the city sprinkled with lustral water. Elsewhere he commanded the demolition of martyrs' chapels in the neighbourhood of temples, and for the same reason—"purification"—he forbade funeral processions during the daytime.

In the autumn of 326 Julian re-exiled not only Athanasius but many other bishops. He seemed about to undertake on his return from the Persian campaign a new offensive against the

---

[1] J. Bidez, *La Vie de l'Empereur Julien*, p. 134.

Church. On the other hand, the pagan world expressed a fore-
boding that his victorious return would totally abolish the
breed of horned cattle in the Empire. He had frequently been
known to sacrifice as many as a hundred bulls in a single day
and it was said that he desired to emulate Solomon, whose
sacrificial animals were counted in tens of thousands.

Julian had shown his courage and genius as a general in
Gaul; it was the army that had chosen him for Emperor,
perhaps against his will. The Persians who had harried the
Empire under Constantius respected Julian and were willing to
make favourable terms with him, but Julian had determined
on a complete conquest. Spectacular victories marked the
beginning of his campaign. Depicted by Persian artists as a
furious lion vomiting forth fierce flames, he was secretly
approached by King Sapor with offers of peace, and might,
Gibbon surmises, have gained half the Persian kingdom
would he but have relinquished hope of conquering the whole.

The Persians, their offer refused, were driven to desperation
and engaged in the devastation of their own country known
today as scorched-earth policy. Amid a starving and discouraged army Julian, severely wounded, displayed, says
Gibbon, "perhaps with some ostentation, the love of virtue
and fame which had been the ruling passions of his life". One
does not know why Gibbon finds ostentation here. At
any rate, Julian seems to have awaited death cheerfully, saying
he had "learned from philosophy how much the soul is more
excellent than the body and that the separation of the nobler
substance should bring joy rather than grief . . . I die without
remorse as I have lived without guilt". He thanked the
supreme Being who had given him "in the midst of an honourable career a splendid and glorious departure from this
world". He would not select for his country its future ruler, as
his choice might not be a wise one. He distributed his private
fortune by a military testament, and rebuked the fears of the
bystanders, reminding them that he would in a few moments
be united with heaven and with the stars.

He then exhausted what strength was left him by entering
on a discussion with two philosophers, Priscus and Maximus, as
to the nature of the soul: he called for a drink of cold water and
after drinking it died painlessly.

THE REPRESSION OF PAGANISM

The attempt at repaganising the Empire died with Julian. Jovian, who reigned only eight months, and Valentinian, proclaimed tolerance of paganism, only reiterating the laws of Constantine against incantations, astrology and magic.

With Gratian's repudiation of the title of Pontifex Maximus and the policy of himself, his brother and finally Theodosius, a new era began. All three stood against persecution of the individual: there was a moment in 384 when all the leading functionaries, civil and military, were pagans. On the other hand a strong campaign opened for the destruction of the pagan temples, which was taken up eagerly by various bishops. St. John Chrysostom, who spoke so magnificently against persecution, reminding his people that Christ was the shepherd of sheep and would nowise remain their shepherd if they turned into wolves, asked for and received an imperial rescript to demolish the temples of Phoenicia (399). The cost of this was borne by some rich Christian ladies—but at least they also paid the expenses of missionaries to the people whose temples were being swept away.

Two centuries later St. Gregory the Great would instruct Augustine not to demolish the temples in Britain, not even to close them, but to bring to the people in the places where they had always worshipped a better kind of worship. By and large this has been the Church's policy through the ages. She is often reproached for taking into her liturgy elements from pagan worship, for being too tolerant in her attitude to the imperfect stammerings in which men had expressed the ABC that was all they knew of religion. But at this time very few bishops seem to have tried even to transform the buildings, far less to leave them as they were. In the towns it may be that the temples were deserted anyway, that only spectacular yearly festivals drew crowds; but the very word "pagan" testified to the hold the old customs had in the countryside. The pagans were the country-dwellers, and for them the rhetorician Libanius poured forth a passionate plea in his discourse *Pro Templis*. A countryside, he says, thus maltreated, is lost. The peasants lose courage when they lose hope. Their work is vain if the gods are gone who crowned their toil with success. Do not the destroyers realise that these sanctuaries where generation has succeeded generation are the soul of the surrounding country-side?

But it was a heathen philosopher, not a bishop who said of the myths of Asia, "Spit them out and then rinse your mouth." We have only to read such a book as *The Golden Bough* to follow a track of blood and horror which, even if it be narrow in relation to the whole, is traceable in pre-Christian religion. The prophet Micheas protests against the idea that Jahve requires human sacrifice, and even if rarer than Frazer indicates, this was not absent from pre-Christian religion.

Besides ritual murder there was in many rites ritual prostitution. Attis and Cybele were served by eunuch priests, so were Artemis of Ephesus and the Syrian Astarte of Hierapolis. Processions in honour of these dieties often included rituals in which the priests gashed their bodies and stirred some of the onlookers to such a frenzy that they then and there castrated themselves in dedication to the goddess. There is a famous poem of Catullus describing a man's feelings on the day following such madness.

Apart from these scenes of horror Christians viewed with deep distrust such things as the *taurobolium* or bath of bull's blood, the phallic signs adorning the temples, the stories concerning various initiations. They believed much of it to be devil-inspired—and who can deny this possibility, if he believes at all in unseen forces warring invisibly for men's souls and for the triumph of good or evil?

But the mistake many Christians made was that they failed to see the immense mass of human cravings which God had put into men's hearts and which flowed into their religion, the revelation of Himself through sun, moon and stars, through water and trees, through the cycle of human life and effort, through rocks and high mountains. Today we sacrifice to speed more victims than were ever offered to any ancient god, but we should feel an appraisal of our civilisation to be unfair in which this was regarded as the chief feature.

Eighteenth- and nineteenth-century scholarship was unfair precisely in this way. Gibbon in history, Frazer in comparative religion, were immensely learned, but from lack of sympathy they failed in proportion and in interpretation. How often

Gibbon invokes as an absolute the civilised modern man for whom it is impossible to enter into the thought processes of these superstitious characters; Anthony the hermit and Julian the idolator are equally despicable, except that Julian had also a practical side which redeemed him despite his superstitions. Again and again Frazer refers in the same way to the modern civilised Englishman, for whom primitive religion can be no more than an amusing puzzle, long outmoded but of antiquarian interest. These writers have no sense of the sacred, no realisation that man as such is valuable, that if in his story a current of thought and feeling runs very strong it *must* have some validity worthy of respectful examination. In such a book as Eliade's *Patterns of Comparative Religion* the wheel has come full circle; it is we who are to be pitied for our "broken and alienated existence". "The modern profane mind" has lost the clue to deepest reality, but "primitive spirituality lives on . . . as a nostalgia which creates things that become values in themselves: art, the sciences, social theory and all the other things to which men will give the whole of themselves."

While Eliade is inclined to soft-pedal the ugly side of pre-Christian religion (you have to look closely to discover in his book the defilements of ritual immoralities and blood sacrifices) he yet realises how inevitable was the attitude of the Jew to the pagan, of the Christian to both pagan and Jew. "To anyone who has received a new revelation"—the Mosaic in the Semitic world, the Christian in the Graeco-Roman world— the earlier hierophanies have lost their meaning as revelations of the sacred and "become obstacles to the development of religious experience". Breaking idols, destroying temples was, he holds, "justified both by their own religious experience and by the point in history where it occurs". In possession of a greater truth "they *cannot* see any religious value in the hierophanies accepted in previous stages of religious development".

Then too, just as Ruskin rebukes the Catholic of the nineteenth century, who "does not care what kind of idol he worships", Clement of Alexandria says: "The Arabs adore stones." Perhaps some of them did, but there was in fact a theology on the subject which he had never tried to penetrate. Sacred stones were adored only as "manifesting a divine presence. They represented God's *house*, they were his sign, his emblem, the repository of his power or the unchanging witness of an act performed in his name".[1]

Clement was remote from the religion of the people not only as Christian but as philosopher. Eliade believes that the Graeco-Roman world, when it did try to turn the old religions into philosophy—from *hierophany* into *idea*—made of them the palest shadows of what they once had been. He instances Julian in his treatise *On The Sun King* and Proclus in his *Hymn to the Sun*. The sun, "one of the mightiest of all the cosmic hierophanies", was reduced by rationalisation to the palest shadow of what it had meant to the primitive. For the man of the mountains, the sea, the countryside, sun, moon and stars, great rocks, trees, the all-embracing sky, the search for the Centre, ways of escape from earthly into real time, made up the rhythm of a life in which daily actions became sacred: sowing and reaping, marrying and giving birth. Things least understood were often most holy. "Contemplating the vault of heaven" is a kind of revelation. "The sky shows itself as it really is: infinite, transcendent . . . 'Most High' becomes quite naturally an attribute of the divinity." Height itself has for the primitive a consecrating power: "High places are impregnated with sacred forces."

Life was lived in an atmosphere of the sacred, if also of dread. Perhaps the peasant could not have explained it, but he was at least well aware that evil as well as good surrounded him invisibly.

It was only in Christianity that philosophy came to terms with the religious instinct of the little ones, but in the final battle against paganism the Christian leaders seem to have been singularly lacking in psychology. Was it likely that men who had seen the centres of their old worship smashed to pieces before their eyes would embrace the religion of the destroyers? Yet this very thing did occasionally happen. St. Martin went through the countryside of Gaul practically hammer in one hand and cross in the other, destroying and building up— and he converted that countryside on a vast scale. The saints could do this amazing thing, but only the saints. St. John the Golden-Mouthed destroyed temples and converted pagans,

---

[1] Mircea Eliade, *Patterns in Comparative Religion*, p. 228.

but Theophilus of Alexandria destroyed temples and provoked revolution.

Meanwhile the legislation grew more and more repressive both in East and West. It was by no means bishops alone who shut or destroyed temples: the Prefect Cynegius went through Syria and Egypt between 385 and 388 shutting so many as to sting Libanius into the vehement protest *Pro Templis* quoted above. Pagans employed by the administration could check destruction, but any Christian functionary to whom the idea appealed clearly had a free hand to carry it on.

Pagan feeling had a lot to do with the revolt of Arbogast in 392—or at least with winning support for it. His pawn Eugenius put back the statue of Victory in the senate, and the prefect of Italy solemnly restored the forbidden worship. At the prayer of St. Ambrose, the victorious Theodosius spared all the revolutionaries but re-enacted the laws against paganism.

Among these laws had been the last and most devastating edict, that of 392, in which throughout the Empire all were forbidden, not in temples only but even privately, to honour by fire or incense their Lares and Penates—household gods who represented the spirits of their ancestors—to honour the genius of people or places by libations, to build altars of sods.

Henceforth only in secret under menace of severe punishment was it possible to practise pagan religion.

Where conversion had indeed kept pace with destruction, this might have meant what was called "the end of paganism". But Christians should have known by experience that to forbid is not to destroy, rulers should have known from history that things repressed go underground and often grow more evil as they do so. Throughout the Middle Ages the Church had to struggle with pagan superstitions, with magic not only white but black. Exiling the innocent myths, the rulers of the Empire had often left merely an empty space—which the demons hastened to occupy. Household gods, however mythical, were better companions; for, as Chesterton has said, though the myths were not solid realities they were an expression of human hunger, and only the Bread of Life can appease it. There were unhappily more enthusiasts eager to destroy temples than there were saints ready to break this Bread to the worshippers.

GREGORY the Great signifies for us the first Pope of that name, but to the Cappadocians of the fourth century the great Gregory was Thaumaturgus—the Wonderworker. He was a century earlier than Basil (329–78), who often spoke and wrote of him; Basil's brother, Gregory of Nyssa, wrote his life. Their grandmother Macrina would often tell the two boys of this great bishop, repeating his very words. We have already met Gregory Thaumaturgus and his brother in the school of Origen at Alexandria, whence they returned to preach the Gospel in their native country.

When Gregory became Bishop of Neocaesarea there were only seventeen Christians there; when he died there were only seventeen pagans. So deep was the impression he had made that Basil tells us how—in an age when the liturgy was rapidly developing throughout the Christian world—men of Pontus and Cappadocia would not lay a finger on the heritage bequeathed by their evangelist. Their liturgy had, he acknowledged, an archaic, indeed an unfinished look, because of this profound reverence for the man who had first brought it into being.

In the countryside Gregory recognised the need to win people to Christianity through a certain gaiety, to transform not destroy their ancient joys. Saints' days were to be kept with high festival; a populace baptised and transformed through the Christian message would learn later to worship with greater awe and solemnity. He was concerned to preach divine truth accurately to these simple folk but not to curtail their pleasures.

How could he announce to worshippers of many gods the Trinity in Unity of the one God of Revelation? It was, as we have seen, in answer to his really anguished prayers that Our Lady appeared to him. With Mary came John the Apostle especially loved by her Son, and Mary told John to teach Gregory how he should unfold this great mystery. This is the

first apparition of Our Lady known to history; the Creed itself
remarkably anticipates Nicaea. Devotion to the Holy Trinity
is marked in the men of Cappadocia—Gregory Nazianzen,
Gregory of Nyssa and Basil himself, all disciples of the Wonderworker—and it is to Gregory of Nyssa that we owe his namesake's creed in its fullness, since the last clause is not found in all
the codices:

And there is one Holy Ghost, who hath His being of God,
who hath appeared [to mankind] through the Son, Image
of the Son, Perfect of the Perfect; Life, the Cause of all
them that live; Holy Fountain, Holiness, the Bestower of
Sanctification, in whom is manifested God the Father, who
is over all and in all, and God the Son, who is through all.
A perfect Trinity, not divided or alien in glory and eternity
and dominion.[1]

Intellectual ardour seems to have been the chief mark of
Basil as he grew into youth and manhood—pursuing his education first at Caesarea in Cappadocia, next at Constantinople,
where he was taught by Libanius, and finally at Athens. Men
of sense, says Gregory Nazianzen, his close friend and fellow-
student, realise that among all good things education comes
first—not only the noblest part of it, which concerns our
salvation, but also that culture which so many Christians reject
as useless and even dangerous. What gift of God is useless, and
what is without danger? he asks, passionately defending in his
famous funeral sermon the mental culture which he and Basil
received together at Athens. "The ignorant and uncultured
want everyone to be like themselves, that they may pass unnoticed in the crowd and escape the reproaches their illiteracy
merits. This principle once laid down and accepted, let us
consider our hero."

When acutely bored by Bossuet's *Oraisons funèbres*, it may
amuse us to remember that this is no original Christian style
but derives with a few turns and twists from the Sophists of
Greece. So, long before, Gregory Nazianzen had studied the
same form closely and applied his studies to the man who was

[1] Bull's translation, given in the *Dictionary of Christian Biography*, art. "Gregory
Thaumaturgus".

his hero. Things must be said that belong to the form—Basil had (for instance) been a fine-looking man before he had begun the conquest of his body by asceticism. Classical allusions must be introduced, comparisons elevating his hero in relation both to the heroes of Greek antiquity and of Scripture. But anything perfunctory in this discourse is conquered by a vitality rising up from the deep affection, the shared life, of those days at Athens.

Gregory had got there first and welcomed Basil, as yet merely his acquaintance. And if Basil owed to his own personality his unique escape from initiation—via a highly undignified ceremonial bath—into university life, Gregory makes it clear that to himself was owing Basil's first triumph in debate. The close friendship they formed was based indeed on this, but far more on their common aim. Both took the road to church even more eagerly than the road to the lecture room, both avoided feasts and shows, both desired philosophy above all else; and for the young Christian philosophy implied the ascetic life.

Basil gathered around him some sort of confraternity which made them, Gregory claims, "famous among our professors and our companions, famous throughout Greece and especially among the country's notabilities . . . both of us were known and praised together; a famous pair known and boasted of as such among our teachers". Of higher fame in fact than any of the noted couples in classical literature—the Orestes, the Pylades, the Molionides of Homer. "But here I am boasting of myself without realising it—a thing I regard as ridiculous in others." He cannot help it. Those days are so much alive. Then he profited through Basil's virtue, today through his glory.

Every effort was made to persuade the two friends to remain in Athens, and Gregory did agree to stay on for a time after his friend left in 355. For a short while Basil taught rhetoric in Caesarea; then came a visit to his home where his sister Macrina and his widowed mother were already living a secluded and ascetic life. His brother Gregory says bluntly: "The great Basil returned after his long education a practised rhetorician. He was puffed up beyond measure with the pride of oratory and looked down on the local dignitaries, excelling in his own estimation all men of learning and position."

Thus the sharp-eyed younger brother, taking note of what might become a critical situation. "Nevertheless," he continues, "Macrina took him in hand and with such speed did she draw him also towards the goal of philosophy that he forsook the glories of this world, and despised fame gained by speaking and deserted it for this busy life where one toils with one's hands."

Somewhere between these two accounts what happened to Basil emerges. He speaks himself of all he owed to Macrina, he speaks of a conversion when, after leaving Athens, it was as though he had awakened from sleep. This is not to deny the excellence of his university life, so much as to show us that something startlingly greater had shown itself suddenly before the eyes of his spirit.

Yet it is difficult to fix the chronology of his early life or to evaluate the various influences working upon him. From Gregory Nazianzen one would judge that they had long determined on leaving the world together and that Basil was only waiting for Gregory to join him. But Gregory would not come; he admits his promise, but to have kept it would have distressed his parents.

THE RULE OF ST. BASIL

Newman attributes to Basil's disappointment at the non-arrival of Gregory, his decision to spend a year studying the ascetic life as it was lived in the wide deserts. But we must not forget the influence of Eustathius, Bishop of Sebaste, who did in fact suggest this pilgrimage, nor yet that of Macrina. Anyhow it was commonsense, having decided to follow the perfect life of renunciation, first to study it in its highest representatives. "And many did I find in Alexandria and many in the rest of Egypt and others in Palestine and in Coelo-Syria and in Mesopotamia." Basil was away for a little more than a year and returned full of admiration, but already he had ideals differing in some respects from what he had been witnessing. A study of his own ascetical writings, and a glance at the contemporary behaviour of hermits and ascetics, show us the weaknesses which Basil became determined to correct in his design for monastic living.

Anthony wrote no rule, but Pachomius did—and for the East it was surprisingly moderate. (What appeared moderate in the East seemed to the Westerner appallingly severe.) But Pachomius looked on his rule as a minimum—his monks were encouraged to go beyond it, each according to his ability. They were often called athletes of Christ, and the competitions that resulted had a slightly comic resemblance to those of modern athleticism. While the young athlete tries to run faster or jump higher than his competitor, the young ascetic tried to fast longer, sleep less, wash less and weave more mats. Even men who cared little for visible prowess in these matters tended to admire and emulate monks famous for asceticism—to feel that they must be the best soldiers in the army of Christ. Basil was among the eminent churchmen who knew in middle life that they had seriously damaged their health and strength by youthful excesses in self-discipline. Gregory Nazianzen was another—and Chrysostom, and Gregory the Great.

In his own monasteries Basil laid it down that the Rule he drew up was enough—no one might exceed it without permission, and such permission was not to be lightly given. The common life, with its daily round of prayer and work, was the ideal: individual exaggeration might easily destroy the common life.

Basil's ideas about the common life developed as he lived it. On his return from his grand tour of monasticism his thoughts turned to the companionship he had first desired. Gregory had hesitated to leave his father, the aged Bishop of Nazianzus, and Basil first experimented with a place near Nazianzus for his monastery. But he abandoned it as too cold and damp. "O clean-footed, tip-toeing, capering man," says Gregory, reproaching him, "you are gentlemanlike and wealthy and a man of the world; I cannot praise it. Say not a word more against our mud . . . or I will match our wading with your trading and all the wretched things which are found in cities."

Finally Basil decided on a site across the river Iris opposite his home, and there he remained. Newman in his *Church of the Fathers* has painted pleasantly the friendship with Gregory, his long visits to Basil and their opposite opinions of Basil's idyllic dwelling.

Basil says:

There is a lofty mountain covered with thick woods,
watered towards the north with cool and transparent streams.
A plain lies beneath, enriched by the waters which are ever
draining off upon it; and skirted by a spontaneous profusion
of trees almost thick enough to be a fence; so as even to
surpass Calypso's Island, which Homer seems to have
considered the most beautiful spot on earth . . . Does it not
strike you what a foolish mistake I was near making when
I was eager to change this spot for your Tiberina, the very
pit of the whole earth? Pardon me, then, if I am now set
upon it; for not Alcmaeon himself, I suppose, would endure
to wander further when he had found the Echinades.
(*Ep. XIV.*)

Gregory, after a visit to his friend, retorts on

. . . the dwelling without roof and without door—the
hearth without fire and smoke—walls, however, baked
enough, lest the mud should trickle on us, while we suffer
Tantalus's penalty, thirst in the midst of wet . . . I have
remembrance of the bread and of the broth—so they were
named—and shall remember them: how my teeth got stuck
in your hunches, and next lifted and heaved themselves as
out of paste. You, indeed, will set it out in tragic style yourself, taking a sublime tone from your own sufferings. But
for me, unless that true Lady Bountiful, your mother, had
rescued me quickly, showing herself in need, like a haven to
the tempest-tossed, I had been dead long ago, getting myself
little honour, though much pity, from Pontic hospitality . . .
(*Ep. V.*)

But now he had hurt Basil's feelings, so he hastens to write
again of "the luxury of suffering hardship with you":

. . . Who shall restore me to those psalmodies, and vigils,
and departures to God through prayer, and that (as it were)
immaterial and incorporeal life? or to that union of brethren,
in nature and soul, who are made gods by you, and carried

on high? or to that rivalry in virtue and sharpening of heart
which we consigned to written decrees and canons? or to
that loving study of divine oracles, and the light we found in
them, with the guidance of the Spirit? or, to speak of lesser
and lower things, to the bodily labours of the day, the wood-
drawing and the stone-hewing, the planting and the draining; or to that golden plane, more honourable than that of
Xerxes, under which, not a jaded king, but a weary monk
did sit? ... (*Ep. VI.*)[1]

During this long visit the two friends collected the passages
from Origen known as the *Philocalia*. Gregory, after leaving his
friend, asks to hear more of his life among the men he has
gathered around him, and Basil is nothing loath to write of
their prayers and labours, their studies of the inspired Scriptures, their night vigils and "variety of psalmody", one choir
answering another. He writes at some length on conversation,
showing that social life within the monastery was in his eyes
an important part of the common life: "To question without
over-eagerness, to answer without desire of display, not to
interrupt a profitable speaker", to study for a tone of voice
pleasantly modulated, to be courteous and amiable. "Harsh-
ness is ever to be avoided, even when censuring."

Basil had at first been drawn to the solitary life—he came to
feel that the monastic was both higher and safer. We get a
hint of one of his reasons when we learn that his decision was
partly based on reluctance to give up his books. And this was
not only because (as Dr. Lowther Clarke has so well shown)
the monastic movement under Basil was recruited from a
different and more educated world. Basil saw that Christianity
is an intellectual religion—Christians are "People of the
Book". If a Basilian monk did not know how to read he would
need to learn—unless, like the great Anthony, he could
accomplish immense feats of memory. In the *Moralia* every
admonition is supported with a dozen Scripture references,
and Basil was the first man to organise the seven hours of daily
and nightly recitation of the Psalms in all his monasteries.

"I think," he says, "it is advantageous to have diversity
and variety in the prayers and Psalms at the fixed hours

[1] I have borrowed Newman's translation of these passages.

because when there is monotony the soul often gets weary and is a prey to distraction; but when the Psalms of each hour change and are variable, the desire of the soul is renewed and attention is restored."

Next in his remedies for extravagance, we may put the great stress laid on obedience. Basil's monasteries were of a moderate size, probably thirty to forty monks. Sometimes small village groups amalgamated—he points out the advantages of one fire, one lamp, fewer messengers to market their goods. And the phrasing of his views on authority seems to suggest that the heads of these groups formed something like a council of superiors. Basil also lays enormous stress on the value of frequent confession—and this more as consulting a soul-doctor than as sacramental. Confession was often made to monks who were not priests.

The third and highest safeguard against excess was the common life—and this involved not only prayer but work. Often there were two monasteries—of men and of women under the one Abbot. The two together could be totally self-supporting, the women weaving and making the men's clothes, bed-coverings, etc., the men building, carpentering and doing the heavier field work. "Generally speaking," Basil says, "one may recommend the choice of such arts as preserve the peaceable and untroubled nature of our lives, needing neither much trouble to get the requisite material nor much anxiety to sell what has been made . . . preferring those arts which preserve for us a life undistracted and waiting continually on the Lord . . . Of them agriculture is the best."

Sometimes their products must be sold at "the functions designated fairs" and then several brethren should go together. But selling and buying at martyrs' tombs is not suitable, and it is better to get a lower price for goods than to make use (as so many do) of a saint's feast and burial place "as a market and fair, and common emporium".

Every man should learn a skill, he who has one should stick to it, for "to gain a mastery of one skill is more useful than to dabble in a number". The care of tools must be "a special consideration to the workman in each occupation".

In his treatment of the details of daily life, one is especially struck by Basil's common sense, and his determination that details should not be made of undue importance. Food is to be simple and cheap; imported goods are only to be bought if essential for living (e.g., oil), the monks should buy the simplest (mainly bread and vegetables) of what is there for the public. There is an agreement here between the rules of Basil and Benedict, one saying of food, the other of material for clothes, that the cheapest and easiest to procure is to be preferred in any district. The extra hard worker can have extra food. (So, too, says St. Benedict.) Doctors should be called in for the sick, but a man must never allow the question of his health to fill his thoughts—must never fuss unduly over it.

Avoidance of fuss is a keynote in Basil's teaching. It is good to offer hospitality, but not to alter the daily simplicity of your life—you accuse your visitor of greed by "piling up the food and fussing over it". Our Lord told Martha not to fuss, He fed the five thousand with simple food. It is good to choose the lowest place, but bad to scramble for it—and perhaps a greater sign of pride. The shorter rules are answers to questions, and to the question, "What are the cares of this life?" Basil answers, "Every care is a care of this life, even if it seems to involve nothing forbidden, unless it contribute to godliness." The test of a man's rebuke of his neighbour's sin is to be "that which is most important, that of sympathy". If all else fails, "let us use at the proper occasion strong indignation with sympathy, in order to benefit and reform the sinners". The question, "Who is the meek?" receives the unusual reply: "He who is unalterable in his decisions upon the things that are done to please God."

Basil chose the life of the monastery with a conviction that it was more perfect than that of the hermitage. Obviously, he says, in the search for perfection, "it is impossible for a man to succeed if he lives in promiscuous intercourse". But if altogether alone he "will not recognise his defects, not having anyone to reprove him and to set him right with mercy and compassion". How can a man show humility with none to compare with, compassion when cut off from other men, long-suffering when no one withstands his wishes? Christ washed the feet of His disciples. Basil says to the solitary: "Whose feet wilt thou wash?"

And how is the complex of all good works to be achieved by

one man alone? While we visit a sick man we cannot be receiving a stranger, while distributing alms we neglect work, work not done means we can no longer feed the hungry and clothe the naked. But by men living in community "many commandments are easily performed . . . Who then would choose the idle and fruitless life in preference to the fruitful life which is lived in accordance with the commandment of the Lord?"

Basil, like most of the Fathers, thought of the early Christians as practising the first form of the religious life—having all things in common, having on conversion laid all their goods at the feet of the Apostles for distribution to the needy.[1] And all solitaries as well as all monasteries held it a duty to give alms from the fruits of their labours.

Priest in Caesarea

Basil, with all his social sense, all his keen awareness of the value of the common life, had conceived of the monastery as its fulfilment, as the place for his life's work and his soul's perfection. But he was too great as thinker, organiser and leader to be left in such times as these in the woods of Pontus. The Council of Rimini, at which Dianius, Bishop of Caesarea, had signed a semi-Arian formula, had caused Basil to break off relations with him, but it was Basil who received the assurance of Dianius' orthodoxy and assisted him in his dying hours. The new bishop, Eusebius, kept Basil in Caesarea and ordained him priest, probably in the year 362, Basil being then thirty-three. Before long, however, he began to be jealous of his popularity, and Basil went back to his monastery.

He could ill be spared by Caesarea. Incapable men tend to be jealous of the capable; Eusebius could not handle his important job unaided, and the threats of the Arian Emperor Valens led Basil's friends to make efforts for his recall. Gregory, himself in favour with Eusebius, wrote begging for him:

> . . . Proud as I am of your notice (for I am a man, as someone says before me), and of your invitations to religious consultations and meetings, yet I cannot bear Your Holiness's

---

[1] For a discussion of the Apostolic life see Jacquier, *Les Actes des Apôtres*. He makes a strong case for the renunciation of goods not having been absolute, but only a total readiness to renounce when called upon.

past and present slight of my most honoured brother Basil,
whom I selected from the first and still possess as my friend,
to live with me and study with me, and search with me into
the deepest wisdom . . . If there is anything you will grant
me, let it be this; and I trust you will, for really it is equitable.
He will certainly defer to you, if you do but pay a reasonable
respect to him. For myself, I shall come after him as shadows
follow bodies, being small, and a lover of quiet . . .
(*Ep. XVI.*)

Before long Eusebius sent for Basil, who became, says Gregory,
"his good counsellor, his able auxiliary, his teacher in the
things of God, his guide in action, the staff of his old age, the
support of his faith. Most active in outside works, most faithful
at home, he showed himself as full of good as he had been
imagined to be of ill will." (*Orat. XLIII.*)

Though he never abandoned his literary tastes and style,
which had in youth become a part of him, Basil's mightiest
achievements lay in three fields: his moulding of eastern
monasticism, his theological teaching—especially of the doctrine of the Trinity—and his vast creation of social services.

Basil brought back, says Puech,[1] what Greek eloquence had
lost: its qualities of "elevation, happy choice and clear development of an image, magnificence of phrase and strong simplicity
of style". Even in translation his sermons are astonishing,
especially if we remember that they were preached not to an
élite but to a crowd of artisans and labourers, to the mixed
population of a large city. In one respect Basil could probably
make contact with these minds more easily because of his dislike of the allegorising which marked the Alexandrians. Belonging more to the school of Antioch—"When I hear grass
spoken of", says Basil in an early sermon, "I take it to mean
grass, the same with a fish, etc."

Always he spoke as one having authority. "You sit around
me as judges not disciples, but you shall listen, not to what
pleases you, but to the truth."

The revolt of Procopius occupied Valens and averted the
threatened persecution for a time. The first great test of Basil's
powers came with the famine which swept Caesarea in 368.

[1] In *Histoire de la Littérature grecque chrétienne.*

Those terrible days come alive for us as Basil describes in a sermon a father forcing himself to sell one child that the whole family may have bread. Would it not be better, he asks himself, for all to die together? Should the eldest be sacrificed, or the youngest? what will the other children feel towards their treacherous father? How can he sit down with them to eat a meal bought at such a price?

Yet it is better than the death of all. He steels himself, but the tears flow down as he takes to the market the best loved of his children—"And you," cried Basil addressing the rich purchaser, "you are unmoved by nature's reproaches. Hunger is driving this miserable wretch and you drag out the business, you bargain, you prolong his agony. He is offering you his heart in exchange for a little food. Your hand does not fall paralysed as you stretch it out with the money, but you haggle with your fellow slave for a lower price."

This thought was familiar with Basil: we are all the slaves of God, fellow slaves with one another. The highly placed is God's steward over his fellow slaves and owes them their share in God's bounties. The very animals set man an example, pasturing together in the same field or on the slopes of the same mountain. You lie, he cries out to the rich young man of the Gospel, claiming to have loved your neighbour as yourself. Long ago the money of the rich would have been shared with others had they really loved their neighbours.

Pitilessly he chases the rich man from one excuse to another. You have not enough to help everybody? "Your tongue swears it but your hand betrays you, silently proclaiming you a liar with the sparkles of your jewelled ring. How many debtors could that ring alone set free? How many crumbling houses could it rebuild?"

Your chest of clothes could cover a whole shivering populace, and you dare to send away the poor with empty hands, having no fear of the Judge's just punishment.

You have shown no pity; there will be no pity for you.

Another claims that he must save for his children's future. "Begin," says Basil, "by giving your soul its rights as the first-born. After that you can divide your wealth among your children." The future is uncertain, says another. "Strange madness," cries Basil, "you dug your gold out of the mines and now you are going to hide it again. And when you have buried your fortune you will find you have buried your heart with it."

All this means that "the Lord is not your master, the Gospel does not rule your life". "But I," says another wealthy man, "will make the poor my heirs, setting them down in my will as masters of all I have."

"When you are far from men you will become their lover, so when I see you dead I will praise your humanity."

But what can dust and ashes do either by display of splendour or by generosity? "No, when the market is closed there can be no more trading. He who arrives after the contest wins no crown. When the war is over so is the time to show courage."

In his life of their sister Macrina, Basil's brother says, "His renunciation of property was complete." But since then his mother had died and we may conjecture that a fresh fortune had come to him from this land-owing family, who had estates both in Pontus and Cappadocia. In his *Funeral Oration* Gregory of Nyssa says that during the famine Basil "sold his possessions and turned the money into food". And Gregory Nazianzen, telling of Basil's skill in opening the purses of the obdurate rich, adds that "with his own slaves, call them if you will his companions in slavery, become in the circumstances his fellow workers", he waited on the needy, solacing body and soul alike. It was a fiercer famine in Caesarea than it would have been in a maritime town, where food could be brought in and merchandise carried out in exchange. The whole countryside was stricken and there were more than enough profiteers buying wholesale and selling at fantastic retail prices.

Comparing him with Moses, Elias, Joseph and Our Lord Himself, Nazianzen describes how Basil saved the city. There were men and women, children and the aged, almost dead from hunger. He got them together and collected "every sort of food . . . cauldrons filled with a purée of vegetables, the home-salted meats which are the food of the poor; and then, copying Christ the servant, who, girded with a towel, did not disdain to wash His disciples' feet", he served them.

BISHOP OF CAESAREA

The threats of Valens and the clamorous demand of his people, much more than Gregory's entreaties, had induced Bishop Eusebius to recall Basil. When Eusebius died in 370, Basil had been in fact governing the diocese for several years. But it was by no means certain that imperial disfavour and Arian intrigues would not prevent him, or any other Catholic, from becoming bishop. Basil has been accused of intriguing from the first to get the vacant see. This is quite possible, but it seems more likely that he had another candidate in mind— probably, he felt, a reluctant one. Unfortunately we have not got the letter which he wrote to Gregory Nazianzen but only Gregory's angry answer.

> You pretended to be very ill, indeed at your last breath, and to long to see me and bid me a last farewell . . . I shed a fountain of tears and I wailed aloud, feeling myself for the first time unphilosophically disposed . . . But as soon as I found that the bishops were in the city I stopped short in my course . . . (*Ep. XL.*)

Basil had not, he felt, treated him fairly, had not guarded himself against evil gossip, had not "remembered that such nominations are deserved by the more religious, not the more powerful or those most in favour with the multitude". Later, when he sees him, Gregory will have "more and graver reproaches to make".

Gregory may have suspected his friend of wanting to make use of him for his own election, but as editors of both his and Basil's letters suggest, it seems far more likely that Basil was planning for Gregory's. As to the illness—his health was always wretched, and Gregory may have read the letter in alarmist mood. The story, however, gives a strong impression of deceit—but of a kind not uncommon in those centuries, when tricking a man into a bishopric was deemed rather praiseworthy than otherwise. To get a first-rate man for Caesarea came before all other considerations.

Gregory, who would later reproach Basil even more bitterly for putting loyalty to a friend too low on his scale of values, did himself realise the importance of this election. He believed Basil the best man for the post and wrote several brilliant letters, supposedly from his father, entreating the support of friendly bishops.

Whether or not Basil had first desired the election of Gregory, he contrasts interestingly at this point with Ambrose, Augustine, and the rest who shrank from the episcopal office. In his own election now lay the best hope of victory for the Faith, and he did not hesitate to try to secure it. The younger Gregory refused to be present; but finally his father, though very ill, was, at the risk of his life, carried in a litter to Caesarea. The people were enthusiastic for Basil, and Gregory's support made the adverse bishops yield; the old man consecrated him and he received the joyful congratulations of Athanasius and the whole Catholic world of the East.

Every battle between bishop and Emperor has something of the same colour, though each has its own details. Valens sent his prefect Modestus to give Basil his choice between banishment or communion with the Arians. He found neither threats nor blandishments got him anywhere, and had to report his total failure to the Emperor.

The dialogue between prefect and bishop had been striking enough.

"You, Basil," Modestus began, "what do you mean by opposing so great a prince and not yielding to him as others do?" On Basil's asking where his fault lay, he was told that it was in his refusal to worship after the Emperor's fashion.

"I have a Sovereign," said Basil, "whose will is otherwise. I can worship no creature—I, the creature of God and called to be a god."

"What do you take me for?" exclaimed Modestus.

"For a thing of nought while you give me such orders."

On Modestus' proclaiming his own rank and position in tones very unlike his name, Basil acknowledged them, but urged the equal dignity of all Christians. Modestus, enraged, asked Basil if he had no fear of his power.

"Fear what?" asked Basil.

"Confiscation, exile, tortures, death."

"Think of something else. What is confiscation if one has

nothing to lose—these garments and a few books? . . . Home is everywhere for God's pilgrim . . . Tortures cannot hurt a body so frail that one stroke would bring death. It would only send me sooner to Him for whom I live . . . to whom I have long been journeying."

"No one," said Modestus, "ever before spoke to me like this."

"Perhaps," Basil answered, "you have never met a bishop."

This famous phrase was followed by the assurance that in all temporal matters the prefect would find Christians humble and submissive. "But when God's honour is at stake . . . fire and sword, beasts of prey, irons tearing the flesh are an indulgence, not a terror for the Christian. Insult, threaten, do your worst . . . Go tell your Emperor. You will not persuade or win me to an impious creed by menaces even more frightful." (Gregory Nazianzen, *Orat. XLIII.*)

On the feast of the Epiphany Valens himself entered the Cathedral while Basil was celebrating Mass. The bishop stood facing the people, his ministers in a semi-circle around him. The thunder of the singing, the immense throng of worshippers totally oblivious of the Emperor and his train, "the unearthly majesty of the scene," a worship "more like that of angels than of men," as Gregory Nazianzen has described it, overwhelmed Valens. Almost fainting, he tried, at the Offertory, to present his gift. The ministers hesitated—for was he not a heretic? —but Basil came forward and took it from his trembling hands.

Valens lived henceforward in a state of perpetual vacillation towards Basil. On this occasion he gave him a splendid present for the hospital he was planning, but shortly after ordered his banishment. Before Basil could depart the Emperor's only son grew ill and he was hastily sent for to pray over the child. He prayed and the child grew better. But soon Valens, breaking a solemn promise, had him baptised by an Arian. The boy grew worse and died.

Presently Valens again yielded to Basil's enemies and tried to sign the decree of his banishment. Three pens split in his hand and he departed from Caesarea leaving the bishop master of the scene. Modestus became Basil's friend and a number of his letters are written to the prefect begging his help for people in distress.

Commenting on the command to love our neighbour, Basil
said, "Man's neighbour is man". He preached and practised a
universal charity, but I wish we had more details concerning
the Basileiad, as his great composite institute came to be
called. Basil was, Ephrem of Syria said, "filled with compassion for the widow and the orphan"—two classes for which
the Church from her beginnings had specially provided.
There were probably buildings for these. Gregory Nazianzen
mentions too Basil's care for children during the famine, and
that it was extended to Jew as well as Christian. Basil invites
a fellow bishop to visit his "refectory of the poor". He made
a special point of himself waiting on lepers. He seems to have
known something of medicine, and his own feeble health
inspired him with special sympathy for the sick.

The swift energy with which he worked seems to have
disturbed Elias, Governor of Cappadocia. Experts date
Basil's letter to him in 373:

> Can it be said that it is against the people's good to have
> raised to our God a magnificently built house of prayer,
> with dwelling-houses around it, one of them specially for the
> bishop, other, lesser houses allotted according to rank to
> God's ministers, but suitable also for use by you magistrates
> and your attendants? Who is wronged by the shelters we
> have built for strangers, for travellers, for those with illnesses
> needing treatment, or by the necessary aids we have provided
> for them—nurses, doctors, pack animals and men to lead
> them?
>
> For these various institutions there must be tradesmen on
> the spot, supplying both the strict necessaries of life, and
> those other things which have been invented to make life
> more livable. There must be other buildings to house these
> industries—and all these things improve the appearance
> of the place and give glory to the Governor, on whom the
> credit naturally falls. (*Ep. XCIV.*)

That the whole thing was on a vast scale we may gather
both from this description and from the Emperor's decision,
recorded by Theodoret, to give Basil "some very fine lands
that he owned in the area". We know it too in another way,

for the Basileiad grew so large it became known as the "new city" and to it shifted Caesarea's centre of gravity. "The new city of Basil", says Sir William Ramsay, "seems to have caused the gradual concentration of the entire population of Caesarea round the ecclesiastical centre and the abandonment of the old city".

Eustathius had already done the same thing on a smaller scale at Sebaste; Basil may have got some helpful hints for his own vast scheme. He saw this not as a single effort. Round the central bishoprics of the big cities were villages with assistant bishops known as *chorepiscopi*. Basil had several of these and he wanted them all to establish similar smaller buildings with their assisting monks. He pleaded with the civil authorities that these be free from taxes.

Here was the perfect fulfilment of the common life—not stopping short in its own group of seekers for perfection, but poured out over a very imperfect world. Basil was the first bishop, Lowther Clarke says, who united episcopacy and monasticism in one social mission. Ramsay compares the Basileiad and other such buildings to the cities founded by the Greek kings, as centres from which the Christian ideal grew and radiated as had that of Greece from its cities. These buildings were becoming the centre of social and municipal life. "The Greek conception of a free people governing itself without priestly interference was dying out and the Asiatic conception of a religion governing in theocratic fashion the entire life and conduct of men was reviving."

In the background of Basil's life as bishop we must see always the woods of Pontus where he had been born, where his sister and youngest brother still lived, ruling the monasteries he had founded. He kept in close touch with these monasteries: sending them vocations, going there to rest and to pray. The two monasteries were in the end one. The nuns had begun in Basil's ancestral home. But finally both men and women were established on the other side of the river under the rule of Peter.

THE YEARS OF TRIAL

Difficulties with the Emperor and his myrmidons were a small fraction of the heavy burden Basil had to bear during the ten years of his episcopate. Many of the surrounding bishops were jealous of his elevation. They were mostly tainted with Arianism and it was only, says Gregory Nazianzen, the pressure of the multitude, faithful alike to orthodoxy and to Basil, which forced them occasionally to make professions of the Catholic creed. Strangely enough Basil's own uncle, although orthodox, was one of the bishops who disapproved his election. I wish there were fewer Gregories in this story— he was another, and Basil's brother, Gregory of Nyssa, embroiled the matter still further. He twice forged letters of reconciliation from uncle to nephew, joyfully received by the one, indignantly repudiated by the other. This well-meant folly Basil felt keenly: his letter to the elder Gregory is curiously beautiful and did finally win him round.

But most of his troubles were less with the men concerned than with their ideas. Newman has called Basil the Job or the Jeremiah of the fourth century, and, writing to Eustathius of Sebaste, he says of himself that he had, like Job, kept a long silence in the midst of afflictions, that, like the prophet, he had for three years been "as one who heard not and in his mouth are no reproofs". He had loved and admired Eustathius, and it was only on conviction that he was heretical about the Trinity that he broke with him—with bitter grief, often expressed bitterly.

We see in his letters to St. Athanasius how heavily the troubles at Antioch weighed on Basil's mind, how keenly he felt the estrangement with Pope Damasus and with the western bishops.

In the chapter on St. Athanasius, the beginning of the schism in Antioch has been told, with Meletius, consecrated bishop in 361, suspected of some tinge of Arianism, and Paulinus also consecrated. There were still (and would be for the eight years of Basil's bishopric and for fifteen years after) two Catholic bishops at Antioch. Paulinus, because of Athanasius' support, was acknowledged by Rome; Basil upheld Meletius. It was to Athanasius that Basil looked to win from Rome a keener interest in the affairs of the East. It was Athanasius who, if he were convinced, would be able to convince Pope Damasus of the real state of things at Antioch. Basil felt bitterly that whereas the slightest sign of heresy among themselves agitated the western bishops, they were apt to be indifferent to the terrible storms shaking the East, yet as he wrote to Athanasius: "The one way of safety for the Churches of the East lies in their having the sympathy of the Churches of the West."

It was suspicion of heresy in Meletius and, as Basil believed, mis-information, that had caused Rome to support Paulinus. The immense distance made it difficult for Damasus and the West to judge an Eastern situation, but, says Basil to Athanasius: "What through all the West is more honoured than your venerable grey hairs? . . . send men of sound doctrine to the bishops in the West . . . Tell them the troubles that beset us. Suggest some mode of relief."

In another letter he tells him that he has written to Damasus asking him, if the calling of a synod is difficult, to exercise his own personal authority and send men able to undertake this laborious journey to examine matters on the spot. A new heretic is arising, Marcellus of Ancyra, who teaches that the Word comes indeed from the Father but "had no existence before His coming forth, nor hypostasis after His return". This was in fact to treat the word *persona* in its classical meaning of a mask and to destroy the reality of the Persons in the Godhead, making the Son only a manifestation of the Father. Basil begs the help of Athanasius lest Christians "struggle as in a night battle, without being able to distinguish between friends and foes'.

Basil had a lack, curious in so immensely intelligent a man, of the most elementary psychology. The letters between him and the Pope are enough to make one weep—probably he himself wept often enough. But his optimism rose unreasonably at the slightest cause. His first attempts had been wholly unsuccessful—partly because Athanasius was supporting Paulinus against Basil's candidate Meletius, but partly also because Basil's own orthodoxy was half doubted in the West.

In his panegyric of St. Athanasius, Gregory Nazianzen makes clear how these doubts had arisen—just as Athanasius himself had shown at the Council of Alexandria that Greeks and Latins were trying to say the same thing in different languages.

We asserted one essence and three hypostases (one of these terms expressing the nature, the other the properties of the three Persons). The Latins thought as we did; but because of the poverty of their language and the lack of vocabulary, they could not distinguish hypostasis from essence. Therefore, to avoid talking of three essences, they brought in the word *persona*. What is the result? An utterly ridiculous, indeed lamentable, disagreement. A trifling difference in terms is seen as a difference in faith: the three Persons have given rise to Sabellianism; the three hypostases to Arianism . . . and as new disputes arise daily, we see the whole world in danger of perishing for a few syllables.

Jerome was also writing from the East begging the Pope to intervene there: "From me, a Roman, the phrase 'three hypostases' is being asked by this Arian brood of rustics . . . Settle the matter, I beg of you . . . No school of secular learning knows any difference between *hypostasis* and *usia*. Who would be so sacrilegious as to speak openly of three substances?"

If, remarks Père Lebreton, even men of learning felt such distrust of the eastern vocabulary, what would the ordinary faithful of the West feel? When Basil sent really intelligent messengers to Rome who could explain the meaning of his letters, he received at last a friendly reply from Pope St. Damasus. It was a situation of immense difficulty for the Pope, but Basil realised this so little that, on receiving a first sign of understanding, he wrote back eagerly asking Damasus to censure three eastern bishops—one of them being Paulinus of Antioch!

But another was Apollinaris of Laodicea. Basil in fact realised earlier than the bishops of the West that a new Christological heresy was arising in the East. Apollinaris is an interesting figure. During Julian's brief reign, when Catholics were forbidden to teach the Classics in the pagan schools, he and his father, another Apollinaris, set out to write Christian Classics. They rewrote the Bible in Homeric verse, most of which has disappeared. The version of the Psalms attributed to the son is dismissed by Puech[1] as of poor literary quality. Violently

---

[1] *Littérature grecque chrétienne*, vol. ii, p. 635.

anti-Arian, Apollinaris stresses the divinity at the expense of the full humanity of Christ, declaring that the Godhead had taken the place of the human soul. The phrase in which the orthodox attacked this heresy was "Nothing is healed that is not assumed"; if Christ had not a human soul, then man's soul would not be healed; but it precisely needs healing first, sin is no mere bodily act. Christ had taken our whole nature.

St. Basil might have been more speedily successful in drawing the Pope's attention to this heresy had the question of *usia* and *hypostasis* been clarified earlier, or had he been content to leave the matter of the Antioch schism alone until or unless he could convince St. Athanasius, the man most listened to by Rome, and thus the great link between East and West.

Pope Damasus did in the end condemn Apollinarianism, but not until 377.

Basil had written to Athanasius of all that a meeting would have meant to him: to be able to talk of the Church's necessities, just to see and know personally the man he so much admired. One feels in these letters something deeper than is spoken—the yearning of a lonely man for intercourse, of a man of tempered steel for one strong like himself. Strong men are few, and Basil lived the years of his bishopric in an increasing solitude.

At first he showed intense activity, visiting all whom he could help, counsel, direct into the right path, but illness increasingly confined him to Caesarea. His letters show how hard it was for him to travel even a short distance, especially in cold weather. To an irate functionary who threatened to tear out his liver, Basil remarked what a kindness this would be since, where it was, he had suffered from it for years. Youthful excesses catch up with some men in middle life; Basil was dying of his youthful austerities.

Duchesne sees in "the distrust and bitter tone of his correspondence" the effect of this diseased liver. Basil enlisted, he says, in the service of a campaign for peace "a temperament both too sensitive and too combative". The way he fought for peace is indeed sometimes disconcerting, but reading his letters as a whole, one is more struck by another element. True, many of them are combative, but even these are written in love for

truth and for souls, while many others are solely letters of
service. With his miserable health, the immense burdens he
was carrying, the feebleness of his friends and the fierceness of
his enemies, the wonder is that Basil could concentrate on letter
after letter of simple charity: letters to tax assessors begging
consideration, that monks and private people may "be relieved
of this many-headed hydra"; letters to Modestus the prefect,
now Basil's friend, begging his protection for the oppressed;
letters of consolation in which Basil is weeping with the afflicted
—a father whose son has died, a man widowed after "a
wedded companionship blended in uttermost harmony, dis-
solved more quickly than a dream". Yet, writes Basil, all must
die and grief at the ending of a perfect marriage "is itself no
small gift among the gifts of God . . . Thus therefore you should
think of her as having gone her way by a certain road that we
all must travel".

If his psychology sometimes failed with popes or statesmen,
it was perfect with friends in distress: he never forgot that
praise of the departed is what the mourner craves. He writes
to a general's widow of "that noble and unconquerable soul"
who had left her "in the full flower of his years and the splendour of his successes", and bids her "give thanks to the Lord
that you have been thought worthy of living with such a man
whose loss nearly the whole Roman Empire has felt", and in
her children and her own eternal future he offers "a noble
occupation for your thoughts".

Asking a favour of a functionary Basil is careful to say "that
this affair will cross over to great Alexandria and supply admiration for Your Honour to the people there is clear even if I do
not mention it". But there was little he forgot to mention that
would be of service to "a friend", "a compatriot", a "son" or
even "on behalf of a stranger"—for consolation "is due to
strangers from Christians". With his intimates we get another
Basil again: "Whether I write or not I bear you about with me
enshrined within my heart," he writes when, "fretful at the
long waning of the winter," he has set his heart on getting a
married couple "to spend the saving days of Easter with us".

A light-hearted correspondence, blending pleasure and
charity, is that with his old pagan master Libanius, whose
answers make him very attractive. Basil sends various young

Cappadocians "to seek after eloquence and learning and to employ you as the master of their training". He is "conferring as great a favour on them as do those who guide the thirsty to a spring". Libanius is delighted, especially when one of them arrives bringing "a letter from the admirable Basil". He was an expensive teacher but not for Basil's poorer friends. "Our services are not measured by money; it is enough that he who cannot give should be able to receive . . . if any man in poverty loves learning he is preferred to those who are wealthy."

Delighted to relive the past, Libanius and Basil revive classical allusions and Libanius questions Basil about their common friends. Then begins what Basil calls a game that Libanius is playing with him. For the rhetorician declares himself vanquished by the greater eloquence of his friend's letters—he has taken a vote on the matter with a group of eminent men who all agreed with him. Basil retorts that Libanius is behaving like a father who encourages his child by pretending he has won a game. But there was "something indescribably delightful in the language you used in your game . . . as if Milo should beg to be excused from boxing against *me*". After all, in this matter of language Basil now associates with Moses and Elias, "who communicate their thoughts to me in a barbarian tongue . . . Even if I did learn something from you, time has made me forget it".

This new letter, however, made those present with Libanius "leap to their feet" when read to them. Whatever Basil may say, "of that which has always been mine and was formerly yours, the roots not only remain but will remain as long as you live and no lapse of time could ever excise them, not even if you almost wholly neglect to water them".

Valens seems to have feared two men only—Athanasius and Basil. The death of the former in 373 was the signal for a fierce persecution in Alexandria. Athanasius had desired for his successor his brother, Peter, and the Catholics ratified his choice. But the Emperor forced upon them the Arians' candidate, Lucius. His intrusion was marked by scenes such as the city had witnessed with George of Cappadocia. Consecrated virgins were violated, paraded naked through the town or put to death; priests, deacons and monks imprisoned, exiled, sent to work in the mines. A young man dressed as a girl danced on the altar of the basilica while another stood naked in the pulpit whence Athanasius had preached, pouring out blasphemies and obscenities.

Lucius came in supported by an official and by the old Euzoius, who fifty years previously had been expelled with Arius from Alexandria by Bishop Alexander, and had come from Antioch to celebrate his revenge. Peter could only disappear. For a while he hid in the neighbourhood; before long he had fled to Rome. But he was not the man to govern a diocese or carry on a fight after his brother's grand style. Nor did he possess the patience and balance that made Athanasius an ambassador of peace. As far as in him lay, he embroiled the Antioch dispute still further, fiercely denouncing Meletius to the council in Rome at which St. Basil's letter was read, and complaining to Basil because Basil's own envoy defended the bishop supported by him.

None of this was cheering for Basil, and his difficulties nearer home were becoming more acute and pressing every day. The vast province of Cappadocia, over which he was Metropolitan, had been, in 371, divided by the Government into two, and Anthimus, Bishop of Tyana, claimed that the civil elevation of his city into a metropolis extended its episcopal authority also over the new province. He began to ordain bishops, to act in general as Metropolitan and to manifest complete disregard of Basil's authority.

What was to be done? No support could be hoped for from the civil authorities, and Basil saw the only solution in a multiplication of sees, not necessarily in large or important cities, but at strategic points. Thus he chose Nyssa for his brother Gregory and Sasima for his friend of Nazianzus. The brother did his best and struggled for many years with circumstances adverse enough. But the friend failed Basil totally, and this incident led to the breaking of his closest tie, to the crowning loneliness of his life.

Poor Basil; yet he should have known better. Almost immediately after his consecration, he had begged for Gregory's presence and help and the answer had been a definite refusal, both for Basil's sake and his own—"that you might not seem to be collecting your partisans about you with indecency and heat as your objectors would say; next, for my own peace and reputation". A poet, a thinker, a recluse, Gregory seems to have been curiously unfitted to deal with the strange, wild world of Asia Minor in the fourth century. Yet so too, by temperament, was Basil. It was only by heroic courage that he had overcome a natural shrinking from all the things his office involved: general society, public functions and disputations. A heretical opponent spoke with contempt of his "retired cottage and closely fastened door, his flustered manner when people came in, his voice and look, the expression of his countenance and other symptoms of fear". If *he* had had to overcome all this, it must have seemed to Basil that his friend could do the same. And lately Gregory had offered to come "if the sea needs water or you a counsellor, at all events to gain benefit and act the philosopher, by bearing ill-usage in your company".

They had in fact travelled together to collect the produce of a farm situated in the Second Cappadocia which belonged to the Church of Caesarea. On their way back the retainers of Anthimus had blocked the pass and attacked them. Sasima was a village or small posting town—important by its position, because whoever held it could more or less assure safe passage for his convoys. But for the rest: a very few houses, a gaol— you could hear, says Gregory, the groans of the victims and their rattling chains. There was nothing green in Sasima, no water, nothing but dust.

Gregory never claimed his bishopric, never ordained a priest for it. When Anthimus put in a rival bishop, Gregory would not contest the see with him, but went back to Nazianzus, where his old father was still alive. "Give me", he wrote to Basil, "peace and quiet above all things. Why should I be fighting for sucklings and birds that are not mine as if in a matter of souls and canons? Well, play the man, be strong, turn everything to your own glory, as rivers suck up the mountain torrent . . . so much shall I gain from this your friendship, not to trust in friends, or to put anything above God." It was probably the heaviest disappointment of Basil's life.

Basil died on the first day of the eventful year 379. He was not quite fifty, though he looked an old man, and all his struggles seemed to have led nowhere. There was still schism in Antioch, Constantinople was in heretical hands, so was Alexandria. Arianism was still strong, though beginning to grow tired, and a whole crop of new heresies were flourishing. The Empire was in confusion after the victory of the Goths at Adrianople. The Church in the West still appeared remote and indifferent. But he never lost hope. "Many times", says his brother, "we saw that he [like Moses] was in a dark cloud wherein was God. For what was invisible to others, initiation into the mysteries of the spirit made visible to him, so that he seemed to be encompassed in the dark cloud wherein knowledge of God was concealed."

And now as he lay "hardly breathing, life almost utterly gone", his friend saw "a renewal of vigour, as he spoke his words of farewell, his words of prayer. He laid hands on the most generous of his servants, giving with his hand the Holy Spirit that the altar might not be robbed of those who had been his disciples, and had borne their part in his own priesthood".

As he lay there dying Gregory Nazianzen saw him, like St. Paul, his course run, like Moses, having heard God's words, "Come up into this mountain." Not, says Gregory, as Moses was told, "to die there", but "to be with Us". But Moses was also told that from the mountain he should "see the land of Canaan which I will deliver to the children of Israel to possess". And it may be that as he laid his hands on his disciples with the sudden strength that appeared miraculous, Basil saw how the failure of his fight would after all issue in triumph. Not merely the momentary immediate triumph of the vast multitudes that thronged around the body of the man they at once proclaimed saint; of the orations which already entitled him Basil the Great; of his feast celebrated as less only than those of the Apostles. If indeed he was less! For listen to his brother: "If Paul preceded him in time and Basil was raised up many generations later this is the work of the Divine Dispensation on behalf of men, not a proof of inferior excellence. Even Moses was born many ages after Abraham, and Samuel after Moses, and after him Elias, and after him the great John; after John Paul, and after him Basil." Few saints have had so instantaneous a personal triumph, but for that Basil would have cared little.

The triumph of the Faith was what mattered, and within three weeks of his death Theodosius had become Emperor, within four months the hesitating Gregory had left Nazianzus and established a Catholic Church in heretical Constantinople. Basil had to wait for time's healing hand to bring the Antioch schism to its end, but doubtless it is easy to wait patiently in heaven. In 380 Theodosius gave his adhesion to the creed of Nicaea and restored the churches of Constantinople to the Catholics, and the following year the Council of Constantinople brought back at least for a time the always precarious peace between East and West.

St. Gregory Nazianzen

Newman tells some of this story in his *Church of the Fathers*, and he remarks quaintly that it appears impertinent for him to be arbitrating between two saints, but that he does feel, looking merely at the external facts of history, that a saint and an ascetic should not have objected to be sent to Sasima because "it was deficient in beauty and interest", although he will allow Gregory to object to the responsibilities involved in becoming the neighbour of Anthimus. But Gregory himself almost saves the historian the need to arbitrate, by his own oration on Basil from which I have already quoted copiously. It was delivered three years after Basil's death. During those three years Gregory had gone through a greater variety of experience than in all his previous fifty.

Historians are puzzled as to how he got to Constantinople; he speaks himself of a call from "many pastors and sheep", which Tillemont reads as meaning the people and the neighbouring bishops. Technically he was still Bishop of Sasima; actually he had even left Nazianzus on his father's death, and the Catholics of Constantinople dug him out of a monastery in Seleucia. Whether legally appointed or not, he poured new confidence into his discouraged flock. He was a brilliant preacher and the Arian population, which began by despising him, raged as his congregations grew too large for the chapel called by him Anastasis, or Resurrection, to express his hope of the resurrection of the Faith in Constantinople. He preached a series of magnificent sermons on the Trinity, which cannot have soothed Arian susceptibilities. During the Easter Vigil, as he celebrated the Mysteries, they broke in and drove out the congregation with a volley of stones. Then they brought Gregory into court with the charge of provoking a riot!

An attempt at introducing another bishop was crushed by Theodosius, who had Gregory solemnly installed in the Basilica of the Apostles. This was confirmed by the Council of Constantinople, and Gregory was enthroned by Meletius of Antioch, who very inconveniently died almost immediately afterwards. As Gregory struggles to end the schism, vainly entreating the followers of Meletius to accept Paulinus and bring peace to their Church, we feel, as we have through these three years, that the mantle of Basil had briefly fallen upon him. "Was it Gregory", asks Newman, "or was it Basil that blew the trumpet in Constantinople and waged a successful war in the very seat of the enemy?"

But alas, wars are long to wage and a defeat or two must not mean withdrawal if they are to be won. Gregory gives the impression of a man living always at fever point. He has none of the calm with which Basil confronted misfortune. He failed to win support for Paulinus. Flavian was consecrated as Meletius' successor, and Pope St. Damasus also expressed his doubts, not about the enthronement by Meletius, but about the canonicity of the transfer from Sasima. Such transfers, he said, "are not made without some degree of ambition, and are contrary to the tradition". The Egyptian bishops, on arrival at Constantinople, refused to take part in the liturgy celebrated by Gregory.

This was the last straw and Gregory saw the horrible spectre of Sasima arising before him again. He threw in his hand and returned to his solitude. He bade farewell in a final and powerful discourse to the town of Constantinople, to the little Church of the Resurrection, to the great basilicas of Sancta Sophia and the Holy Apostles, to the East and West, for whom he was suffering persecution, to the guardian angel of his Church, and—very curiously—to the Trinity, whom he had untiringly made known to his people.

He was succeeded by Nectarius—an old senator, not baptised when he was chosen—and he, in due course, by the great John Chrysostom.

Before his total retirement, Gregory preached in Caesarea the eulogium of Basil which is so revealing about them both. And in it he defends Basil's action in creating new bishoprics when his province was divided. He speaks of the wild confusion that ensued, of the robberies committed, of the priests who upheld Basil being expelled. But Basil "made the dispute serve the Church's development and gave to evil the best possible result by adorning his fatherland with a greater number of bishops. What came of this? Three results, all excellent: greater care for souls, the possession by each town of its own bishop, hence the end of the war."

Even now, however, after so many years, he cannot wholly forgive Basil for making him a pawn in the game. "From this have arisen all the irregularities, the agitations of my life. This made it impossible for me to be a philosopher or to win the reputation of being one—not that this last matters very much." But while at the time he had blamed the pride and ambition of Basil, he can say today: "His thoughts were above the thoughts of men; detached from this world while still in it, he referred all things to the Holy Spirit, and knowing how to respect friendship he only despised it from the moment that he was obliged to put God's honour before all things and place our hopes of eternity above perishable things."

This was a generous judgement, and we may well ask whether Basil had perhaps, like many great men, forgotten that no man is expendable even in the service of others. But there seems to have been at this period the curious idea that one did nothing but good to a man by forcing him to accept the grace of ordination, and with it responsibilities for which he might well be unfitted. Although thousands were flying into the deserts to seek the life of contemplation, the principle that a man might have simply a contemplative vocation was often curiously ignored.

And it must be admitted that, in theory, both Gregorys made this attitude easy for Basil. They both insisted that only the man who fears high office is worthy of it. Nazianzen especially, in his eulogy of Basil, descants at length on the damage to the Church wrought by ambitious men grasping at episcopacy. The humble must be exalted, not the proud. The elder Gregory of Nazianzus forced the younger to become a priest, Basil pushed him into being a bishop. They both claimed that the needs of the hour were urgent, that no man should put his own spiritual life above the general need of Christ's people for the Bread of Life, given in sacraments, given in teaching. But it looks as though for Gregory Nazianzen, the call of solitude was altogether too strong. He could leave it to meet an emergency, but he could not live in the series of emergencies through which the great Basil prayed and fought his way to the very end. He ends his eulogy:

This, O Basil, to you from me; receive this offering from a tongue once very dear to you, your peer in honour and in age. Look upon me now from on high, divine and blessed man, and hold back by your intercession that thorn in the flesh given me by God for my discipline, or else gain for me the courage to endure it. Direct my whole life to my greater good, and when I die may you receive me where you are dwelling. Living thus together and contemplating ever more clearly and perfectly the holy and blessed Trinity whose faint reflection is all we have yet seen, may our desires be thereby sated and the reward bestowed for the fights we have waged or that others have waged against us. But when I die who will praise me as I have praised you?—always supposing he could find anything in me worthy of an oration, in Jesus Christ Our Lord, to whom be everlasting glory. Amen.

St. Macrina had been a second mother to all her brothers: Gregory of Nyssa wrote her life, describing her influence upon Basil, whom she converted, on Peter, whom she educated, and on himself, whom she described as naturally quite unfitted for the splendid position he attained after Basil's death. She told him this on his last visit to the monastery and he described himself in all simplicity as rejoicing at the wisdom and beauty of her words. But her death was very near and as the evening drew on, she tried with failing voice to repeat the prayer sung at the lighting of the lamps. When "her hand brought to her face to make the Sign had signified the end of the prayer, she drew a great deep breath and closed her life and prayer together".

Macrina died shortly after Basil; Gregory of Nyssa and Peter both outlived him for several years. Peter too was made a bishop, succeeding Eustathius at Sebaste. A man of great practical ability, he managed to secure a harvest even in the famine years, could do anything with his hands, and ruled his diocese most capably. Gregory, far less efficient, was great as preacher and as a profoundly mystical writer. Rufinus said of them that the two together were equal to Basil; Gregory in word and doctrine; Peter in works of faith. But saints though they both were it would, I think, take many Peters and even Gregorys to equal Basil the Great.

VIII: ST. JOHN CHRYSOSTOM

JOHN, later called Chrysostom or the Golden-Mouthed, was born at Antioch in the year 347, in the same year as St. Jerome and seven years before St. Augustine. His father Secundus was a pagan and *Magister Militum* of the imperial army of Syria. He died soon after John's birth, and the child was brought up by his Christian mother Anthusa, yet, like all his contemporaries, attended a pagan school and university. We have met Libanius as friend of both Julian and of Basil. He had taught in Constantinople and in Athens, but Antioch was his home and he was now living and teaching there. He thought highly of his pupil. Asked whom he would choose as his own successor, he is rumoured to have answered, "John, if the Christians had not stolen him." They did not, however, "steal him" immediately. He was enjoying life and also ambitious of success in the law. He wrote later explaining to his closest friend why their intimacy grew so slowly: "It was impossible for a man who attended the law courts and was in a flutter of excitement about the pleasures of the stage to be often in the company of one nailed to his books and never setting foot in the market place."

Antioch was a marvellous city for a young man bent on fame and pleasure. Breathtaking in its beauty, it was crossed from east to west by a broad avenue four miles long; marble colonnades, red granite paving, golden statues between the pillars. It was as light, says Libanius, by night as by day. "Only the quality of the light was different." Some citizens worked all night but many more played. The river Orontes flowed through the city, high mountains stood around it. The groves of myrtle and cypress just outside, where a temple of Apollo commemorated the god's pursuit of the nymph Daphne, reminded men of the city's two-fold character. For close to the gigantic ivory and jewelled statue of the god had lain the bodies of the Christian martyrs Ignatius and Babylas. It was in John's childhood that Julian, trying to fan to life the dying embers of paganism, had a "revelation" that the bones of the martyrs were angering the gods and insisted on their removal. John may have witnessed the great Christian procession bringing the bodies into the city. "The market places were empty of men," he said in a sermon on St. Babylas, "the houses were empty of women." And he reminded his listeners of the thunderbolt that struck and destroyed Apollo's shrine.

Nominally the population of Antioch was half pagan and half Christian but for the most part the pagan element just enjoyed life and were indifferent in their attitude to the gods.

John was only twenty—he had entered the university at fourteen—when he joined the class of catechumens and, after about three years, was baptised, in 370. He was longing for the ascetic life, but his mother begged him not to leave her yet. She spoke of the fearful anxiety she had experienced in bringing him up, of the expenses of a liberal education made more difficult by the harsh exactions of tax collectors; of designing relatives, of the rascality and laziness of domestic slaves. She compared the miseries of a widow's life to an "iron furnace" —the biblical phrase for the Egyptian captivity, meaning a furnace fierce enough to melt iron.

Next to the divine helps that had strengthened her had come the sight of John, "a living image of him who had gone". "Do not plunge me into a second widowhood," she pleaded, "do not revive my grief." Sitting beside her son on the bed where she had given him birth she entreated him to stay with her until her own death, which she believed was not far off. John could not resist these pleadings, but very soon after his mother's death he did for six years embrace the ascetical life —four years with a group, two years as a solitary in a cave near the city. Like St. Basil and St. Jerome, he was not meant for it; he undermined in those years what must have been a remarkably strong constitution.

PRIEST IN ANTIOCH

Bishop Meletius had long wanted this solitary for the priesthood; he ordained him deacon, and Flavian, successor of

Meletius, ordained him priest. This was in 386. John was nearing forty.

Schism still divided the Catholics of Antioch. It had been rumoured that whoever died first, Meletius or Paulinus, had promised the succession to the other. But on the death of Meletius at Constantinople his followers, despite St. Gregory Nazianzen, chose Flavian to succeed him. Presently, Paulinus, feeling the approach of death and in defiance of canonical regulations, consecrated Evagrius without even a single assistant bishop. Alexandria and the West refused to recognise Evagrius, while still not formally acknowledging Flavian. Most of the years of John's priesthood at Antioch were spent in a divided Church, with discontented laymen—and especially laywomen—moving from one group to the other.

But with the non-recognition of Evagrius, the end of the strangest schism in church history was in sight. Ambrose especially pressed Theodosius to get the two men to Italy, where their case might be judged by a council. Flavian would not hear of this and the matter was finally left more or less in the hands of Theophilus of Alexandria, who summoned a synod. Rome had never made an issue of the schism; though themselves supporting Paulinus, popes remained in communion with men in communion with Meletius and Flavian, and acknowledged bishops consecrated by them. Pope Siricius now did all he could to make matters easy, stating specifically in a directive to the eastern bishops assembled at Caesarea in 393 both that Nicaea had decreed the necessity of several bishops for an episcopal consecration and that there must be at Antioch one bishop only, and he must have been consecrated in due form. The synod decided that this meant Flavian. Theophilus was not present, but a deputation was sent to Rome and the decision was accepted.

Part of John's clinging to his solitude had come from fear of the magnitude of the priest's office. "Great", he says in his *Six Books on the Priesthood*, "is the conflict of the solitary, great his toil. But compared with those of the priesthood rightly exercised, the difference is as wide as between king and commoner." And he paints vivid pictures: a low-born cripple called to wed a king's daughter; a shepherd boy chosen to command an army or a fleet. The boy has witnessed the blood, the mutilations and all the horrors of war, he knows the danger of captivity and slavery worse than death. "Order him immediately to mount his horse and command the army. Would he not be dismayed?"

It is now that John begins to earn his second name, Chrysostom. And it is interesting to learn that he had to work hard before it was his. Readiness in speech, he says, is needed by the preacher even more than by contending barristers. And, though a man may have natural ability, "since preaching does not come by nature but by study, if a man reaches a high excellence he will soon lose it if he does not cultivate his power by steady hard work and exercise".

"A passion for sermons" possessed, he says, pagans and Christians alike. They came as to the theatre, they listened critically, wanted novelty, punctuated a successful sermon with bursts of applause. And, like Augustine, Chrysostom was an orator who drew forth this applause again and again. "I know not", he says rather pathetically, "whether any man ever succeeded in the effort not to be pleased when he is praised."

Chrysostom's sermons give no impression, during the first year of his priesthood at Antioch, of any major troubles. The first heavy blow came not from an ecclesiastical but from a political cause: the famous riots of 387 commemorated in his lenten sermons "Concerning the Statues".

The Emperor Theodosius issued an edict taxing the city to produce a large sum of money for the benefit of the army. Every soldier was to receive five gold pieces. The edict was read on February 26th and received for a moment in stunned silence. Then began mutterings—according to Libanius there were professional trouble-makers in the crowd. Gradually feelings became more and more inflamed; there was a rush to the Baths of Caligula, where lanterns were smashed and trees cut down, then a rush back to the Prætorium. The prefect had disappeared from the audience hall, Bishop Flavian was at his sister's sick bed. There was no one to control or soothe the mob. A stone was thrown at the gold statue of Theodosius and soon all five statues of the royal family had been stoned, torn down and dragged through the streets.

Then came the day, the many days, of reckoning. *Lèse-majesté* was no light offence; the punishments could be limitless. Men were executed, others were tortured, the groans of prominent citizens were heard through the prison walls, their goods were seized, their wives and children thrown on the street. Meanwhile the prefect sent messengers to Constantinople to report the crime to the Emperor. It was a hard winter, with heavy snow blocking the mountain passes. And while this delayed the messengers, the aged Bishop Flavian set out, determined to push through the snow, arrive first and plead for his flock. For rumour had it that Antioch was to be totally destroyed.

Eight hundred miles of bleak country buried in snow through which this old man was making his forced marches against time—John missed nothing of the drama. "There is a silence", he said, "big with terror, and utter loneliness everywhere." Day by day he stood before his audience, for in Lent there was a daily sermon, to strengthen and encourage them. In this holy season, he told them, Flavian would show the Emperor the blessedness of forgiveness; the very sight of the venerable old man would dispose him to mercy. "Let us help him with our prayers, let us make an embassy to the King who reigns above, an embassy of tears."

Their fast itself would be a great help—but they must also learn not to fear man too much. God knew what they could bear and when to remove their trials. He reminded his people that they had done worse things than destroy statues. "How many men have not only thrown down, but trodden under foot, God's images. When you throttle a debtor, strip him, drag him away, you are trampling under foot the image of God." God had now allowed these terrors to come upon them, he says, using Basil's favourite phrase, "through dread of a fellow slave".

Thus boldly he told them that the Emperor too was God's slave, that their first prayer must be to the Lord of all. He rebuked them for the luxury and the love of money which he held to be the root of the rebellion. They would only have spent the tribute money on girls and horses, theatres and more splendid houses. Now no bawdy songs were to be heard, no drunkards seen reeling through the streets. The city looked like a desert, the forum was empty but the church was filled. "Our Mother the Church will console us with the multitude of her offspring . . . the chorus of the brethren . . . and will drive away all despondency." "The rulers threaten, therefore must the Church give comfort."

Lent was halfway through when the imperial commissioners from Constantinople, Hellebicus and Caesarius, entered the city. They had brought with them decrees of punishment that were severe enough: the theatre and hippodrome, shut already, were not to be reopened. The baths, too, were to be shut, the free grants of corn were to cease and Antioch was to lose its metropolitan rights. The insignificant town of Laodicea was to supplant it. And the horrible scenes of questioning and torture began again. Crowds stood weeping in the streets, listening to the groans of the accused and praying silently, not daring to speak to one another lest informers might be among them. But when Libanius, the head of the pagan school, ventured in the evening to approach the commissioners, they whispered to him that they were going to put no one to death. They wanted only to terrorise the people into profound submission and repentance.

The next day a strange sight startled the royal commissioners. Hordes of ragged hermits poured into the city and boldly approached them. One man, seizing the bridle of Hellebicus, imperiously ordered them both to dismount. This was not well received until his sacred character was explained. Whereupon the two commissioners, both Catholics, knelt before the strange-looking saint and reverently clasped his knees. The statues, he told them to remind the Emperor, were now restored and replaced, but it was beyond human power to restore God's image if they put to death another man. The hermits entreated permission to go themselves to intercede with Theodosius. Their efforts were seconded by the local clergy and neighbouring bishops, who approached the commissioners on their way to court, kissed their hands, clasped their knees, and implored clemency, holding them fast until they had definitely promised to be merciful. While refusing to allow the strange embassy of hermits to go to Constantinople, the commissioners agreed that Caesarius should return there immediately, taking with him a petition for mercy written from their dictation. Meanwhile the court should be closed and no more trials take place until the answer to the petition came.

Chrysostom, in a sermon describing these scenes, rather unfairly forgets the courage of his old teacher, and indulges in a sarcasm which seems to have been very much part of his character. What, he asks, had become of the professional philosophers while the fate of their city hung in the balance? "Where are they, with their long beards and threadbare cloaks, and the staves in their right hands?" Describing them as abject in soul, lower than the dogs under the table, he tells how they ran away. While the monks flocked in to save the town, the philosophers sought safety in the caves the monks had left. Probably Libanius had been an honourable exception, but it is a bitter little sketch, however well deserved.

Libanius and Chrysostom, pagan and Christian, relate the same story with different additions or omissions, one ignoring Flavian, the other Caesarius, who both had their share in winning the pardon which both orators agree was undoubtedly won! Travelling night and day, Caesarius reached Constantinople in less than a week. He found that Flavian had already softened the Emperor either in one scene, as dramatically described to his people by Chrysostom, or, as seems more probable, in a series of interviews. Flavian did not attempt to excuse what had occurred; he began by standing silent before Theodosius, listening to his reproaches, not trying to stem his own tears. Tears springing from the thought of his people's suffering were by the Emperor held to spring from that of their grievous sin. He reproached Flavian for his people, but already more in grief than anger. Why had they forgotten his own past kindness, but why, above all, had they desecrated the memorials of the dead?

Curiously enough, Libanius also agrees with the idea then put forward by Flavian—it was by the instigation of demons that the rioters had acted. But Flavian even now spent little time in excuses. He urged rather the motives for a generous forgiveness. This was the part of a Christian, he told Theodosius. The pagan world would stand amazed at the sight of a magnanimity which only his religion could inspire. "Great", they would exclaim, "must be the God of the Christians who makes men into angels and raises them above the limitations of humanity." He reminded the Emperor that he, too, would be judged on the Last Day, that forgiveness for him would depend on whether he had forgiven. He reminded him that Christ had forgiven even those who slew Him.

This last thought was dwelt on by Theodosius as his motive when he consented to pardon a crime which had perhaps been already overexpiated. Caesarius presented the petition of the hermits, adding his own strong recommendation to mercy. And all its privileges were restored to Antioch, all the citizens were granted a free pardon. Now in generous mood, Theodosius promised a visit to Antioch, and bade Flavian hasten home that he might bring the message of peace and joy in time for Easter.

The last of these lenten sermons "On the Statues" are happy ones; Flavian was returning, was home again among his people. "Who could have thought that in so short a time he could have arrived, had audience with the Emperor, averted our destruction and be back in time to celebrate the Pasch with us?" And, continues John, what if our city has lost some worldly splendour? What should be the real root of our pride in being citizens of Antioch? "If you would glorify the city speak not of Daphne, the multitude of its lofty cypresses, the water of its fountains. Speak not of the city's great populace, of its market place thronged up to midnight, of the wealth of goods for sale." Does the dignity of a city rest on its splendid arcades and porticoes, its large and beautiful buildings, or even on its title of metropolis?

Perhaps not, but John was very conscious that he was a citizen of no mean city. What was Alexandria, what was the upstart Constantinople, compared with Antioch? But he will only allow that pride is justified by its Christian history.

The splendours of a city are "material things, lasting for this life only". But it is a glory for eternity that here at Antioch the disciples were first called Christians. "This dignity none of the cities of the whole world possesses, even the city of Romulus." And a second dignity was theirs, that in time of famine they thought not of themselves, but ministered to the Church of Jerusalem. And yet a third dignity was that from Antioch went the embassy to Jerusalem of Paul and Barnabas, so that "pure doctrine cleansed from all Jewish imperfection

might go forth to all parts of the world". The true glory of
Antioch lay in this past, and in the present of "almsgiving,
vigils, prayers, sobriety, true wisdom of soul: for these things
commend the city".

Flavian's return had been gloriously celebrated. Lamps were
lit and green branches spread, the forum was garlanded with
flowers. Chrysostom exhorts his people to thank God always
for His mercy and the true glory of their city.

John contrasts interestingly with the Cappadocians in the
ease with which he dropped his Classics. He had studied for a
much shorter time than they; literature meant far less to him,
and despite his use of the word for the Christian religion, he
cared little for philosophy. That the label "Origenist" should
later have been attached to him is almost comic, for his treatment of Scripture was wholly in the Antioch tradition, not the
Alexandrian. He would never, like Basil or Gregory, have
composed the *Philocalia*; he cared nothing for the great
Alexandrians.

Where he did resemble St. Basil more than any other of the
Fathers was in his passionate love for the poor, in his hope to
change the ordinary careless Christian into a man with an outlook like his own. Aimé Puech says that the sermons of his
Antioch period are characterised by a balance and moderation
at first unnoticed because of the torrential eloquence. This is
true if he means that John only urged men to give freely, only
attacked ill-gotten riches. But he stretched the idea of ill-
gotten riches very far: even if you had not robbed the poor
yourself, were you sure about the wealth you inherited? And
he demanded charity on the scale of the Gospel. "You make
no difficulty about boarding and lodging soldiers at the
demand of the civil authority; you will not do the same for
the poor at the demand of Christ. Yet the poor are your
defenders against the devil, as the soldiers are against the
barbarians. All of you should have guest houses in proportion
to your income; set apart a room in your dwelling for the guest,
that is, for Christ. Put a servant in charge—choose the best
you have—to receive the poor and sick and to wait upon them.
If you will not make this sacrifice and let Lazarus sit by your
family hearth, at least shelter him in your stable. Yes, give

Christ shelter in your stable. Ah, you shudder at this idea—but it is far worse to shut the door in His face."

There was already at Antioch a Church centre for the needy. It was not enough for Chrysostom—he wanted them welcomed voluntarily at the town gates and taken *home*: not for their own sakes only but for the good of their hosts. If the clergy alone help the poor, the layman will soon be expecting the priests to do all his praying for him too.

In John Chrysostom's ideal world there would have been community of goods, slavery would have disappeared, above all there would be much praying. He urged frequent attendance at a liturgy into which he had introduced antiphonal singing, he urged in a very early work—the *Apologia for Monastic Life*—that young men should make a retreat in a monastery before entering on active life. "Those who live in the world," he said once, "except for marriage, and despite of marriage, ought in everything else to resemble monks." The rich should learn habits of poverty, not only giving generously, but living detached from their wealth. He warns a rich woman of the Judgement "when Christ will make you pay the price for those pearls and bring the poor who have perished with hunger into our midst". But to the poor he cries: "Weep with me! Weep for your plunderers, who are more to be pitied than you."

He who had once loved the theatre became the vehement opponent of shows of any kind. Fights of wild beasts and even gladiators still went on in the amphitheatre at Antioch. The best actors were brought from Tyre or Beyrout, the best dancers from Caesarea: in the theatres were shown, John says, impure scenes which dwell in the soul and stimulate sensual passions—better have the actress or prostitute in your house; your wife would soon drive her out, but your wife cannot banish your secret memories. Once after a vivid description worthy of some pagan satirist, he cried out, "Did you feel nothing while I was speaking? Do not blush and be ashamed at what nature urges. But if listening here to a priest you are overcome, what of the theatre? Would you still dare to say that you remain cold as marble?"

The sermons on the statues had been preached in Lent, so they urged the keeping of the fast, but John held abstinence, as he once said, to be the least of virtues. It was far more important to abstain from swearing—a matter on which he felt keenly—than from food; to serve your neighbour and to pray. He urged coming to church as an alternative to the theatre, and it would seem that while he preached, men often felt it so. That he went deep in his doctrinal teaching is shown in his instructions to catechumens.

"Christianity is no child's play," he says, "yet a handicraftsman and a poor man can be a philosopher." We have seen in Christ "our nature borne upon the Cherubim". Going forth from these Christian assemblies we should move "as from a sacred shrine, as from heaven itself, poised, philosophical, doing all in right measure . . . you have been enrolled in the choir of angels, conversed with the Lord, been in the company of Christ".

In the instruction "to those about to be illuminated" he speaks of the meaning of baptism. We are not merely cleansed but made new, like some golden statue cast into a furnace. God "sending forth, not fire but the grace of the Spirit, brings us forth with much brightness, renewed and made afresh, to rival the beams of the sun". Nor is all yet lost if man, thus renewed, spoils God's glorious work in him. On repentance, God will again bring back those who have received the power of the Spirit and have fallen away. "But this is no time to talk of repentance . . . may you always keep unsullied the beauty and the brightness you are about to receive."

At the head of all John sets the supreme belief—all these teachings are what he calls in another sermon "growing germs of doctrine" for his hearers' minds. "The King shall give the cup into your hand—that dread cup full of much power, and more precious than any created thing. The initiated know the virtue of this cup and you will know it a little while hence."

BISHOP OF CONSTANTINOPLE

It has been said that Chrysostom, like Julian, despised the pleasure-loving, excitable, changeable populace of Antioch, but his sermons certainly show how much he loved them. They were his people, this was the country where he had been born, where he had always lived, in solitary places or in the heart of the city. And his people loved him—as the Alexandrians had loved Athanasius. When it came into the mind of Eutropius, court favourite and chief imperial chamberlain, to make John Bishop of Constantinople, he knew that it could be done only by a trick.

Eutropius was of the lowest birth, had been castrated as a boy slave, had been sold to a general, who employed him as a pander and then gave him to his daughter for a wedding present. His duties were those of a lady's maid—to comb her hair, to prepare her bath. There followed some sort of misconduct, after which he was found starving in the streets of Constantinople. All this is a little puzzling. Now that Roman Law was "christianised", a slave could no longer be put to death by his master—but he could still be sold. It seems that the mistress of Eutropius had just thrown him away! Such life as he had had seemed over. An officer at the Court took pity on him and employed him in some menial job. Step by step he climbed—first into the rank of lowest imperial chamberlain, finally into that of highest. Theodosius was succeeded by his son Arcadius, a man of weak mind and weaker character, and the eunuch's influence over him was boundless. To the horror of the Romans, the Emperor made Eutropius a Consul.

The poet Claudian ends a list of strange phenomena—monstrous birth, showers of blood, double suns, etc.—with the line *Omnia cesserunt eunucho consule monstra*—"An eunuch for consul, monstrosity can go no further." This horror is, he feels, a symptom of the depravity of the Greek mind. The Senate applauds, and the Greek populace and their rulers: *O patribus plebes, digni consule patres*—"O populace worthy of your nobles, nobles worthy of your consul." Gibbon notes in this verse "the first symptoms of jealousy and schism between old and new Rome, between the Greeks and Latins".

The Bishop of Constantinople had died, and Palladius describes a crowd of candidates, "some battering at the doors of officials, others offering bribes, others again going on their knees to the populace". All this to the great scandal of the serious laity, whose petition to the Emperor was for an experienced priest to become their bishop. Perhaps Eutropius had heard John preach, perhaps merely heard echoes of his fame. He suggested to Arcadius that the governor of Syria should arrange to meet him at a famous shrine. There John could be kidnapped, brought to Constantinople and consecrated. Everybody was reluctant in this affair except the plotting chamberlain and his Emperor. John did not want to leave Antioch, his people did not want to lose him; above all, Theophilus of Alexandria did not want to consecrate him. It was said that only by threatening exposure of some disgraceful secrets he had discovered, did Eutropius force Theophilus, early in 398, to perform the ceremony. The Court had chosen its own bishop; the Court was satisfied. But not for long.

John was a man of enormous gifts, of great holiness, but not a man of easy character. He insisted on ruling this see which had been forced upon him—and he was successor to a pacific easy-going bishop who had been there sixteen years. One of his first acts was to sell the splendid furniture of his predecessor and give the money to the poor. The clergy had grown wealthy and luxurious, a rich laity set no bounds to extravagance: golden tables that took several men to lift them, marble floors gold-dusted, golden bits in the mouths of their horses. All this we learn from John's sermons: he became in the pulpit a scourge of God against the city's wealth and luxury, against the neglect of its poor.

At Antioch John had been a valued assistant; here at Constantinople he was master in his own house. There was much to be done and he was in a hurry to do it. There were no hospitals or asylums in this great city and John, admiring and emulating Basil, founded several, supplying them, says Palladius, with a large staff of doctors, superintendents and nurses. The countryside lacked priests and churches; he urged the great landowners to work at conversion of the pagans, to provide each one a church and priest on his own estate. "Give the dowry of a daughter to this church, which will in good truth be your daughter." He toiled himself at the conversion of the Goths, of whom there were many in the city—soldiers with their wives and dependents formed quite a population. Gathering them in a large church, John had Mass said for them in their own language—sometimes preaching to them through an interpreter.

Unfortunately his zeal against heresy led on occasion to riots and bloodshed. The Arians, having been by Theodosius deprived of all churches inside the city, had formed the habit of assembling in various squares and courts and forming a procession, to end with a meeting outside the city walls. John saw fit to emulate these gatherings by Catholic processions: psalms were sung, magnificent silver crosses carried—but of course in time the two bands met. Stones were thrown as well as hard words and when one of his eunuchs was wounded Arcadius shut down the Arian processions.

Perhaps there is something about the air of Constantinople; St. John Chrysostom, like St. Gregory, now seems for the first time a little feverish. His reforms were many of them overdue, but he was certainly in a tremendous hurry to make them.

To the generous rich he gave the interesting counsel— become your own almoners, do not give the money to the clergy to distribute. In part this may have been to get them into personal contact with the poor—"blessed is he that *understands* concerning the poor and needy". But he made no secret of his doubts of what would happen to money entrusted to the priests of Constantinople. He tried to stop legacies to the Church. Above all he forbade the custom of "spiritual sisters"—albeit under vows of chastity—keeping house for priests.

Overeating and drinking was another habit in his new see. John refused all banquets and ate alone. In the whispering campaign started against him one item was the suggestion that he ate in solitude lest his own intemperate habits be noticed. The sight of his emaciated face and figure showed the absurdity of this story, but his enemies were not slow in inventing others. For John soon had a host of enemies—but also a group of most devoted friends and the enthusiastic admiration of the vast crowds who listened to his sermons. Eutropius was soon questioning his own wisdom; this bishop was not pliable. Enemies of the eunuch had sought asylum in the church and Chrysostom had protected them. Eutropius persuaded the Emperor to abolish the law making this possible—henceforth the Church could protect no one from the State.

Hubris is something more than ordinary pride—it is an exaltation that makes a man feel himself unconquerable, untouchable. There is no height he cannot reach; he has forgotten to guard against enemies, against fate. He believes himself a god. And the gods are jealous.

Eutropius, eunuch and consul, had risen from the depths to a height inconceivable. It was not wonderful that *hubris* had clouded his judgement, blinded his eyes. Earlier favourites had exercised a vast and hidden power, but he blazoned it before the world. Described on monuments as the third founder of Constantinople, "this infamous broker of the Empire", says Claudian, "hung up in his office a chart of the price at which he was prepared to sell each province". He was confident of his ascendancy over Arcadius, oblivious of the men he had ruined, the hatreds he had aroused, and, most strange of all, of the growing jealousy of the Empress Eudoxia. She owed her throne to Eutropius; but a man who had disgraced or murdered so many of his own benefactors could hardly be so simple as to think that this fact guaranteed his safety. Eudoxia's opportunity came with the advance of a barbarous army upon Constantinople. Eutropius undertook the conduct of the war; of the two generals he chose one was incompetent, the other disloyal. Worked upon by his fears and by Eudoxia's private accusations, Arcadius consented to sign the condemnation of Eutropius. The eunuch fled the palace; he took sanctuary where he had abolished it, at the altar of God.

Curious to the western eye are the tent-like curtains screening the sanctuary in an eastern church. On the Sunday following the disgrace of Eutropius Chrysostom stood in the ambo outside them and preached on the vanity of human greatness as shown in the fall of the late favourite. "Vanity of vanities, and all is vanity" was his text, as he asked what had become of the delights of high rank: the dancing and the feasting, the applause at theatre and hippodrome, the garlands and the flatteries, the feigned friends at the man's wine parties, the brilliant performances of his cook. As he speaks he shows it all fading like flowers, vanishing like smoke—and we become aware of the great orator addressing the fallen favourite, we are conscious of the vast, excited crowd, wondering where Eutropius was, whether their bishop had protected him or had given him up. Then suddenly the curtains part and there he is crouching beside the altar. "Even the harlot", cries Chrysostom, "took hold of the feet of Jesus", and he points to "the harlot-face, lately radiant with the prosperity of extortion, looking uglier than any wrinkled old woman. Adversity, like a sponge, has wiped it of its paint and its enamel".

How cruel, we feel—he has received the fugitive only to mock him; could not the golden mouth of the great orator have formed words of pity at such a time? The sermon goes on— and we see something else. Here is an audience thirsting for blood. What were the insulted dignity of Eudoxia, the fears of Arcadius, compared with the anguish of oppression this man had inflicted on the people of Constantinople? Chrysostom was showing them this cowering wretch, not to humiliate him but to win their pity. And he succeeded. "Have I softened your passions?" he asks. "I think I have, from the way your tears are falling." He will not deny the wrongs and insults they have suffered, but "how will you handle the holy mysteries and repeat that prayer which commands us to say 'Forgive us as we also forgive our debtors', when you are demanding vengeance?"

Chrysostom had saved Eutropius from the mob: had the eunuch remained he could, he claimed, have saved him even from the Empress. But the situation could not last indefinitely and Eutropius was induced by promises of safety to leave sanctuary and go in exile to Cyprus. Shortly afterwards he was brought back to Constantinople, tried, and executed for treason.

EXILE AND DEATH

St. John Chrysostom did not suffer from *hubris*—his eye was single and his sight was clear. He had found early favour with the Empress but this did not for a moment lead him to put his faith in princes. And he certainly did nothing to placate them. The only question is, might he have been just a little more accommodating, a little less uncompromising? There are disadvantages in being a great orator, the words pouring out in a mighty flood are not always those prudence would have chosen. And the excited listener adds conclusions. After a few windings the stream of words would not be recognised at their source. The gestures, the eyes of the preacher, are interpreted— Chrysostom was seen to look towards the royal tribune as he denounced luxury and neglect of the poor. His alleged sayings flew from mouth to mouth. And, too, Eudoxia was jealous: she had destroyed Eutropius only to find a more powerful rival, for Chrysostom was beginning to gain influence over the weak mind of her husband.

Theophilus of Alexandria, who both feared and hated John, was ever ready with plots against him. The story, too involved for a short sketch but of absorbing interest, is told by Palladius, of how he was sent for to Constantinople by the Emperor that John might judge his conduct, how John refused to do so, and of how Theophilus bought his way into the royal favour until he felt strong enough to judge the man who had refused to judge him.

Of this incident Bury says: "Though it appeared merely to concern Chrysostom personally, it really decided that in future the Patriarch of Constantinople was to be dependent on the Emperor." The Emperor in the East was to be not within the Church but above it.

It was not too difficult to make contact with John's enemies. Two deacons disgraced by him for murder and fornication respectively, bore false witness against him. And Theophilus, besides being well supplied with money for bribes, had brought with him, as John told Pope Innocent, "no small multitude" of Egyptian bishops. There were thirty-six of them; not enough to outvote the local bishops, but the local bishops were not invited to the highly uncanonical synod gathered by Theophilus —known as the Synod of the Oak from the name of the house where it met. The accusations brought against John were numerous and confused. He had deposed a deacon for beating a slave; he had taken under his protection some pagans who had injured Christians; he had treated clerics as men of no worth; he had encouraged sin by telling the sinner, "As often as you sin come to me and I will help you"; he had eaten a pastille immediately after celebrating Mass, and had dressed and undressed on his episcopal chair. Earlier Theophilus had attacked John as an Origenist, but at the Oak this accusation was dropped. He had, however, it was said, used in his sermons expressions savouring of paganism, speaking for instance of "a table full of Erinyes".

What would the synod have made of the Cappadocians if one little classical allusion could so stir them? The quality of his judges becomes clear enough through the very pettiness of most of the accusations. Moreover, as John wrote to Pope Innocent, "It is not fitting that one belonging to Egypt should judge those of Thrace, a man moreover who is himself under an accusation and is an enemy and an adversary."

Before the synod ended his enemies had played their trump card: John was a traitor "encouraging the multitude to revolt". It was also alleged, says Palladius, that he had called the Empress "Jezebel".

While all this was in progress Palladius, himself present, tells us how John's friends, a company of forty bishops, were sitting with him when he told them in the words of St. Paul, himself "inspired by the Spirit": "The time of my departure is at hand." They kissed him, weeping. But John told them:

". . . It was often said that I should lose my head for being too outspoken. I think you will remember if you look into your memories, that I always used to say to you, This present life is a journey, and its joys and sorrows are ever passing away. What is before our eyes is but a fair; we finish our buying and selling and we move elsewhere. Are we better than the Patriarchs, the Prophets, the Apostles, that this state of life should abide with us forever?"

Then one of the company sobbed aloud, saying, "Nay, we lament our orphaned condition, the widowhood of the Church, the confounding of ordinances, the ambition of those who do not fear the Lord and leap upon high offices in the Church, the defenceless state of the poor, the famine of teaching." The Christ-loving bishop tapped the palm of his left hand with the forefinger of his right, a familiar gesture when he was in deep thought, and said to the speaker: "Say no more, brother, only remember what I said; do not desert your Churches. The teaching office did not begin with me, nor will it come to an end in me. Did not Moses die, and was not Josue found? Did not Samuel end his days, and was not David anointed? Jeremias departed this life, but was there not Baruch? Elias was taken up, but did not Eliseus take his place as prophet? Paul was beheaded, but did he not leave behind him Timothy, Titus, Apollo and countless others?"[1]

[1] Palladius, *Dialogue Concerning the Life of Chrysostom.*

John's refusal to appear at the Oak was judged a confession of guilt. The synod deposing him stated that dealing with the accusation of high treason did not lie within their competence; they begged the Emperor himself to punish this crime. John was banished, but he had only gone one day's journey when an earthquake shook the palace. Eudoxia, terrified, sent messengers to recall him. Theophilus fled. Prudent for once, John wanted to wait for a decision by another and more authoritative synod, that he was authorised to return to his see after the deposition at the Oak. But the people were so violently inflamed that the Court insisted on his immediate enthronement. John described all this in a sermon surprisingly laudatory of the Empress, and for a short while the reconciliation seemed perfect. It lasted two months.

And then a magnificent silver statue of Eudoxia was set up opposite the Senate House, within a few steps of the Cathedral. In honour of this event games, dancing and dramatic representations, held by John to be licentious and idolatrous, were held on a vast scale. In vain he complained to the prefect—the near neighbourhood of the square where all this was taking place to his church gave him an obvious right to protest. But as repeated to the Empress, his protests became treasonable. "Again Herodias dances," he was supposed to have said, "again she demands the head of John."

These words are found in a certainly spurious sermon written later—perhaps by the men who wanted to see to it that he never returned again from exile. But something he may have said to which the words could be attached. Whether she again danced or not, Eudoxia certainly again demanded John's exile. This time there was to be no recall but the problem was how best to get him away.

It is a little difficult to form a clear picture of that last fearful Easter Eve, because Palladius, and John in his letter to the Pope, want to throw the blame on Theophilus and his ecclesiastical sycophants rather than on Arcadius or even Eudoxia. Soldiers, John says, by contrivance of the plotting bishops and against the Emperor's wishes, attacked that night the Christians keeping vigil, the neophytes receiving baptism. Women "stripped for baptism fled naked . . . many were wounded . . . the baptismal pools were filled with blood . . .

The soldiers penetrated into the place where the sacred vessels were stored . . . the most holy blood of Christ was spilt upon [their] garments . . . when day dawned the city was empty. Outside the walls under the forest trees the people like scattered sheep were celebrating the feast."

All this John wrote to Innocent before he left the city himself. "I beseech Your Charity", he says, "to rouse yourself, show compassion and do all you can to put a stop to the mischief at this point." He was willing to stand trial on the accusation of Theophilus before a lawful tribunal, but none such had ever been held.

Chrysostom could, had he chosen, have been a demagogue. The masses of Constantinople were already aroused in his defence and he had clergy in plenty and many rich and influential people among his friends. But while he refused to leave merely at the Emperor's private request, he accepted the official decree of banishment, and leaving his mule standing where the people awaited him, at the west door of the church, he went out quietly by the east. Only more bloodshed, more suffering for his flock, could have come from a prolonged resistance.

A painful journey brought him near to death but he just managed to reach Cucusus, a bleak spot chosen by Eudoxia for his place of exile. Here, with unfailing optimism he began to build up his life again. Antioch, his old home, was only one hundred and twenty miles from Cucusus. When his enemies, says Palladius, "saw the Church of Antioch migrating to the Church of Armenia and the gracious philosophy of John chanted from there back again to the Church of Antioch, they longed to cut short his life". The world had thought of him as already dead, but they saw important men "turning pale and writhing in fear of a priest, alone, disfranchised, infirm, exiled. . . . Here is a formidable dead man who frightens living men, and those in authority, as bogies frighten children".

Confident that he would return to Constantinople, John continued to write directions to his clergy, to console his friends by long letters, to busy himself with the conversion of Huns and Persians, to help the poor. He wrote letters to the West, he again laid his case before the Pope. In fact, he was altogether too busy to please either the usurper of his see or the imperial rulers. They had hoped the bitter cold of the place would kill him (he did in fact spend the winter enclosed in one small room, half choked with smoke in the attempt to get it warm), but after three years he was still very much alive. It is touching to see from his correspondence how he and his friends tried to conceal their sufferings from one another. Olympias the deaconess and other close friends had been banished for their support of him, and neither Hun nor Vandal could have done much worse than did the imperial torturers who tore the flesh of a young lector of John's with hooks, and then scorched him with torches until he died.

In his second letter to Innocent, John speaks of "the magnitude of what has to be done. For the contest now before you has to be fought on behalf of nearly the whole world, Churches humbled to the ground, people dispersed, clergy assaulted, bishops sent into exile". Theophilus, too, had appealed to Rome but the Pope, having examined both sides carefully, decided that the Synod of the Oak was invalid. He suggested the summoning of a General Council. But neither the Pope nor the Emperor of the West could achieve anything, so Innocent finally broke off relations with John's adversaries and did his best to console the unhappy exile.

To his friends John tried to sound a cheerful note, but to Innocent he speaks of three years "exposed to famine, pestilence, wars, continual sieges, indescribable solitude, daily death". At Constantinople all were banished who refused to communicate with the new bishop—but there were far too many of them to please the Court. An end must be put to it—who would rid them of this turbulent priest? "He was in their hands," says Newman in his brilliant study of Chrysostom, "they had sentenced him to die and only hesitated how his death was to be brought about. . . . Cucusus promised to spare them the odium of his murder." Since he still lived, "he must be carried off to some still more inhospitable region; he must undergo the torture of a still more exhausting journey. Cold and heat, wind and rain, night air, bad lodging, unwholesome water, long foot-marches, rough-paced mules—these were to be the instruments of his martyrdom. He was to die by inches; want of sleep, want of rest, want of food and medicine, and the collapse certain to follow, were to extinguish the brave spirit which hitherto had risen superior to all sorrows."

Palladius, although no longer an eyewitness, tells the story vividly: how John was hustled forward through pouring rain and under blazing sun, allowed no halt in any town where a bath was available—a comfort which in Constantinople had appeared for him a necessity of life. He was past sixty, always since his hermit years in poor health, unable to eat coarse food or undergo great exertions; his journey was arranged by men for whom, says Palladius, "it appeared as if their promotion depended on his dying in the course of it".

And so most probably it did. One of the two guards showed him by stealth an occasional kindness, the other was consistently brutal. Pityontes on the eastern shore of the Euxine was their destination, but John soon realised he would not live to reach it. "They approached Comana", says Palladius, "but passed through the town as men cross a river by a bridge and lodged outside the wall at the shrine of a martyr, five or six miles from the town." That night Basilicus the martyr, once Bishop of Comana, stood beside John and said, "Be of good cheer, brother; tomorrow we shall be together." It is said that the priest of the shrine had also an intimation: "Prepare the place for Brother John, for he is coming."

John asked his guards next morning to stay a while at the shrine—but no, still this mad drive onwards, still this strange new torture of death by marching. The march lasted this time about four and a half miles and then a sharp attack of illness forced them to bring John back to the shrine. Here, like a neophyte preparing for baptism, he asked for white clothes and changed everything, even his shoes. "Then, having communicated in the symbols of the Lord, he made the closing prayer 'On present needs'. He said his customary words 'Glory be to God for all things'; and having ended it with his last Amen, he stretched forth those feet of his which had been so beautiful in their running, whether to bring salvation to the penitent or reproof to the hardened. . . . And shaking off this mortal dust he passed to Christ."

Eudoxia had died before the man she had persecuted. Thirty years later Theodosius II had his relics brought back to

Constantinople. The Bosphorus was all bright with torches and a great multitude of the faithful were, says Theodoret, "crowding the sea" with boats. The Emperor laid his face upon the coffin and entreated that his parents might be forgiven. But the Church at Constantinople remained in bondage to the Court. The triumph of Ambrose was never won in the East.

GOVERNOR OF MILAN

AURELIUS AMBROSIUS, father of St. Ambrose, was Pretorian Prefect of the Gauls, ruling over France, Spain, Portugal, part of Germany, Britain, Sardinia, Corsica and Sicily. From his palace in Trèves he administered this vast area as the absolute representative of his sovereign—even military officers of high rank kneeling in his presence. Here at Trèves Ambrose was born, probably at the beginning of the year 339. He went through the usual education of a patrician boy of the period—elements, grammar, rhetoric. He may have also studied philosophy and it seems almost certain that at Rome, where he completed his education, he took an advanced course in jurisprudence.

The son of a prefect would naturally follow in his father's footsteps, and the law was the best stepping-stone to the heights of the civil service. Ambrose and his elder brother Satyrus were soon practising in the Court of the Pretorian Prefect of Italy—and in the year 370 Ambrose himself was appointed "Consular" or Governor of the Province of Aemilia-Liguria, the capital of which was the city of Milan. Ambrose was now technically a member of the Roman Senate and in the third order of the official aristocracy, his title being that of *Clarissimus* or Worshipful. The road was clear ahead for a position as great as his father's—indeed, his dreams might have soared higher yet, for his family was among the great ones of ancient Rome which had given consuls as well as prefects to the Republic.

Milan was, at the beginning of the fourth century, the seat of the Imperial Government in the West, later to be succeeded by Ravenna. It boasted a magnificent circus and theatre, splendid baths built by Maximinian, fountains everywhere, an imperial palace, many temples and several Christian basilicas—

besides the ancient baptistry where Augustine, his son Adeodatus, and Alypius, were one day to be made Christians.

When Ambrose took up his post as Governor, the Church at
Milan was in great distress. In 355 Dionysius, the Catholic
bishop, had been sent into exile by Constantius, who had
named an Arian in his place. This man, Auxentius, was still
reigning, despite the vehement efforts of Hilary of Poitiers,
Eusebius of Vercelli and others, to get him removed. St.
Jerome commented optimistically: "Auxentius, that curse of
the Church, was buried, so to speak, before he was dead," but
Auxentius in fact remained very much alive until 373; on one
occasion a visiting Catholic cleric, Philaster of Brescia, who
attacked him, was flogged by the Arians and turned out of the
city.

It is not surprising that on the death of Auxentius, the
Governor of Milan should have felt concern over the election
of his successor. Catholics and Arians were both determined
to get their man in, and it was not unlikely that there would be
riots. Ambrose decided to go down in person to the basilica
where the election was to take place. We can imagine him
leaving the court of justice at which he was presiding, setting
aside, perhaps, pressingly urgent business, and wondering how
much time he would have to waste on calming his fellow
citizens.

He had begun to address the crowd when suddenly a voice
was heard above his—the voice, it is said, of a child—chanting
the words "Ambrose, Bishop! Ambrose, Bishop!" Instantly
the whole church took up the cry, Catholics and Arians together repeating the words "Ambrose, Bishop! Ambrose,
Bishop!"

Ambrose was no cleric; he was not even baptised. He was a
career man whose career was prospering; he had no faintest
desire to be a bishop, he had in fact a violent repulsion against
the idea. Leaving the cathedral, he went back to the courts
and, against his custom, though in accord with Roman law,
he ordered several suspects to be put to the torture. But the
people, who had followed him in hordes from the basilica,
instead of reacting as he had hoped and repenting their hasty
choice, all cried out: "Your sin be on us! Your sin be on us!"

More and more troubled, Ambrose, after a vain effort to

withdraw on the plea of retirement for philosophic meditation, decided to shake public confidence in his moral character. He ordered several prostitutes to be brought ostentatiously to his dwelling. But again the crowd swarming round the house cried out: "Your sin be on us! Your sin be on us!"

This was getting serious and Ambrose next attempted to escape by night and fly to Pavia. Through the darkness he drove, but the dawn saw him again approaching Milan by the Roman gate. He had taken the wrong road in the darkness and had driven right round the city. Now the people, taking him back to the governor's residence, set a guard around it to keep him safe. Messengers were despatched to the Emperor requesting his immediate confirmation of the election of his own high official to be bishop of his capital city. Before the Emperor's letter arrived, Ambrose had fled again and hidden himself in a friend's house. But his secret was betrayed and he was brought back. At last he yielded, "recognizing the divine will concerning him", says his biographer Paulinus.

Valentinian was delighted to have a troublesome question settled so peacefully. The Church authorities were no less compliant—for they felt this was a case of God's choice. Ambrose was baptised and confirmed on November 24th, received minor orders, diaconate and subdiaconate on succeeding days, was ordained priest, and on December 1st was consecrated bishop.

It would be fascinating to learn something of what his former religious life had been. A man who rose to sanctity so fast, becoming one of the greatest of the Fathers, establishing the spiritual authority of the Church when it had been so fearfully shaken—that such a man should have entered upon his vast task at a mature age yet still only a catechumen is startling in the extreme. He would up to now have been present only at the first part of Mass, would have listened to what were then long readings of Scripture, have taken part in prayers varying with the season. But it is hard to picture a man of deep religious belief who had done all this from boyhood and never received Holy Communion. No word suggests that Ambrose had led other than an exemplary life; the Christians of Milan made choice of him, the clergy accepted him. But what a gulf he crossed when he received the four sacraments of Baptism,

Confirmation, Holy Communion and Holy Orders. It is a pity Ambrose never wrote the story of his own life.

To his fellow bishops in East and West he sent news of his election and a statement of his own orthodoxy. He had asked for delay in his consecration, but had only insisted that his consecrator be a Catholic, not an Arian. Of Basil he begged the favour that the body of his Catholic predecessor Dionysius be brought back from Cappadocia, where he had died and where he was venerated as a martyr. Basil replied, joyful at the choice of Ambrose and authenticating the relics, "Let no one dispute, let no one doubt. Here you have the victorious athlete . . . known to the Lord. These bones He will crown, together with that soul, in the righteous day of His requital."

Bishop Malgré Lui

If he had to be a bishop, Ambrose was not the man to do it in a half-hearted way; that week of intense inpouring of divine grace probably brought with it a keen illumination of the mind, as well as a powerful strengthening of the will. The new bishop gave all his goods to the poor, keeping only a provision for his sister; he set himself again to study—this time Scripture and the great Christian writers—Origen especially and Basil. Most bishops had been able to lay a foundation of such knowledge before taking up the burden of office: Ambrose read immensely, but he often spoke of the huge difficulty of learning while obliged constantly to teach. He prayed much, especially at night; he fasted. Though welcoming visitors to his table— hospitality was a duty even for a poor man—he would not, he said, waste time dining out, constrained to listen to worldly talk and to refuse repeatedly the refilling of his glass.

Ambrose took very seriously the primary duty of father and teacher of his people. He himself prepared catechumens for baptism, labouring at this, says Paulinus, more than his five successors put together. Every Sunday he preached. Every day he offered Mass for his flock. When he heard confessions he would weep with the penitent.

St. Augustine, coming to Milan, "attended carefully" when Ambrose preached, "to judge whether his eloquence was equal to his fame . . . I enjoyed the charm of his speaking,

though for all his learning it was not so pleasing and capti-
vating as that of Faustus. I refer only to the actual speaking:
for the rest, there was no comparison at all. Faustus was
simply straying about amongst the fallacies of the Manichees.
Ambrose taught the doctrine of salvation most profitably."
(*Confessions*, v. 13.)

The bishop's door was always open. Anyone at all could
enter at any time, but the room was often so crowded that
many were beyond the sound of his voice. When no one spoke
to him Ambrose would fill the time with reading, and Augustine
awaited the moment, that never came, when he could find the
bishop fully at leisure. For the ancients reading normally
meant reading aloud, and Augustine speculates on why
Ambrose read silently. Was it to spare his voice? Was it to
avoid questions on what he was reading? "Whatever his
reason for doing it, that man certainly had a good reason."

How St. Ambrose managed to write in so overworked and
distracted a life is a mystery—but even more how he could
think so deeply, when not even his own room was a place of
solitude. He must have been a reader before he was a church-
man; he knew the Classics well. Probably as a lawyer he had
formed the writing habit and had had to use his mind constantly on practical matters. None of this accounts for the full
depth of his writing, but it does explain his having written.
For he was still the Roman lawyer, the practical man applying
his powers to a fresh situation. One book came into being for
an almost comic reason. A broken-hearted young widow was so
successfully comforted by Ambrose that she began to think of
marrying again. The bishop, in alarm, wrote the treatise *De
Viduis*, depicting the greater blessedness of the widow's state.
We do not know whether he succeeded in undoing his earlier
success.

But on a wider scale he had a greater need to fill—the provision of a Christian literature in Latin for his clergy and his
people.

Modelling himself on Cicero, Ambrose wrote for his clergy
De Officiis Ministrorum. Called a classic by Augustine and Cassiodorus, used by the medievals as a text book, this is, of all his
works, nearest to the Greek apologists in its use of pre-Christian
truth as a path to the truth of Christ.

For Ambrose all goodness stems from a relationship between the soul and God. Man is "the glory of God", His "most precious work", "consummation and flower of creation". Man must learn *about* God. Ambrose regarded an understanding of the doctrine of the Trinity as essential to the virtuous life. He must cultivate in himself a likeness to God. And no one who has studied Ambrose can doubt in which virtue he will find this likeness best shown. Mercy, he says, "makes men perfect".

And no longer have we to look, as did the ancients, to imaginary models: Plato's philosopher-king, Aristotle's moral expert, the wise man of the Stoics. God has given to the Christian the perfect model, the pattern of perfection. Christ, the God-Man, is our exemplar. Nor need we search painfully to spell out from nature the duties and virtues proper to man, for Christ has revealed them to us.

The peace of the Church had brought a flood of catechumens to her doors, and with it an immense problem of instruction and discrimination. Many of them were like the "devout men" of old, who admired the Jewish faith but had no intention of taking on the burdens of the Law. We have seen how Origen's father had his infant son baptised, although the deferring of baptism was already beginning to creep in. By the fourth century the child of Christian parents might go through life as a catechumen. In *Hypatia* Kingsley has brilliantly depicted the terrifying effect of the fearful discipline of penance through which post-baptismal sin could, once only, be held forgiven *by the Church*. Even Christian parents were getting the outlook that it was best to let their young sow their wild oats first and then come, sobered and serious, to the font.

Meanwhile, most bishops seem to have accepted for instruction only those catechumens who had written down their names for baptism. We have seen how Ambrose toiled over them; of the twenty-nine works listed as genuinely his by Dudden, several are collections of catechetical sermons or treatises written for their instruction before and after baptism. One book rejected by him but included by many authorities— *De Sacramentis*—is probably reported sermons.[1]

[1] See the Intoduction to *St. Ambrose on the Sacraments and on the Mysteries*, by J. H. Strawley.

Perhaps the most touching tribute to Ambrose as a teacher is the only letter we possess from the young Emperor Gratian— the first Roman Emperor to refuse to be Pontifex Maximus of the still established paganism of Rome. To Gratian's choice the Empire later owed the great Theodosius, but had he not been murdered in early youth one suspects that Gratian might have shown himself at least as great. This letter reveals how, in West as well as East, the thoughtful layman was beset with the problems introduced by Arianism and anxious for theological enlightenment.

I greatly long to enjoy the bodily presence of him whom I ever bear in mind, and with whom I am present in spirit. Therefore hasten to me, religious priest of God, to teach me the doctrine of the true faith. It is not that I am eager for controversy, or that I wish to apprehend God in words rather than with my mind; but I would have my heart opened more fully to receive the abiding revelation of His Godhead. For He will teach me, whom I deny not, whom I confess to be my God and my Lord, not cavilling at the fact that He took upon Himself a created nature like my own. . . . Weak and frail, I glorify Him according to my powers, not according to His divine majesty. I request you to send me a copy of the same treatise which you gave me some while ago, enlarging it with an orthodox dissertation on the Holy Spirit. Prove, both by Scripture and by reason, that He is God. God keep you for many years, my father and servant of the Eternal God whom we worship, even Jesus Christ.[1]

In *De Fide* Ambrose answers the Emperor's request for a supplementary treatise on the Holy Spirit. No Western writer had yet done this. Ambrose's teachers were Athanasius and Basil. Jerome, in his caustic fashion, spoke of Ambrose as decking himself like a jackdaw with other birds' plumes and spoiling the good things he stole from the Greeks. ("There is an upstart crow", said Robert Greene of Shakespeare, "beautiful with our feathers . . .")

Jerome's verdict was prejudiced and unfair. Theology, like all sciences, progresses by one man learning from another, and

[1] *Gratiani Epistola*, prefixed to Ambrose's letters. The letter was written by the Emperor with his own hand (*Ambros. Ep. i*, 3). I have used Dudden's translation.

Ambrose, while constantly declaring himself a learner, built an essential bridge between the Greeks and Latins and advanced beyond his predecessors. On this very doctrine, for instance, he anticipated the teaching of the Procession of the Holy Ghost from both Father and Son. St. Augustine has spoken of how much he learnt from St. Ambrose. He read Greek reluctantly, if not with difficulty: Ambrose was a first-class Greek scholar and read it with enjoyment. "The importance of Ambrose as a theologian," says Dudden, "has not hitherto been adequately realised. He has been thrown into the shade by Augustine. The lesser genius has been absorbed by the greater."

Ambrose and his brother Satyrus, who remained a layman, were linked in closest friendship. Satyrus never married. The sermon preached by Ambrose at his funeral is deeply moving— his loss was the greatest sorrow of the archbishop's life. Their only sister Marcellina was vowed to virginity, and on this subject Ambrose is as exuberant as Jerome though less violent. Four of his works are devoted to the subject. To foster vocations to virginity and the ascetic life was one of his highest aims. Making it a part of his deep devotion to Our Lady, he sees her as the mirror of all virgins: "Through one woman He came down, but many women has He called."

Newman has noted that development, in the case of Our Lady, has had little to do with doctrine though much with devotion. Ambrose is only one of a long line of Marian theologians, but he specially loves to dwell devotionally on Our Lady. He compares her with the earlier Mary, who with Moses and Aaron "led the march of the Hebrew hosts through the waves of the sea ... taking once more the timbrel [she] will awaken the virgin choirs as they sing to the Lord of their passage over the sea of the world." The name Mary signified the bitterness of the sea, but through Mary God had come, "that the bitterness of man's state might become sweet, tempered by the sweetness and grace of the heavenly word". Mary, says he, is at once the daughter of the Church, as its greatest member, and its mother, since she gave birth to Christ. "A virgin espoused, she conceived us in the spirit."

"Christ before the Virgin, Christ from the Virgin; born indeed of the Father before creation, but born of the Virgin for the sake of creation." "Mary was the temple of God, not the God of the temple." "She who had given birth to God desired to know God."

"She was alone and wrought the world's salvation and conceived the redemption of all." "The everlasting came into the Virgin."

BORN ADMINISTRATOR

Heavy as was the burden of episcopacy on the purely spiritual level, Ambrose must also have been thankful for his years of administrative experience. The fourth century revealed plainly enough in the West that the Empire was decaying. Buildings were falling down, land going out of cultivation, there were bandits on the great Roman roads, the postal service was disordered. Starvation was not uncommon; it was not only in a year of famine that parents sold children into slavery to get bread. The native population was declining and a kind of caste system, whereby the son of a baker must bake, the son of a farmer farm, weighed down all ambition.

Lethargy and despair were induced by a crippling taxation administered by officials both cruel and corrupt. In the law courts a man rich enough could always buy a verdict. The poor man had no chance.

Lactantius compares the coming of imperial surveyors into a district to an invasion by a hostile and plundering army. The middle classes were disappearing—small farmers hired themselves to great land-owners, ceding their land in return for protection. Others even moved to districts under barbarian sway. For the failure of Roman government was opening the road to other races, looking eagerly towards what remained of the imperial order and civilisation.

During a long period of conquest Rome had absorbed many nations, and the Romanised Celt or Iberian or Gaul had come to think of himself primarily as a Roman. Paul from Tarsus, Augustine from Africa, Patrick from Britain were all "Romans" —and the Catholic religion only added a more profound meaning to the title. "It was more, apparently," comments Bury, "to have been called the city of St. Peter, than to have been the city of the Caesars."[1]

---

[1] *The Later Roman Empire*, vol. i, p. 52.

Long before the coming of the Goths *en masse*, the Roman army had begun to be filled with them. They made excellent recruits and had been for some time replacing the old citizen army of the Republic. The army, in the third century mainly Illyrian, was, by the fourth, fed largely by adventurers from beyond the Rhine and Danube. Many of these soldiers became established with their families inside the Empire, so that certain districts were almost entirely settled by them.

And then in the middle of the fourth century came the first large-scale migration—the first real break-through. The Visigoths in 376, fleeing panic-stricken before the Huns, begged the Emperor Valens to let them cross the Danube and give them land in the Balkan provinces. The soldiers and their families camped in their multitudes on the banks of the river while awaiting the Roman answer. "Quite suddenly," says Bury, "without any time for thinking out the problem or for any preparation, he was called on to admit into his dominions a foreign nation, of barbarous habits, armed and warlike, conscious of their national unity: to provide them with food, and to find them habitations."[1]

He decided to attempt the vast task, but the Roman military and civil authorities were both greedy and inefficient, and it failed. Very soon Romans and barbarians were at war. At the battle of Adrianople, the Roman legions were defeated by the heavy cavalry of the Goths. The Emperor Valens was probably among the slain, and in the chaos that followed Gratian did the only possible thing—summoned to his aid the great general Theodosius and begged him to become his colleague in governing the Empire. Theodosius agreed, though with real reluctance, and received from Gratian the Eastern provinces.

But now the Goths were no longer mere beggars for the imperial bounty: Theodosius made a treaty with them whereby they paid no tribute for their land but even received certain pensions from the Government. They were to serve the Empire if called upon as federate soldiers under their own leaders. This was in 382. "The reception of a whole people . . . strikes what was to be the characteristic note of the dismemberment of the Empire, namely, disintegration from within."[2]

---

[1] *The Invasion of Europe by the Barbarians*, p. 57.   [2] Bury, *Invasion*, p. 61.

Theodosius was both strong and diplomatic, he saw the danger but was able to control it. He made great use of the Goths and chose them for the highest posts in his army. Stilicho was his favourite, and became commander-in-chief. Alaric had high promotion and the promise of higher. The Empire was, says Bury, "almost a necessity of thought" to these barbarians. It was, says Fustel de Coulanges, "not an enemy but a career". A career is seldom a man's primary loyalty and Alaric, disappointed in his career, would later turn his arms against Rome. The Empire was no longer strong enough to change these *foederati* into Romans. While Theodosius lived they kept the borders well enough and held back more dangerous foes, but we must see their menace as a background to all the activities of Church and State. Christians are ruled, councils are assembled, Popes are consulted, all the vast work of the Church goes on in a world rarely and precariously at peace, in a civilisation gradually falling apart.

We must beware of thinking of a bishop in this unusual period in terms of the modern or the medieval world. In the West even more than the East, the failure of the State had forced the emerging Church into a position unique in history. The State had become in most men's eyes simply something to which you paid taxes; personal liberty was smothered by bureaucracy, initiative and patriotism were both dead. The Church had for Christians become a new *patria*, awakening energy and self-sacrifice. Augustine, in one of his sermons, remarks characteristically, "How many say, 'The Government has taken away all I own, so I shall die in want.' How few say, 'Christ has taken away all I own, so I shall never die at all.'" Yet in fact, multitudes were found enthusiastically giving to Christ all they owned, while on the other hand the Church had created a new citizenry of the slave, the derelict and the outcast. These above all were Christ's people.

The charge of the poor was passing more and more into the Church's hands. Every basilica was a centre of public relief and had its list of the poor supported by it. Hospitals, orphanages, hostels for travellers, were being built everywhere. There were Church banks. There was Church provision of dowries for poor girls. Despite the crippling taxes, vast sums were poured out on these works of charity.

Ambrose held that private property, slavery and monarchy were all results of the Fall. An ideal society would be a democracy consisting not of wealthy and comfortable but of poor and contented men. None would be perpetual rulers, none perpetual workers. In the world as it is today we must obey our rulers, but he admonishes them also. An emperor should not deny freedom of speech, "should not abolish liberty, even in the case of those who owe him a military obedience. The difference between good and bad rulers is that the good love freedom, the bad slavery".

The institution of slavery was not intended by God but is the result of man's sin and folly; yet Ambrose oddly seems to think that in this unsatisfactory world slavery is best for some men. In any case justice demands of all the total gift of self in service first of the Christian community, then of the State. Justice becomes "charity, which regards others rather than itself, not seeking its own". "The Church is, as it were, the form of justice."

The bishops were taking the place of the People's Tribune of old days. They protected the poor, stood out against unjust laws, spoke boldly to rulers. We have seen how St. Basil, confronting a hostile proconsul with calm assurance, told the astonished tyrant: "You have never met a bishop." Like Basil, Ambrose did not hesitate to confront officials: he held that intercession for the condemned and defence of the oppressed were among a bishop's highest duties. "If any be a bishop," he wrote, "let him rescue by his intercession and influence the man who is being dragged to death." Getting no satisfaction from a subordinate, on at least one occasion he made his way into the Emperor's presence and, pleading with him face to face, won the pardon he sought. After the battle of Adrianople he melted down and sold the Church plate to provide money for the vast multitude of prisoners to be ransomed, a task which he called "the highest liberality". The Arians cried out "sacrilege", but Ambrose answered, "It is far better to preserve souls for the Lord than to preserve gold."

A law of Constantine allowed bishops to hear and judge civil cases. Since the church courts were cheaper and incomparably more just than those of the State, the people flocked to them. Augustine's biographer speaks of the grievous burden which this became since at times he was kept both morning and afternoon hearing and judging. Probably Ambrose, with past long experience, could decide more swiftly which cases really merited the expenditure of his time—he laid down as a principle that in matters of property it was not always necessary that a bishop should arbitrate, but that he must never refuse to do so in really important cases involving the law of God or the interests of the Church. Perhaps he remembered as he sat in judgement that when he first entered upon the office of prefect, his former chief had said to him, "Act not like a prefect but like a bishop."

AMBROSE AND THE ARIAN EMPRESS

When in 382 Gratian issued a decree disestablishing and disendowing the pagan religion, money hitherto spent on vestal virgins, priests and temples was not transferred from pagan to Christian worship but diverted to the Imperial Treasury and the Prefect's Exchequer. Gratian refused even to see a deputation of the majority of the Roman Senate protesting against this decree. He had probably already received from Pope Damasus, through Ambrose, a vehement counter-petition from the Christian minority—but it is unlikely that anything but his own conscience guided Gratian. The Senate must, the pagans realised, bide its time; but within a year it seemed that the angry gods were themselves taking vengeance. A successful revolt dismembered the Empire of the West. Gratian was horribly murdered. Maximus the usurper reigned in Gaul. The crops failed in Egypt, Africa, Spain and central and southern Italy; there was not food enough for the local populations, far less to supply Rome, where famine began to threaten.

The moment seemed propitious for a fresh petition to the boy Emperor, Valentinian II. He was only thirteen, and the great Symmachus drew up the appeal with such skill that Ambrose himself praised the "golden tongue" of his adversary. News of the petition had been kept from the bishop till it was too late for him to summon a synod or invoke the aid of the Pope. He must act alone, and he did so in a letter to Valentinian showing the intensity of his faith and of his anxiety. It was probably the force and character of the man that chiefly worked on the young prince—perhaps also the suggestion that he should consult Theodosius ("your father", Ambrose calls him), Emperor of the East, a sincere Christian and a man of experience. But one paragraph of the letter must have rankled, unless Valentinian was unlike any other schoolboy. "The altar of Christ", wrote Ambrose, "rejects your gifts because you have made an altar to idols. . . . The Lord Jesus refuses and rejects your service, because you have served idols; for He has said unto you, *Ye cannot serve two masters.* What will you answer to these words? That you fell into sin because you were only a boy? But no childhood is recognised in faith, for even little children in the face of their persecutors have fearlessly confessed Christ."

The letter did its work: Valentinian refused to undo the act of Gratian. But this was only to be the first round in a fight between Ambrose and the imperial power. And Justina, mother of Valentinian, Empress-regent, would certainly remind her son, if he ever forgot it, that he had been called by Ambrose a mere boy and compared with little children.

An episcopal tendency to liken troublesome empresses to Jezebel was an element in what Dudden calls the "spirited manner" of fourth-century controversy. Ambrose did not resist it. He compares Justina also with Herodias, and Paulinus speaks of her violent rages. She was no pagan but a convinced Arian, and she detested Ambrose both religiously and from jealousy of his influence with Valentinian. It was hard on her to see a city so long held by her co-religionists turned overnight into a Catholic stronghold. All the basilicas of Milan were now in the hands of the Catholics and there were hardly any Arians among the townsfolk. But in the Palace Justina could point to Arian courtiers and officials, and the considerable number of Gothic troops quartered in the city were almost all Arians.

The reason for this is an interesting one. A young Cappadocian named Ulfilas, born in the second decade of the fourth century, had been made captive by the Goths, in one of their raids on the Empire. While still a boy he was sent as a hostage to Constantinople and brought up among Arian Christians. Eusebius of Nicomedia consecrated him bishop and he went back to evangelise the Gothic people. He created a Gothic alphabet and translated the Bible into Gothic. Ulfilas was, says Christopher Dawson, "the founder not only of German Christianity, but also of Teutonic literature". Creator of the first Christian Church among the Goths, it was from this Arian that their religion took its source, and Arians they continued for centuries, often persecuting the Catholics, often persecuted by them.

For these men and for her court, Justina demanded of Ambrose in the name of the Emperor that one of the Catholic basilicas should be turned into an Arian church. Summoned to a privy council at the beginning of Lent 385, Ambrose was ordered to hand over the Portian Basilica outside the walls. He refused—and the people of Milan, getting wind of the affair, backed their bishop in noisy fashion, shouting outside the palace, "We are ready to die for the faith of Christ." There does not seem to have been any suggestion of asking anyone to die for anything, but the demonstration became so vehement that Ambrose was finally asked to quiet the people. He did this by assuring them that no one should "invade the basilica of the Church". It was said afterwards that he had himself contrived the riot, but for the moment the matter rested until near Easter, when Justina resumed her efforts.

Ambrose had a habit, quite specially infuriating for the Court, of taking his flock publicly into his confidence. Asked again to yield a basilica—this time the one known as "New" and the most important of his churches—Ambrose answered briefly, "A bishop cannot give up the temple of God." On the following Sunday he reported his action from the pulpit and the church rang with the applause of the congregation, in the midst of which the Pretorian Prefect of Italy appeared. Then and there abandoning the demand for the New Basilica, he tried to persuade Ambrose to give up at least the Portian Basilica which, after all, was only a suburban church. The people shouted in protest and the prefect withdrew to report to Valentinian.

Ambrose was told that the Emperor, in demanding the Basilica, was acting within his rights, "for he has sovereign power over all things". But Ambrose answered, No. Over all things temporal—"my land, my money, anything that is mine

I will not refuse . . . But not even the Emperor has sovereign
rights over what belongs to God . . . drag me to prison or death,
I will go joyfully. I will not hide behind the thronging people.
I will not lay hold of the altar and beg for my life. For the
altar's sake I will gladly be a sacrifice." And after spending the
day in church, he went home to give them the chance of
arresting him.

It was a dilemma for the Government. No need for Ambrose
to "hide behind" a people who were wholly his supporters.
An Arian priest had been mishandled by the crowds; Ambrose,
hearing it, wept and prayed that no blood but his own should
be shed. But the rich merchants of Milan, thrown into prison
and fined as a reprisal, said, "We will gladly pay this [perhaps
£50,000 in our money] and as much again if we may keep our
faith." Gothic soldiers set to guard the Portian Basilica proved
to be more Catholic than Arian and, hearing a rumour that
Ambrose had excommunicated them, rushed tumultuously
into the Basilica in the middle of Mass to make their peace with
him. The terrified congregation feared a massacre but the
soldiers cried, "We have come to pray, not fight", and the
congregation started a singular chant as though the Emperor
himself were there: "We petition you, Augustus, we do not
fight, we do not fear, but we petition."

The arrest of Ambrose was out of the question; even the fine
on the Catholics was remitted and soldiers again burst into
the church (this time the New Basilica) bringing the news and
kissing the altar in sign of peace. The Court had capitulated,
but his officers found Valentinian in a sulky and furious mood
when they entreated him to go in state to the Cathedral on
Easter Sunday as a sign of reconciliation. Ambrose, he said,
was "a usurper and worse"—and to his advisers: "You would
give me up in chains if Ambrose bade you."

The Grand Chamberlain Calligonus introduces an Eastern
touch at this point by sending a message to Ambrose: "Do you
dare to flout Valentinian while I am alive? I will take off your
head." To which Ambrose answered: "God grant you may
do what you threaten. I shall suffer as bishops suffer and you
will act as eunuchs act." But in the West even an imperial
eunuch had not imperial power. And not long afterwards
Calligonus was himself executed.

Valentinian was once addressed by the usurper Maximus as "Your Most Serene Youth". At the moment he was far from serene. He had been dragged by his mother into a struggle with the redoubtable archbishop, had been made to feel and to look a fool; his one wish was to get away—from Milan and its triumphant people. The rest of the year he spent in Venetia—and in all probability he would never have ventured to resume the war with Ambrose. But Justina thought otherwise. She had a new ally, named, like Ambrose's predecessor, Auxentius, also an Arian and a bishop, the disciple indeed of Ulfilas. Expelled from his see of Dorostorum on the Danube by Theodosius, he had taken refuge at the Court of Milan, and he and Justina together worked out a plot to get rid of Ambrose. First a law was drafted giving right of public worship to all who accepted the Council of Rimini, and treating anyone who opposed such right as guilty of sedition and punishable by death. Ambrose merely continued to hold all his churches, in perfect confidence that no Arian would dare to seize one. Next the Government summoned him to debate with Auxentius the points of difference between them—each disputant to choose lay umpires, the Emperor himself to be supreme arbiter. If Ambrose would not come he must leave Milan—which meant in effect handing his see over to the Arian.

Ambrose flatly refused either alternative. It was unheard of that a bishop's doctrine should be judged by a layman—and in this case the arbiter was to be a mere boy, not yet baptised and ignorant of the sacraments of the Faith. If lay opinion were wanted, let the debate be held before the instructed Christian congregation in the basilica. He would not be jealous if his people chose Auxentius. But they, indeed, had already given judgement when they petitioned Valentinian I to make Ambrose their bishop. And the Emperor had promised he should not be molested if he accepted the see.

The very reluctance with which Ambrose had accepted his position gave immense force to the stand he was now making. He would be judged by a synod of bishops only—and indeed he had already consulted the local episcopate—he would neither go to the Court nor abandon his see. After sending this letter Ambrose remained day and night in the New Basilica, surrounded by his people. The Court set a guard of soldiers who

allowed whoever wished to enter but no one to leave the church.
One can only suppose that those who entered brought food to
those already there, for the siege lasted for several days. Wild
rumours ran through the crowd: "They have a carriage ready
to carry the bishop into exile"; "His death is decreed and
executioners are on the way." And then suddenly they would
be shaken with rage and cry "Away with Auxentius", or with
fear that the bishop would himself desert them and choose
exile rather than death.

To keep up his people's spirits, to inject the note of prayer
and confidence, Ambrose encouraged them in singing psalms
and hymns. We are reminded of Athanasius—but the psalmody
of Ambrose, although coming originally from the East, was an
advance on that of the great Bishop of Alexandria. The earlier
singing was hardly more than rhythmic speech—and the people
only answered the celebrant. It was probably Flavian and
Diodorus (the men who mobilised the monks in their mighty
musical onslaught on Arianism) who first introduced the
usage taken up by Ambrose of two choirs, one answering the
other; but Ambrose himself who created the music. Imagine
the immense basilica—the excited and harassed people, short
of sleep, of food, of drink, yet trained and mobilised by their
bishop, "ready to die with him", as St. Augustine tells us.
"Then it was," Augustine says, "that the practice was instituted of singing hymns and psalms, after the manner of the
Eastern churches, to keep the people from being altogether
worn out with anxiety and want of sleep. The custom has been
retained from that day to this and has been imitated by many,
indeed in almost all congregations throughout the world."
His mother, Monica, "bearing a great part of the trouble and
vigil, had lived in prayer", while he himself "was stirred to
excitement by the disturbed and wrought-up state of the
city".

Not psalms alone were sung, but the hymns written by Ambrose himself, which were also something new in Christian
worship. Some of them are still in the Breviary today, both
those certainly authentic and a number of imitations. The
Arians, Ambrose said, complained that by his hymns he be-
guiled the people. "I certainly do not deny it. . . . For what
is more powerful than the confession of the Trinity, daily

celebrated in song by the mouth of the whole people? All alternately vie with one another in making profession of their faith; all know how to proclaim in verses the Father, the Son, the Holy Ghost. So all have become teachers, who were scarcely fit to learn."

The hymn used on Mondays at Lauds is said by Bede to be one of Ambrose's own and we can imagine how, as the sun rose after another weary night, the people sang:

> *. . . Cedant tenebrae lumini,*
> *et nox diurno sideri,*
> *ut culpa quam nox intulit,*
> *lucis labascat munere.*
>
> *Praesta Pater piissime,*
> *patrique compar Unice,*
> *cum Spiritu Paraclito*
> *regnans per omne saeculum.*

Every hymn ends with some form of invocation of Father, Son and Holy Ghost. But it may be that the teaching in song went further: a fascinating theory, held by some weighty authorities, is that Ambrose himself wrote the creed called by the name of Athanasius. Arranged in short stanzas this profoundly theological creed could, like the hymns, be chanted, and would, even more than the hymns, instruct through liturgy and devotion a people hungry for truth.

The tireless bishop relieved the exhaustion that singing must at last bring by a powerful sermon in which he assured his flock that nothing but force would take him from them, that he would yield to the Emperor all his goods, but not his see, not his Church. He told them the story of Peter meeting Christ as he was leaving Rome: "*Quo vadis,* where are You going, Lord?" And Christ to Peter: "To Rome, to be crucified again." The lesson of the story is, he told them, that Christ desires to suffer again in His servants.

Ambrose would render to Caesar the things of Caesar but not the things of God. And in this sermon, he uttered for the first time the great principle for which he was prepared to die. "The Emperor is within the Church, not above it."

Again the Court yielded. Auxentius disappeared and the
basilicas remained with the Church which had built them, the
people offering to God the worship of that Church by the hands
of their bishop.

AMBROSE AND THEODOSIUS

In 387 the growing ambition of Maximus brought about his
fall, for he invaded Italy, and in 388 Theodosius marched west
with extraordinary speed and captured Maximus at Aquileia,
where the soldiers—probably without the consent of the
Emperor—put him to death. Although Theodosius confirmed
Valentinian in his position as Emperor of the West, he evidently
thought the boy incapable of ruling—he would always be in the
hands, if not of his mother, then of some other strong personality. Theodosius had insisted on Valentinian's reconciliation with the Church as a condition of his remaining Emperor,
and he (though not Justina) had become also fully reconciled
with Ambrose. But Theodosius was now, in effect, sole
Emperor, and in future the masterful archbishop would have
to deal, not with a woman and a boy, but with a no less masterful Emperor.

It was difficult for churchmen in this changing world, where
the Church had passed so quickly from suffering to dominating,
to determine the principles whereby each new problem in the
relations between Church and State must be solved. Up to
now, Ambrose had stood upon two principles—God's churches
belonged to God and not to the Emperor; the Emperor was
within the Church, not above it. The statement of these
principles might sound startling to the successor of Constantine,
but to the convinced Christian, even if he happened to be an
Emperor, they were clear and undeniable.

The first contest between Ambrose and Theodosius involved
far more mixed elements—and in similar circumstances
Gregory the Great was to give in future years an opposite
judgement. The Christians of Callinicum on the Euphrates
had (with the hearty encouragement—indeed, at the instigation—of their bishop) burnt down a Jewish synagogue, first
seizing various objects they found there. Furthermore, a group
of monks had burnt a village chapel belonging to a Gnostic

sect in the same neighbourhood. Theodosius first decreed that
the bishop must rebuild the synagogue at his own expense, that
the stolen property must be restored and the monks punished.
None of this appears at all unreasonable, but even so he
presently modified the ruling by saying the town as a whole
should bear the expense of rebuilding the synagogue.

The principles acted on later by Pope Gregory when he
ordered the restoration to the Jews of a synagogue seized by
Christians were that Jews must be allowed to worship as they
had in all their generations and that the synagogue was Jewish
property. Ambrose had an intense desire to win forgiveness for
all men. He had even interceded with Gratian for pagans
attacking anti-pagan legislation. He had earlier attacked
furiously the inhuman conduct of the bishops who won from
the imperial power the execution of Priscillian and his followers
on charges of magic and immorality, but really for heresy.
Yet it is hard to see on what principle he now opposed the
orders of Theodosius. We feel there *must* be some element unknown to us as we read the amazing letter he wrote and the
sermon he preached in the Emperor's presence.

"Will you give the Jews", he wrote, "this triumph over the
Church of God, this victory over the people of Christ? Will
you give, Sir, this joy to unbelievers, this festival to the Synagogue, this sorrow to the Church? The Jews will place this
solemnity among their feast-days . . . in memory of the triumph
which they won over Christ's people."

Ambrose demanded of Theodosius that no reparation be
made to the Jews either by individuals or by the Christian
community, that no punishment be decreed against the
rioters. When the Emperor did not answer his letter—refused,
it would seem, even to grant him an audience—Ambrose
carried out a threat he had made, and addressed him directly
from the pulpit.

"Cherish", he begged, "the body of Christ, which is the
Church; pour water on His feet and kiss them, not merely
forgiving those who have been taken in sin, but also by your
pardon restoring them to peace and rest. . . . In plain words,
honour the least of Christ's disciples and pardon their faults
that the angels may rejoice, the apostles exult, the prophets
be glad. Every member of Christ's body is necessary to the

body. Do you, therefore, protect the whole body of the Lord Jesus, that He also of His divine mercy may preserve your kingdom."

Coming down from the pulpit, Ambrose stood before Theodosius, who said, "You have been preaching against me." He then explained the change in his orders, but Ambrose pressed urgently that the episode be totally forgotten and at last declared that he would go on to celebrate the Sacrifice relying on the Emperor's honour. This he repeated twice and Theodosius answered, "You may celebrate in reliance on my honour."

The courage was splendid, but great harm was done by this stand of Ambrose in a matter so dubious—for Theodosius, who had been disposed to rely on the great archbishop's advice, became sore and angry. He had received a public rebuke. He had felt obliged to yield, not because his conscience urged it but because it would have been highly impolitic for a newcomer to Italy to withstand the idolised archbishop. But, as he had remarked to Ambrose, the monks were "always offending". The council known as the Latrocinium showed later that there was a very real danger in yielding to their violence—and it was, alas, true that very little incentive was needed to encourage a Christian riff-raff in persecuting Jews. The most unfortunate effect of this episode was its indirect contribution to the Thessalonica massacre. For Theodosius laid strict orders on the members of his consistory that they should not— under pain of death—tell the bishop anything of their secret deliberations.

In the year 390, serious riots occurred in Thessalonica. Large numbers of barbarian soldiers were quartered in the town and were not popular with the civil population. Botheric, the commandant of the town, had imprisoned for immorality a popular charioteer and refused to let him out for the approaching games. Whereupon the enraged citizens murdered Botheric. It somehow came to the ears of Ambrose that Theodosius was meditating a fearful vengeance and, unpopular though he knew himself to be, he managed to have several talks with him. Condemning as "most atrocious" the idea of a massacre, he got from Theodosius some vague reassurance that made him believe it was abandoned. But surrounding the Emperor, really deep in his councils, were men who urged on him that a hideous vengeance was the only road to future peace. Theodosius gave, then quickly countermanded, orders for a general massacre in the circus of Thessalonica. For three hours the soldiers slaughtered indiscriminately and at least seven thousand were killed, guilty and innocent, citizens and visitors perishing together.

Ambrose, when he heard of it, was presiding at a council of bishops from Gaul and Italy; all were filled with horror, but it was for Ambrose to act and he prayed, with much anguish, that he might act rightly. Until he was clear about what he ought to do, he left Milan and stayed in the country. One night he dreamed that he was in the Cathedral preparing to offer Mass. Theodosius came in and he found himself powerless to offer the sacrifice. This seemed to Ambrose a divine indication of what his course should be, and in a most remarkable letter, he intimated to Theodosius that he, like any man with blood upon his hands, must do penance publicly before he could attend Mass again. The letter itself was intensely private—even Ambrose's biographer did not know of it. "I write with my own hands," Ambrose said, "what I wish to be read by yourself alone." It begins with every expression of respect and affection, with explanations of why Ambrose had of late refrained from frequently seeking the royal presence; but the Emperor was reminded too that Ambrose *had* remonstrated, had called "atrocious" the thing about to be done, that the Emperor's own attempt to cancel his order witnessed to the reproach of his own conscience. His zeal for the Faith was great, Ambrose acknowledged, but the violence of his temper ungovernable. "I would to God that those about you, even if they do not moderate it, would at least refrain from stimulating it."

Recalling the example of David, Ambrose begs his royal master to follow him in repentance as he had followed him in sinning. "Do not, Sir, take it ill if the same words are addressed to you which the prophet addressed to David—*Thou art the man.* For if you heed them well and answer *I have sinned against the Lord* then to you also it shall be said *The Lord hath put away thy sin.*"

The heart of the letter lay in the definite statement "I dare not offer the sacrifice, if you determine to attend. For can it possibly be right, after the slaughter of so many, to do what may

not be done after the blood of only one innocent person has
been shed?''

Exactly what happened next it is hard to know. While contemporary historians all agree that Theodosius did penance,
they differ widely about the when and the how. I follow here
the reconstruction made by Dudden in his admirable Life of St.
Ambrose. It would seem that at first the Emperor ignored the
archbishop's letter, but did not venture to go to the Basilica.
But, deeply religious as he was, his conscience was tormenting
him and he earnestly desired absolution and reconciliation.
Already in August, two months before his formal penance
began, he issued a new law—that thirty days must in future
intervene between the condemnation and execution of a
criminal. This law was issued from Verona. Back in Milan, he
appears to have sent Rufinus, Master of the Offices, as an
ambassador to Ambrose. But no compromise could be reached
on the main point—that the Emperor must do public penance
before he could again receive Communion. The period was
shortened as the humiliation would in his case be so great—
but it still remained a matter of weeks.

Laying aside his imperial ornaments as a sign of mourning
Theodosius was allowed, according to the forms customary in
Milan, to enter the church for the sacrifice although not to
communicate. He knelt publicly lamenting his sin with tears—
and his amazed subjects wept with him. At Christmas came the
public reconciliation and the Emperor once again received the
body and blood of the Lord in whom, despite his many sins, he
fervently believed.

Honourable to Ambrose, the story is perhaps even more
honourable to Theodosius, especially as it was followed by a
steady friendship between the two men—Theodosius henceforward often asking counsel of Ambrose. Accustomed to the
subservient court bishops so common in the East he would,
unlike his degenerate son, have appreciated Chrysostom. ''I
know no one'', he once said, ''except Ambrose who deserves
the name of bishop.''

Ambrose, on his side, had always recognised the existence of a
political field, in which the bishop was a subject, owing obedience to the Emperor. While insisting that in faith and morals

the Emperor owed obedience to the Church, he was, especially
after the stupendous victory he had won, careful not to go outside his own field or give Theodosius any reason to suspect him
of doing so.

LAST YEARS AND DEATH OF AMBROSE

The boy Emperor Valentinian II is a historical figure of
almost unbearable pathos. When Theodosius returned to the
East he left him in Gaul and, although nominally his co-
Emperor, placed him under the tutelage of a rough barbarian
named Arbogast.

It was difficult for Theodosius to know how to act. Best, of
course, would have been to leave Valentinian with Ambrose—
but then there was always Justina, and the past had shown that
she could sway her son against all the moral suasion of the
archbishop. Theodosius does not seem to have recognised that
Valentinian was beginning to grow up. He had spent much
time shooting and hunting, but suddenly decided to give up
sport entirely. He rather spectacularly demonstrated his self-
control in the matter of sex by summoning a beautiful actress
to the Court and then refusing to see her. He combatted his
greed by severe fasting. Above all, he refused to oppress his
subjects by increasing the existing heavy taxation. And his
letter to the Senate rejecting their request that he should
abrogate the ruling of Gratian and restore pagan worship to
Rome had been both firm and intelligent.

But against the bullying Arbogast, Valentinian was helpless.
The barbarian gloried in putting the young Emperor to shame,
cancelling orders he had given, making it plain that he had no
authority in his own court. Valentinian wrote repeatedly to
Theodosius, who was always slow to move; having experience
of Arbogast only in submissive relation to himself, he probably
thought his young colleague was painting a very exaggerated
picture. Ambrose, on good terms with Arbogast, could have
helped, but hesitated to act against what might be the wishes
of Theodosius until he received from Valentinian a letter of
vehement entreaty.

The strange thing, according to our ideas today, is the main
reason Valentinian gave for his request that Ambrose should

come at once to Vienne: he desired baptism at his hands. Theodosius had made it a condition of his rule that Valentinian acknowledge the orthodox creed. He was now twenty-one; yet he might, one supposes, have gone on like Ambrose himself to the age of thirty before asking for the sacrament. But this was a clear reason for Ambrose to act, totally within his sphere, and he started at once, only to learn on the road that Valentinian was dead (15 May, 392), Arbogast declared by suicide, most people thought by murder at his guardian's instigation.

For two months Valentinian's body remained unburied, while the court at Vienne awaited the orders of Theodosius. Finally he wrote ordering the funeral to be held at Milan but making no comment on the position or conduct of Arbogast. Ambrose preached—and his confident assertion of the salvation of Valentinian has in it two interesting elements. He could hardly have made it had he really believed in the suicide story— and it is perhaps the earliest assertion of the Church's teaching on baptism by desire.

"I hear", he said, addressing Valentinian's two sisters, "that you are grieved because your brother did not receive the sacrament of baptism. But tell me what more can we do than desire and ask? . . . Grant therefore, O holy Father, to Thy servant Valentinian that gift which he longed for, that gift which he asked for . . . He had Thy spirit; how, then, can he have failed to receive Thy grace? . . . As well might one argue that martyrs, who suffer while they are still but catechumens, are not crowned. But if the martyrs are washed by their own blood, then Valentinian also has been washed by his piety and earnest desire for baptism."

Gratian and Valentinian, all the boys and girls whose shining youth has no issue but the grave, are seen by Ambrose as by St. John in that innumerable multitude for whom joy unending has been won by the blood of God. Only faith in immortal glory redeems the tragedies of history.

Theodosius should have marched at once—his trusted Arbogast now proceeded to put up a new claimant for the Western Empire, a Roman official called Eugenius—and for a while he looked like succeeding. Clearly, he half hoped that Theodosius would accept his man or, failing that, that he might bargain to keep, like Maximus, the lands west of the Alps.

Eugenius had been reigning several months before it became clear that Theodosius did not intend to acknowledge him. Eugenius then threw in his lot with the pagan party. He tried to make the best of both worlds by veiling his subsidies for the re-establishment of pagan worship as gifts to his personal friends and at the same time sending presents to the Christian bishops. Ambrose was hardly the man to be deceived by this pretence and for the last time he drew the sword of the spirit against the imperial power.

"Consider, Sir," he wrote, "how great God is. He sees the hearts of all. Do you expect to hide anything from God?" However ardently the senators had urged him to re-establish paganism, was it not his duty to resist "out of reverence for the most high and true and Living God, and to have refused what was flagrantly against the sacred law. How can the priests of Christ dispense your gifts?"

Ambrose had left Milan to avoid Eugenius and this letter was a warning of excommunication. In his life of St. Ambrose, Paulinus tells us that the Church did in fact reject the gifts of Eugenius and refused to let him join in Christian worship.

It was almost two years before Theodosius had made his plans and completed his preparations for the overthrow of Eugenius. Barbarian was matched with barbarian, for Arbogast was the real military power behind Eugenius and the army of Theodosius contained great numbers of Goths and Vandals led by their own chieftains, including the terrible Alaric. The Vandal Stilicho was second in command of the whole army. Theodosius hesitated. Again Ambrose waited. Theodosius marched into Italy and on September 8th, 394, after a four-day battle he defeated Eugenius and, amid his cries for mercy, had his head struck off by a soldier. Arbogast had taken his own life.

Ambrose offered Mass at the request of Theodosius in solemn thanksgiving and sent him a letter of somewhat extreme flattery but having for main point the entreaty that no more blood should be shed, "that by your clemency the Church of God, as it rejoices in the peace and tranquillity of the innocent, may also be gladdened by the pardon of the guilty".

He wrote two more letters pressing the same point and then, having apparently received no answer, went in person to

Aquileia to intercede. Theodosius, rejoicing in his victory, was in clement mood, and himself kneeling before Ambrose, declared his own indebtedness to the merits and prayers of the archbishop. At his request he granted a free pardon to all who had fought for Eugenius, to all who had declared their adherence to his cause. And Ambrose hastened back to Milan to receive the Emperor in his capital.

Neither man was to live much longer. Exhausted by the fatigues of his campaign, Theodosius fell ill. Before leaving Constantinople he had sent to a noted prophet, John of Lycopolis, to ask him about his fortunes; and John had answered that he would conquer Eugenius but himself die in Italy. It may well be that the Emperor's power of resistance was weakened by his faith in the prophecy. The weather, too, was especially evil—earthquake shocks were felt and fog shrouded the city. Whatever the reasons, Theodosius lived only to welcome his son Honorius, and to plan for the future of both his sons under the guardianship of Stilicho (nothing would cure him of relying on his barbarian allies). He also placed Honorius specially under the care of Ambrose, who took the charge very seriously and was fully prepared to stand up to Stilicho should it become necessary. But Ambrose lived only two years longer.

It is difficult in sketching such a life as Ambrose's to keep the proportions right. One reminder of this is the death of Valentinian. We imagine Ambrose waiting, if not at the end of a telephone at any rate in some such fashion—absorbed, unable to think of anything else, asking himself constantly, should he go, should he wait. But the archbishop's life was never like that. Deeply concerned as he was over the young Emperor, his life was one life, his soul one soul, among the thousands for whom Ambrose must work and pray and suffer. The sick must still be cared for, the traveller lodged and fed, the poor must be succoured, the oppressed protected, the captive redeemed.

On all this, the archbishop, as he grew older, never relaxed, while his spiritual tasks grew heavier every year. The chant that had come into being in an inspired hour was now organised into something very much like the canonical office of later years. The Hours were kept in Ambrose's basilica; he complained sometimes that his people did not pray enough, especially at the vigils, which lasted all night, bringing in the greater feasts. And Ambrose still offered the holy Sacrifice daily for his people, still preached to them every Sunday. During Lent, he still instructed daily the catechumens he would baptise at Easter. He still wept with the penitent and threw his door open to all, that no need of any least member of his flock should go unanswered. History has dwelt upon this great man as the chastener of an Emperor, has seen him chiefly as a political figure, but his real life was elsewhere; glimpsed by his people but hidden also in Christ with God.

The last public acts of Ambrose were ecclesiastical. As Metropolitan, he had to go to Vercelli to reconcile quarrelling factions and preside at the election of a bishop. Honoratus was chosen—perhaps at Ambrose's suggestion, for he was one of the clergy of Milan. Early the next year (397) he consecrated a new Bishop of Pavia—did he remember his attempt to flee to that city to escape his own episcopate? Returning home, he felt unwell, but began to dictate to his secretary and future biographer an exposition of Psalm xliii (A.V. xliv), *Deus auribus nostris audivimus.* The note of triumph in God's power—"Through Thy name will we tread them under that rise against us"—passes into the appeal of man's weakness and loneliness. He broke off at the verse "Wherefore hidest Thou Thy face?" and soon after was obliged to take to his bed. The rumour of his illness spreading, Stilicho, who had at first opposed him but now regarded him with a kind of superstitious awe, sent to Ambrose some of the leading citizens of Milan on a curious embassy. He is said to have cried out, "The death of so great a man will be the ruin of Italy", and now his messengers entreated Ambrose to pray for his own recovery. Ambrose answered, "I have not so lived among you as to be afraid to live on, but I am not afraid to die, for Our Lord is good."

A little before his death he told a friend that he had seen the Lord Jesus come to his bedside and smile upon him. On Good Friday he remained constantly in prayer, from five in the afternoon lying with his arms stretched out in the form of the Cross. At some time after midnight Honoratus, who had been with him but had gone away to bed, heard a voice crying "Honoratus! Honoratus! Honoratus! Rise, make haste, he is departing." He ran down and was just in time to anoint Ambrose. There seems often a great significance in the day God chooses to call His servants. Ambrose died on Easter Eve 397—that day on which he had anointed so many with the first anointing of the chrism of salvation and had poured on so many heads the waters of baptism.

X: ST. JEROME

EUSEBIUS HIERONYMUS was born probably in 347, the same year as Chrysostom and a few years after Ambrose, ten years after Constantine's death, at Stridon, a town later so completely destroyed by the barbarians that today its exact site remains uncertain. We do know that it was not far from the city of Aquileia. It may be taken as certain that Jerome was an Italian, coming from that wedge of Italy which seems on the old maps to be driven between Dalmatia and Pannonia. Jerome did not love his birthplace. From the desert he wrote to friends, "My country is a slave to ignorance—*rusticitatis vernacula*. For God they have their belly; they live from day to day; the richest is the holiest." Among those rich may very well have been his own parents: they were certainly well-to-do. They were mildly Christian, after that fashion of Christianity produced by the peace of the Church and the social fusion between pagan and Christian that came with it. They were certainly much disconcerted when all three of their children, disdaining a worldly career, embraced the ascetic life.

Nor did this appear at all probable in Jerome's boyhood. He was an ardent scholar, eager and ambitious for learning and its triumphs. His parents sent him to Rome when he was twelve and there he stayed till he was twenty, first in grammar school under the famous Donatus and afterwards as "a student of the rhetoricians". He learnt the Greek and Latin Classics, the elements of the sciences, a little music.

When Julian the Apostate died Jerome was sixteen. Diligent in study, he also delighted in games and spectacles and had quite his share of sexual pleasures. Later, in the desert, he was to repent these years bitterly, finding their imprint on his imagination, seeing himself back in Rome "among bands of girls". We must allow for Jerome's natural tendency to rhetoric and the stereotyped biblical phrases in which he laments his sins. He may have exaggerated his youthful vices.

With no strong religious feelings to control him, he was not likely to be different from other boys in fourth-century Rome, but even before religion came into play, ambition and hard work set bounds to pleasure; for Jerome was adding to his regular studies a work of real magnitude. He had begun to build the library that became later one of the most famous in the world. At that day building a library meant, unless one were vastly rich, copying the books. Night after night, Jerome sat writing: he became so steeped in the Classics that he could say later, "Dye the wool purple and no water will cleanse it. I must drink the water of Lethe if I am to be blamed for remembering the poems that once I knew."

How swiftly must have passed the time of this double enchantment: the joys of great literature taken in copious draughts, the pleasures of youth enjoyed in youthful company. But by Roman law every youth must, as he neared the age of twenty, be sent back to his province. Before he left Rome Jerome was baptised. Only later did he become fully aware of all that his baptism signified, but already in Rome two things deeply affected him: the enthusiasm of the congregations in the churches—especially the ardour of their loud "Amen"; the mystic atmosphere of the catacombs, where lay the martyrs who had died for Christ.

To the Desert

It was on the track of the exiled Athanasius that Jerome first heard the story of the ascetics in the desert, experienced conversion and determined to follow them in his life. Outside the town of Trèves he found solitaries; in Aquileia itself he joined a group of young ascetics. His brother and sister he won over to the same ideal. There followed three years of profound happiness. The little group—Bonosus, Niceas, Rufinus, Evagrios and the rest, living companionably a life of prayer and study—was later described by Jerome as a "choir of the blessed". What bombshell fell to scatter them we do not know. The ascetics were not too popular with run-of-the-mill Christians; the Arians were strong and trouble-making. Jerome was not a patient man and his skill in epigram was too ready in finding his opponents' weak spots. Anyhow, the band broke up, Jerome turning his steps towards the desert, but planning to meet some of the others at Antioch where Evagrios had a property. He went overland by the postal road.

Worn out when he reached Antioch, he fell ill and all but died. Saved by Evagrios, he lingered with him, postponing the desert and continuing, although with prayer and fasting, to copy and read the Classics. The city was an important centre, Evagrios a rich man, and opportunities were all around for adding to his culture—and to his library. Months were growing into years. The desert beckoned but the Classics held him.

Then one night Jerome had a dream. Already very ill, he fell into a deep unconsciousness; his friends believed him dead.

Suddenly I was rapt in spirit and brought before the tribunal of the Great Judge. There was so much light, such a radiance of glory in those who stood about Him, that I fell upon my face, not daring to raise my eyes. I was asked of what condition I was and I answered "Christian." Then said the Judge: "You lie. You are a Ciceronian, not a Christian. Where your treasure is, there is your heart." Immediately I fell silent. In the midst of the blows (for the Judge had ordered that I be beaten) I was tortured still more by the fire of my conscience. I recalled the verse of the Psalms: "In hell, who shall speak for thee?" Nevertheless I began to cry out, and in my lamentation I said over and over again: "Have pity on me, O Lord, have pity." These words resounded amidst the noise of the rods. At last those who stood by fell at the knees of the Judge. They prayed him to pardon my youth, to permit me to repent of my error, only to chastise me later if in the future I read pagan books. And I, who in so great distress would have promised much beside, made a solemn oath, calling upon the name of God: "Lord, if ever I touch profane books, if I read them, I shall have denied Thee." (*Ep. XXII.*)

He awoke, convinced that he had had no vain dream: he still ached from the beating. In this same letter, written fifteen years after, Jerome tells his pupil Eustochium that he had never read the Classics since. But he kept his precious books and, ten years later again, we find him not only reading them but teaching them and having others copied at a high price. Rufinus, who from a friend had turned to a bitter enemy, reproached Jerome with being forsworn. Jerome retorted that if we are to go by dreams he had had plenty. In dreams he had flown above the earth, in dreams he had assuaged his thirst with the ocean, but on waking he had still been thirsty, had still found himself wingless. Rufinus, he rather cruelly added, had dreamed of himself as a Confessor of Christ, but no man knew the name of the judge before whom he had borne witness. It was a rash man who picked a quarrel with Jerome, unless he was seeking a dubious immortality.

The dream, or vision, drove Jerome into the desert; twenty years later it had done its work. The Vulgate was completed, his convents of Scripture scholars had come into being in Bethlehem. Jerome, as he went into solitude, was beginning something of vast importance for the Church, though as yet he did not know it.

The desert is very beautiful, but it can be frightening, its clear air can entice, its mirages bewilder. But by the hermit the desert's moods go unrecorded; what counts for him is the felt presence or seeming absence of God. Jerome's feelings ran up and down the scale from joy to misery. He writes to Heliodorus begging him to join him, painting in brightest colours the delights of the solitary life, and addressing him as *delicate miles* for fearing its combats. At other moments he records moods of near-despair.

Like all hermits he lived a life of immense austerity; he slept on the ground, he ate only bread and herbs, often fasting for several days on end. Elegant Roman that he had been, he wore rough clothing and gave up bathing; his skin, he says, grew parched and dry. He suffered temptations and met them by praying, weeping, imploring God's mercy, beating his breast, redoubling his fasts; even leaving his cell to wander alone into the deeper parts of the desert. In all this he was like the other hermits but in another aspect most unlike. They lived in narrow cells or huts, laboured with their hands on mats or baskets, had few books. Jerome's dwelling was spacious enough to hold his library and a band of copyists brought from Antioch. He had books made for himself, he paid his way by having them made for others. He borrowed books to copy. He hurled himself with immense energy on the study of Scripture and Scripture commentaries.

Two things led him on to his next undertaking. He discovered the need of Hebrew to get to the bottom of many Scripture problems—and he found in this most difficult study a novel means of overcoming the temptations of his lively imagination. Impassioned over the Classics, he had hated the structure of scriptural Greek and had turned with relief to the majesty of the Greek and Latin poets. Now he found himself studying a language full of words that "hissed" and "gasped". He engaged a rabbi to teach him and set resolutely to work. No hermit took much sleep; Jerome's days were given to Scripture, the greater part of his nights to an immense correspondence. To one friend who wrote him too brief a letter he remarked that a very long letter could easily be written in the course of one night! In his spare moments he wrote that little gem of poetry, the Life of St. Paul, the first hermit.

Jerome's complaint about his particular desert was that it was not deserted enough. It was not the number of hermits that irked him so much as the kind of men they were. They did not speak civilised languages; he would have to learn a barbarous tongue to converse with them. They were painfully and argumentatively preoccupied about the wording of the profession of faith in the Holy Trinity, and we can imagine the problems of such a discussion carried on in a mixture of Greek, Latin and the "barbarous tongues" of the desert dwellers. The question of the claimants to the see of Antioch was mixed in with the theological dispute, and Jerome says they would not leave him alone on either. Their account we have not got, but we know Jerome was not the man to let an argument expire for want of fuel.

In 382, leaving his solitude, disillusioned and disgusted because he had found no peace there ("Better", he remarked, "live among wild beasts than among such Christians"), Jerome made his way back to Antioch, to Constantinople, to Rome. And Pope Damasus made him his secretary and set him to translate the Bible. In later life Jerome often sighed for the desert with the sighs of the romantic. But delicate in body, ardent in intellect, he was not the man for such a life. Five years was enough. A little longer and it might well have killed him.

IN ROME

If the little world of Stridon had seemed evil in the eyes of the strict Christian, how much more the larger world of Rome. Here, too, mixed marriages and daily contact had made Christian society and pagan almost one thing; and it was not, Jerome thought, a very nice thing, especially among the patricians. Surrounded by a court of slaves and eunuchs, dressed in the lightest and most elegant silk robes, reclining in a litter as they were carried to the baths or shops, their highest duty was entertaining themselves and others. Women, as well as men, had courts of slaves and eunuchs who assisted in large numbers at an incredibly elaborate toilet. Artificial colouring for face, lips and finger-nails is not unknown to us today, nor methods of enhancing the eyes' lustre. Added to all this was a building-up of the hair (sometimes increased by borrowed tresses of another colour) into a high curled structure surmounted by a sort of mitre. Gold figured largely both in the hair and on the feet. Gold slippers clacking on the floor were a summons to admiring youths to gather round. When some kind of silk dress was in fashion depicting scenes of history and mythology, Christian ladies had scriptural scenes woven into theirs. There were even priests, complains Jerome, who curled their hair, dressed themselves up and danced attendance on patrician families, hoping for legacies. A Christian emperor, by the Pope's desire, passed a law to forbid legacies to the clergy, but ways were found to evade it.

Damasus was a reforming Pope; largely for this reason his election had been disputed and an attempt made to introduce an anti-pope. Violent scenes of bloodshed culminated in the firing of a basilica. Every accusation was brought against the Pope, including a persistent one of immorality, and it was many years before he could get a council to take the matter up and clear his character publicly. Meanwhile he worked steadily at reform of the clergy and at raising the level of Christian learning.

As the wave of luxury sweeping Roman society in the fourth century came from the East, so too did the first powerful impulse towards reform. Luxury from Constantinople, asceticism from the desert. When Athanasius came to Rome

during his first exile he brought with him two men who had
been hermits. With them he visited the great Christian
families and told them of the desert. And he left behind him
his *Life of St. Anthony.* Among his hosts had been Albina, a
widow of noble family with a small daughter, Marcella, who
listened attentively to the stories and took possession of the
book. Albina, though a Christian, was a worldly one, and
arranged a grand marriage for Marcella. But after only seven
months of marriage her husband died and Marcella steadily
refused to remarry. Instead, she made of her palace on the
Aventine a place of prayer and retirement and a centre for
like-minded women. They wore sober clothes, sang the
Psalms together, fasted, prayed and studied.

It was the first convent of Rome. There were other young
widows—Furia for instance, to whom Jerome later wrote,
Fabiola, who gyrated between the religious life and the world,
Asella, an older woman addressed by Jerome as *Mi Domina,*
and above all the great St. Paula with her daughters Blesilla,
Paulina and Eustochium. Besides these and a few more who
lived in this "church in the home", as Jerome called it, many
others, both men and women, came and went, joining the little
group in prayer, study and care of the poor. They had all
heard of Jerome and were eagerly awaiting his arrival. His
letters had been read and admired. Fabiola later recited
to him his own letter to Heliodorus in praise of the desert;
she had learnt it by heart. They asked his help in understanding Scripture and his counsels on the ascetic life.

Pope Damasus loved Jerome's writings, even copying them
with his own hands. He wanted his help in the work of reform.
Above all, he wanted him to revise the Latin New Testament.
The existing Latin manuscripts were full of variants; all
copies had to be collated and corrected with constant reference
back to the Greek. We have seen in earlier chapters the
language problem in relation to theological definition: we
shall meet it again. But with St. Jerome and the Scriptures
we have something more like a picture; words are colours, they
are shapes. Christianity makes a new and vivid literature,
as a great artist creates a new sort of painting. This new
supernatural art is expressed not in definitions alone, but even
more richly in the liturgy and the Scriptures, as they are given

to one race after another in forms suited to the genius of their different tongues but all alike coloured by the supernatural.

At the beginning of the Christian era Greek was the language of the educated; Justin, born in Samaria, and Clement of Rome, wrote in Greek as naturally as the Alexandrians; so did Irenaeus. The first Christian Latin writer was probably the great Tertullian and even he used both languages, translating his own work from Greek into Latin. De Rossi holds that down to the end of the third century the liturgy was in that language. But it was a language less and less familiar to the uneducated, less and less spoken even by the educated. Much earlier than liturgical change came the realisation that, if the common people were to understand Scripture, they must have it in their own tongue—and that tongue, for most of the West, was Latin.

At least two Latin translations existed before the end of the third century: Tertullian uses the one made in Africa, although also translating many passages straight from Greek. There was no thought at this early date of an "authorised" version. The Italian Latin translation was made possibly a *little* later than the African, the two affected each other as the work of copying and collating went on. St. Cyprian did not vary his quotations like Tertullian, but used steadily the early African, which would seem by his date to have become almost official. But St. Augustine speaks of a great number of translations, and anyone felt at liberty to "improve" the version he was reading if a better phrasing occurred to him.

The Latin language itself was changing. Cicero claimed the right to speak of new ideas in new words—*imponenda nova novis rebus nomina*. St. Jerome, claiming Cicero's authority, remarked in his commentary on the Galatians that in much shorter books Cicero had used more new words than he did. And yet, Jerome might well have added, Cicero had not ideas as new as those of the Christian writer to set down in his new words.

Agonia, apostata, apostolus, baptisma, blasphemia, catholicus, diabolus, diaconus, ecstasis, eremus, episcopus, eleemosyna, homilia, laicus, martyr, monachus, schisma—all these are quoted by De Labriolle and many more could be added, concerning whose origins we seldom reflect but which we could hardly do without. Of Hebrew words we have *hosanna, cherubim, rabbi, alleluia, gehenna, pascha, sabaoth* and others.

Old Latin words too had taken on a new meaning: *devotio, aedificatio, praevaricatio, remissio, vocatio. Virtutes* was used of miracles, *tentator* had become the devil, *tingere* meant to baptise, *absolvere* to forgive or absolve. There is a fascinating field for study here for all those who love words: it did not, one feels certain, escape that lover of words, St. Jerome.

Enchanted by his work on the New Testament, the Pope insisted that he go on to the Old. He must have worked fast, for this happy period lasted only until the death of Damasus three years later. Marcella and her companions helped him; they all knew Greek and were learning Hebrew. He boasts that sometimes he himself could learn from his learned pupils. When enemies complained that he made too much of these women, he asked rather acidly for men-pupils to come forward. Eustochium (whom he calls the "first virgin of Rome") and the young widow Blesilla he describes as his "apprentices".

During these years Jerome was at the height of his glory, being even spoken of as probable next Pope. He was the fierce defender of the ascetic life and the upholder of Christian scholarship. When he talks (at great length) of fasting he becomes a little tedious, when he abuses marriage he is intolerable; one would think he believed that the devil, not God, invented this particular sacrament. Criticised for attacking marriage, he answered sardonically: "I am all for marriage and the married life, because it produces the virgins I want." He added that marriage was of the old law, virginity of the new.

But when he can forget fasting and marriage, when he speaks as a scholar, classical and Christian, St. Jerome is enchanting. Part of his charm lies in the fashion in which he mingles the two, part in his way of introducing daily life and its details, great part in the skill and force with which he uses language. Erasmus said he preferred him to Cicero—but surely he is more like Tacitus in his phrasing. In these letters he has all the wealth of the Classics in memory, and the Bible in hand and in mind. No one reading the breviary homilies could guess at the charm of the correspondence which brought the Roman world to Jerome's feet. He was the first great Christian humanist.

In the year 384 everything broke up at once. Always in a great popularity, or in a general hatred, there are undertones—of jealousy, dislike, even loathing in the one case, of love in the other—that dare not let their discords be heard against the chorus. A few in every crowd are waiting for a change of ruler, a change of emphasis, to give them their opportunity. From "Hosanna" to "Crucify", the interval was five days. Pope Damasus died—and at a moment most fortunate for the enemies of Jerome.

Among the members of the "church" in Marcella's house, Paula and her daughters stood out conspicuous for learning and nobility of lineage. Paula's family boasted descent from Agamemnon; her husband had claimed Aeneas as his ancestor. Relatives on both sides were annoyed at Blesilla's refusal to marry again, and even more at Eustochium's refusal to marry at all. Once they persuaded her to let them dress her up in lovely silks. They painted her lips and face, curled her hair and then showed her her own beauty. Eustochium let them have their way and then, quietly resuming her rough garments, returned to her convent home.

Suddenly Blesilla died, and her mother was shattered with grief. Jerome, himself weeping, tried, for long in vain, to console her. The one thing in which she seemed interested was the idea of going to the Holy Land. At this the family opposition broke out violently and every kind of ugly rumour began. Blesilla had been killed, said some, by her fasts and austerities; her mother's grief was sharpened because she herself was to blame and because too she would now have no grandchildren from this daughter of hers. But most to blame was Jerome, who had bewitched them all and was going to carry Paula off to the East. The new Pope had dismissed him from his post; in the streets the cry was raised of "Greek!" and "Impostor!" He was even accused of misconduct with Paula. Triumphantly acquitted, he still realised that Rome was no place for him now that Damasus was dead.

A Roman priest, several monks who believed in Jerome, and his own brother, decided to leave with him. A crowd of admirers of the late Pope's reforming party accompanied them to the ship. As he went on board he wept bitterly; then, taking up a pen, he wrote his farewell to the dear family church of the

Aventine. *"Mi Domina Asella"*, he begins, pouring out his gratitude and prayers that God may reward her goodness to him. But not for long is this gentler note held. The burden of the letter is the anguish into which he has been plunged by the savage attacks upon him. "I am an evil liver, tortuous and slimy . . . a liar who deceives men through the arts of Satan . . . Men who used to kiss my hands were secretly biting me with viper's teeth . . . Before I visited the house of the holy widow Paula the whole town spoke well of me. Almost without exception they declared me worthy of the Papacy. Damasus (so happy in my memory) and I spoke as one. I was holy, I was humble, I was eloquent: now I am no longer any of those things." (*Ep. XLV.*)

"The whole town", he says, "delights in making up stories about those women who have lifted up the standard of the cross—who will not go to fashionable resorts perfumed and elegant with the common crowd of sinners. Let them go to hell in their own way, says the world, dressed in the sackcloth they have chosen."

The letter ends, as it begins, on the tender note of the departing father and friend. "Greet Paula and Eustochium, mine in Christ whether the world likes it or not. Greet Albina my mother, Marcella my sister . . . keep me in your memory, noble friend, model of virginal purity: and calm for me by your prayers the raging waves of the sea."

AT BETHLEHEM

At Antioch Jerome waited for Paula and Eustochium, who brought with them from Rome other women desiring a dedicated life in the Holy Land. They decided to settle in Bethlehem, where they built three monasteries, two for women, ruled over by Paula, and one for men, under Jerome. To these they added a free hospice for travellers, "for," said Jerome pleasantly, "if Mary and Joseph came they might not find a lodging", so vast was the concourse of pilgrims. The hospice was soon so full that there might still have been no room for the Holy Family. St. Jerome also opened a free school and taught Greek and Latin to the children of Bethlehem, as his master Donatus had of old taught them to him.

In the monasteries, all sang the Hours of the Canonical Office, all were supposed to know the Psalter by heart and to learn daily some fresh portion of Scripture. Jerome praises Paula's zeal in physical labour. The women did their own housework and made their own clothes. Far from using her rank or seniority as an excuse for repose, Paula would lift and carry with the youngest, cook the vegetables, and do any other work that was rough and hard. Bread and vegetables were the only food, and if he ate before sunset Jerome did not consider that he was fasting. Above all, the two monasteries were an assembly of the learned in which only prayer was rated above study.

Before the buildings were put up Jerome chose his own study: a large cave next to that of the Nativity. Here Paula and Eustochium came to ask for further teaching in the Scriptures. They were soon established as his assistants as fully as in Rome. Before his death Damasus had set Jerome to work on the Psalter and he had completed its revision. But many copies had been made and copies of copies—already full of errors. The two women gathered all they could, collated and corrected them. They sat surrounded by manuscripts, devoting many hours daily to the task.

Meanwhile St. Jerome was going forward with the other books of the Old Testament. The Hebrew surroundings of Palestine helped him. He again acquired a rabbi as master, and several as friends. Among his enemies the rumour ran that he was selling out the Faith, while the rabbis on their side risked death from their own people by visiting him. When it came to the Book of Daniel he found that to understand Hebrew was not enough: it was written partly in Aramaic. His master knew the language, and translated the Aramaic into Hebrew for him, but was that enough? Jerome decided to learn Aramaic himself. If Hebrew had been a task, what a toil was this. Again and again Jerome was tempted to abandon it, but he steeled himself to continue.

Now there was a fresh task for Paula and Eustochium. Jerome made them check the translations, for they were now first-rate Hebrew scholars. Meanwhile he poured out commentaries on the different books of Scripture, which he dedicated to his faithful assistants. Again the complaint was heard about making so much of women, and again Jerome countered it indignantly. Had his detractors, he asked, never heard of the great women of the Old Testament; of Deborah and Judith and Esther? Did they not know the genius of Sappho among the Greeks, or had they not heard of Aspasia and Themistes? And in Rome were not Cornelia and the wife of Brutus illustrious?

So little did the Middle Ages like this friendship, sealed by learning and made sacred by asceticism, that they painted Jerome with an imaginary lion and wrote chronicles of weird miracles rather than show him with the companions of his choice, Eustochium and Paula, as they sat in a cave and toiled over Hebrew and Greek manuscripts. Medieval copyists sometimes erased the dedications in the books, substituting the words "Venerable Brethren", but Christian history can never omit the story of this friendship and of the immense impetus that it gave to learning as well as to the religious life. No one, said Jerome in his moments of discouragement, would attack me if I just made baskets.

When Paula died he wrote a lovely eulogy, echoing in one phrase Horace's certainty of immortality: "I have built a monument more enduring than bronze. Age cannot destroy it. Wherever our language goes, the reader will know you as I have praised you."

This was a period when even a peaceful man would not have found peace easy, for the formulating of the creeds had to be done amid the hostile voices of heresy and the confusion of many sincere thinkers. It may be said of St. Jerome that he seldom started quarrels—but he always prolonged them, if only by his amazing skill in words. One such quarrel was with St. Augustine, who ventured to criticise the new translation.

Jerome was the first of the Western Fathers to learn Hebrew —and indeed there was very little knowledge of it even in the East. The Septuagint was held to be itself inspired: it was so called from the story that seventy translators worked separately but miraculously found their results to be identical! Christian translations into other languages had all been made from the Septuagint.

Augustine wrote to Jerome protesting about a work that must be futile—for how could there be anything in the Hebrew undiscovered by so many men so learned in the language? We marvel to find these correspondences pursued when each letter might take months to arrive, but Jerome defended himself, and Augustine wrote again.

The combat between these two—the philosopher fencing with the scholar—is more an expert display of swordsmanship than a duel to the death. And the fight issued in a warm friendship. Far otherwise was it with the endless quarrel with Rufinus, once his close friend, which is part of the saddest story of Jerome's life.

The greatest churchmen of the East deeply admired Origen, but they realised that much in his writings must be taken with caution. Basil and Gregory had, as we have seen, selected in the *Philocalia* some of his most striking passages. St. Ambrose, in the West, knew and loved the *Philocalia*; St. Jerome was at first an intense admirer of the great Alexandrian, but less, I fancy, of his ideas than of his immense learning, especially in Jerome's own field—the Scriptures.

Duchesne has pointed out that whenever there was no outstanding heresy to fight, combative churchmen fell back on Origen and started a campaign against his errors. One of these warriors was St. Epiphanius, Bishop of Cyprus, an ardent collector of heresies. His charity and asceticism had won the old bishop world-wide renown. He was very simple, very excitable, very good—not at all intelligent and therefore valuable to such a man as Theophilus of Alexandria, who could hide his own crafty designs behind this man of obvious sincerity.

Unfortunately, Epiphanius also thought of himself as a crusader for orthodoxy, and as such entitled to search out heresy everywhere. Visiting Jerusalem, he preached in the presence of the bishop against Origenism, with the obvious implication that he had noted its presence in his city. The somewhat irritated bishop preached in return against anthropomorphism—for it seemed to many that, in reaction against Origen's teaching, his enemies were seeing God as the old-man-with-a-beard of certain later painters, were seeing Scripture so literally as to lose its spiritual meaning.

Epiphanius went down to Bethlehem and Jerome was probably not too happy to receive him there—for he was at that point on good terms with his bishop, and Epiphanius suspected both John of Jerusalem and Rufinus of heresy. Rufinus, with their other old friend Melania, had a double monastery in Jerusalem. They had there most cordially received Jerome, Paula and the rest of their company when they first came to Palestine. However, as the quarrel grew more acute, and it became necessary for him to choose a side, Jerome embraced that of Epiphanius. I have a suspicion that with him close personal contact had more effect, and therefore ideas less, than is usually assumed. Rereading Origen under the old man's wing, he discovered the heresies which he came to believe he had seen from the first. Epiphanius was an awkward ally. John had refused any longer to supply a priest for the Bethlehem communities; so when Paulinian, Jerome's brother, was on a visit to his Palestinian monastery, Epiphanius ordained him priest. He first tied up the reluctant Paulinian hand and foot and gagged him; could such an ordination have been valid? Apparently it was accepted as such, and he officiated for the monasteries of men and women that Jerome and Paula had built. Naturally the bishop was enraged, and the Bethlehem monasteries narrowly escaped destruction.

Meanwhile, Rufinus was persuaded to undertake the translation of Origen's *Peri Archon*. As we have seen, he omitted or changed much that was heterodox but seemed to be giving to what he retained the stamp of his approval; and in the Introduction spoke of Jerome as the man who should really have made the translation, quoting his earlier enthusiastic praise of Origen. This alarmed Jerome's friends in Rome, who begged him to set himself right with the orthodox world. He and Rufinus had already had one quarrel, followed by a reconciliation, and Jerome was really reluctant to break the peace again. But when he decided to do so he did it with great thoroughness, and the attacks on one another of these two old friends make melancholy reading.

Rufinus stopped first—for his last ten years he was silent, but rumours coming from Jerome's friends kept Jerome from realising this. "The many-headed hydra", he said when Rufinus died, "has for a moment ceased to hiss against me."

Once Epiphanius and Jerome had agreed that Origen was heretical, anyone could make use of them against anyone suspected of Origenism. Curiously enough, Theophilus of

Alexandria, who was later to use them both, began by being against Epiphanius and the "anthropomorphites", on the side of Rufinus and Origen. A quarrel in his own locality, however, produced a sudden shift and Epiphanius wrote joyfully to Jerome that Theophilus had raised the flag of orthodoxy in Alexandria. On his decision to attack St. John Chrysostom as an Origenist, Theophilus found them both most useful allies.

But very dramatically a change was wrought in Epiphanius in the very midst of the campaign against John that had brought him to Constantinople. Arriving at the Church of the Apostles to preach against Chrysostom, Epiphanius was met on the threshold by Serapion, who in the name of his archbishop solemnly adjured him to reflect on the enormity he was about to commit. Perhaps Serapion spoke of John's love of the poor, of the austerity of his life, of the love of God that should have drawn these two saints to one another. Exactly what he said we do not know, but Epiphanius, thunderstruck, left the people waiting and the sermon unpreached, turned back, went to his boat and set sail for Cyprus. He died on the voyage.

It was otherwise with Jerome who, to the end, believed Theophilus; attacking Chrysostom, he deemed himself to be attacking heresy. He thus made the most tragic of all his mistakes. For once Chrysostom was safely buried, his enemies in the East had it all their own way. "Iniquity", says Duchesne, "held carnival." Theophilus poured out "works of hate" which not only revived the old accusation of Origenism, but called John impious and sacrilegious, a Judas and a Satan for whom the tortures of hell were too good. These pamphlets were by St. Jerome translated into Latin. But the Pope had pronounced in John's favour and many Johannite bishops were being warmly entertained by the leading Christians of Rome, who realised fully how cruel the persecution was in Constantinople. "Jerome's correspondence with his Roman friends", Duchesne comments, "appears at this time to have slackened."

One's first feeling is of horror—must not the man translating such slanders have been utterly callous and cruel?—yet it is quite certain that Jerome was neither. Towards Rufinus he was indeed bitter, thinking he had betrayed him—but Jerome had no personal feelings about Chrysostom. Once involved in a quarrel, however, he always did his best (or worst) for his own side; once he had espoused a cause he went all out for it.

And we must not forget the pressure and the stresses of his life. Perhaps his story teaches us, in a different way from Basil's or John's, that the emphasis on fasting and watching was too great in the fourth century, especially for a man who worked at every waking moment. Almost certainly it teaches us the value put by the Church (even if faults of character remain) on total devotion to God's service. The positive achievement of Jerome's life is stressed in the collect for his feast: "O God, who didst deign to give to Thy Church for the expounding of Sacred Scripture blessed Jerome, Thy Confessor and mighty Doctor, grant that by his prayers and merits we may be strong to carry out with Thy help what he taught by word and work."

LAST YEARS

The fourth and fifth centuries were a period of violent contrast between a vigorous growth of Christian thought and the disintegration of the world around. We can see the fiery scholar of Bethlehem as he sits in his cave writing day and night, despite controversies and ecclesiastical intrigues; we can watch him still writing through tragic news from the West and threatenings of barbarian inroads at his doors.

Neither Jerome nor Augustine lived in an ivory tower; both wrote directly on the tragedy of the age, and reflect it indirectly in their other work and in their letters. Who could comment on Jeremias without piercing awareness of the fate of Rome? And while the philosopher wrote *The City of God*, the historian wrote a chronicle of Rome from 325 to 379—reserving the rest "for a much larger historical treatment . . . For while the barbarians are spread throughout our lands, all is uncertain". In his Chronicle Jerome declares himself, although a Christian, still a patriot of Rome, and his love of the Eternal City breathes through every line of his writing. But the depth of his anguish shows most clearly in his letters—that day-to-day chronicle written for his friends of "the frail fortunes of human life. The soul", he writes, "shudders to tell of the downfall of our age. For twenty years and more the blood of Romans has been daily shed between Constantinople and the Julian Alps. Scythia, Thrace, Macedonia, Thessaly, Dardania, Dacia, Epirus, Dalmatia and all the provinces of Pannonia, sacked, pillaged and plundered by Goths and Sarmatians, Quadrans and Alans, Huns and Vandals and Marcomanni. How many nations, how many of God's virgins . . . have been the play-thing of these beasts? Bishops made captive, priests killed, churches destroyed, horses stabled at Christ's altars . . . The Roman world is falling . . . I am not writing history but weeping a little over our miseries. Even Thucydides and Sallust would be silent in face of such a story." (*Ep. LXXVII.*)

This letter was written in 396. Three years later he returns to the chronicle of horrors and tells of the threat to the East when "swarms of Huns had poured forth from the distant sea of Azov, midway between the icy river Tanais and the savage tribes of the Massagetae. . . . Flying hither and thither on their swift steeds, said our informants, these invaders were filling the whole world with bloodshed and panic . . . they outstripped rumour by their speed, spared neither religion nor age, even for wailing infants they had no pity". (*Ep. LXXVII.*)

Jerome and his friends had ships prepared for flight: Fabiola, on a visit to Palestine, did return to Rome but Jerome clung to his home in Bethlehem. And two later letters show Rome first threatened and then pillaged. In 408 and 409 Alaric was bought off by large sums. But in 410 he seized and sacked Rome—sparing the churches, because he was a Christian, but allowing his soldiers to plunder, rape and destroy for three days.

> All that lies between the Alps and the Pyrenees, the Rhine and the Ocean, is devastated by the barbarian . . . Who could believe that Rome on her own soil fights no longer for glory, but for her existence; and no longer even fights, but purchases her life with gold and precious things? (*Ep. CXXIII.*)

Finally the blow falls: "The city which had taken the whole world was itself taken; nay, it fell by famine before it fell by the sword . . . men tore one another's limbs, and the mother did not spare the baby at her breast, taking back into her what she had just brought forth." (*Ep. CXXVII.*)

At Bethlehem they waited for news. Marcella had been tortured. Other friends had died, none knew how, houses and estates had been ravaged, girls violated. Many died of hunger. Those who escaped were robbed and sold into slavery by the officials of the Roman provinces through which they had to make their way. This is less startling, though no less tragic, if we remember the numbers of these officials who were Romans only by adoption. For long the Empire had been absorbing the barbarians. At last the process had gone too far and the tribes within the Empire and those outside were tearing it apart.

Presently the flood of refugees began to pour upon Bethlehem. Paula's princely fortune and Jerome's own small estate had been deeply reduced by maintaining their monasteries and by lavish almsgiving; it was an immense problem to house and feed the multitudes arriving from Rome. The holy sanctuary of Bethlehem had, said Jerome, to receive "as beggars, nobles both men and women, formerly abounding in the goods of this world. We ourselves, hardly able to help them, can at least share their grief and mingle our tears with theirs". And Bethlehem, filled to overflowing with these refugees, was itself under threat of invasion.

Jerome wrote on steadily, reflecting in his letters and his commentaries his anguish of sympathy, his grief for Rome, and his fears for the world. Never did man fulfil his vocation more completely than this monk and scholar. It seems strange to read that in his youth the Bishop of Antioch insisted on ordaining him priest—which makes the odd story of his brother's ordination even odder. Jerome agreed reluctantly, on condition that he remain a monk; it is almost certain that he never exercised his priestly powers. Medieval painters created him a cardinal, but Jerome remained in fact solely a scholar and a monk. He ardently pursued learning even when daily awaiting death. He urged asceticism and spurred on both men and women to undertake the adventure of monasticism. This was his vocation and he lived and died carrying it out to the full.

For thirty-six years Jerome lived in Bethlehem. Paula died in 402, Eustochium sixteen years later. Jerome survived her for two years. He was probably only seventy-two—by no means the immensely old man of art and legend, but aged by his labours and his sufferings. A man who steadily devotes night and day to labour and spends almost no time in eating or social intercourse has lived almost two men's lives; it is no mistake to see him bowed with the weight of years. His profound grief at the death of Eustochium breathes in his last letter to his African friends Augustine and Alypius. To Augustine he entrusted the carrying on of his fight with heresy— after this last grief he felt too old. But Eustochium had not left him without a family. Paula, her niece, remained, and at Jerusalem were the second Melania and her family. The grandchildren of the first Melania and the first Paula were now good friends; Bethlehem was at peace with Jerusalem. With all his harsh theories about sex Jerome found it easier to be at peace with women.

He was thin, almost transparent, his voice grew gradually more feeble; bit by bit movement became impossible without the help of the pulley with which he raised himself on his bed; he directed to the end the ordering of his monastery. That feeble voice will always be heard in Christendom, for its cadences have passed into our language. As Catholics we sing in it, we read in it. But Jerome shaped not only the Latin of the Church: he set his mark also on all the languages of Europe, their structure, their vocabulary and their modes of thought. If Augustine has most deeply affected the thought of Christendom, it was the voice of Jerome that gave it speech.

XI: CLERICAL CELIBACY AND THE
FOURTH CENTURY

S T. JEROME was among the men who, by their enthusiasm
for virginity, helped to stimulate in the fourth century
the acceptance of celibacy as an essential element in the
priestly vocation. At first it had not been so.

St. Paul, while elevating virginity above marriage, had
insisted only that a bishop should not be a twice-married man
—and in the early Church the only law in regard to clerical
marriage was that no priest or bishop could marry a second
time. A priest was not a monk, and for several centuries the
adoption of the ascetic life, including celibacy, was for clergy,
as for laity, a matter of individual vocation. It is fascinating
but not at all easy to trace the gradual change that took place, in
the West mainly during the course of the fourth century, in
the East even later and never completely.

"The Church", says Clement in the third century, "fully
receives the husband of one wife, whether he be priest or
deacon or layman, supposing always that he uses his marriage
blamelessly; and such a one shall be saved in the begetting of
children." (*Strom.*, iii. 13). And Socrates, the Church historian,
though saying that a different custom prevails in Thessaly and
Greece, declares that in the Eastern Church neither priests nor
bishops have any obligation to separate from their wives.

As martyrdom became rarer and asceticism took its place as
the ideal of the enthusiastic, the Church had more often to
restrain ardour for sacrifice than to stimulate it—she had, for
instance, to condemn the teaching of the Encratites that
baptism was equivalent to a vow of virginity. Marcion held—
and claimed that St. Paul had said—that "there is no resurrection except for those who have kept their virginity".

The Synod of Gangra was probably held about 340, and its
decrees included an anathema on anyone who should maintain

"that when a married priest offers the sacrifice no one should take part in the service". And another strikes those who condemn a married priest for sleeping with his wife.

Fifteen years earlier an attempt had been made, at the Council of Nicaea, to bind the clergy by a law of celibacy. It was defeated by Paphnutius, a bishop in the Upper Thebaid, who had been tortured and banished for the Faith. Although approving the celibate clergy he opposed any law forbidding priests married before ordination to continue to live as married men. In the West the Spaniards had already, at the turn of the century, passed at Elvira (between 295 and 302) a rule binding deacons, priests and bishops. If they continue to live with their wives and beget children they are to be deposed. "This would seem", says Father Thurston, "to have been the beginning of divergence between East and West." But it was only a beginning.

THE PRESSURE OF ASCETICISM

There is no doubt that in East and West alike the attitude of the clergy was being deeply affected by the ascetic movement. Gregory Nazianzen was the son of a bishop: he returned to his native place to help his father and finally succeeded him —but we cannot conceive of St. Gregory as a married man. St. Patrick was the son of a deacon, grandson of a priest, but himself ardent in the cause of virginity.

There are many examples in the fourth century of husbands and wives, still living in the same house, but without intercourse, after the husband had received orders. Eucherius and Galla went to Lerins where their two sons, educated in the monastery, both became bishops, probably during their father's lifetime. Eucherius himself ended as Bishop of Lyons for sixteen years.

Paulinus of Nola, even better known, retired with his wife to his family estates, being later made Bishop of Nola. St. Jerome writes to him and his wife praising their resolution to live a life of continence and exhorting them to perseverance. We do not know whether, when Paulinus became bishop in 408, his wife Therasia was already dead. Tillemont doubts it, but for the most part after the husband becomes a bishop the wife tends to fade out of the picture. Two slightly comic exceptions are Sidonius Apollinaris, with whom his wife found fault for giving away the episcopal plate to the poor, and Priscus, Archbishop of Lyons. Priscus is known as a saint, was given the title, very rare in the West, of Patriarch, and was present at all the local councils of his time. But St. Martin of Tours accuses him, "with his wife Susanna", of persecuting the friends of the previous archbishop, St. Nicetius.

It is clear from the account of Nicaea given by Socrates that already the marriage *after ordination* of priests as well as bishops was held to be contrary to the tradition of the Church —and at the local Councils of Ancyra in Galatia (314) and of Neo-Caesarea in Cappadocia (315) this was expressly stated. While this was an absolute law for priests, Ancyra made a reservation for deacons. If a deacon declared at the time that a celibate life was above his strength he might afterwards marry, tacit permission of the ordaining bishop being assumed.

In the East, as late as the Council of Trullo (692) a law forbidding priests and deacons to marry *after* ordination, together with another that orders a *bishop*, on his consecration, to part from his wife, makes it clear that priests and deacons could remain married. This is still the rule today in the majority of Eastern Churches, although some of the Uniates have adopted the Western custom.

In the West, by the time of Leo the Great, clerical celibacy was practically universal. Under Pope Siricius an edict was passed (in 386) forbidding priests and deacons to have intercourse with their wives. Subdeacons apparently ranked with acolytes and need not separate from theirs before the age of thirty, when they would be ordained deacons after a short period of testing in relation to their strength in keeping continence.

All these laws came into effect only gradually. St. Ambrose, in *De Officiis*, notes that, in outlying country districts especially, married clergy were still to be found. G. T. Stokes says that "a careful review of the councils and canons will shew that in Britain and North Gaul there existed no prohibition of clerical marriage in the last quarter of the fourth century." And in 404 St. Exuperius of Toulouse wrote to Pope Innocent I asking how he should deal with married priests who had had children subsequent to ordination. Innocent, in his reply (February 405), refers to the decree of Siricius, but himself permits the clergy of Toulouse to continue to live with their wives if they had contracted marriage in ignorance of papal legislation.

The Church was slow to press the rule *as* a rule; but as early as Nicaea another question was raised which had a considerable bearing upon its necessity. Nicaea condemned what were called *mulieres subintroductae*—women themselves under vows, living with priests and helping them with their missionary work, or even simply housekeeping for them. No woman, the council decreed, must live with a priest except his mother, sister or aunt, unless she were of an age to make scandal impossible.

Obviously enough, it would be far harder for a man and woman under vows who had previously lived as husband and wife. The usual expression, to live "as brother and sister", covers a world of intense power of emotion unimaginable by the life-long celibate. The Church had to learn to be realistic; and synods of the sixth and seventh centuries, giving these former wives the honourable titles of *episcopissa*, *presbyterissa* and *diaconessa*, laid down very strict rules for their relations with their former husbands. The bishopess must not live in the same house as the bishop, and rules were laid down in the case of the higher clergy—as that their subordinates should sleep in the same room with them in order to obviate all danger of scandal.

The gradual progress in the direction of entire celibacy came at least as much from the choice of the clergy themselves as from any urging from above—celibacy was the principal item in that ascetic life which was to set them free to serve God totally. And fellowship was another. St. Ambrose, who himself established one, speaks of Eusebius of Vercellae (consecrated bishop in 340) as the first to have a monastic household. This was an inspiring ideal rather than a mere system of regulation and safeguard.

In the eyes of a secular ruler there was another interesting reason for a celibate clergy. While the Church was from the first vehemently opposed to anything like a hereditary priest-hood, the tendency to create one often showed itself. Apollinaris the Elder, priest of Laodicea, had a son Apollinaris the Younger who became bishop of the same city. Gregory of Tours, bishop from about 573–94, was great-grandson of Gregory, Bishop of Langres, and most of the former bishops of Tours had belonged to his family. But Justinian's Code of Civil Law forbade any-one with children or even nephews being consecrated bishop, for fear that his natural affections should warp his judgement.

Julianus, Bishop of Eclanum, was the son of an Italian bishop called Memorius. Gelasius of Cyzicus, who wrote the history of the Council of Nicaea, was the son of a priest. For son to follow father in his profession is natural enough; it is the line of least resistance. But Justinian was expressing the Christian mind as well as dealing practically with a practical problem. For the priesthood is not a mere profession, and priests are made to beget spiritual children.

Some of the stories of renunciation strike a note of great tenderness and beauty. Salvianus, a priest of the fifth century, was called by Hilary of Arles "the most blessed man Salvianus the presbyter". When Gennadius wrote of him in his extreme old age he called him *Episcoporum Magister*; he was held in highest honour as a perfect type of monk and scholar. As a young man Salvianus had married Palladia, daughter of Hypatius. They had one daughter and after her birth they both adopted the monastic life. This enraged her father, Hypatius, who refused to have anything to do with them for seven years. One of Salvianus's letters is an earnest appeal from them both and from his little granddaughter that he would give back to them his love and friendship.

That such a thing exists as a vocation to marriage was seldom mentioned in the fourth century—so great a wave of enthusiasm was sweeping men and women into deserts and monasteries. The life of shared celibacy was a third and heroic way. But one cannot escape the feeling that for every one really called by God there were many only carried away by the powerful stream of other men's vocation and that this accounts in part for the problems with which the Church had to cope. Who could read Jerome or listen to Augustine unmoved? Their genius stirred enthusiasm powerfully in the imagination and some at least mistook this stirring for a call to the soul.

THE STRANGE STORY OF SYNESIUS

Among many surprising stories in this strange period is that
of Synesius, Bishop of Ptolemais in the Libyan Pentapolis.

Born at Cyrene about the year 365, Synesius inherited large
estates, served in the army, was passionately addicted to field
sports. Leaving the army, he went to Alexandria and under
the tutelage of Hypatia became a neo-Platonist. Then he went
on to Athens, because it was held that no young philosopher
could be fully equipped save at that university—but he was
bitterly disappointed with the city and its professors. Hypatia
remained his "most venerated teacher". Returning to his own
estates, he divided his time happily enough between sport and
study till public affairs called him into action.

Synesius was a pagan but a pagan far more affected by
Christian ideas than he at all realised. He prayed in Christian
churches to "gods" who were in fact conceived by him as the
Christian would think of patron saints; beyond them he saw
the one supreme God. "I prayed," he writes, "to all the gods
Thy ministers . . . whom Thou hast crowned with angelic rays,
Thy holy servants." Conversely, when he married a Christian
wife and became a Christian, his mind remained soaked in
Platonic ideas.

Contemporary of Eutropius, who had hung up in his office
a list of the provinces and their prices, Synesius cannot have
been surprised, though he was furiously angry, at finding that
a local scoundrel was "on his way to us" as governor. He wrote
vehemently and vainly to Constantinople. The practical
provincials realised that they themselves must act. A strong
bishop alone could stand against such a governor—and they
urgently demanded Synesius. Horrified, he wrote to his
brother, ". . . I am in every way unworthy of the dignity of the
episcopate . . . I now divide my time between amusements and
study. When engaged in study, especially religious studies, I
keep entirely to myself, in my amusements I am thoroughly
sociable. But the bishop must be godly and like God have
nothing to do with amusements. A thousand eyes are on him
to see that he observes this duty. In matters religious, however,
he cannot live apart, but must be thoroughly sociable, as he is
teacher and preacher of the law. Singlehanded, he has to do

everybody's work or bear the blame of everybody. A man of strongest character is needed to carry such a burden of cares without the overwhelming of his mind or the quenching in his soul of the divine spark by the infinite variety of his employments. Still I will submit to this if it be God's will."

What he will not agree to is the concealment of any of his philosophical ideas which appear different from those of the Christian multitudes. These he will make known to Theophilus. "There shall be no contradiction between my thoughts and my tongue."

But the crux of the letter is the question of celibacy, and it is especially interesting as coming from the East as early as the beginning of the fifth century. "God and the law and the sacred hand of Theophilus gave me my wife. I therefore declare openly to all and testify that I will not separate entirely from her or visit her secretly as an adulterer . . . I shall wish and pray to have a large number of virtuous children."

This was written from Alexandria—there could be no return to Libya for Synesius without acceptance of the episcopal office, and he put himself wholly in the hands of his bishop. Theophilus ordained him and sent him back. His letters reveal a bitter struggle with an extortionate and cruel governor, inventing new modes of torture, deaf to all expostulations, defeated at last only by the powerful weapon of excommunication. Later Synesius pleads for his fallen enemy—"Justice has perished among men. Formerly Andronicus acted unjustly, now he suffers unjustly."

Letters alone make the story of a man's life at once vivid and difficult to follow. The friends to whom he is writing are in possession of facts unknown to us. He is not telling his own history, but commenting on it and we have no clue to some of the comments. But we do learn that the years of Synesius' bishopric were burdened and melancholy, full of private sadness and public calamity.

Earlier he had spoken of the social and sporting life he must abandon; in a letter a year after his consecration he talks of his intolerable loneliness. His wife is not mentioned, but as he speaks of losing "the last comfort" of his life, his little son, we may infer that she too had died. Overburdened with work,

missing the fresh air and exercise of the sports he had relinquished, he grew more and more ill. The last letter we possess
is to Hypatia: "You have been to me a mother, a sister, a
teacher . . . My bodily sickness comes from sickness of the
mind . . . would to God I could either cease to live or cease to
think of my children's graves." After accepting the heavy
weight of rule he lived only three years. Poet, orator, sports-
man, philosopher, soldier, statesman, bishop—all with success
in the eyes of the world, he was in his own eyes a failure. "O
Christ," he wrote in his last hymn, "Son of God most high,
have mercy on Thy servant, a miserable sinner. Release me
from the sins that have grown up in my heart, which are implanted in my polluted soul. O Saviour Jesus, grant that hereafter I may behold Thy divine glory."

Acts of contrition come alike from saint and sinner, but so
far as we can judge Synesius was no saint, nor had he scarlet
sins of which to repent. But he was a misfit. He had not, it
would seem, the strength of an Ambrose, who accepted man's
will forcing him as God's voice calling him.

But after all, what do we know from a handful of letters?
Only, perhaps, a little more of the strangeness of the period,
more especially in the East. A country gentleman must
abandon his home if he will *not* consent to be made into a
bishop. But if he consents he need not abandon his wife. The
Bishop of Alexandria accepts his conditions of a certain theological latitude and a continued family life. And the theology
of Synesius was definitely that of Origen, on suspicion of which
this same Theophilus began his persecution of St. John Chrysostom. Finally, a Christian bishop, instead of trying to convert
her, hails the famous pagan Hypatia as his mother and his
teacher. And Hypatia, a few years later, is torn in pieces by a
Christian mob in a Christian church.

LATER CHANGES

Synesius is especially interesting in a discussion of celibacy
because he comes at a turning point in history; a little later
celibacy was enforced on bishops everywhere. The East, as
we have seen, remained satisfied with this compromise, and

retained a married parochial clergy, most of their bishops being drawn from monasteries. But in another way a historical turning point had been reached—between the order of imperial Rome and the multitudinous variety and confusion of the barbarian kingdoms. When we say that the clergy in the West accepted, or even for the most part welcomed, the Church's legislation in this matter we are still thinking of Romans in the wider sense: men of whatever race who had adopted Roman ways of thinking and living. The word *Romania*—Romanity!— is first heard at the end of the fourth century. And when St. Augustine, besieged by the Vandals in Hippo, received letters from the bishops of the province asking his advice on their behaviour towards the invaders, his biographer Possidius describes them as *illos Romaniae eversores*. These barbarians were overthrowing, were destroying, the Roman thing.

This Roman thing the Church would rebuild out of the very men who had ruined it, but it would be a long and laborious task. The history of celibacy now becomes a part of the history of the Dark Ages and the emergence of Christendom. The chief builders of it were the monks: the monks of Ireland, the monks of Benedict.[1] There was also, around the great cathedrals, a development of the common life among the secular clergy. The Rule of St. Chrodegang approved by the Council of Aachen in 816 "formed", says Father Thurston, "the basis of the cathedral chapters in most of the dioceses throughout the dominions of Charlemagne".

But the period called "the iron age" followed only too closely on the first shaping by the Church of the turbulent Franks, Lombards and other warrior tribes. Three elements are present from the sixth century onwards which grow worse before they begin to improve. Romans were often cruel enough, but with the barbarians came new horrors of torture— such as cutting off the noses and ears, not of criminals only, but of possible rivals or of captives. Sexual excess was rampant. Simony reached new heights and after the breakdown of the Carolingian Empire, bishoprics were even given as fiefs to soldiers and handed down by them to their sons. "Impurity, adultery, sacrilege and murder have overwhelmed the world", cried the Council of Trosly in 909.

[1] See below the chapter " The Creative Spirit".

Many clergy in this period married, had children and handed on to them their worldly possessions—including bishoprics. The situation by the eleventh century was such that in several local councils (Rouen 1063 and 1072, Lisieux 1064, Winchester 1076) permission was given to the rural clergy to keep the wives to whom they had been previously married, thus allowing eastern custom to prevail in the West.

Exactly how far this went it is difficult to know, as we may see by the example of Anglo-Saxon England. Married *preosts* or priests were common enough, and to be a priest's son was no disgrace—but then we realise that the word "preost" by itself meant only cleric. Abbot Aelfric wrote that a "priest of the common order" may marry but that all conjugal relations are forbidden to "a Mass-priest or a deacon". (Aelfric, *Homilies*, vol. ii, p. 94 in Thorpe's edition.) "Priests of the common order" meant those who had merely received Minor Orders, and this included almost all educated young men who might, did a benefice come their way, go on to ordination. The state of the marriage law being at that date somewhat ambiguous, they could fairly easily break off their marriage; should they decide to abandon the clerical career they could legitimatize it.

This, of course, does not mean that the marriage of actual priests may not have been tolerated in certain places and periods. But the ambiguity of words does seem to have led to exaggeration on the part of some historians. In theory a married clergy was not accepted by the popes or by the Western Church as a whole. Leo IX, Gregory VII and their successors made a very strong stand against it. One curious law, apparently passed by the Council of Pavia in 1018, declared all children of priests' marriages (in our sense of priest) Church property, never to be enfranchised. And Gregory VII interdicted married priests from saying Mass.

This is no place to carry the story through the Middle Ages, but perhaps certain lessons emerge from the Church's action and the thinking of her wisest children at different times and under different circumstances.

Brought up as we have been in a western civilisation, taking for granted what we have always lived with, it came as a shock to many of us when we first discovered a married clergy. In one American city where a large number of Catholic immigrants

of Eastern Rite had settled, accompanied by their married pastor
and his wife, the bishop drove round the parish in an open
car with the couple beside him in order to convince the local
American Catholics that the situation was wholly regular.
They appeared only to be convinced that their bishop was
sharing in the guilt of another's sin.

The same shock affected many Catholics when Pope Pius
XII allowed certain Lutheran convert clergy to be ordained
priests and to keep their wives. We had not learnt to distinguish
between a Church law, changeable by the Church which made
it, and the immutable moral law of God. And perhaps we had
not meditated enough on the nature of vocation and the pro-
founder meaning of virginity.

To some degree a celibate clergy has been seen by the
Church's rulers as a practical provision to further their work
for souls. An Anglican, Bishop Bickersteth of Tokyo, wrote in
one of his letters: "In Japan a Roman priest gets one-seventh
of what the Church Missionary Society and the Society for the
Propagation of the Gospel allow to an unmarried deacon."
How much greater must the gap have been between that
seventh and the allowance for the married clergy? Bishop
Bickersteth admired the priests' courage in facing extreme
poverty in their solitude. But even above the need for more
money if a family is to be kept, comes the need for time to
devote to them. The Church, placing high the rights of wife
and children, has often feared to let these natural rights interfere with the needs of souls which press upon the priest. Should
two such heavy burdens (the Western Church asked) be laid
on one man's shoulders?

A vocation means a call from God—what He is asking each
of us to make of our lives. In the widest sense everyone has a
vocation, but of all these vocations the highest for the Church's
needs is the priest's, the highest for the individual soul is that
of virginity. Not even in Western Christendom have these
vocations been held necessarily to imply one another. Many
monasteries in the Church's history have had only one or two
priests among a large number of monks. And conversely, a
vocation to the priesthood is not held in the Eastern Church
to mean of necessity a vocation to celibacy. For those who have

this vocation there are always the monasteries. These are two vocations, not one—a man may have one and not the other. He may have both.

The Church has varied in the application of her laws, but always she has seen virginity as a path of penance; also, a state of perfection which is the answer to a call from God.

XII: ST. AUGUSTINE

T HE chief problem in these slight biographies is to make
clear the historical and geographical background. As
we watch the growth of the Church through the eyes of
her greatest children we move from one country to another;
we are carried forward in one study to a date beyond that at
which another begins. Nor can we be content to tell any man's
story starting from his first appearance on the scene, for the
meaning and significance of his life can be understood only in
relation to much earlier elements that went into his making,
and into the making of the world he lived in. Above all, each
one of these lives is a part of that great composite life of the
Mystical Body which we call the history of the Church.

THE CHURCH IN AFRICA

The Church in Africa belonged to the West, although in
its geographical position slightly isolated.

We do not know when or by whom it was founded, but we
find, in 180, twelve martyrs dying for the Faith at Scillium.
They had with them the Epistles of St. Paul, and as it seems
morally impossible that these simple people should have been
able to read Greek this is an indication of the early date of
the African Latin version of Scripture. A few days earlier
others had died in another place under the same proconsul,
this short persecution being followed by a respite, during which
the Church grew at a tremendous pace.

"If we chose to offer ourselves to death," wrote Tertullian
to the proconsul Scapula about 212, "what would you do with
so many thousands . . .? How many stakes, how many swords,
would you need? What would become of Carthage, decimated
by you, as men recognised their relatives, their neighbours,
men and women, it may be, of your own rank, the foremost
citizens, the parents and friends of your friends?"

Between these dates had come, about 202, the martyrdom of SS. Perpetua and Felicity, the *Acta* of which is one of the most beautiful and celebrated that we possess. In its final form it is probably the work of Tertullian, who was the father, not only of African but of all Christian Latin writers. For Africa, where Latin was being used while Romans proper were still writing in Greek, produced in the early centuries by far the richest harvest of Christian Latin literature: Tertullian, St. Cyprian, St. Augustine are the three giant figures, but there are, too, Minucius Felix, the humanist so much admired by Renan, Pontius, secretary and biographer of St. Cyprian, Arnobius, Lactantius, Commodian, and the champions alike of Montanism and the Catholic opposition to it. North Africa was, says De Labriolle, "down to the fourth century the centre of Christian thinking in the West".

Tertullian

Even here the question of language was at first in the balance. Tertullian wrote in both, but his Greek works have disappeared and he finally settled for Latin. Tertullian was for the Church in the West very much what Origen was for the East—St. Vincent of Lerins makes the comparison—a powerful yet suspect originator of some of the best thought of those that followed him. "Da magistrum"—"Hand me the Master"—that other great African, St. Cyprian, would say when he wanted, almost daily, to read him. And none can doubt the debt owed him by St. Augustine.

Tertullian probably began his career as a lawyer: born at Carthage, his father an official, he was a convert from paganism, a married man but without children. At some time he became priest. His learning was immense in philosophy, law, pagan and Christian literature; his memory stupendous. If he was like the Alexandrians in all this, and in his enthusiasm for Christian ideas, he was most unlike them in his fierce opposition to anything whatsoever coming from the pagan world. "What has Athens in common with Jerusalem," he demands, "the Academy with the Church"—or, he adds, "heretics with Christians?" At first using all the powers of his rhetoric against paganism and heresy, he later used them against the Church.

What a strange tormented nature his was, fierce, uncompromising, possessing and perhaps possessed by, a torrential eloquence which carried him into strange positions. He had nothing of Origen's patience and sweetness of character: *miserrime ego*, he once said, admitting his own impatience. But, like Origen, he was a pioneer in Christian thinking.

"Where is learning like Tertullian's," says St. Jerome, "where a keener mind?" "His Apologetic and his battles against the heathen contain all the learning of the age."

Could he have been nothing but intellect, it seems unlikely that Tertullian would have left the Church. It was the life of living men that defeated him. Baptism he believed, as do all Christians, to be a total cleansing, a making-new, of sin-stained humanity. Jesus Christ had brought us to the Father, and in this company our life should be all-new. He was totally possessed, as were all the Montanists, whose sect he joined, by the belief that the end of the world was at hand; he could almost see Christ returning in glory. Could not then the Christian, for that brief time, live a life of perfect purity and undimmed courage?

In his earlier years Tertullian had boasted of the immense numbers of Christians in every quarter of the town, in the palace, the senate, the forum, the army—"we have left you nothing but the temples". But later, with great fierceness, he tried to close to Christians almost every avenue for a living or for a life among their fellows. No trade must be practised which might even remotely contribute to the worship of false gods. Christians must not read profane literature. They must not take public office or serve in the army. No form of words must be used that smelt of paganism, hardly any trade was safe, since nearly all were based on covetousness or fraud and were so often proximate to idolatry. Mixed marriages between pagans and Christians were abominable. Public spectacles of whatever sort must be shunned—not only the fighting of gladiators, but athletic contests, the circus and the theatre; all these things were akin to paganism and its delights.

It appeared to him that fundamental human weakness had become unthinkable, flight from persecution intolerable; second marriages were to be abhorred, the life of asceticism should be lived by all. The Donatists added further fasts to those (very few at that date) ordered by the Church. Above all, Tertullian attacked the possibility of restoration to the fold of those who had, after baptism, committed adultery or fornication. "The stains on the body made after baptism cannot be washed away by penance." He furiously attacked Pope Callistus, who was teaching that they could, as an innovator; he accused of gluttony and worse those clerics who would not accept the Montanist asceticism—he exhausted himself in bitter and angry rhetoric.

But it was not sin only that Tertullian found intolerable. It seemed to him that redeemed man, for the short time that remained, should live the life of an angel. He forgot that men, unlike angels, have bodily appetites; not by accident but by God's plan. In one amazing passage, insisting that Christians cannot in conscience attend the public games, he offers instead the joys of prayer. The need to relax the tight-drawn bow of the intellect while it depends upon the easily-wearied body seems never to have occurred to him. It may be that in his rhetoric he found some slight relaxation. But surely it was the overtaxed mind and body that sought relief in bitter sarcasm towards the Church and its teachers, in cruel accusations of bad faith and moral corruption.

The Montanist heresy started about the year 172, and was in principle a revolt against authority. Mystical, especially ecstatic, experiences were to be substituted for the divine guidance of the Tradition. The two chief colleagues of Montanus were women—Priscilla and Maximilla. The end of the world, he declared, was at hand. Christians must prepare for its coming by a tremendous austerity of life. There was at first no innovation of doctrine, but the claim to divine guidance given by ecstasy soon turned into a defiance of the bishops' teaching and authority. The founders died, their prophecy unfulfilled, but the sect grew and lasted into the fourth century.

Montanism had given this angry man a curious compensation for worldly amusements and for the peace of Christian brotherhood in the vicarious joy of heavenly visions. Female prophets were quite a feature of Montanism—and the Church's disapproval of them stemmed less from the contents of their vision than from the frenzy into which it threw them. Montanus,

too, claimed to receive revelations and finally to be himself
the Paraclete; he claimed that in these women were renewed
the ecstasies of the early Church. But it is strange to think of
the brilliant lawyer and philosopher solemnly setting down how
one "sister", after a sermon of his, had seen the soul "light and
shining and of the colour of air, shaped like the body".

In the end Tertullian, breaking with official Montanism,
gave his own name to a new sect. Called Tertullianists, they
lingered on until the last of them were by St. Augustine
reconciled to the Church.

The date of Tertullian's death is unknown. He wrote and
flourished (if the word can be used of so gloomy a person)
from 197 to at least 212, more probably until 223. This
period was marked by sporadic outbursts of persecution,
which gave him the opportunity for some of his most powerful
invective and his highest claims. Tertullian was the first to
use the words *testimomium animae naturaliter Christianae*. Yet how
much higher, he declared, could that soul soar with the graces
given in the Church—"All men love their friends, but only
Christians their enemies." Men condemned for crime have
commonly to be hunted out, but Christians go willingly;
while they are tortured they pray for the Emperor at whose
orders they are slain. Their only interest in this world is to
leave it as soon as possible. Yet they are so many that did
they choose to fight society, "without arms, without revolution", simply by going away to some far-off spot, "the loss of
so great a multitude would fill with shame the world's rulers,
would be adequate punishment for them".

If Tertullian reread these words in purgatory he must have
blushed for his fellow Africans. For, with the long peace that
followed his death, came a slackening of the Christian enthusiasm which ill prepared them for the persecution under
Decius in 250. This long peace of the Church meant that
everywhere Christians were beginning to have by custom the
rights that only under Constantine became theirs by law. They
could accumulate property, they could hold high office—a
Christian could even be a titular high priest of paganism, with
exemption from the obligation to offer sacrifice. It was held
to have become a purely civic function; the Church had at
the Council of Elvira to condemn the practice. St. Cyprian

complains that too many bishops are business men, taking charge of estates, frequenting fairs and exercising usury ("usury" in church language covers any lending of money for interest, be the rate low or high).

Christians in general had got so thoroughly mixed in with the pagan world as almost to justify Tertullian's passionate separatism. They lived with pagans in a country where living could be very pleasant; a spirit of relaxation had crept upon them, and when persecution broke out there were apostates in vast numbers. The imperial orders were that all must offer incense to the Emperor—and St. Cyprian tells us that Christians were to be seen bringing their children to the tribunal, that others arriving late would beg the officials to defer the closing hour that they might immediately carry out the law. They were eager, says St. Cyprian, for death—the death of their souls. One priest, even, arrived leading his flock to burn their incense all together. Others, who shrank from actual apostasy, bought certificates—*libelli*—saying that they *had* sacrificed. Doubtless the officials made a good thing out of these *libellatici* as they were called.

St. Cyprian of Carthage

Tertullian had said something else which this persecution disproved: that it was sinful to fly from the danger, sinful to hide. For the greatest figure of those terrible years was Cyprian, Bishop of Carthage, who spent many months in hiding and was able, like St. Athanasius, to keep in being a flock, demoralised indeed, but not totally destroyed. St. Cyprian was a late convert and his greatness had only the brief period of ten years for its rich and full development. Born in Africa of pagan parents, normally educated in the Classics and rhetoric, after a youth which he avowed had not been spotless, Cyprian was converted in middle life by a priest called Caecilius or Caecilianus, whose name he added at baptism to his own. Giving most of his goods to the poor, he was ordained priest and in 248 or 249, just before the Decian persecution began, he was chosen by popular acclaim for bishop. Newman's *Callista* gives us a glimpse of Cyprian, in hiding in the natural catacombs developed from caves in the countryside, going forth at night to gather in his flock. The strengthening of Agellius, the converting of Callista, are pictures developed by the Cardinal from lists of the African martyrs. The book is, Newman insists, a tale, but the atmosphere is even more wonderfully conveyed than that of early Christian Rome in Pater's *Marius*. We see the heavily Roman Jucundus, the exquisite Polemo with his rose and his litter, the Greek brother and sister exiled in a small African town, the Roman soldiers, and the rough mob of African peasants. The black magic of Gurta and many of the incidental touches give us a picture which at a more outspoken date could have been even more vivid, of the dark underworld of paganism. Against this background we see the great bishop who had so much to do before he could die for his faith.

The story of St. Cyprian as far as we know it is short in years but too eventful to be told in what is merely an introduction to the life of a greater bishop still. To summarise, he had to struggle, when persecution stopped, with those who bitterly blamed him for not having suffered himself, with the arrogant confessors or near-martyrs, who claimed the right to reconcile all the lapsed, with the Tertullianist element who desired no reconciliation for any of them. Thanks to him, a middle course of penance, yet mercy, was taken by a council at Carthage.

The schism led by Felicissimus and the priest Novatus against Cyprian made his task no easier. About the same time, the Novatian schism broke out in Rome. Cyprian rallied the Church in Africa to the side of Pope Cornelius. Novatian in Rome was maintaining fierce penitential discipline for apostates, Novatus in Carthage was the partisan of laxity—but the two made common cause against the Pope and against Cyprian. The fierce energy of Novatian swept all before him; like a whirlwind he ordained schismatic bishops everywhere. In Africa, Italy, Spain, the East, was set up what St. Cyprian called "a human church over against the Catholic Church". These schisms inspired Cyprian to the writing of his treatise on unity, a unity which he himself imperilled later by his dispute with Rome on the invalidity of baptism by heretics.

As Bishop of Carthage, Cyprian had a vast task, for though in theory Carthage did not hold the position of Antioch or Alexandria, it was in practice the metropolis of all Africa, nor was there at this time any other bishop comparable with Cyprian. "A whole people", it has been said, "lived by his words. His every sermon, his every speech, was an act." So great did he become in the eyes of the African Church, that Augustine had later to remind his own adversaries that Cyprian's writings were not actually canonical. Cyprian was one of the ten Fathers on whom the Council of Ephesus based their condemnation of Nestorius.

While his spiritual care of his flock came first, he was deeply concerned, too, with their human needs. He collected money to ransom Numidians who had been carried into captivity. He organised, like St. Basil, a service of relief during the pestilence which in its fierceness troubled the faith of Christians and called from pagans the familiar claim that Christians were angering the gods.

The effect of Cyprian's ministry could be seen when, in 257, the Valerian persecution began. It had seemed under Decius that the Church in Africa would be totally lost, but now it had rallied, and Cyprian judged that he need not again hide himself to continue his work. "Such was his passion for preaching," says Pontius, his biographer, "that he hoped in the day of his longed-for martyrdom to perish in the midst of a sermon while speaking of God."

If a sermon, it was the shortest he had ever preached. "The divine emperors", said the proconsul Galerius Maximus, "have ordered you to sacrifice." "That I will not do," said Cyprian.

THE PROCONSUL: "You'd better be careful."
CYPRIAN: "Carry out your orders. In so clear a case I need no time to deliberate."
THE PROCONSUL: "We order that Thacius Cyprianus be put to death by the sword."

"Thanks be to God," said Cyprian. He ordered twenty-five gold pieces to be given to his executioner and went to his death surrounded by his flock. The pagans watched in a respectful silence, and none was dragged to prison or to death while bringing linen cloths to dip for relics in the blood of Cyprian. They carried his body to a private cemetery, singing hymns of triumph as they went. This great bishop had re-created a Christian people.

THE DONATISTS

By a deliberate and happy anachronism Newman, in *Callista*, gives us a glimpse of Arnobius as a young man, and Lactantius as a boy rescued by him from a schoolmaster whose cruelty the lad takes with surprising lightheartedness. Arnobius was a specimen of the ardent uninstructed convert; he gave little idea of the Church's teaching, but was, says De Labriolle, "a kind of Voltaire", less subtle but equally ironic and mordant, making a mock of mythology as Voltaire later mocked at the Bible. His pupil Lactantius, in *De Mortibus Persecutorum*, did in the West what Eusebius was doing at the same time in the East. His history is of great value for the later historian—not from the conclusions he draws but from the facts he relates. Born at Sicca about 250, taught by Arnobius, he too was a convert and he too taught rhetoric, chiefly at Nicomedia, which became from 285 the central residence of Diocletian. Losing his pupils, perhaps when the first signs of persecution were showing, he took to his pen. During the persecution he suffered from starvation if not worse—his friend Donatus, to whom he dedicated *De Mortibus*, had been tortured nine times under three governors. Both men had emerged into happier times, and it was at the court of Constantine, as tutor to his son, that Lactantius wrote down the story of the bitter years now over.

Diocletian had begun his reign as a non-persecuting emperor. Lactantius says it was his Caesar, Galerius, who stirred him to persecution. There may have been other elements. He certainly hated the Manicheans, and they announced their creed as a synthesis of Christianity and the oriental religions. A fierce edict against them was put forth in 296, and shortly afterwards there were signs of a changing attitude to the Church.

There remained always a strong current of anti-Christian feeling among the pagans—witness the fierce *Against the Christians* of Porphyry, a work in fifteen volumes which appeared between 270 and 280. Nor was Porphyry the only one, while Christians like Arnobius, Lactantius and Commodian did nothing to sweeten hostile opinion. One notes in these African writers far less enthusiasm for Rome than in native Romans, whether Christian or pagan. Tertullian and Lactantius both believed the world and the Empire would end together; Rome was mighty but she was not lovable.

According to Lactantius, Diocletian was finally terrified into persecution by an incident at Antioch in 302. The priests declared after a sacrifice that the omens were bad because the Christians present had made the sign of the Cross. Diocletian, terrified, issued an edict against them. At first he tried to avoid blood; Christian churches were to be destroyed and the sacred books seized. This war on the books is a chief reason why so little Christian literature earlier than the fourth century remains to us. Vast quantities were burnt. Mensurius, Bishop of Carthage, managed to save his by putting heretical works in their place and hiding the Catholic. As time went on bishops were imprisoned and even lost their lives rather than hand over their sacred volumes. A group of laymen in Numidia died for the same reason. Others, however, did hand them over and were called *traditores*, "handers-over", the origin of our word "traitor". And the unjust accusation of their having done so became a chief weapon in the hands of the Donatists against the Catholics.

During the illness of Diocletian in 304 Galerius accentuated the persecution; all were given the choice: "Sacrifice or die." Rivers of blood flowed. Only Gaul and Britain, where Constantius Chlorus was Caesar, were exempted. The African list of martyrs becomes at this date an imposing one, and Egypt was even more heavily oppressed, becoming, in the words of Ruinart, the China of the ancient world.

The African bishops dared, in the spring of 305, to gather in council for the election of new bishops in place of the martyred or the traitors. The death of Mensurius of Carthage, and the consecration of his deacon Caecilianus as his successor, gave an opportunity that Donatus, Bishop of Casae Nigrae in Numidia, a man of intense ambition, was not slow to seize. Many of the confessors felt that while they had been suffering Mensurius had escaped by being just a little too clever. Caecilianus, too, had, by his bishop's orders, moderated the wild enthusiasm of his flock for some of these confessors. The

Numidian bishops, always extremists, began to accuse Mensurius as a *traditor* and to assert that Caecilianus had been consecrated by another *traditor*, Felix of Aptonga, and was therefore no true bishop.

Like the Montanists, the Donatists were soon busily ordaining bishops everywhere. Monceaux describes Donatus as a powerful orator, a skilful diplomatist, intensely conscious of his own superiority, a man who longed to dominate the whole of Africa. Over against the official Church stood his "new Church claiming to be the true Church, the Church of the martyrs",[1] although too often it became in fact a school of robbery, hatred and murder. But the universal Church in other countries, though maintaining communion with Caecilianus, was not bestirring itself to bring the schism to an end.

There was some excuse for Constantine's intervention, although in the end he did far more harm than good. As we have seen, he firmly believed that God had made him judge over all human affairs. And careless of the principles involved, his one idea was to bring about peace and unity in the Church for the sake of peace and unity in the State. Soon after the victory of the Milvian Bridge he sent presents to Caecilianus, describing him pointedly as the legitimate Bishop of Carthage. But when the Donatists approached him he agreed to their request that some bishops from Gaul, not being involved in the dispute, might judge the issue. Constantine asked the Pope to preside, and Pope Miltiades added some Italian bishops to those from Gaul. This small council listened to ten bishops from each side and to a number of witnesses, and decided unanimously in favour of Caecilianus. They did their utmost to keep the peace in Africa, by condemning Donatus only and allowing the other Donatists to keep their sees, unless there had already been another bishop there first. Naturally, this did not satisfy Donatus. Back went his followers to the Emperor, claiming that the French bishops had been drowned in a sea of Italians, and had not, moreover, examined at all whether Felix of Aptonga had been a *traditor*—whether, therefore, the ordination of Caecilianus was null and void.

Constantine had the folly to listen to these complaints: he set aside the decision of the tribunal he had appointed, and

[1] Monceaux, *Histoire littéraire de l'Afrique chrétienne*, vol. iv, p. 20.

summoned a larger Council at Arles in 314. We have all heard of this Council: for at it there were three British bishops!

The papal legate was there and many other matters were discussed besides Donatism. The council agreed that should a man be proved to have handed over "the Scriptures, the sacred vessels or the names of his brethren", his name should be erased from the list of the clergy. But all the same it went much further than Rome had in its condemnation of the Donatists, calling them "crazy fanatics, a danger to Christianity". Nevertheless, ordinations made by Donatist bishops were valid, and the African Church must no longer rebaptise people baptised by heretics if their first baptism had been given in the name of the Trinity. This decision went against the custom of the African Church—which St. Cyprian had upheld; and it cut at the root of the Donatist heresy—that unworthy ministers made a sacrament invalid.

The decision was utterly clear, but the Emperor was again annoyed. In his eyes the Council was a failure, because the Donatists would not accept its findings! As one account of the proceedings has it, he "became weary of the business and bade the bishops return to their sees, Amen". To the renewed appeal of the Donatists, he replied that he would himself judge this interminable dispute, and by the end of the year 316, he at last got around to doing so. His decision was the same as that of Rome and of Arles, but with astonishing naïveté, he seems really to have believed that, though councils had spoken in vain, he, the mouthpiece of God, had only to speak to be obeyed.

He was not only the mouthpiece, he was also the strong arm, of the Lord! When his orders were not obeyed, that basilicas seized by the Donatists should be given back to the Catholics, the Roman governors of Africa, civil and military, did not hesitate to seize them, massacring the rebellious Donatist congregations. This action gave fresh saints and martyrs to the Donatist Church, which, however, received an almost mortal blow when it was clearly established, a few years later, that while Caecilianus had *not* been a *traditor*, some of the Donatist leaders had. Sylvanus, of Constantine in Numidia, was accused by his deacon and clearly proved on trial to have been ordained by *traditores*, and to have engaged in various kinds of shameful and dishonest traffic. He had had accomplices both in Numidia and Carthage. He was sent into exile, and the blow struck at Donatist morale was as heavy as might be. For it proved the foundations rotten on which they had built. The pure Church was impure, the protesters against treason proved to be the traitors.

This was in 320, and in the following year Constantine reluctantly and contemptuously halted the persecution and gave the Donatists freedom to worship in their own way. Their own way involved as fierce an attitude towards Catholics as the civil power had shown towards them. Pagans and Catholics were all one, but Donatus approached the Arians with a skilful tract on baptism and the Trinity, which showed his readiness to win any allies he could against his chief foe. This did not save him from the zeal of Constantius, who did battle for his own conception of the Faith by re-opening the persecution. When, in 347, he began his campaign by sending two imperial commissioners into Africa to reconcile the contending Christian bodies, Donatus received them with words very like those later used by St. Ambrose: "What has the Emperor to do with the Church?"

Much Donatist blood flowed at the hands of this semi-Arian. In Passions of their martyrs which still survive, wild statements were made that the commissioners were making Christians adore the idols of paganism. Bandits attacked the soldiers, who in revenge massacred the villagers. Donatus and the other leaders were exiled. Unity, after some fifteen years, appeared to be established by force. And then, in 361, came Julian the Pagan.

Now it was the Donatists' turn to be on top. Julian, in response to their appeals, annulled all the laws against them, ordering "that all things be established as they were formerly". What exactly was "formerly"? The Donatist bishops came pouring back; basilicas were returned to them and were solemnly washed with salt water for their purification. The seizures were made by force and Optatus declares that rivers of blood flowed at the hands of those whom the State had so lately crushed. Julian's representatives, especially when pagans, were not disposed to interfere. Julian's death meant another change, but Valentinian was in the main neutral, and after Julian follows a period when Catholics and Donatists alike were consolidating their positions and fighting with words rather than swords. During this time each side produced a writer of quality, Parmenian the Donatist and Optatus of Milevis the Catholic.

It has often been said that the Circumcellions, who went about massacring Catholics and ravaging property, were the left wing of the Donatist party. It seems established today that they were of independent origin, although happy to lend their hand to any disturbing element. Their speciality was a belief that, as they would go straight to heaven if killed for their faith, they must take measures to secure this death. Any passing citizen might be met by a Circumcellion with the demand to kill him—with the alternative of being himself killed.

Altogether the Africa in which the small boy Augustine was growing up was a country where violence always lay little below the surface.

AUGUSTINE IN TAGASTE AND CARTHAGE

Both from the *Confessions* and from casual remarks in letters and sermons, one gets the impression that the smiling surface was for many years all that Augustine observed of his native land.

Born at Tagaste in 354, he grew to manhood in an almost wholly Romanised society. As fully as our own, and perhaps more skilfully, that Roman world was geared to pleasure. Under the blazing sun of Africa, work must have been even less agreeable, amusements even more alluring, than in a more temperate climate. From ruins and museums we can picture cities built not for business but for the happy life of citizens, conceived after an increasingly material pattern. "What are your interests?" Augustine cries out to his people. "Eating and drinking, luxurious living, gaming and hunting . . . Of course we know well that these things are pleasant. Who would question it?" The mosaics of North Africa, floorings from houses on which Augustine may himself have walked, are rich in scenes of hunting, fishing and animal life: men lasso deer, drive an ostrich into a net, pursue a stag, a boar or a leopard; others are shown holding the fish they have caught while dolphins play round in the water.

Like the mosaics, Augustine's sermons mirror the world of
nature and man with a wide sympathy for human life and all
that surrounds it. Yet none was more aware than he of how
superficial the pleasant living of the Roman had become. *In
cordibus aruerat*, Gregory the Great would later say—it had lost
its roots in the souls of men. Even before the barbarians
became a serious threat, this withering had begun: the religion
and patriotism which had been the basis of society had almost
disappeared. The middle classes in Africa, as in Italy, were
crushed by overwhelming taxation while the great city populations were kept contented by free shows and doles of bread,
oil and other necessities—sometimes even of money.

The old City State had drawn its people into a unity; they
were conscious of a common life and aim, of solidarity; religion
and patriotism were a shared experience. But, by the time of
the later Empire, religion (except among the Jews and Christians) was a solitary adventure for the few that chose to seek it.
Most men had become sheer materialists. Since joy was lost,
they grimly pursued pleasure. "They do not trouble," says
Augustine in *The City of God*, "about the moral degradation of
the Empire, all they ask is that it should be prosperous and
secure . . . Let there be plenty of public prostitutes . . . Let
there be gorgeous palaces and sumptuous banquets . . . Let the
noise of dancing be heard everywhere, let the theatres resound
with lewd merriment and with every kind of cruel and vicious
pleasure . . ."

All great men have first to be men. Augustine's completeness
as a man dominates the mind at a first reading of the *Confessions*
and is deepened at each fresh reading. He had everything:
vast intellectual curiosity, philosophic power, human passions
for love and friendship, imagination and, what goes with it, a
wide tolerance of minds unlike his own. Even in boyhood,
though often needing to be beaten to his lessons, he had begun
to think. Child of a pagan father and a Christian mother, he
begged during an illness for baptism and it was about to be
given him; "but I made a sudden recovery. This caused my
baptismal cleansing to be postponed: for it was argued that if
I lived I should inevitably fall again into the filth of sin: and
after baptism the guilt of sin's defilement would be in itself
graver and put the soul in graver peril". Against this Augustine

protests, "In the matter of the body's health we do not say: 'Let him be wounded worse, he is not yet cured.' It would have been far better had I been made whole at once." Confessing the sins of his childhood, he yet gives us a pleasant picture of the boy he was. "In my small thoughts upon small matters I had come to delight in the truth. I hated to be wrong, had a vigorous memory, was well trained in speech, delighted in friendship, shunned pain, meanness and ignorance. In so small a creature was not all this admirable and reason for praise? Yet all these were the gifts of my God, for I did not give them to myself. All these were good and all these were I . . . But in this lay my sin: that I sought pleasure, nobility, and truth not in God but in the beings He had created, myself and others."

Physical manhood comes early in Africa and before he was sixteen Augustine had begun the life he was later so deeply to lament. A year of idleness, while his parents were saving the money to send him to Carthage for higher studies, was his undoing. They had immense ambition for him, and he relates how even his mother, Monica, later a saint, allowed that ambition to influence her. "She had urged me to chastity", he says, but "she did not want me married, because she feared that a wife might be a hindrance to my prospects".

He went to Carthage where he became "a leader in the School of Rhetoric, enjoyed this high station and was arrogant and swollen with importance". Here too "a cauldron of illicit loves leaped and boiled about me. I was not yet in love, but I was in love with love".

But at Carthage also came an impulse to something higher: reading the *Hortensius* of Cicero, he felt an intense desire to devote himself to philosophy—understood in its true meaning as love of wisdom and hence of the God who is all Wisdom. He began to read the Scriptures but "was repelled by their simplicity". He derided "God's holy servants and prophets. And I gained nothing by mocking them except that I should myself be mocked by You. Gradually and inevitably I was drawn to accept every kind of nonsense".

This is how Augustine describes his adoption of the creed of the Manichees, which held him for so many years, and indeed the details he gives of it do make it seem incredible that a man of his intellectual powers should have lived so long in that weird world of Aeons and Elements, light particles and the rest. He confesses two chief reasons. Very few men have ever possessed at once so powerful a mind and such strong physical passions. In the school of Mani Augustine could continue to indulge the lust against which he ought as a Catholic to struggle constantly. Intellectually too, he had immense difficulty in conceiving of God as pure spirit. This kept him back from the Christian conception of infinite Godhead, nor was he helped at all by the Catholics he talked to—until, years later, he met St. Ambrose.

The Manichees believed in two principles of creation, one good, one evil. Aeons of light on the one side fight with demons on the other. Men can co-operate with either. All use of matter is bad, above all the act of generation. But only the small number of the Elect can refrain from sensual acts. The others, called Hearers, "were urged to virtue, but if they fell into sin they had the consolation of knowing that these sins were something they were not responsible for but the acts of a foreign power working in them".[1]

Augustine embraced this teaching of Mani with all its other complexities, too many and elaborate to detail in a short sketch. At eighteen he returned to Tagaste, where he taught rhetoric and where he also took a mistress. He lived with her for fifteen years. They had one son, called Adeodatus, whom he deeply loved.

I wonder whether Monica took pleasure in her grandson. I think she must, even if a mixed pleasure, for she was an intensely feminine woman. Her husband Patricius was now dead—he died a Catholic—and Monica's ambitions for Augustine had been lifted on to a more supernatural level. To see her son a Catholic Christian before she died was her chief longing. To this end she prayed and wept and ran around consulting bishops. Her chief confidant gave her an answer that has echoed through the ages and to which she listened "as if it had sounded from heaven". But Augustine tells us that the bishop who gave it did so "losing patience" with the widow's importunity. "Go your way", he said, implying a desire to be let alone, for she had been beseeching him to argue

[1] See the foreword to F. J. Sheed's translation of *The Confessions of St. Augustine*, London, 1944.

with Augustine. "It is impossible that the son of these tears should perish."

Monica in these years is immensely touching. Over-anxiety had the usual devastating effect on her judgement and her tact. Augustine, wanting to leave Carthage for Rome, had to steal away secretly. From Rome he went to Milan where through the offices of Symmachus, devotee of the gods and opponent of St. Ambrose, he had obtained a professorship, and there Monica joined him. When Augustine told her that though not yet a Catholic he was no longer a Manichee, Monica's confidence grew stronger. But she was still asking too little of God. No vision of the future bishop seems to have crossed her mind; she prayed much for him to make a good marriage. And curiously enough, Augustine tells us that she wished him first married and *then* cleansed in the waters of baptism. She seems almost to have felt he must first be made respectable, then sanctified. Marriage was still thought of by both as a help to worldly advancement. "I was all hot", he says, "for honours, money, marriage."

This may be part of the answer to the question why no one even considered his marrying the mistress he loved, who had given him a child and been faithful to him for fifteen years. But it is certainly only a part. He agonised over the separation just as she did—she was, he says, torn from his side, and he deeply admired her greatness of soul in vowing she would never know another man. But Augustine, so ready to abase himself in the *Confessions*, never suggests that any wrong had been done to her. There must have been some reason unknown to us making marriage between him and his mistress impossible. Is it conceivable that she had a legal husband when she first joined her lover and that he was still alive?

Anyhow, Monica chose a wife for Augustine—and, of all incredible things, a girl two years below the legal age for marriage. "I liked her," says Augustine, "and agreed to wait." But his passions proved too strong for him and he very soon took another mistress. Monica must again have wept over the failure of her plan and of her prayers, but again we can hear the words spoken by Augustine to God in reference to leaving her behind in Africa. "You did not do what she was at that moment asking, that You might do the thing she was always asking."

The double action on Augustine's soul cut deep: he felt anguish at parting with the woman he loved; he felt, perhaps, a deeper anguish as he realised how much he was tied in the bonds of the flesh, so that neither grief for his mistress nor anticipation of marriage could set him free. It was becoming less and less an intellectual, more and more a moral, struggle.

Conversion at Milan

At Milan Augustine first saw Ambrose. "I regarded Ambrose", he says, "as a lucky man, by worldly standards, to be held in honour by such important people: only his celibacy seemed to me a heavy burden. I had no means of guessing, and no experience of my own to learn from, what hope he bore with him, what struggles he might have against the temptations that went with his high place, what was his consolation in adversity, and on what joys of Your bread the hidden mouth of his heart fed."

The young African often listened to the Roman patrician as he preached and "would draw aside the veil of mystery and lay open the spiritual meaning. . . . Nothing of what he said struck me as false although I did not as yet know whether what he said was true".

A vivid impression is given in the *Confessions* of his unsuccessful efforts to establish any close contact with the great bishop. Longing to discuss his problems with Ambrose, Augustine frequented the ever-open room, but, "I could not ask of him what I wished as I wished, for I was kept from any face-to-face conversation with him by the throng of men with their own troubles whose infirmities he served . . . The agitation working in me required that he should be fully at leisure if I were to pour it out before him; and I never found him so."

Augustine describes how he and his mother would find Ambrose silently reading and "after we had sat long in silence, unwilling to interrupt a work on which he was so intent, we would depart again".

Sometimes the two men did talk, for Augustine says, "When he saw me he often broke out in praise of Monica . . . congratulating me that I had such a mother, not realising what sort of son she had." But it does not seem that Ambrose guessed at the greatness of the man who sat there day by day, silently imploring an alms for which he could not just stretch out his hand. No doubt the bishop had often been told about brilliant young men in Milan who might become Catholics—but somehow never did; perhaps Augustine's friends were a little too enthusiastic, perhaps the African accent grated on Roman ears, perhaps—indeed, this seems almost certain—Ambrose, preparing his sermons, felt that in them he could go far more effectively to the root of any man's difficulties than in a conversation which must be curtailed because of the needs of the waiting throng.

And it was, in fact, in church that the young African received the help he was seeking. As he listened to the weekly sermon, Augustine learned from St. Ambrose that the Catholic religion was wholly different from what he had imagined. He learned the meaning of God infinite and spiritual, transcendent and immanent, he learned to read the Scriptures rightly. "I was filled with shame," he says, "but joyful too, that I had been barking all these years not against the Catholic faith but against mere figments of carnal imagination."

Augustine was not alone. With him were a group of young men, his friends and disciples, who with him had long been full of worldly ambitions and with him were soon to change. To them came a friend from Africa who told them about "the great groups in the monasteries, and their ways all redolent of You, and the fertile deserts of the wilderness". It was in this life of complete asceticism, not in the half-measure of even a Christian marriage, that Augustine found himself at last. A fierce struggle began within him; "wild in look and troubled in mind", he cried out, "What is wrong with us? The unlearned arise and take heaven by force, and here are we with all our learning, stuck fast in flesh and blood! Is there any shame in following because they have gone before us; would it not be a worse shame not to follow at once?"

Close to tears he rushed out into the garden to be alone with his anguish. There he heard the voice of a child repeating again and again, "Take up and read, take up and read." He wondered in what game children used these words and could remember none.

Damming back the flood of my tears I arose, interpreting
the incident as quite certainly a divine command to open my
book of Scripture . . . I snatched it up, opened it and in
silence read the passage upon which my eyes first fell:
"Not in rioting and drunkenness, not in chambering and
impurities, not in contention and envy, but put ye on the
Lord Jesus Christ and make not provision for the flesh
in its concupiscences." [Rom. xiii. 13.] I had no wish to
read further, and no need. For in that instant, with the
very ending of the sentence, it was as though a light of utter
confidence shone in all my heart, and all the darkness of
uncertainty vanished away. . . .

Then we went in to my mother and told her, to her great
joy. She saw that You had given her more than with all her
pitiful weeping she had ever asked. For You converted me
to Yourself so that I no longer sought a wife nor any of this
world's promises. (*Confessions*, xii, 12.)

In the Lent preceding their baptism, the bishop himself
instructed his catechumens day by day. And on Easter Eve,
24 April, 387, Ambrose baptised Augustine. In the story,
traceable back to the eighth century, that, inspired by the Holy
Ghost, they uttered alternately the verses of the Te Deum, we
have the expression by a later age of all that this occasion held.
It was the greatest moment of Ambrose's bishopric, of Augustine's life—but one wonders which would have been more
surprised to look into the future and see themselves as Doctors
of the Church forever linked in the minds of men.

At least Augustine appreciated to the full "the excellent
steward of God whom I venerate as a father, for in Jesus
Christ he begot me through the Gospel, and through his
ministry I received the washing of regeneration—the blessed
Ambrose, whose grace, constancy, labours, perils for the
Catholic faith, whether in words or in works, I have myself
experienced, and the whole Roman world unhesitatingly
proclaims with me".

The *Dialogues* give a pleasant picture of the next few months.
Monica mothered the whole group of friends, looking after
their bodily needs, praying with them, taking part in their

discussions. She declared that philosophy was not meant for women, but Augustine told her that in loving wisdom she showed herself truly a philosopher. She cared for them, he says, with the serenity of great age. Actually she was fifty-five! Nor does serenity seem quite the right word for her rather restless activity. Once, persuaded to join them, she broke in on their conferences with perpetual demands for explanations. On the occasion of her son's telling her she was a philosopher, she remarked "blande et religiose", "I have never heard you tell such a big lie in your life." The question whether St. Augustine had a sense of humour seems to be solved in the affirmative when he is talking of the mother to whom he was so entirely devoted.

Most of us see mother and son in imagination, not so much in the years of her sorrow or the peaceful months of fulfilment as in that last scene when they rested at Ostia on the road back to Africa. On that day when "they stood leaning in a certain window" mother and son, in an immense elevation of the supernaturalised intellect, glimpsed the beatitude of heaven. How often, even with those utterly beneath the saints, is the moment of a great loss chosen by God to give to His children a swift intuition of eternal joy. A few days later Monica fell ill and died.

MONK AND BISHOP

Augustine continued on his way to Africa and settled at Tagaste, where he founded a monastery. Picturing him as a monk we are drawn to thinking of him as a friend—for great powers of friendship are needed to make a real success of monastic life. "All kinds of things", Augustine says of his early friends, "rejoiced my soul in their company—to talk and laugh and do each other kindnesses; read pleasant books together, pass from lightest jesting to talk of the deepest things and back again; differ without rancour, as a man might differ with himself, and when most rarely dissension arose, find our normal agreement all the sweeter for it; teach each other or learn from each other; be impatient for the return of the absent, and welcome them with joy on their homecoming; these and such-like things, proceeding from our hearts as we gave affection and received it back, and shown by face, by voice, by the eyes, and a thousand other pleasing ways, kindled a flame which fused our very souls and of many made us one." Imagine all this with the light of God upon it and you can fancy St. Augustine as a very happy monk.

His first biographer, Possidius, tells us that with his return "the Catholic Church in Africa began to lift up its head". Men's eyes were upon him: the Bishop of Hippo was an old man and Augustine, unwillingly ordained priest in 391, four years after his conversion, was still more unwillingly consecrated as coadjutor bishop in 395. On the death of his superior shortly afterwards he was chosen Bishop of Hippo, and so he remained until his own death in 430. In one of his sermons he tells the story of how it all began:

> So much did I dread being made a bishop that when I found that God's servants were talking seriously about the reputation I had made I was careful not to go to places where I knew there was no bishop . . . but I came to this city to see a friend whom I thought I could win over to God's service and who might perhaps enter our monastery. I felt quite safe since a bishop was in occupation of the see. But I was caught and made a priest, and once that step had been taken I was made a bishop.

He shed tears as he thought of his broken solitude, his lost leisure. He had been in the habit of reading almost daily half a book of Virgil; the Classics must go. How much time would there be for philosophy or even for Scripture? "My ecclesiastical preoccupations", he wrote to St. Jerome, "completely keep me from any other study than what is needed for the instruction of my flock." And again, "Morning and evening", he says, "I am eaten up with other men's affairs."

To Paulinus of Nola, who had written in wild excitement over the rumour of his consecration, Augustine answered, "I cannot bear it calmly, for if I did no one could calmly bear me. What has happened to me is marvellous but true." And in a sermon on the office of a bishop he told his flock, "I want to rejoice in you, not to be puffed up by your praise."

This at least he was determined to avoid, and it was one of

his reasons for writing the *Confessions*. To a friend who had
asked for a copy he replied: "Here is a portrait of me which
will prevent you from over-praising me ... He made us, not we
ourselves; rather had we made shipwreck of ourselves, had not
He who made us re-made us . . . pray for me that I fail not
but may be brought to perfection . . . pray, my son, pray . . .
you will be robbing me of a very great help if you do not."

Augustine, as a bishop, did not give up community life, and
Possidius gives a few details of his daily habits. He dined at
eleven (the usual hour in fourth-century Africa), except on
fast days, when the first meal of the day was taken at three.
Visitors were frequent and the food was plentiful. But the
amount of wine for each person was strictly limited and anyone
who swore was docked of one cup. Swearing had been one of
Augustine's own bad habits, and drunkenness was, as he
repeatedly reminds his congregations, a distinctly African vice.
But above all he was strict about charity. Over the table
was inscribed,

> *Quisquis amat dictis absentem rodere vitam*
> *Hanc mensam indignam noverit esse sibi.*[1]

Once when malicious gossip began, Augustine rose and said,
"That inscription must be rubbed out or I leave the room."

Although, as bishop, Augustine was obliged to receive guests,
he would not allow his monks to dine out and he urged, though
he did not compel, his secular clergy to live, like himself, a life
of poverty. He had given up his patrimony and would never
accept a legacy. At a time of scarcity he imitated St. Ambrose
and melted down the church plate to sell for the poor.

It is noted as unusual that Augustine had been empowered to
preach while only a priest. Preaching was the bishop's office.
Reversing modern custom, he sat while the audience stood.
But they by no means stood still or silent; they moved, they
applauded, they interrupted. "I am glad you shouted,"
Augustine told them when they acclaimed a text, "for it shows
you know the Scriptures." And again: "Your applause shows
that you understood." And another time: "I see by your

[1] "Whoever wants to backbite an absent person should know that this table is
not the right place for him."

acclaim that you have run ahead of me. Your shouts show
you know what I am going to say." If moved by the preacher's
words, they would beat their breasts; they might draw attention
to some distinguished visitor; they showed when they wanted
more of the sermon or if they were getting too much. "I
have wearied some of you; I can see that. But some of you
think I have ended too soon; I can see that too. Let the
weaker listeners forgive the stronger and the stronger pray for
the weaker."

The demonstrations of his people Augustine not merely
tolerated but encouraged. He would ply them with questions
to test their grasp of what he had said. He would ask them to
pray for light that he might expound the subject well, sometimes he would ask their opinion: "If any among you has a
better interpretation, then let him teach me." Expounding a
long psalm, he breaks off saying, "Go out and take some
refreshment, not for your spirits which appear tireless, but go
out and give some little refreshment to your bodies; and when
you are refreshed, then come back to your real food."

"When I approached this subject", he says, preaching on
the Holy Trinity, "I was filled with fear. Yet I see you
listening with deep attention . . . you not only understand what
I am saying but even anticipate what I am going to say.
Thanks be to God."

Scripture was the supreme source of Augustine's preaching.
"I meditate", he says, "on the Law of God, not indeed day
and night like the Psalmist, but during the brief moments I
can snatch; and lest I forget the ideas that come to me I pin
them down with my pen." It was the ideas that mattered;
eloquence was secondary. "What is the use of a golden key
if it will not open the door?" "Just as the soul is of more
importance than the body, so are ideas more important than
words."

But Augustine was an orator: once the ideas were thought
out the words would flow. Probably few men have ever had a
happier gift of phrasing. Like Chesterton's, his very puns (and
he was fond of punning) are fraught with meaning. *Petrus
flevit amare quia novit amare* is lost as a pun in English, but the
bitter weeping that sprang from the deeps of love can be
heard in any language. And again *Milites non militia sed malitia*

prohibet benefacere—"Not military life but malice stops soldiers from doing good."

He was insistent that the lectors should be well trained and should take real trouble to give out the lessons—*pronunciare*—and on these readings the sermons were usually based; they, too, were part of the liturgy; together with the Holy Eucharist they were "the Lord's table; he who ministers there has no right to defraud the guests".

CONTROVERSIES

The life of a fourth-century bishop was, as we have seen with Basil and Ambrose, no narrow one. Besides feeding his flock with the sacraments and the word of God, he was responsible for a vast economy of charity, he was expected to hear and to judge civil cases in the courts, he was the arbiter of conscience of great multitudes.

Augustine aimed at even more; he was Bishop of Hippo, not of the Catholics only, but of heretics and pagans. It was his business to win them to the Faith. So to his sermons he added public debates with Manichees and Donatists, which were listened to by immense audiences. This popular practice was strictly regulated: a challenge was sent out to the chosen adversary and a chairman selected. An equal number of reporters represented each side. Stenography was so skilful among the ancients that not only the speeches, but the questions, interruptions and reactions of the crowd, were all recorded. When the reports had been compared and fair copies made, both speakers would sign them as correct.

These debates called for great alertness of mind. Augustine tells us how once, when his opponent produced a document he had not heard of, Alypius prompted him, reading rapidly over his shoulder. But in general Augustine was more than ready, not only by his powers of mind, but by the vast resources of his memory and his ready wit. One of his opponents complained bitterly of "the clatter of his endless, pointless questions". But to others these appeared very pointed indeed, and his minute knowledge of the Bible, his experience in the courts, his close accuracy, made him a formidable opponent. These debates became spectacles, bringing the civil authorities as well as the heads of the dissident Churches and an ever-growing audience.

A risk for a less skilled speaker, these encounters paid enormously. Felix, a prominent priest of the Manichees, after five days of debate declared himself not merely conquered but convinced of the falsity of his position. In the supreme debate with the Donatists held at Carthage in 405—the report of which still exists—Augustine spoke sixty times. And on these occasions, even when he did not convince his debating opponents, he strengthened his friends, persuaded a large mass of waverers, and converted other Donatists in the audience. On this occasion Marcellinus, chosen by the Emperor to preside, closed the debate by a solemn condemnation of Donatism which was followed by edicts of proscription.

Augustine, unlike Jerome, had the utmost intellectual consideration for his opponents. Only such consideration could have made a man of Felix's standing throw in his hand as he did; Augustine made friends with men while combating their opinions. "Do not imagine," he once said, "that heresies are the product of little minds; it takes a big mind to make a heresy." And he respected big minds. But he said, too, "A heresy is a schism grown old." For this heresy had started as a schism. A universal Church, said Augustine, could neither be a Church of the pure alone nor of Africans alone—but as he showed this, he won men instead of alienating them. But if we imagine Augustine filled with horror at the action of the Emperor's representative in proscribing the Donatists, we find we are wrong.

He had begun his bishopric with an ideal of total toleration, but he came to think that with the Donatists (constantly referred to as a murderous and lawless sect) some measure of repression was reasonable. As De Labriolle has pointed out, this conclusion fell far short of what the Middle Ages made of it. Their deductions, he believes, would have horrified Augustine; but undoubtedly he did become convinced, against his earlier judgement, that mass conversions, worth having, resulted from the action of the State. Was it perhaps that the leaders of the sect had terrorised populations which were only too glad of an excuse to escape them? "Formerly", he wrote to the Donatist Vincentius, "it was my conviction

that no one should be brought by force into the unity of Christ;
we should act through the word, fight by argument, conquer by
reason. Otherwise we should have false Catholics with us
instead of honest heretics against us." Facts had changed this
conviction. His native town, Tagaste, formerly wholly Donatist, had, from fear of the imperial laws, become totally Catholic: "Now it is so hostile to your sect of hatred and death that
it seems to have been always alienated against it." And the
same had happened in many another town.

The two great heresies with which Augustine had to contend
led to another element in his speaking and his writing, which
we today find a little difficult to understand. Much time as
he had devoted to Donatism, Augustine needed both more
time and more mind for two heresies as important and as
different as Manicheism and Pelagianism. In the comparisons
sometimes made between him and St. Thomas this element of
time is seldom stressed. Yet it is immensely important. True,
St. Thomas died young, but while he lived he could, in the
quiet of the cloister, devote his whole mind, for the whole of
every day, to God and theology. St. Augustine had to legislate,
to preach, to dispute, to guide his flock to heaven, to deal with
statesmen and soldiers, to carry on a vast correspondence. His
health was bad: he suffered from bronchitis and had sometimes
to beg his lively audience to remember the weakness of his
voice. He suffered from insomnia—and often dictated letters
half through the night.

De Labriolle has listed the works of St. Augustine, written
against all these obstacles, which still remain to us; there are
119 of them, besides many hundreds of letters. And if some are
mere pamphlets there are also books: *De Trinitate*, which is long,
The City of God, which is very long. Both these were written
over a period of years, as and when he could find leisure.
Others were put out in preparation for a debate—men need
not come to hear him with vacant minds, but with some
knowledge of the subject under discussion.

But when we come to the specific answers given to the
Manichee and the Pelagian, we find in St. Augustine what
we can only feel to be a contradiction. The Manichee believed
in an evil element in creation, saw man as bound to fate. To

him Augustine preached of creation by a good and loving God, and of man's free will. The Pelagian believed in man's innate goodness and that he could take his first steps towards heaven under his own power. Later grace would come—measured in the proportion of man's merit. To him Augustine preached the Fall, and the utter need of grace.

He had too much experience of his own struggles to doubt his need. "What have you," he cries to man, "that you have not received?" And to God, "Give what Thou commandest and command what Thou wilt." "Draw us to Thyself." All is given, not measured parsimoniously in response to man's puny effort, but poured out beyond all he could desire or hope. Pelagianism was in many ways a noble conception, directed towards good works, pragmatic in its outlook, very Roman in its spirit, acceptable especially to those educated in the school of Stoicism—an exaggerated answer to the equally evil exaggeration of faith without works. But logically it became destructive of the spirit of mysticism, of the whole life of prayer, and above all of the sacraments.

Had this been all that St. Augustine so superbly stressed, we should not have been troubled. And it is comforting to come upon a beautiful passage in *De Trinitate* in which he begs his admirers not to treat his writings as Scripture; they must try to understand and they may do well to criticise.

St. Augustine, perhaps, even more than the other great men we have studied, was deeply concerned with the mind. *Intellectum valde ama*, he wrote to Consentius. God forbid that we should think He does not love that in us by which He has made us capable of knowing Him. To know God was Augustine's most passionate desire—*noverim me noverim te*. And "passionate" is the right word, for he did not believe philosophy or theology to be "a work of the intellect alone"; the end of philosophy is the God of love.

Perhaps the stresses of his life prevented him from bringing together and working out to their conclusions these two lines of thought. One is haunted by the horror of his *massa damnata*. As doctrine has developed the Church has seen it as incompatible with other clear teachings: God's great love, His death for all men and His desire for their salvation; man's free will and hence his responsibility.

Was it Prosper of Aquitaine or was it not rather the great St. Leo himself who wrote, twenty years after Augustine's death, *De Vocatione Omnium Gentium?* Much disputing had gone on not only in the lifetimes of Pelagius and Augustine, but between their followers after their death. The semi-Pelagians had softened down the one, the extreme Augustinians had fathered their interpretations on the other, the people had continued to believe in prayer and in sacramental efficacy which can only be blocked by our own deliberate action. A man in a shower of rain can put up an umbrella, otherwise the rain will wet him.

But not so much this did St. Leo (if he it was) stress as that God's help "under the most varied forms, hidden or visible, is offered to all. If many reject it theirs is the sin. If many receive it this is the result of grace and of their own will".

"The City of God"

Next to the *Confessions*, St. Augustine's best-known work is *The City of God*. The occasion for the writing of it was the sack of Rome in 410. St. Jerome's letters bring home to us the fearful effect of this event on the imagination of the Roman world. Rome, the Eternal City, was in the hands of the barbarian Goths who had been paid to fight her battles. Again the cry was raised that the wrath of the gods was roused against a people who had forsaken them. Christianity, pagan Rome cried and the pagans of the provinces cried with it, was destroying the Empire.

St. Augustine began at once to answer them; the completing of the answer took him thirteen years, but he published the separate books as he went along, which is probably one of the reasons for the many repetitions, another being the difficulty in finding time, in gathering his thoughts together amid the pressure of his life. He was at the same time writing *De Trinitate*, in which one seems to feel his relief in turning from the confused world men had made for themselves to the Creator of the "city that hath foundations whose builder and maker is God".

These words from the Epistle to the Hebrews mirror the most conscious of Augustine's inspirations in his task. ". . . That most glorious society and celestial city of God's faithful," he begins the first book, "which is partly seated in the course of

these declining times, wherein 'he that liveth by faith' is a
pilgrim among the wicked; and partly in that solid state of
eternity, which as yet the other part doth patiently expect."

But Augustine had, too, another inspiration, and of all his
books this is the one which most fully warrants the statement
"His conversion was the conversion of an age". He had been
educated in Platonism, and the thought of an ideal city "laid
up in heaven as a pattern" is found in Plato, and echoed by
Marcus Aurelius. "The poet saith, Dear city of Cecrops. Will
you not say, Dear city of God?" Clement of Alexandria, also
educated in the school of Platonism, pictured an archetype
and ideal of human cities where man should enjoy a social life
resting on righteousness. But Versfeld, in his brilliant *Guide
to the City of God*, sees truly that it was not in the Alexandrians
but in Augustine that the conversion of a culture took place;
if that conversion may be seen embodied in one man he was the
man, the *City of God* the book. "Philosophy," Versfeld continues, "required a new substance to express, faith sought to
find expression in new languages and new ways of elaboration."

The *City of God* came next to the Bible for the medieval
world. In the libraries of Europe there are more than five
hundred handwritten copies of it, sixty-two of them illuminated
and illustrated. Between 1467 and 1495, printing being in its
infancy, twenty-four editions appeared. It was, says Sir Ernest
Barker, "a philosophy of history in answer to pagan murmur-
ings . . . a justification of the whole *philosophia Christi* in answer
to the human philosophy of the ancient world". Yet it was,
too, the bridge so greatly needed between old and new.

The *City of God* is heavy going to the modern reader. The
Confessions is the most modern of books, for it deals with a man's
soul, but all who have taught the *City of God* to students recognise the difficulty arising from the immense change in our modes
of thought. Reading it is, in fact, rather like reading the Old
Testament. Barker suggests "steeping" oneself in a single book,
Versfeld suggests starting a first reading at Book IX. I think
myself it is best to start at the beginning and plough on, marking
the magnificent phrases and passages that occur here and there
and returning to them for further meditation. Augustine is
more like Clement than like Newman in the frankness of the
glimpses he gives us at the world of temple prostitutes and

sodomites, the "anointed heads, painted faces, relaxed bodies and lascivious paces up and down the streets of Carthage", of the "timbrels, turrets, eunuchs, ravings and symbols" of the Mother Goddess. In general some light relief is afforded to the modern man by the descriptions of the ways of the gods that diversify the great Augustinian justification of the ways of God.

"Let this city of God remember", we read (bk. i, ch. xxxlv), "that even among her enemies, there are some concealed that shall one day be her citizens: nor let her think it a fruitless labour to bear their hate until she hears their confession; as she hath also (as long as she is in the pilgrimage of this world) some that are partakers of the same sacraments with her that shall not be partakers of the saints' glories with her, who are partly known and partly unknown."

This important passage gives us a clue to one of the difficulties in understanding the book. The two cities, says Augustine (bk. xi, ch. i), "in this world lie confusedly together", and yet he seems in other places to be identifying the city of God with the Church, the human city with the Empire. "Glorious things", he quotes, "are spoken of thee, thou city of God", and "the Most High has sanctified His tabernacle, God is in the midst of it unmoved". He continues: "These testimonies and thousands more teach us that there is a city of God whereof His inspired love makes us desire to be members . . . And the only sure, plain and infallible highway is this Mediator, God and Man: God our journey's end, and Man, our way unto it." (xi. i.)

In Augustine's eyes the perfection of the city is in heaven; angels are its inhabitants as well as men. Here on earth we have its beginnings. There is a fight between good and evil, led by good angels and bad, "the one inflamed with God's love, the other blown big with self love". For two loves build two cities. The *civitas Dei*, opposed to the *civitas terrena*, is indeed partly mixed on earth, but there is a general trend: in Hebrew history we see a progressive building of the *civitas Dei*, in Roman history a rooting of the *civitas terrena*. So, too, with the Church: the *civitas Dei* is not perfected till after the Resurrection, but is in the building, despite man's sins.

The position of the barbarians within the Empire had entered upon a new phase with the gradual establishment of regular kingdoms under Roman lordship. First the grant of lands, then the more regular structure of barbarian settlements, were based on the old Roman principle called *hospitalitas*—the quartering of the army on reluctant citizens. The owner had to give one-third (usually) of his produce to these guests. "Transactions," says Bury, "which virtually meant the surrender of provinces to invaders were, in their immediate aspect, merely the application of an old Roman principle, adapted indeed to changed conditions. Thus the process of the dismemberment of the Empire was eased; the transition to an entirely new order of things was masked; a system of federate states within the Empire prepared the way for the system of independent states which was to replace the Empire. The change was not accomplished without much violence and even continuous warfare; but it was not cataclysmic."[1]

While this is true from the point of view of the Empire's constitution, the raids from without and the rebellions within must have appeared utterly catastrophic to anyone living through them. No man has ever paid homage more powerfully to the value of thought than Augustine as he continued to preach, to discuss and to write his great philosophy of history, not in the tranquillity of order but in the midst of barbarian invasions and the manifest destruction of civilisation. But in the spring of 428 the Vandals crossed the straits of Gibraltar and poured into Africa. Although they, like the Goths, were often employed in the Roman army, they did not enter Africa as *foederati*. In Spain, indeed, a grant of land had been made to them; they owed military service to the Empire. But the Roman commander Boniface treacherously invited their support in a rebellion, and they were brought by him to Africa as enemies intending to conquer this rich province and wrest it away from Rome. As savage as the Huns, Arians by religion, they burnt churches and monasteries, violated cemeteries, tortured the clergy in the hope of obtaining hidden treasure. One bishop was burnt alive, another laid on red-hot plates of iron. No African bishop could reach the Council of Ephesus; clergy, monks and nuns were scattered through the ravaged country which rape, murder, loot, and the destruction of food had made into a desert.

[1] Bury, *Invasion of Europe by the Barbarians*, pp. 110–11.

Three cities were for a time untouched—Carthage, Cirta and Hippo. Augustine was now seventy-four; for almost forty years he had been ministering to the Christian people; he was aware of approaching death. "It was as if," says Newman, "the light of prosperity and peace were fading away from the African Church, as sank the bodily powers of its great earthly ornament and stay."

His fellow bishops appealed to Augustine as to whether they should flee before the foe or remain at their posts; he answered that they should remain unless they could take with them the flock they shepherded. "When the people remain and the ministers flee and the ministration is suspended, what is that but the guilty flight of hirelings, who care not for the sheep?" The escape of Athanasius had been urged as an example— but while he had been the personal object of the persecutor there had been many to take his place at the altar.

"O that there may be a quarrel between God's ministers, *who* are to remain, and *who* is to flee, lest the Church should be deserted whether by all fleeing or all dying."

Boniface had intended to divide Africa between himself and the Vandals, but the horror of them was probably too much for him. He became reconciled with Rome and tried, too late, to repel the foe he had invited. Hippo, filled with panic-stricken fugitives, was under siege in May 430 and Boniface was seeking advice and help from its bishop.

In the third month of the siege Augustine fell ill. Possidius was with him and he has told how he "set himself to write out the special penitential psalms of David, and to place them four by four against the wall, so that as he lay in bed, in the days of his sickness, he could see them. And so he used to read and weep abundantly". Until now, Possidius says, "he had been able to preach the word of God in the Church without intermission, with energy and boldness, with healthy mind and judgement". But now he asked them to leave him alone except for the visits of his doctors or when his food was brought him. "This was strictly attended to and all his time given to prayer." In prayer he died, "while we stood by, beheld, and prayed with him. We took part in the sacrifice to God at his funeral, and so buried him".

After Augustine's death the siege was lifted for a time. But then the Vandals defeated the united Roman armies, took Hippo and burnt it to the ground. When Carthage fell in 439 Italy trembled, Constantinople was uneasy, Rome, Naples and the shores of the Bosphorus were all put into a state of defence. The Mediterranean was no longer a Roman lake. Nor could the menace of Persia be neglected, while on the other confines of the Empire Anglo-Saxon invasions had begun in Britain.

The world was entering into the Dark Ages, but thanks to Augustine and the other Fathers of the Church, both West and East, an immense spiritual renascence had been accomplished before the darkness became total.

The withering of hope and faith in that materialistic civilisation had made men ripe to fall under the barbarian onslaughts; but the work of the Christian intellect made the Church ready even to accept and convert these barbarians. As Christopher Dawson has noted, the giant task had already been accomplished of integrating the classical culture into Christian thought and of developing that thought into a world philosophy able to outlive violence and destruction. *The City of God* was stronger than the Vandals because it was stronger than any City of Man.

XIII: ST. PATRICK

IT was strange that the Empire, which had for so long persecuted the Church, should appear now so closely linked with her fate. Christians could "look up and lift up their heads". The year 431, which seemed to them so late in Church history, seems to us still early. They had from the first been longing for Christ's return on the clouds, and the dissolution of all earthly things was the prelude to this return. But they were very certain that the fall of Rome *would* mean the end of this world and with it the end of the Church's life on earth.

St. Augustine was dead, and with him there almost died the Church in Africa. But that year the Church universal began at Ephesus her great affirmation of Christ's One Person in two natures, from which theology could develop into all the richness of Thomas and Bonaventure. In that same year Palladius, in the following year St. Patrick, landed in Ireland.

St. John in his Gospel often gives us echoes which link the beginning with the end of a story, like notes or chords building up a dominant theme. So can a life's music be planned, so do we find it with St. Patrick in the two writings he has left us. The young boy sold into slavery to a barbarous people sees his own fate repeated when in his old age the children of his spiritual begetting are slain and enslaved—this time by men of his own race. The Irish barbarians have become Christians, the British Christians are the barbarians. He writes to the soldiers of Coroticus; he will not call them his fellow citizens or "fellow citizens of the holy Romans, but fellow citizens of demons . . . gorging themselves with blood, the blood of innocent Christians, whom I in countless numbers begot to God and confirmed in Christ . . . O most lovely and beloved brethren and sons whom I begot in Christ . . . What shall I do for you? . . . Thanks be to God it was as baptised believers that you departed from the world to paradise".

Even more than in the better-known *Confession* do we get in this *Letter* the "feel" of St. Patrick, the realisation of the kind of man he was and of the kind of time in which he was living. Coroticus was the type of Romanised barbarian common in the Empire's decay. He had made himself an ally "of the Scots and apostate Picts". The terms "fratricide" and "parricide" applied to his behaviour show that he was also a Christian; and Patrick demands that the letter be read aloud "in the presence of all the people, yea, in the presence of Coroticus himself so that even though late they may repent . . . and may liberate their baptised women captives so that they may deserve to live to God".

Coroticus "has stained his hands with the blood of the sons of God whom He recently purchased in the ends of the earth". This phrase St. Patrick often uses of Ireland. The *orbis terrarum* was the Roman Empire: Britain was Patrick's home, but Gaul, where he had studied, Italy—where Rome was and the Pope, Father of Christians, and the centre of Empire—had all seemed close at hand and had all been abandoned.

"Was it without God, or according to the flesh, that I came to Ireland? Who compelled me? *I am bound in the Spirit* not to see anyone of my kinsfolk. Is it from me that springs that godly compassion which I exercise towards that nation which once took me captive, and made havoc of the menservants and maidservants of my father's house? I was freeborn according to the flesh; I am born of a father who was a decurion; but I sold my noble rank—nor am I sorry—for the profit of others . . . I am a slave in Christ to a foreign nation for the unspeakable glory of the *eternal life which is in Christ Jesus Our Lord*."[1]

And in the *Confession* he adds that, should he leave Ireland to go to his fatherland and kindred or "as far as Gaul to visit the brethren and to behold the face of the saints of my Lord—God knoweth that I used to desire it exceedingly", he would be guilty in God's sight, for "Christ the Lord commanded me to come and be with them for the remainder of my life".

[1] The Letter, in *Writings and Life of St. Patrick*, ed. Newport J. D. White.

BOYHOOD

How intense a life lay between these two searing experiences.
Patrick seems as a boy to have taken nothing very seriously—
he did not, he says, listen to the priests who were set over him,
he did not know God. All through his writings he laments
his lack of culture (*rusticitas*). He did not have the chance
so many have to repair in youth a boy's neglect of letters. His
father owned a farm and to this farm came raiders who carried
Patrick off to Ireland, where for six years—from his sixteenth to
his twenty-second—he was a swineherd. "I went into captivity
in language [also]," he says. "I have not studied as others have
who . . . have never changed their speech from their infancy . . .
my speech and language is translated into a tongue not my own."

St. Patrick's *Confession* is not an autobiography; it is a
hymn of thanksgiving to God; only those things are told which
seem to Patrick relevant and significant. No dates are mentioned,
very few places or people. His father, he says, had a property
at Bannavem Taburniae, which cannot be identified, but which
was certainly in the fully Romanised part of Britain. His
father, Calpurnius, was a Briton and also a Roman citizen.
He was a small landowner: a minimum of sixteen acres
obliged a man to take the office of decurion and with it responsibility for collecting the imperial taxes. He was also a deacon,
and Patrick's grandfather Potitus was a priest. In some parts
of the Empire and at some periods the holding of Orders
could bring release from municipal burdens; we have no
means of knowing whether Potitus and Calpurnius had this
in mind. Celibacy was not yet obligatory in all parts of the
Church, and we do not know how seriously their religious obli-
gations weighed on the clergy. Anyhow, Patrick's home was
both Christian and cultured—a culture and a Christianity
brought by Rome. "Peaceful folk in Britain in those days",
says Bury, "could have imagined no more terrible disaster than
to be sundered from the Empire: Rome was the symbol of peace
and civilisation and to Rome they passionately clung. The worst
thing they had to dread from year to year was that the Roman
army should be summoned to meet some sudden need in another
province." Like Paul the Asian Jew, Calpurnius the Briton
would have made it his boast, *civis Romanus sum*.

And, however annoying Roman taxes were, Roman arms were increasingly needed for the protection of Britain against three fierce foes—the Picts, the Scots and the Saxons. Calpurnius had experienced the years when all three attacked simultaneously and the Roman general Theodosius came in haste and defeated them all, pursuing the Scots across the sea so that, as the court poet sang, "Icebound Hibernia wept" for the heaps of her slain children. Under Maximus (383) a great part of the army was withdrawn into Gaul and the inroads began again. After his fall five years later the Emperor Theodosius (son of the general) came to Britain's rescue by sending the famous Stilicho, who set the island in a thorough state of defence and brought with his legions a truce of several years. During this truce Magonus Sucatus Patricius—to give him his full title, as the register would state it when he became of citizen's age—was born—probably about 385.

But before that time arrived, another raid had taken place and a band of Irish freebooters had carried off the boy Patrick.

In captivity Patrick found the God he had neglected in his free and happy childhood. "Love of God", he says, "and fear of Him increased more and more and faith grew and the spirit was moved." He would say a hundred prayers by day and nearly as many by night. "And before daybreak I used to be roused to prayer, in snow, in frost and in rain."

Then came the intimation in sleep: "You are soon to return to your native land", and presently, "Your ship is ready", which Patrick obeyed by making his escape and walking the two hundred miles that lay between him and the place where the ship was to be found. A series of minor miracles brought him into safety and liberty.

Preparation for the Apostolate

The next years of Patrick's life present something of a puzzle. They were spent in Europe, mainly in Gaul, apart from a short visit to his kindred in Britain. A "saying" traditionally preserved is, "I had the fear of God as my guide through Gaul and Italy and moreover in the islands which are in the Tyrrhene Sea." And Tirechan says, "He was in one of the islands which is called Aralanensis."

St. Athanasius had visited Gaul as well as Rome and it is
probable that at Trèves he had sowed the first seeds of the
ascetic and monastic life. Anyhow, spontaneously it would
seem and simultaneously, monasteries were springing up and
rules being shaped all over France and north Italy during the
last half of the fourth century. Besides Athanasius there came
from the East Cassian in person and St. Basil through his
writings, spread by St. Ambrose and others. Ambrose himself
built a monastery near Milan and he speaks of little islands off
the Italian coast where the sound of monastic choirs mingled
pleasantly with the sound of the waves. Like deserts, islands
were greatly affected by monks. One marvels, visiting those
of Lerins off Cannes, how the most ascetic community could
grow food enough to live—but perhaps with fish and vegetables
they might be independent of the mainland.

These island monasteries produced men of learning, produced
especially bishops. The founder of the Lerins community,
Honoratus, became Bishop of Arles, where he was succeeded
by his disciples—first Hilarius and then Caesarius. Eucherius
of Lyons, Valerian of Cimiez, Maximus and Faustus of Riez—
the only Briton to be called a Father of the Church—were all
the product of this surprising island, and also the famous
Vincent who gave as the test of a doctrine that it had been
believed *semper, ubique, ab omnibus*.

Was "Aralanensis" Lerins? The presence of the British
Faustus makes it probable, and Patrick's sojourn at Lerins
was long taken for granted in all his biographies. Lately the
identification has been questioned by Père Grosjean and
others, partly on chronological grounds, partly because
another island monastery has been suggested, near Auxerre
at the mouth of the Yonne. This would bring Patrick, on his
first visit to Gaul, under the same master as he had, we know,
on his second: St. Germanus.

"After a few years," the *Confession* tells us, Patrick was again
in Britain, "with my kindred who received me as a son." The
word "as" suggests, though not conclusively, that his own
father was dead and that it was other relatives who urged
upon Patrick that "after the great tribulations I had undergone
I would not depart from them anywhither." He did not want
to; his love of home and kindred shows clearly enough in his

story, and there must have been also a love of the ordered
existence which had followed the horrible years of slavery—
the opportunities of prayer and thought offered by the monastery
or even by the life of normal Roman civilisation. No, it was not
by his own choice that Patrick "sold himself into captivity"
once more.

He had a dream: a man stood by him in the night with a
heap of letters in his hand. "And he gave me one of these,
and I read the beginning of the letter which contained 'the
voice of the Irish'. And as I read . . . I heard the voice of the
folk who were near the wood of Voclut nigh unto the western
sea. And this was the cry: 'We pray thee, holy youth, to come
and again walk among us as before'. I was pierced to the
heart and could read no more; and thereupon I awoke."
(*Confession*, xxiii.)

The subject of the saints and time could make a fascinating
study. They will never waste a minute; time is a gift of God
more precious far than gold. Yet they are never in a hurry:
time belongs to God and not to them—He will show them when
they are ready, when and how they should act. Patrick knew
his dream was a call from God, but he knew equally well that
he could not rush off and convert Ireland by a few mass
meetings. He must be sent with all the authority of the Church
behind him, and to be sent he must be prepared intellectually
as well as spiritually.

A contrast between Western monasticism and that of the
East is seen in the comparative calmness of its controversial
spirit. An abiding enthusiasm for service brought, as we
have seen, many of these monks, in troubled periods, into the
greatest office of the Church's activity—the episcopate.
Earlier than the foundation of Lerins, St. Martin of Tours
had left his hermitage to become a bishop, had founded
monasteries; and when he died two thousand monks followed
him to the grave. And he, like St. Augustine, may be said
to have taken his monastery into the episcopal palace. Basil's
ideal of the monk-bishop was fulfilled in the West perhaps
more perfectly and frequently than in the East.

In these few centuries when the new life of the Christian
Church was mingling with the old life of the Roman Empire,
men from the imperial army and civil services became monks

and bishops; Martin from the army, Ambrose and Germanus from the administration stand out in Italy and Gaul—and Germanus in his turn was the master of Patrick.

For whether Patrick was ever at Lerins or not, we know for certain that he was at Auxerre—under its famous bishop, Germanus. Formerly provincial governor of Gaul, Germanus was, like Ambrose in Milan, forced by the clergy and the people of Auxerre into becoming their bishop. His biographer Constantius speaks as though it all happened quite suddenly: *repente mutatur ex omnibus.* His wife became to him a sister. He gave all his goods to the poor, himself embraced poverty. René Louis points out[1] that the details given by Constantius show a man already inured to extreme austerity. Germanus gave up cheese, vinegar, oil and salt, drank no wine, ate only barley bread which he baked himself, wore the same garment by day and night, sleeping on planks and cinders with his cloak thrown over him. This degree of austerity might suggest that although not a priest he was already a monk before being made bishop—but such transformations were not uncommon in the Church's early centuries. *Quod est difficillimum,* adds Constantius, was that "the most blessed man continued among crowds to lead the life of a solitary, and, living in the world, to dwell in the desert".

He transformed his episcopal dwelling into a religious house. He also established, either earlier or during his episcopate, a monastery on the right bank of the Yonne, to which, as bishop, he frequently retired. There was, says Constantius, a holy rivalry between these two families of his, the bishop, as the leader of a heavenly army, urging them on "that they should vie in zeal, challenging each other to the glory of perfection".

The river monastery, built on ground almost surrounded by water, could, René Louis thinks, be in fact the Aralanensis of Tirechan. I am not skilled enough to follow his derivations from French and Latin place-names. But whether Patrick ever lived at the "island" monastery or not, he would most certainly, like his bishop, have visited it; have made, to use a modern term, retreats in its solitudes. The length of time he spent with Germanus remains a problem. The *Vita Secunda* speaks of

[1] " Le Séjour de Saint Patrice à Auxerre " in *Mélanges d'histoire du moyen âge,* ed. C. E. Perrin.

thirty years—but this figure thirty is perhaps used like *sescenti* in Latin or *trente-six* in colloquial French, merely as meaning a large number. It was perhaps fourteen years.

I have always loved the thought of Patrick at Lerins, and even made pilgrimage to it as the scene of his formation. But the more one studies Germanus the more one comes to feel that his was the chief formative influence on Patrick. Here in Gaul Patrick was far closer to the Roman Thing, Christian and cultural, than he had ever been in Britain—and he was close to it under a man who had passed from the imperial service to that of Christ. Here he was being initiated into the life of a missionary bishop who was at the same time a fervent monk. And surely the later developments of Irish monasticism owed much to the old warrior who made such war on his body, as well as to the eastern influences that, through Athanasius and Cassian, had trickled into Gaul.

No man has ever felt more deeply than Patrick his lack of learning; he insists on it constantly. The monastic life of prayer and manual labour, above all the study of the one book he really did get to know—the Bible—must have filled his days and drawn on all his energies. But of course not all the time was spent in study—there were difficulties to be overcome, men to be persuaded, material to be got together, before he could set out. Bede lists the equipment with which St. Augustine later started for England: sacred vessels and altarcloths, adornments for the churches, relics of the Apostles and martyrs, and a large number of books. Patrick tells us in the *Confession* that many tried to hold him back, feeling him unfitted for the work by his illiteracy. "And I did not quickly", he adds, "recognise the grace that was then in me. Now that seems meet in my eyes which I ought to have done before."

What complicated things was that there were already small groups of Christians in Ireland; it was not a question of a wholly heathen land to be converted. Probably the Christian Irish were asking Rome for a bishop. Germanus had been sent to Britain by Pope Celestine to combat the Pelagian heresy, and Patrick tells us that in Britain a friend had in his absence "fought" for him, Patrick, as the man to be sent to Ireland. This unnamed one had said, "You are to be raised to the rank of a bishop." But the choice fell instead on the deacon Palladius, and Bury, who connects Patrick's rather obscure narrative with this incident, comments on how natural it was that Celestine should have chosen the older, more experienced and more learned man. Palladius had, too, fought successfully in Britain against a subtle heresy which might well be undermining Irish Christianity also.

Three churches, tradition says, were founded by Palladius in Leinster, but he died a year later and Patrick was chosen as his successor. "The Lord", an old Irish saying expressed it, "gave Ireland not to Palladius but to Patrick."

But were there others than Irishmen, Christians from Europe, who then or later raised difficulties more subtle than the opposition of the heathen? The Leyden Glossary speaks of "Huns and Vandals, Goths and Alans, at whose devastation all the learned men on this side of the sea took flight, and in transmarine parts, namely in Ireland and wherever they betook themselves, brought about a very great increase of learning to the inhabitants of those regions". These men would have been, suggests Kenney, contemporaries of Patrick, "well educated in the Latin tongue, who regarded with scorn the illiteracy of the Saint and even questioned the legitimacy of his mission".[1] It is perhaps these men Patrick apostrophises in the *Confession* as "ye lordly rhetoricians". God had exalted him, Patrick, "fool though I be, from the midst of those who seemed to be wise and skilled in the law, and powerful in word and in everything else".

Paradoxically enough, while we are certain of the authenticity of the *Confession*, what it tells us is disputed vehemently. Patrick certainly assumed that those to whom he addressed it knew the background and the general outline of his life. We, alas, do not. I have read the *Confession* many times over—both in Latin and in translation—and I am still at the mercy of the last treatment of it by an expert on the points chiefly in dispute; and especially the question of the dating and surroundings of Patrick's betrayal by his false friend.

The very man who had put his name forward for the episcopate revealed a boyhood sin confided to him by Patrick.

---

[1] Kenney, *Sources of Irish History*, p. 143.

Some scholars hold that this took place before Palladius was chosen, and was a chief reason for the choice. "Fifteen years after" are the words in the *Confession*—and this may mean fifteen years after the sin or fifteen years after the confidence. His elders, Patrick says, urged his sins as well as his illiteracy "against my laborious episcopate"—and while one school of thought declares that the mention of elders proves the early date, the other school holds that after rather than before his toils Patrick would speak of his "laborious episcopate". Then, too, were these "elders" in Britain, in Gaul or in Ireland?[1]

As with the arguments from internal evidence which divide Scripture critics, one scholar will urge that Patrick's tone is far too anguished for the telling of a tale long past. Another will hear in it the voice of an old man for whom the past is more living than the present.

Probably we shall never know. But though the suffering meant much to Patrick the dating of it means very little to us:

. . . Must Thou char the wood ere Thou canst limn with it?

and Patrick was an instrument charred by God for one of His greatest designs.

BISHOP IN IRELAND

The story of St. Patrick's achievement might be told in many different ways. The historian sees it as part of a larger scene; for Patrick succeeded, where all the power of Empire had failed, in integrating lonely and remote Hibernia into the Roman orbit. The fact that Christianity was now the imperial religion doubtless gave it a high authority in the eyes of all the surrounding barbarians; they respected the Empire even when they were fighting it, they went in awe of it even when destroying it. Rome was a name of power long after we, looking back, can see her doom at hand.

Patrick came at the turning point when the Church was just

---

[1] An interesting suggestion is made—very tentatively—by Kenney. In the Annals of Ulster (441) we find "Leo ordained Bishop of Rome and Patrick the bishop approved in the Catholic faith": he suggests this may refer to the attacks on Patrick, thus placing them about nine years after his arrival in Ireland.

beginning to replace the Empire, Rome to be greater as a
spiritual than as a military, commercial or imperial force. But
it was still Rome, and the amazing thing is that it was a Briton
who sealed Ireland as Roman, it was a "deeply ignorant" man
who made the chief means of that sealing a Latin liturgy.
"Church of the Scots, nay of the Romans", a traditional
"saying" of St. Patrick begins. Because he insisted on this the
Irish clergy became part, and an increasingly important part,
of the culture of the Western Church. Because of this Irish
unity with Rome remained unbroken. We have only to compare the story with that of the various Eastern Churches to see
how unity was strengthened. We have only to read the
correspondence of Columbanus with Gregory the Great or
glance at the effect of the Irish monks on Western monasticism
to realise that for many years they were in the forefront of the
Church's culture and learning. British boys, Bede tells us,
were sent to the schools of Ireland to learn the Faith and good
behaviour. Columbanus and his monks put to shame the
Church of France.

Or we can tell the story quite simply as Patrick tells it, as
one of spiritual conquest made by God through Patrick, of
the triumph of Christ over all the forces of evil. The famous
Breastplate utters in poetry what the *Confession* speaks in
prose:[1]

> I arise today:
>> in vast might, invocation of the Trinity,
>> belief in a Threeness;
>> confession of Oneness
>> of the Creator of creation.
>
> I arise today:
>> in the might of Christ's birth and His baptism;
>> in the might of His crucifixion and burial;
>> in the might of His resurrection and ascension;
>> in the might of His descent to the Judgement of Doom.

---

[1] In its present form it is probably ninth century. But "its composition by St.
Patrick is a possibility that should not be rashly dismissed". (Ludwig Bieler,
Works of St. Patrick, p. 67.)

against incantations of false prophets;
against black laws of paganism;
against false laws of heresy;
against deceit of idolatry;
against spells of women and smiths and druids;
against all knowledge that is forbidden the human soul.

He writes in the *Confession*:

I am a debtor exceedingly to God who granted me such
great grace that many peoples through me should be
regenerated to God and afterwards confirmed and that
clergy should everywhere be ordained for them, for a people
newly come to belief which the Lord took from the ends of
the earth . . . they who never had the knowledge of God,
but until now only worshipped idols and abominations—how
has there been lately prepared a people of the Lord and they
are called children of God? Sons and daughters of Scottic
chieftains are seen to become monks and virgins of Christ . . .

He had "baptised many thousands", he had journeyed
"through many perils even to outlying regions beyond which
no man dwelt and where never had anyone come to baptise or
ordain clergy"; even there he had "initiated everything carefully and very gladly" for the salvation of this new people of
God. He had refused gifts lest his ministry should be defamed,
he had bestowed gifts on kings and judges, he had been
plundered and bound with irons and he daily expected "either
slaughter or to be defrauded or unfair attack of some kind".
But through all this Patrick entrusted himself to the hands of
God and to Christ, the Sun of Righteousness, in whose "clear
shining" he expects to rise again. And, he adds, against the
sun-worshippers: "For that sun which we see with our eyes,
by the command of God rises daily for our sakes; but it will
never reign nor will its splendour endure." It was not he,
Patrick the unlearned, whose ignorance had done "whatever
trifling matter I did". Everything had happened "in accordance with God's good pleasure; but judge ye, and let it be
most truly believed that it was the gift of God. And this is my
confession before I die".

Patricius, says Tirechan, *cui Hibernia tota credidit, qui eam pene totam baptizavit*—all Ireland believed in him and he baptised almost all of it. We should like more details about this stupendous achievement.

Two centuries after Patrick's death we are given these details in plenty by his earliest biographers, Muirchu and Tirechan. Even though two centuries is an immense gap they are judged by many of the best authorities to have been drawing on a living and in the main reliable tradition. Bury, Gougaud, MacNeill, Grosjean, accept this tradition wherever contemporary evidence does not contradict it. And it is interesting to realise how much can be squeezed out of the *Confession* and *Letters* themselves by close examination and a feeling for historical detail; MacNeill builds his short *Life*, Bieler his study, almost wholly upon them. But the tradition, even when it begins to grow legendary, helps us immensely to fill in the outline, to make the dry bones live.

It is interesting to note that bishops were included among the manual workers of Patrick's household. "The holy bishop Assicus", says Tirechan, "was Patrick's metal worker, and he made altars and quadrangular book covers. He made patens also . . . and I have seen three . . . And his monks, seeking him, found him where his artificers were working in the mountain valleys."

Three bishops from Gaul came to Ireland to join Patrick, and Tirechan gives an immense list of others ordained by him; the native clergy he was quickly building up. Sons and daughters of chieftains became monks and nuns, as Patrick himself tells us twice. With his own hand, it is said, he wrote out three hundred and sixty-five copies of what early biographers call sometimes an *abigitorium* (late Latin for an alphabet) or abecedary, sometimes *elementa*; perhaps, in fact, a summary of Christian doctrine and rules, one of which he left with his converts in every place.

But in several accounts of a boy adopted by Patrick or brought to him to become a monk, Marrou translates simply, "he baptized him and *gave him an A.B.C.*" St. Patrick is an example of the Church's attitude to education outside the Roman world. Ireland had in many respects a high culture when he came, but not a literary culture. As with pre-Homeric

Greece, her poems were sung, her laws created, long before they came to be written. But the Christian religion demands at least a minimum of literacy. Long before Patrick, the Church had given to Copts and Syrians a native liturgy and the Gospels in their own tongue. Many Greek words are embedded in them, for at that time the central Church was still Greek-speaking. She raised Ethiopian to a written language and also Armenian and Georgian. For all these peoples Christianity created a written culture into which much or little of the old classic culture seeped, much or little of their existing unwritten law and legend. St. Patrick did more. Whether his A.B.C.'s were in Latin or Irish, he both made Ireland learned with a Latin learning and stimulated the creation of written Irish. And the chief reason that his work spread so rapidly seems to have been the monastic structure it took from its earliest beginnings.

Converted Druids often received the tonsure and became monks, the daughters of kings became nuns and probably helped to elevate religious life socially. Brigid would later rule a monastery with a bishop to help her! Not only did every monastery demand its own bishop; the office seems at times to have been merely one of honour. Other bishops were not local but missionary. Apart from the swiftness with which the monastic life came into its own, the story of St. Patrick's Ireland and his "first order of saints" keeps reminding one of the beginning of Christianity itself. Then also bishops were missionary. Then also dedicated women—virgins and widows—had some place in the ecclesiastical order as well as in missionary activities.

Later accounts made St. Patrick the builder of seven hundred churches—which would mean one a fortnight during the whole period of his mission. Others offer the more modest figure of three hundred and sixty-five (the same number as the abecedaries), but probably the least reliable thing in any of these chronicles is the figures: "He read all the ecclesiastical *ordo*", says the writer of the notes to Fiacc's hymn, "in one night, or fifteen days as some declare"—and this is typical of their attitude to numbers.

"Thrice now did Patrick wend across the Shannon into the land of Connaught. Fifty bells and fifty chalices and fifty altar cloths he left in the land of Connaught, each of them in his

Church. Seven years was he preaching to the men of Connaught." This is from the Tripartite Life (probably as late as the eleventh century). By then the Patrick legend was growing and burgeoning. But it grew largely as a picturing and an explanation of a work the variety and vastness of which cried out for explanation and illustration. A missionary today converting a new country writes home for the things he needs; apart from what he may first have brought, Patrick had to create these things as well as the churches and monasteries they furnished.

Imagine the numbers of men and women mobilised all over the country as Patrick drove in his chariot from one chieftain's dwelling to another, sometimes (as he tells us) bribing these petty kings to let him preach the Faith, sometimes winning them over to it, but oftener only their sons and daughters, and then establishing in each area a fully equipped Church. It was a vast creation of art and industry—the bells, the chalices and patens, the writing out, the illuminating and binding of the books, the teaching of new craftsmen, for the household of Patrick could not possibly have been large enough for all the work required. Patrick, as he gave Christianity to Ireland, was creating a new world. One of the reasons we can never think of him as other than an Irishman is the very fact of this creation. Patrick was indeed the first Irishman because he was the creator of Christian Ireland. It is hard to think of any missionary who won such a place in the minds and hearts of his people as Patrick. As monasteries and places of learning grew up all over the country, boys who went there were said to be given by their parents "to God and to Patrick". We can imagine them seeking this new land of spiritual adventure with the prosaic companionship of the cow which was to pay for their schooling. We can still see groups of the beehive huts which so amazingly housed these ascetic scholars, who remembered Patrick's even more austere beginnings. The Hymn of Fiacc declares:

> He sang a hundred psalms every night, to the
> angel's King he was a servant.
> He slept on a bare flagstone then with a
> wet mantle around him.

Patrick preached to the Scots: he suffered much
labour far and wide.

The transgression cast them down
into the great low pit:
Till the apostle came to them: he
went the way of a rushing wind:
He preached for three score years Christ's
cross to the tribes of the Feni;
On Ireland's folks lay darkness: the
tribes worshipped elves:
They believed not the true godhead
of the true Trinity.

He put an end to night, for light
was not consumed with him.
To a year's end bided radiance,
this was a long continued day.

In an eighth-century catalogue of the saints who were the
first fruits of his mission it is written, "They were very holy
and filled with the Holy Spirit. They had only one head,
Christ, and only one chief, Patrick." Some of these primitive
saints, many of those who came later, were also poets. . . .
The last, which is perhaps the truest, way of telling Patrick's
saga, is the way of the poets. We must never forget that
Hibernia was the land which most highly honoured her poets.
For in that country they were entrusted with the making of
the laws as well as of the songs. To some extent it must be
admitted the poets remade Patrick—giving to his childhood,
for instance, the surroundings and incidents proper to a childhood in their own land, making a man essentially gentle
terrify by his dooms. Yet even in these legends, many of them
late, "historical tradition", says Bury, " was also present,
determining and contributing . . . we can detect genuine
details handed down by tradition, and embedded like metallic
particles, in the myth".
And the same men who recked little of numerical disparity
and cared little about dates had keen eyes for the poetic truth
of history. Bury sees this, despite his disbelief in what was for the

poets as well as for Patrick a struggle between spiritual forces. Patrick had come in response to the cry of a people to save the soul of a people. And the first story told by his earliest biographer is an intensely dramatic first scene in the struggle.

Miliucc had been the master of Patrick the slave boy, and Patrick the apostle approached his dwelling with the "gracious purpose" of offering him ransom money and also the gift of faith. But Miliucc, fearing that he would be forced to adopt a religion he hated and become subject to his slave, gathered his goods around him and committed himself to the flames "in the house in which he had lived as king". St. Patrick, as he drew near, saw the blazing pyre and was silent for two or three hours. "And then with sighs and tears and groans . . . he said, 'I know not; God knoweth. As for this king-man who hath committed himself to the flames lest he . . . should serve the everlasting God—I know not, God knoweth;—none of his sons shall sit as king upon the throne of his kingdom'. . . ."

This answer of the dying pagan to the life-giving faith is not the only story where fire bears its part. For St. Patrick celebrating his first Easter in Ireland "kindled a divine fire, very bright and blessed, which as it shone forth at night, was seen by almost all dwellers on the plain".

> And his magicians said to the king, "O King, live for ever. As for this fire . . . unless it be put out on this night on which it has been lighted up, it will not be put out for ever. Moreover, it will overcome all the fires of our religion. And he who has kindled it, and the kingdom that will follow, will overcome both all of us and thee too, and it will draw away all the men of thy kingdom and all kingdoms will yield to it, and He will fill all things and will reign for ever and ever."
>
> When King Laoghaire had heard these things, he was, like Herod of old, sore troubled and all the city of Temoria with him . . .

Echoes of the Gospels, echoes of the Classics, are heard in these stories because life gives out these echoes and poets have an ear for them. The contest between Patrick and the Druids recalls the apocryphal stories of St. Peter and Simon Magus, and is told as a contest between true and false miracles. The druids bring deep snow over the land, but cannot take it away. "And the saint said: 'Thou art able to do evil but not good: I am not of that sort.' Then he blessed the whole plain round about and the snow vanished quicker than a word could be uttered, without any rain or cloud or wind." They brought darkness over the land but only Patrick could bring back the sun. The young Benignus, "one of St. Patrick's lads", contended with the magician in a contest by fire and "as it is told about the Three Children the fire did not touch him at all", while the magician was destroyed by it.

Into their stories the poets who write of him weave many threads of the vast tapestry of Patrick's life and work. Patrick himself becomes a poet as he speaks of God who "created springs in the thirsty land and dry islands in the sea", who "set the stars to serve the greater lights". But he was a teacher also of truths above nature, and the way of his teaching is shown in their stories; and the sheer power of the man as he poured forth the Spirit with whom he was filled.

From the old lists of the bishops of Armagh it seems that Patrick resigned to Benignus, the Irishman, his office as head of the Church of Ireland. For Benignus became bishop in 457 and Patrick died in 461.

The tomb of St. Patrick has been claimed for Glastonbury—did he come home in the end to his own people? We do not know: the *Confession*, whatever its date, was, he tells us, "composed in Ireland"—and God's people there had become more his own than the race which by birth was his. "Let it not happen to me from my God", he cries, "that I should ever part with His people which He purchased in the ends of the earth. I pray God to give me perseverance, and to vouchsafe that I bear Him faithful witness, until my passing hence . . ."

At the beginning of his mission Patrick had striven with the dark spirit of paganism, and the poets telling that story go on to tell another that must have been the crown of his life.

On the mountain now known as Croagh Patrick he had prayed and fasted forty days and nights. And God said to the souls of the saints, not only of the dead and living, but of the still unborn, "Go up, O ye saints, to the mountain which is higher than all the other mountains of the west, and bless the folk of Ireland."

Then the souls mounted, and they flitted around the lofty peak in the form of birds, darkening the air, so great was their multitude. Thus did God give to Patrick a glimpse of the vast fruits of his work.

For the saints of Ireland who came to him in vision were of his own creating.

XIV: ST. LEO THE GREAT

WHAT a century of great men the fourth was: Athanasius, Ambrose, Augustine, Jerome, Chrysostom, Basil, Gregory of Nyssa and he of Nazianzus, the popes Julius and Damasus; the emperor Theodosius. One feels of that time what Chesterton once enunciated as a general principle—that the great man appears when we are all feeling great, when we think we could very well have done without him.

As the fifth century draws on the supply diminishes, but two men stand out of stature as high as any that preceded them. Remote from one another, Patrick was at the limits of the Roman world and Leo the Great at its centre. Both felt the barbarian impact from their boyhood, both clung to the ordered ways of Rome. Both were probably born about ten years before the fourth century ended.

St. Leo may well have witnessed the horrors described by Jerome in the sack of Rome, when children were stabbed to death in their mothers' arms and women tortured. But of his boyhood we know nothing; an acolyte called Leo mentioned in the letters of St. Augustine was sent in 418 from Rome to the Church of Africa. If this was the future Pope nothing could link him more fittingly into the chain of history than to have met Augustine, heard his sermons, drunk in his memories of Ambrose and the Church of Milan, perhaps of Damasus and the Church of Rome.

Under Pope Celestine (422–32) Leo became Archdeacon of the Roman Church. He wrote at this time to Cassian, begging from him a treatise on the Incarnation. Cassian, in his reply, calls Leo "the ornament of the Roman Church and of the divine ministry". There exists also a letter to Leo from St. Cyril, entreating his influence in preventing the Bishop of Jerusalem from assuming the style of Patriarch.

These glimpses are both significant, for Leo had throughout his life two driving ideas and purposes. The lesser of these was the maintenance of order, discipline, tradition. He had, Bishop Gore says in his brilliant little book, a "large and imperial purpose" in the service of the Church—and his sense of law and order was no small part of that purpose.

But Leo's deepest thought was of Revelation—the revealed truth of the Incarnation. He wrote, he meditated constantly, on the Word made flesh. He was the true successor of St. Athanasius in his devotion to this central dogma of the Faith and this devotion affected his attitude to all the heresies he encountered. He hated Arianism because it made Christ less than God: "Whatever is less than God", he said, "cannot be God." He hated Manicheism as a philosophy that held matter essentially evil—and could not therefore come to terms with the Incarnation. How could God take to Himself a material body if matter was evil?

But already the first stirrings were felt of another heresy against Christ's divinity, known as Nestorianism. It will be remembered that a strong effort was made after Nicaea to stop further disputes by insisting on a verbal adherence to the creed there formulated. But, fortunately or unfortunately—according to whether you believe in thought—men's minds simply will not stop working. "No one doctrine can be named", says Newman, "which starts complete at first, and gains nothing afterwards from the investigations of faith and the attacks of heresy. The Church went forth from the old world in haste, as the Israelites from Egypt 'with their dough before it was leavened, their kneading troughs being bound up in their clothes upon their shoulders'."

NESTORIANISM AND THE MOTHER OF GOD

One result of the defeat of Arianism was development in the theology of Our Lady and the saints. "God became man", said Athanasius, "that men might become gods." But Our Lady especially was exalted. Already she had been called *Theotokos* as early as Origen, who spoke of her also as given by Christ to us as our mother in the person of St. John, called the second Eve by the early Fathers, called sinless and ever virgin. Arianism had made Our Lord only a creature, though the chief of creatures—its defeat left, says Newman, a throne empty in heaven. The distance between the God-Man and the highest of creatures is infinite. But there *is* a highest of creatures. And Mary is seen by Catholics as occupying that throne. St. Proclus had called her "God's only bridge to man," St. Fulgentius "the window of heaven because through her God poured the true light upon the world, the heavenly ladder because through her did God descend upon the earth".

"The votaries of Mary", says Newman, "do not exceed the true faith unless the blasphemers of her Son come up to it. The Church of Rome is not idolatrous unless Arianism is orthodoxy."

When Nestorius was made Bishop of Constantinople in 428 he began his rule by a furious drive against the heresies with which the city teemed. He shut the Arian church and persuaded the Emperor to issue an edict against all heresies. He also exchanged letters of communion with the Pope and with St. Cyril of Alexandria.

But Nestorius came from the school of Antioch. Theodore of Mopsuestia, called throughout further Asia, "the great commentator" or "the interpreter", had been his master. This meant both that he abhorred any allegorical interpretation of Scripture and that his theological terminology differed from that of Alexandria, which was almost always the terminology of Rome and the West. Nestorius was soon causing horror, even among his own monks, by preaching against the title Theotokos and saying that Mary was not the mother of God but only of the man Jesus. St. Cyril of Alexandria at once got into action, warning the monks of Egypt and writing urgent letters to the Pope.

The teaching of Nestorius was "the man Jesus is the Temple, the vesture of the Word. God did not die"; "If Mary is called the mother of God she is made a goddess." And, even in a phrase often used by uneducated hecklers today, "A mother cannot bear a son who is older than herself."

Pope Celestine, after careful examination of Nestorius' letters and sermons, wrote a condemnation which he sent to St. Cyril to communicate to him. Unfortunately he did not, as St. Leo so magnificently did, give any indication of what exactly was wrong in the teaching of Nestorius. St. Cyril therefore delayed for several months the delivery of the Pope's decree and drew up in addition twelve anathemas to which he demanded the signature of Nestorius. These anathemas were written in pure Alexandrian phraseology. As formerly with *hypostasis* and *usia*, so now with *physis*, the two schools of Antioch and Alexandria attached different meanings to one word. For Antiochenes, *physis* meant simply nature; for Alexandrians it signified personality or reality. In this matter, despite the "poverty" alleged by Gregory Nazianzen, Latin was clearer than Greek; *natura* would have been unambiguous, but when Cyril spoke of "one incarnate *physis* of God the Word" he appeared to those educated in the school of Antioch to be saying that there was in Christ only one nature—to be reviving with little difference the Apollinarian heresy.

That Nestorius was teaching heresy no theologian could doubt, but even he was asked in the twelve anathemas to deny more than he need, and the way in which the affair was handled lost to the Church many others who were perhaps not heretics at all.

Nestorius demanded a council. The Emperor was sympathetic to him, the Pope agreed, and a council was summoned at Ephesus for Pentecost, June 7th, 431. Cyril and Nestorius both arrived early at Ephesus, but they made no attempt to meet. St. Cyril, of course, knew quite well that the council was intended by the Emperor to be an instrument of condemnation not of Nestorius but of himself. A rabble from Constantinople had come with Nestorius, but the sailors and *parabolani* (a sort of Red Cross worker) of Alexandria were equal to any rabble in their addiction to violence, and there were constant fights in the streets between the two crowds of camp followers.

The Pope had sent legates but they had a long way to come. Over forty of the Asiatic bishops, the chief supporters of Nestorius, were also late, but they had sent messengers explaining their delay and begging the council to await them. In those days of slow travel long waits were inevitable, but despite their pleas and those of the Emperor's representative, Count Candidian, Cyril waited only two weeks and then insisted on opening the council. He assumed his right to do so on account of the Pope's earlier commission to him. But the Pope was now sending legates, so his standing was doubtful. Count Can-

didian, after a final entreaty for delay, was driven from the
building; Nestorius refused to appear in the absence of so many
bishops. He was thrice summoned in vain. Nearly two
hundred bishops were present. They refused to listen to the
protests of the few present who supported Nestorius. The
Nicene formula was read, the first doctrinal letter of Cyril, a
letter from the Pope to Nestorius, and the famous twelve
anathemas. The words of Nestorius were quoted, that he
"would not recognise a God at the breast, a God of two or
three months old".

When the bishops had pronounced the condemnation and
deposition of Nestorius, they had, in the eyes of the Christian
people, affirmed again the glory of Mary. The bishops were
escorted to their lodgings by a joyous crowd carrying torches
and burning incense. The whole town was illuminated to express
the delight of her children in the glory of the Theotokos.

But now the latecomers began to arrive. John of Antioch
led forty-three bishops who, enraged at the refusal to await
them, held a meeting of their own, Count Candidian with
them, and in their turn excommunicated and deposed Cyril
and his chief supporter Memnon, Bishop of Ephesus. Last of
all came the papal legates. More majority meetings were held,
at which they were present, and the condemnation of Nestorius
was confirmed.

When reports of the council reached Theodosius II he
confirmed all three depositions and treated the meetings of the
forty-three as of equal authority with those of the majority. The
supporters of Nestorius rejoiced, those of Cyril were dismayed.

Cyril knew something of the diplomatic approach—he first
gave magnificent presents to those nearest to the Emperor. He
then wrote privately to Dalmatius, a leader of the desert monks,
who issued forth for the first time for forty-eight years from his
monastery. The Emperor had often visited him and he did not
love Nestorius. He now approached the royal palace, surrounded by a vast crowd of monks and acclaimed by the people.
When he left the palace, Cyril's cause was won with Theodosius.

But Cyril learnt something else during the months that
followed. He earnestly desired the peace of the Church and

realised that he must make some concessions. While entreating
the Easterners to accept the deposition of Nestorius, he unob-
trusively dropped the Twelve Anathemas and tried to moderate
his own followers. He approached John of Antioch, and together
they drew up an Act of Union. John further made a profession
of faith which Cyril accepted. Written in Antiochene terminology, it was clearly orthodox, even in the eyes of an Alexandrian.
The Easterners accepted the Theotokos, but the phrase "one
single *physis*" was replaced by "one single Person, union of
two natures"; the principle of interchanging idioms was
accepted. It was Cyril's doctrine but no longer in Cyril's
words.

But the Act of Union came terribly late and the Twelve
Anathemas remained dear to all Alexandrians—remained,
too, inscribed on the records of the Council of Ephesus.

St. Leo, Pope

Athanasius the Deacon had been the glory of Nicaea. He
had returned to Alexandria with the bishop he was shortly
to succeed; he was already intensely occupied with theology.
We do not know if Leo the Deacon was even present at Ephesus.
He was to be the worthy successor of Athanasius, but we meet
him first as diplomat and administrator. The year after
Ephesus Celestine I was succeeded by Sixtus III who still
kept Leo at his side and in all probability looked on him as his
own successor.

The weakness of the central government was both exemplified
and increased by frequent quarrels among its officers, military or
civil. In 440 the Roman commander Aetius quarrelled with
Albinus the Prefect of Gaul. This might have proved a matter
of no importance but might equally have afforded opportunity
to the barbarians outside the Empire for some fresh incursion,
to those inside it for some extension of their power. It was
not uncommon for churchmen to be used on such occasions as
ambassadors. St. Ambrose had twice served the Imperial
Government on embassies to Maximus. Now St. Leo was sent
into Gaul to pacify Aetius, and while he was absent Pope Sixtus
died. No other name was even suggested as his successor.
"For more than forty days", the chronicler Prosper writes,
"the Roman Church was without a bishop, awaiting with

wonderful peace and patience the arrival of the deacon
Leo."

St. Leo does not seem to have felt anything of the reluctance
of an Ambrose or an Augustine; like St. Basil when made
Bishop of Caesarea, he realised calmly his own fitness for the
post. He was not plagued by the powerful imagination with
which St. Augustine might have pictured dramatic possibilities
of his own failure. He had not, as far as we know, had any
fierce battle with his passions. He had not embraced the
monastic life; he had not, on the other hand, embarked on a
worldly career. His seems to have been a character of unusual
poise and balance—the ancient Roman's ideal, on which the
Christian character was harmoniously grafted. In that character he spoke, acknowledging his total dependence upon God
in the task he was accepting. "We are not without hope . . .
because we count not on ourself but on Him who works
in us."

Leo was very much aware of his mission; he had been made
Bishop of Rome, but he saw himself central, like his city and
the basilica of Peter; he was as Peter's successor, "Father of the
Universe and Rome", having a profound spiritual relationship
with all souls, a profound responsibility for their welfare. He
was intensely aware of God, his Father and theirs; two of his
favourite words, *devotio* and *pietas*, express at once the act of
religion looking towards God and of self-sacrificing love looking
towards man. He speaks of almsgiving as *sanctissima oblatio*, it
is something "celebrated" in the likeness of an offering made
to God. "We aid our fellow-servant", he says in a sermon *De
Collectis*, "and the Lord thanks us".

There were already other basilicas in Rome, of which the
Lateran was the greatest and nearest to the Pope's dwelling;
there were already the twenty-six parish churches called
tituli; there were other churches, and Leo himself built at least
one. But St. Peter's was the shrine of the chief Apostle, con-
taining his relics, and as such claimed the Pope's first care. For
the perfect carrying out of worship there, he established a
monastery; for the care of the relics and treasure, he established
a service of guards—called *cubicularii* after the body-guards of
the Emperor. Leo's name has been associated with work on
the growing liturgy, much of which is probably not actually his.

Duchesne thinks that the words in the Canon, "sanctum sacrificium, immaculatam hostiam", were inserted by him. But the real liturgical greatness of St. Leo is seen in his sermons, phrases from which still echo in prayers and hymns on the feasts he loved so much. Thus "Celebrato proximo die quo intemerata virginitas humani generis edidit salvatorem"— "The inviolate virginity of blessed Mary brought forth the Saviour of the human race"—appears in the *Communicantes* of the Midnight Mass of Christmas with *huic mundo* substituted for *humani generis*. And in the Secret of the same Mass is echoed Leo's "in ipsius nos inveniamur natura quem adoramus in nostra". Again at Epiphany the hymn-phrase

Non eripit mortalia
Qui regna dat coelestia

—"He does not grasp at earthly kingdoms who gives us heavenly"—surely echoes Leo's "The Lord seeks no temporal kingdom, who gives one that is heavenly."

The Lenten collects are marked throughout by his thought of Lent as a time not merely of bodily fasting but of the soul's combat with the devil (see especially Ash Wednesday). But above all we can meet St. Leo liturgically in what are perhaps the Breviary's most beautiful lessons of the year—not even excepting those of St. Augustine.

Seeing the teaching of his flock as the great aim, Leo accepted the existent three ways in which this teaching was given—the Bible, the liturgy, the sermon. Liturgy and sermon, beside the kind of teaching special to each, mediated the Bible after their own fashion. There were far longer Scripture readings than today—"the very reading", said St. Leo in a sermon on the Passion, "has become a kind of seeing". The sermon was closely linked with the reading, but in St. Leo's case, even more with the liturgical season and the meaning of the doctrine celebrated. His sermons are all short—some of them very short. It has even been asked whether what we have are only notes. But on a close reading that seems impossible: there is a subdued eloquence, a rhythm growing with the interest of the subject, a perfect phrasing to be found in a written sermon or on the tongue of an orator but very seldom in a notebook. The sermons are short because, like many listeners but not so many preachers, St. Leo preferred short sermons. Milman, in his *History of Latin Christianity*, says that they "singularly contrast with the florid, desultory and often imaginative and impassioned style of Greek preachers. They are brief, simple, severe; without fancy, without metaphysical subtlety, without passion"—to me it seems that the passion *is* there, but strongly controlled.

Into single sentences, reminiscent sometimes of St. Augustine, a wealth of meaning is packed. "Grace not given *gratis* is not grace," he says, answering Pelagius. Against Arius and Nestorius he calls Christ "the Author of His own ancestry". We could not be saved by Him "if the Virgin's Son were not His mother's Creator"; "In His human nature He received what in His divine nature He gave"; and again, "In taking our nature He became the stair up which by Him we can ascend to Him". "The Lord of David became the Son of David"; "In our Lord Jesus Christ were present both true Godhead for the working of miracles and true manhood for the endurance of suffering"; "Holy men did not give crowns, they received them"; "Anyone less than God is not God."

These phrases would stick in men's memory, they have stuck in the memory of the Church. The liturgy grows from one century to another, but the great lines were already there— the only notable alteration in structure being that the Church's year begins now with Advent, began then with Christmas. The winter fast was its end. The great cycles are the same— that of Christmas and that of Easter. Over ninety sermons, certainly authentic, remain to us and many more which claim the name of Leo, for Christmas, Epiphany, Lent, Passiontide, Easter, the patronal feast of St. Peter and the yearly sermons for the collections to aid the poor.

The greatness of God's work made Leo cry out, "What makes it impossible to stay silent is precisely what makes it almost impossible to speak". He wants his hearers to progress in a knowledge that will be everlastingly inexhaustible; but the layman is not to be content to say simply "I believe"; his religious life is to be lived "not by believing only but by understanding".

St. Thomas Aquinas thanked God that he had understood

every page he had ever read, but few men can utter that prayer. St. Leo was aware that Revelation must be explained, if the ordinary Christian is to understand, in words and phrases that are understandable; we must never lose this clue to his life; spiritually, intellectually, even materially, he was father and nourisher of his flock.

Christmas was the keeping of a promise—"At the end of ages was fulfilled what had been planned before time was", ". . . nor did the righteous men of the earlier times ever hope for salvation save in the Lord Jesus Christ". "So believing, we are true Christians, true Israelites, truly adopted into the company of the sons of God." Christ's birth is also ours, for we are His body—"His conception is the origin of the Christian people, Head and body have one same birthday."

In some of the old collections of Leo's sermons, no distinction is made between those for Lent, for Passiontide and for Easter —all are called paschal. And he says in one of them, "We ought rather to honour the Lord's Passover as present than remember it as past". Paschal joy must not be absent from the weeks of preparation; fasting is always linked with worship, meditation and almsgiving; as well as a combat, these weeks are a prolonged retreat for the whole Christian people in which to think about God and our souls and the glory of Christ's victory. "If what you love is beneath you," he tells them, "you will go down to the depths: if above, you will attain the heights," a perfect expansion of Augustine's *amor meus, pondus meum*. We must therefore "strive with a great effort both of body and mind". "None but they who love the world can have peace with it." The Christian's is another world; and of those who deny Our Lord's humanity he says, ". . . although they dare to use the Christian name yet are they repelled by that whole Creation which has Christ for its Head."

Lent was the time when catechumens were receiving instruction—Leo speaks of the many who will, on Easter Eve, become Christ's members. From end to end of the world "thousands of thousands are preparing themselves to be born again in Christ". These sermons are not instructions for catechumens, but they were preached immediately after the Gospel and the unbaptised would still have been present. He may well have been thinking of them in such a phrase as "It

was much to have received a form from Christ, but it is more
to have a substance in Christ".

Churches are adorned for Easter, people rightly wear their
best; should not the Christian soul, living temple of God, adorn
herself? The pious emperors have decreed the opening of the
prisons. All criminals go free (except, remarks the edict,
"those who would destroy the common joy"; this included
blasphemers, adulterers, magicians and homicides). Let not
then the citizen be more strict than his ruler. "Forget your
grievances, forgive your wrongs, let no thought of revenge
remain; that the sacred feast may find us all joyous and clean."

In his sermons Leo does not very often speak of heresies by
name, but is always aware of the doctrine they menace. As
Bishop of Rome he was early called upon to deal with the
problem of the Manichees, a flood of whom were pouring into
Italy from Africa as a result of the Vandal invasion. Leo
seconded the civil authorities, and even urged them on, in
banishing the leaders. In one sermon he attacks the Manichees
by name and even calls it an act of devotion to denounce them.
Much as he hated their doctrinal errors, he had earlier discussed them quite calmly. One philosophy might be countered
by another and a better. But what examination had now un-
covered was the horrible effect already wrought on society by
this heresy. The idea that matter was evil had two opposite
results—severity of life or total depravity. There seems no
trace in St. Augustine's works of what was happening in
Rome—ritual prostitution of a girl of twelve was one apparently
typical incident, confessed to publicly. St. Leo speaks of an
amalgam of "the unholiness of pagans, the blindness of the
Jews after the flesh, the illicit secrets of magic". He warns
bishops throughout the Christian world; he urges his own
people to avoid social relations with Manichees.

These sectaries were a menace to morals and to the stability
of society, more mortal than Attila, but should not the State (it
has been asked) have been left to do its own office while the
Pope concentrated on preaching that truth and purity which
must in each human soul conquer falsity and obscenity?
Bishop Gore speaks of Leo as a man "who could make the See
of Peter take the place of the tottering imperial power . . ."
and we see the State's weakness almost forcing the one strong

man of the period into all the offices that demanded strength. The rulers who had sent him to placate Aetius were calling upon him again as this greater crisis developed, as they would once more when Attila stood before the gates of Rome.

St. Leo and St. Hilary of Arles

St. Hilary of Arles was a man of devouring zeal, with the severity that often goes with it; in some respects like St. Basil, he was more hasty and impulsive than the great bishop-monk of the East. He was a zealous reformer, trained in the rigorist school prevailing in the monasteries of southern Gaul.

In the year 444 there arrived in Rome the Bishop of Vesantio (Besançon), Celidonius, to appeal against his deposition by a synod summoned by Hilary. He had been accused of an un-canonical election—he had been married to a widow, and while still a layman he had inflicted the death penalty. This sometimes inevitable part of the magistrate's duty was a canonical impediment to the reception of Holy Orders. In his letter to the bishops of Gaul, Leo said that he would uphold the verdict were the facts as stated. But as the facts were not established beyond reasonable doubt, Leo decided to reopen the case in the Roman ecclesiastical courts. Hilary walked across the Alps in the midst of winter to be present at the trial. His former verdict was read aloud and he was invited to state his case but, according to Leo, he had nothing "reasonable" to say but "switched over to such speeches as no layman could utter and no priest listen to". And Celidonius, through "the clear answers of witnesses given in his presence, proved that he was unjustly deprived of his bishopric".

At this point it seems Hilary abruptly left the Council. His biographer claims that he had spoken with all due deference to the Pope, had found himself treated as a prisoner under arrest, and felt there was nothing to be done except depart. But, as Jalland points out, the *Vita Hilarii*, written around the end of the century (i.e., more than fifty years later), is definitely a panegyric.

Celidonius was reinstated, but now more complaints began to pour in. Hilary had entered the diocese of Projectus, another bishop of southern Gaul, an old man and dangerously ill at the time. Hilary hastily consecrated a successor, but Projectus did not die and was in his turn appealing to Rome. Hilary was now not even present to state his own case, and the same court that had restored Celidonius decreed that Projectus should be left in possession of his see. In the letter sent by Leo to the bishops of Gaul he does not merely object to the thoroughly uncanonical act of intruding a bishop into a see already occupied; he urges as an even greater objection the fact that Hilary had brought his candidate from a distance and had not allowed the local clergy and laity to select their own bishop. Leo lays down the principle, "he who is to rule all, must be chosen by all".

Hilary had come (the complaint ran) surrounded by an armed guard to force his candidate upon an unwilling Church. Perhaps a guard was needed in the disturbed state of the countryside, but it is not surprising that Leo, in the light of what had happened to Athanasius and others, should be suspicious of such an accompaniment to an episcopal election.

Other complaints came with those of Projectus; a long letter from his flock was signed by many hands. Hilary appears to have been rather free with excommunications—Leo remarks that no Christian should lightly be deprived of Communion, nor should it be done at the will of an enraged bishop. The judge should inflict it unwillingly and with sorrow—for no trivial matter, but only for a grave sin; "the soul for which Christ shed His blood" should not be wounded by such a penalty. And when it *is* justified it should be inflicted only on the sinner himself.

Before touching on this point, Leo indicates the astonishment felt by the people over Hilary's whirlwind progress through their midst.

"He arrived without warning among people who had never heard of him, and was off again at once, making, we are told, journey after journey at racing speed, tearing through remote provinces so pointlessly that he obviously won a reputation not for priestly good sense but for mere swiftness. One letter sent us by the citizens uses the words 'He was gone before we knew he had come' . . . It looked as if Hilary's object was not to consecrate a new bishop but to kill off the sick bishop already there and to keep the new one unaware that he was not validly consecrated." (*Ep. X.*)

Leo lays down that as a result of the twofold intrusion (indeed he seems to suggest there had been more than two sees in question) Hilary is no longer to act as a metropolitan. Vienne is to take the place of Arles as the leading town of the province. Hilary may keep his own bishopric but no longer consecrate others, no longer summon synods. Leo suggests to the Gallic bishops—though not insisting: "si vobis placet" —that should future synodal meetings of more than one province be necessary the approval of the senior bishop be obtained, so long as the privileges of individual metropolitans are not thereby affected.

A detailed account is given by Trevor Jalland,[1] who concludes that "in the interests of peace and unity in the Church as a whole, it is clear that the measures taken by Leo were inevitable", that he had "not only the right but also the duty of intervention". He goes on to point out that in all these politico-ecclesiastical questions Leo "consistently refused to act on expediency rather than on principle". Much later— in the case of Anastasius, Bishop of Thessalonica, who was his own vicar—Leo severely rebuked the exaggerated use made of his position, speaking of it as tyranny. His suffragans are "brothers and fellow bishops whose rights must be respected".

A sidelight on the Hilary story comes from a letter written a few years later by Auxiliaris, prefect of Gaul. He speaks enthusiastically *of* Hilary *to* Hilary and then goes on to mention that he had talked with "the holy Pope Leo. At this point I imagine your temper beginning to rise." And then, after further praise of his humility and other qualities, he adds, "But it upsets people if we say all we think. And Roman ears are humoured by a little politeness: if Your Holiness would condescend to this you would gain a great deal and lose nothing. Do this for me if you will, and banish small clouds by the sunshine of a slightly altered attitude."

Hilary in fact submitted, and Leo wrote of him after his death as "Hilary of holy memory". At the petition of his successor Leo restored to Arles part of its former jurisdiction, without, however, entirely depriving Vienne. The province was divided.

It seems worth while trying to answer the question why there

---

[1] *The Life and Times of St. Leo the Great.*

was for long so strong an inclination, even among professed admirers of St. Leo, to condemn him in the contest with Hilary. Bishop Gore, for instance, speaks of "almost unpardonable ferocity towards the saintly Hilary", "reckless disregard of Gallic rights", and "the irresponsible absolutism of the Roman pontiff"; Dr. Bright, of "hasty injustice and absolutism". Tillemont is quoted on the ease with which the Pope believed the stories brought to him. Yet this is not what the contemporary record suggests.

Part of the answer lies in the unfortunate language used in Leo's letter. A bare statement of the facts would be more impressive than constant criticisms of Hilary's "arrogant statements", "the pride of his mind", "his insolent retorts". And again: "Hilary the invader . . . considered his brother's tardiness in dying as an impediment to his presumptuous plans."

Moreover, Leo's letter to the bishops of Gaul was followed a few months later by an imperial rescript sent to Aetius by Valentinian III, speaking for the West, and Theodosius II for the East. In it they assert strongly the headship of Rome over all other Churches and her claim on their obedience. "What limit can there be to the authority of so great a bishop in the Churches . . . whosoever shall fail to appear when summoned to judgement by the Roman bishop, shall be compelled to present himself by the governor of that province, and those privileges conferred on the Roman Church by our divine parents shall in all respects remain in force."[1]

Such phrases are ill-sounding in Anglican or even Liberal ears, and it is pointed out that Leo was claiming and being accorded a greater authority than earlier popes. But we are mercifully getting a little beyond the stage in which every papal movement or utterance was received with the cry of "papal aggression"—and the equally unintelligent retort of "Protestant prejudice". To prove that from one century to another papal prerogatives increased, popes became more aware of what the Papacy involved, new situations in the Church and in the world required new answers, external events pushed the popes into surprising positions, that some of them, being human, were ambitious and unscrupulous—all this is

[1] Jalland, *Life and Times*, pp. 125-6.

only to say that the Papacy is a living reality in a living human society. The fact of growth alone does not prove its divine origin—but it certainly does not disprove it. And it is today at least seen as possible that, in the words of Newman, "the early condition, and the evidence, of each doctrine respectively, ought consistently to be interpreted by means of that development which was ultimately attained".

The Papacy had been for Newman the main argument against Rome; he had thought of the Pope as Antichrist, he had taken refuge in antiquity from the monstrous growth of papal powers and authority—and in antiquity he found what he was trying to escape; he saw his own face in the mirror of the fourth century—saw that he was a heretic. "Rome stood where she is now." This moment of blinding revelation was followed by years of anguished study, issuing in *The Development of Christian Doctrine*: the one wholly essential book for the understanding of the Church's growth in those first four hundred years, a book which may be said to culminate with the reign of Leo the Great.

Already, writing on the Arians, Newman had become aware of development. No single doctrine had been given by Christ to the Church full-grown; the Holy Ghost was to guide and safeguard the growth of the seed to its flowering and its fruit. But there are conditions of a true development, and he lists seven: preservation of type, continuity of principles, power of assimilation, logical sequence, anticipation of its future, conservative action on its past, chronic vigour. He does not, of course, deal with the Papacy alone. He is concerned with showing how he came to realise that there must *be* development in a living idea. "It is elicited and expanded by trial and battles into perfection and supremacy . . . Its beginnings are no measure of its perfection and its scope . . . In a higher world it is otherwise, but here below to live is to change and to be perfect is to have changed often."

There would always have been for Newman the possibility of a scepticism of the Gibbon sort. "To be deep in history", he said, "is to cease to be a Protestant"—one moves towards scepticism or Catholicism. He found in the Church's story, as all honest enquirers must, much to perplex, much to sadden; God has still to guide a stiff-necked people. But as he studied the early centuries he became increasingly aware of that guidance.

The Church is no merely human thing: she has been entrusted with a divine revelation and is divinely protected so that it should never be lost. "We have no reason to suppose that there is so great a distinction between ourselves and the first generation of Christians, as that they had a living infallible guidance and we have not." "A revelation is not given, if there be no authority to decide what it is that is given." And, "Apostles are the harbingers of Popes."

EUTYCHES AND THE MONOPHYSITES

Foremost in the attack upon Nestorius had been one Eusebius and his friend and ally Eutyches. Eutyches was archimandrite or abbot of a monastery in the suburbs of Constantinople, seventy years old at the time of the Council of Ephesus, and renowned for the austerity of his life. But as time went on Eusebius, now Bishop of Dorylaeum, clearer minded and better educated than Eutyches, began to be uneasy over what his old friend was teaching. It seemed to him that under cover of the attack on Nestorianism, a new heresy was arising.

Eusebius seized the opportunity offered by a synod at Constantinople in 448 to launch an attack on Eutyches, calling him, after the fashion of the age in characterising one's theological opponents, a blasphemer and a madman, and requesting that he be summoned before the synod. Flavian, Patriarch of Constantinople, was deeply shocked. "Your petition astounds us", he said, "when we consider the reputation of the man against whom you bring it." To his suggestion that Eusebius deal privately with Eutyches, Eusebius answered that he had tried repeatedly to warn his old friend and could listen no longer to his blasphemies.

Reluctantly Flavian agreed to summon Eutyches, who twice refused to come—his monastery, he said, was his tomb and he could not leave it; and Eusebius was his personal enemy, attacking him in malice. He would sign the decrees of Nicaea and Ephesus; above all, his faith was scriptural. "After the Incarnation he adored one nature of God made man." Still Flavian was for gentle measures; he talked to the assembly of the return of the lost sheep, he continued to hope that Eutyches would come to the synod in a spirit of repentance for his errors. Still Eutyches, summoned again and again, refused to come. Still Eusebius raged and demanded he be brought by force; compared with Eusebius, said Flavian, "fire was cool".

But it was Eutyches who, as if in pictorial prophecy, came at last to the synod in force: a crowd of monks, soldiers and officers surrounded him—to protect him, he said, from Eusebius.

Eutyches was regarded as a kind of patriarch among monks. His godson Chrysaphius was the Emperor's chamberlain, and his own influence at Court was enormous. His heresy was a reaction from that of Nestorius. Our Lord was indeed truly God, said Eutyches, but there were not in Him two natures. He took St. Cyril's formula "one incarnate *physis* of God the Word"—and he was now using *physis*, not as Cyril had used it, meaning "reality", but as Cyril's opponents had used it, meaning "nature". Christ had not, Eutyches inferred, a human nature like ours, but the divine nature only. Hence came the name of his heresy, Mono-physite, meaning "of one nature".

Dioscorus, successor of Cyril in the See of Alexandria, supported this heresy with all the prestige of the saint's name to strengthen him. Eutyches had from the first accused his opponents of Nestorianism. The Court had supported him, deposing one bishop who had attacked him, ordering another to confine himself in his own city. None knew better than Flavian how small his own influence was with the Emperor compared with that of Eutyches. He had hoped to avoid strife, but he was a man of integrity when the testing came. Taking his life in his hands, he had cited a court favourite to answer to the charge of heresy. The bishops, after cross-questioning Eutyches, deposed him for his refusal to acknowledge two natures in Christ, unfrocked and excommunicated him.

Eutyches appealed to Pope Leo, who at first was disposed to take his part—but not on the hearing of one side only. "Judging", he wrote to Flavian, "by the statement of Eutyches," he did not see with what justice he had been separated from communion with the Church. "Send, therefore", he went on, "some suitable person to give us a full account of what has happened and let us know what the new error is."

Naturally the Pope was puzzled, for in his letter Eutyches had explained how he was asked to use the *words* "two natures"; "But in the light of your decrees I was afraid to add to or detract any word from the faith as set forth by the most holy Council of Nicaea, for I knew that our holy and most blessed Fathers, Julius and Felix and Athanasius and Gregory, holy men and bishops, steered clear of the label 'two natures'. And I did not dare to discourse on the nature of the divine Word, who came into the flesh in the last days in the womb of the Virgin Mary, in the way in which He willed, not lessening Himself nor suffering change, but putting on the real nature of man, not just an apparition; nor did I dare to condemn our Fathers mentioned above. Since, then, these matters were thus being dealt with, I asked that they be brought to your attention so that you might decide what course I ought to follow and I agreed to follow in every detail what you approved of."

He added a condemnation of "Appollinaris, Manes, Valentinus, Nestorius and all heretics back to the time of Simon Magus", and a strong appeal to Leo to save him from being "shipwrecked by rivals now that I am at the very end of my life". Flavian denied later that the offer of submission to the Pope had been made at the synod; the cross-questioning of Eutyches had been taken down *verbatim*. He had handed in a written statement that seemed orthodox enough but in the end he stuck firmly to the denial that there were two natures in Christ.

He admitted a real humanity in Christ, but he would not agree that, once united with the divinity, it was a nature. One sees what his difficulty was. He was not theologically trained. If the whole matter could have been explained to him slowly, patiently, in private, by one single theologian, he *might* have seen that his difficulty was met by the orthodox doctrine. But to have a lot of people questioning him in public—even if some were trying to help him—called for theological equipment and theological skill that he lacked. He simply stuck to his refusal to use the phrase that orthodoxy required.[1]

---

[1] Tixeront thinks that even for Dioscorus the heresy was not really doctrinal but an obstinate refusal to accept the two-natures terminology.

While it was vitally necessary to safeguard every word in the statement of the Faith, one wishes that at this early stage Leo had already had the matter in hand. Flavian was, after all, imposing a new formula: it was required to state an old truth now being attacked, but a merely provincial synod was perhaps not the place for a new formula. Eutyches was stupid, was obstinate, but he did really believe he was holding the faith of St. Cyril and the Fathers. If a letter from St. Leo had been slowly read to the old man—or the catena he later made of passages from the earlier Fathers showing how his words were solely a clarification of theirs—Leo might have prevailed. Yet even then it might have been too late. Eutyches was not the sole source of his ideas (if indeed he had any clear ideas at all). The new doctrine was in the air. By the time the Pope could get to grips with it, it had spread like a forest fire, at first called Eutychianism but taking, as did Arianism, other forms, and other names, drawing away immense masses of Eastern Christians. Victory over this heresy was won at a terribly high price—and this was due largely to the local patriotism of Alexandria, but partly perhaps to the total lack of psychology with which a stupid old monk was handled. He had only, he told the Pope, got away in safety thanks to Leo's prayers and the protection of a bodyguard of soldiers. And he probably believed what he was saying; like modern Europe, he armed himself through fear, and fear would lead in the end to violence.

It was not difficult for Flavian to satisfy the Pope about what the synod had proved—the problem was to satisfy Dioscorus, and the Emperor—in other words his chamberlain, the eunuch Chrysaphius.

Theodosius II annulled the proceedings and agreed to the request of Eutyches that a council be summoned from West as well as East to judge his case. The Emperor invited Leo to be present, but he decided only to send his legates carrying with them full instructions.

St. Leo had few hopes of this council, also held at Ephesus, and it turned out even worse than he had expected. He had sent to Flavian the letter known as his *Tome*, which furnished the phrasing in which a later council would condemn the heresy —but this council did not even read it. Dioscorus presided, officers of the court took charge. The papal legates were ignored; incredibly enough, they knew no Greek, although it must have been obvious that Greek would be the language spoken. A vague profession of faith was made by Eutyches; his accusers were not allowed to speak. The sentences against him were annulled and he went back to his monastery. Pope Leo christened this council the *Latrocinium* or "gang of robbers" and as such it has gone down to history. "Dioscorus", says Newman, "had been attended by a multitude of monks, furious zealots for the Monophysite doctrine from Syria and Egypt, and by an armed force. These broke into the Church at his call; Flavian was thrown down and trampled on and received injuries of which he died the third day after. The Pope's legates escaped as they could; and the bishops were compelled to sign a blank paper, which was afterwards filled up with the condemnation of Flavian . . . The proceedings ended by Dioscorus excommunicating the Pope, and the Emperor issuing an edict in approval of the decision of the Council." But, as Newman points out, the actual members of the Council "certainly did acquit Eutyches". When the acts of the synod were read in which Eusebius had asked him whether he accepted two natures in Christ, "the Fathers broke in upon the reading: 'Away with Eusebius: burn him, burn him alive; cut him in two, as he divided, let him be divided.' The Council seems to have been unanimous, with the exception of the Pope's legates."[1]

In answer to vigorous protests from Leo against this council, "an insult to the Faith, a blow to the entire Church", Theodosius suggested that the East could look after its own affairs without the help of the revered Patriarch of Rome.

The Council of Chalcedon

The sudden death of Theodosius II by a fall from his horse changed the whole picture. His sister Pulcheria and her husband Marcian, who became the rulers, were both real Catholics. Flavian's body was brought back to Constantinople with immense ceremony, all the exiled bishops reinstated. There was a hasty disavowal of their votes by most of the Latrocinium who had, it seemed, all been terrorised. Eutyches

[1] Newman gives in his *Development* a most brilliant description of this scene and a searching analysis of the doctrinal problems involved.

was sent into retirement. But more was needed than a reversal of imperial policy and the hasty change of position easily achieved by a courtier even if he be also a bishop.

"There had been a time", says Newman, "in the history of Christianity when it had been Athanasius against the world and the world against Athanasius. The need and straitness of the Church had been great and one man was raised up for her deliverance. In this second necessity, who was the destined champion of her who cannot fail? Whence did he come and what was his name? He came with an augury of victory upon him which even Athanasius could not show; it was Leo, bishop of Rome."

At Chalcedon (451) more bishops met than had ever before come together, five hundred and twenty. Nor until the Vatican did any subsequent council show so large a number. In his *Tome*, St. Leo had not discussed the arguments used on either side; he had simply set forth in the clearest possible language what the tradition had always held, "what the Catholic Church universally believes and teaches". This teaching is that Our Lord is one Person possessing two natures, the divine and human. These natures are not confused or mixed, but the one Person acts in both, so that, as the Creed states, the only Son of God was crucified, was buried.

When the *Tome* was read the bishops broke out in great enthusiasm crying, "This is the faith of the Fathers; the faith of the Apostles . . . Peter hath spoken through Leo."

The *Tome* is an exciting document revealing in Leo what I can only call a passionately theological love of God. He makes his reader realise, as he did, that theology—knowledge God-given of His divine being—is food, is light: light in which to pray, food by which to live. The *Tome* often falls into the very phrases in which Leo was wont to offer this light and food to his own people in his sermons.

He pours out with sheer delight the poetry of the Incarnation—the littleness of the Almighty—but in the poetry he never forgets the greatness of the mystery which we can only know by knowing theologically what that mystery is.

. . . His life begins like the life of men, whom Herod sought to slay, but He is Lord of all, whom the Magi adored;

and when He came to be baptized by John, the hidden divinity is revealed by the voice from heaven. As man, He is tempted of Satan; as God, He is ministered to by the angels. To hunger, to thirst, to be weary, to sleep—this is evidently of the man; but to feed the five thousand with the five loaves, to give the Samaritan woman the living water, to walk upon the sea, to subdue the tossing waves—this, without controversy, is of the God . . . to lament with pitiful feeling the dead friend, and removing the stone which had hid him four days in the grave, to wake him to life again at the command of His voice—or to hang upon the cross, and to make all the elements tremble, turning day into night—or to be pierced with nails and to open the gates of Paradise—or to say, "I and the Father are one", and "The Father is greater than I".

Yet never must the one Person be lost sight of, the two natures confused.

He, the same Christ, is begotten eternally of the Father and born in time of His Mother, inviolable in His own divine strength, and subject to suffering in our weakness—the same, rich while He is poor, omnipotent while He is outcast, impassible while He is suffering, immortal while He dies; nor was the Word in any part of Himself *converted into flesh or soul*, for the nature of God is simple and un-changeable, remaining entire in His own essence, admitting neither of diminution nor increase. Why should it seem improbable or impossible that the Word and the flesh and the spirit should form one Jesus Christ, and the same should be Son of God and Son of Man, when the flesh and spirit, which are of natures so unlike, apart from any incarnation of the Word, make up one person in man? The Word was not therefore converted into flesh, or the flesh into the Word, but each nature remains in the one Person, and the One in each nature, not sundered by their dis-tinction, nor confused by mixture—not one Christ from the Father, another of the Mother—but one and the same, begotten eternally in one way and born in time in another.

If two natures be denied to Christ, does Eutyches hold, like Apollinaris, that Christ's soul is divine? Or has he fallen into the "Manichean madness" of holding that all His bodily actions are mere appearances? Or else he becomes an Arian— for Christ is said to be exalted and rewarded: if He be God only, this makes the Son less than the Father in His divine nature.

Even children know in the Church of God that they receive the very reality of Christ's body and blood in Communion. "This is what is taken in that mystical distribution of spiritual sustenance, so that receiving the power of the heavenly food, we are transubstantiated into His flesh who was made our flesh."

Above all, on this twofold nature of God the Son, man's redemption depends. How otherwise can He be "a real mediator unless, equal to the Father in the form of God, He shares in our nature too in the form of a servant, so that through one new man, the old should be renewed, and the bond contracted by the fall of one should be loosed by the death of One who alone owed nothing to death? For the shedding of the blood of the Just for the unjust was so powerful in privilege, so rich in value, that if all the captives should believe in their Redeemer, the chains of the tyrant could keep none of them back. Now what hope can they have in the protection of this Sacrament who deny the reality of human nature in the body of our Saviour? By what sacrifice are they reconciled, by what blood redeemed?"[1]

The ease with which so many bishops changed sides is a little startling. There can be no doubt that some of them had really never understood the doctrine before it was expounded to them with such crystal clarity by St. Leo. But there were also many for whom the union of Pope and Emperor was an irresistible argument. Leo far away in Rome they could ignore, Leo backed by Constantinople was a different affair altogether.

But the handful of Egyptian bishops, who cast themselves on the ground after the council, crying out that their people would never endure the deposition of Dioscorus or the abandoning of the doctrinal terms originally used by St. Cyril, did in fact largely represent eastern opinion. They represented in particular immense numbers of monks.

---

[1] I have used the translation of Bishop Gore, in *Leo the Great*, pp. 64–5.

These desert monks of the East, strange successors to St. Anthony, were becoming increasingly the shock troops of heresy and orthodoxy alike. Theodosius I certainly had some reason for his feeling that they swarmed too frequently and smashed things too easily. They seemed ready at any excuse to leave their monasteries—and indeed many of them had no monasteries. After Chalcedon a trouble-making group were investigated in Constantinople by the civil authorities, helped by the superiors of the neighbouring monasteries. Sixteen out of twenty proved to belong nowhere. It was only too easy for men with no vocation to the religious life to win admiration by installing themselves in desert caves. And even in the huge "lauras" and monasteries were many men not really contemplatives at all, and these welcomed any excuse to abandon prayer for activity and excitement. If they are sympathetic figures when entering Antioch to save the townsfolk from punishment, they are less so when pursuing St. John Chrysostom in his exile. The defence of the Faith always gave them a splendid excuse. It was their tradition to support their bishop *en masse*, whether he was Athanasius, Theophilus, Cyril or Dioscorus. Cyril had brought many of them to Ephesus, and had awakened also the sympathy of those of Constantinople, who walked in procession in a great demonstration of orthodoxy and a plea for him to the Emperor. Every convent in the neighbourhood was emptied. In this procession Eutyches had been prominent and at the Robber Council the roles were reversed. Now Dioscorus was leading against the really orthodox party the monks of Alexandria, whose test of orthodoxy was loyalty to their own patriarch. He had with him also a crowd from Mesopotamia and Syria and was backed by all the monks of Palestine. For throughout the East the majority of monks— although most of them with little theological knowledge— were increasingly Monophysite. The Armenian monks had repudiated Cyril and marched in procession against him when he signed the act of union with John of Antioch. Later they repudiated Eutyches because he did not go as far as they did in teaching what they held to be the only truly spiritual view of the Incarnation. To maintain one nature in Christ meant a *real* affirmation of His Godhead, and the utter repudiation of Chalcedon was the hallmark of Monophysite orthodoxy.

Unfortunately, the monks did not confine themselves to processions as an expression of faith. They exhibited the strangest combination of violence and the claim to advanced spirituality. After Chalcedon, especially, they could in many areas be used by troublemakers to an almost unlimited extent. At Jerusalem the ex-empress Eudoxia was only too ready to foment rebellion—especially when directed against the Council of Chalcedon (which was the council of her successor, the Empress Pulcheria). She helped to stir up the monks, many of whom were always to be found in Jerusalem, mostly wanderers from no known monastery, famous only for their fierce asceticism, to repudiate their bishop, Juvenal. By accepting Chalcedon he had, they said, betrayed the Faith. Returning from the council, he found Jerusalem in a ferment; the monks had shut the gates and were mounting guard on the walls. Inside the city the prisons had been thrown open and the criminals let out; murder and arson were the order of the day. Juvenal escaped narrowly but one of his fellow bishops was murdered. The body of a deacon was dragged through the streets.

Eudoxia was, says Duchesne, the soul of the revolt, which spread rapidly through Palestine. Pope Leo in vain wrote her a letter which Duchesne calls a *"chef d'œuvre* of diplomacy", assuming her desire for law and order and that she must be making every effort to bring the monks back to a sense of duty. His words were as futile as the efforts of the Government, which sent troops to quell the rebellion and to bring Juvenal back to his see. The monks marched to meet them, "as it might be the Machabees against the generals of Antiochus". Every attempt to placate or convince them failed; they chose death rather than submission and it was only by military force that Juvenal was brought into Jerusalem and peace more or less restored.

When, much later, there was question of the acceptance at Alexandria of Zeno's *Henoticon* we learn something of the numbers that were involved in some of these terrifying disturbances —for thirty thousand monks gathered in Alexandria to stage a mass demonstration. By this date Gibbon's words receive their justification. The monks of the East, once so powerful in their peaceful holiness, were indeed darkening the face of the earth.

Then, too, while the theological outcome of the Council of Chalcedon was matter for rejoicing, in the realm of church government Leo was not happy about it. For, against the protests of his legates, the imperial See of Constantinople was declared second to Rome, being thus lifted above the great historic and apostolic cities Alexandria and Antioch. Leo refused to ratify the canon; it was another two hundred years before his successors reluctantly consented to accept it. Why did they mind so much?

In Leo's case the first reason was certainly the Tradition; only by absurd fabrications could this new town be called apostolic. But there was also the enormous danger—which later became a reality—of schism. So great a position given to a bishop who was often enough the tool of the Emperor, and who could in any event be exiled or executed if he refused to obey the Emperor, must involve peril to doctrine throughout the East. Emperors had already forced Arianism on vast tracts of the Christian world, had prompted Monophysitism; what could they not do if the power of the see was augmented to match that of the Court? In Antioch and Alexandria men of holiness and learning had always been found to fight the heresies, while the very rivalry of the two sees had often provided a powerful antidote.

The next step might well be an assertion of the supremacy of Constantinople over Rome. As yet no one had dared to utter such a thought; but it seems unlikely that no Emperor, no court prelate, had thought of it, when Rome would not accept as a first duty to the Emperor, as a first principle, imperial infallibility.

GOTHS AND VANDALS

It was well that the West was not, like the East, torn by theological storms. Leo had refused to go himself to Chalcedon largely because of the barbarian menace at his own doors.

Attila the Hun had invaded northern Italy. He had burnt Aquileia to the ground and was driving forward burning and destroying all the cities in his path. The road to Rome lay open before him. Aetius appeared to ignore the danger, at least he was making no move to protect the city. In despair, Valentinian and the Senate decided to try sending an embassy to Attila: two leading senators and the Pope. In the *Liber Pontificalis* it is said that the embassy was Leo's own suggestion. In a story current two hundred years later, St. Peter stood beside him and filled Attila with awe and fear. Thus Raphael has painted the scene. But even if we do not believe this, we can well believe in a spiritual power working on Attila. He was perhaps approaching Rome with some measure of awe; Alaric the Visigoth had sacked the city and had himself died soon afterwards; not only Christian but pagan antiquity had held Rome holy. It was a name of majesty to the barbarians within the imperial orbit. But there was something else.

Not long ago an American Jew visited the Vatican and had an audience with Pope Pius XII. On his return his friends asked him whether he, a Jew, had knelt before the Pope. And he answered, "When I meet a man as holy as that I find kneeling more comfortable." Even as we glance at some few episodes of Leo's life, read some few passages of his works, we become aware of this majesty of holiness and we can well believe that the presence of Leo rather than senatorial arguments turned back the barbarian army at the very gates of the city.

Attila died the next year. But Rome was soon menaced by another barbarian. Though Aetius had failed to stop Attila he was Rome's best hope; but his growing power invited jealousy. He had many rivals, especially when the invaders had withdrawn and it seemed safe to aspire to high office. One of these, Petronius, worked on the weak mind of Valentinian and succeeded in convincing him that Aetius was a traitor. At a private audience, the Emperor slew Aetius with his own hand. It was mad folly, for Petronius himself proved the real traitor. When he was not given the succession to Aetius as *magister utriusque militiae*, he began to plan Valentinian's death. At a military review in the Campus Martius, an assassin hired by Petronius stabbed the Emperor. Petronius now bribed his way to the supreme power, forcing the widow of Valentinian to become his wife.

But within ten weeks the Vandal Genseric had landed in Italy and Petronius, coward as well as traitor, struck not a blow in the defence of Rome and only tried to escape as the Vandals entered the city. He was himself slain by the enraged populace. There was now no emperor, no army, to save Rome from destruction. Again St. Leo came forward; again he confronted the barbarians.

While not as fully successful with Genseric as with Attila, the victory he did win seems almost more remarkable. For Genseric belonged to a race which had a history of almost uniform success in its contests with the power of Rome. The name Rome would raise no awe in the soul of Genseric—and indeed he would not consent to spare its splendours: for fourteen days the city was ransacked of its treasures, many important captives were taken, many buildings damaged.

But the great basilicas kept their treasures, probably in deference to Leo's request, and he won from Genseric a threefold promise which was on the whole kept faithfully. The Vandals were ardent torturers—Genseric promised there should be no torture. He promised there should be no massacre and that no buildings were to be fired.

After the fourteen days Genseric departed with his army, and the *Liber Pontificalis* has much to tell of Leo's work in restoring to the churches all he could of their former splendour.

His last years cannot have been very peaceful. As soon as the Goths in Gaul heard of the sack of Rome and the death of Petronius, they chose a new Augustus—Avitus, who had been appointed by Petronius successor to Aetius. He in turn appointed the Goth Ricimer as his own successor—and this was in fact the beginning of the Gothic kingdom in Italy. Ricimer rapidly became so powerful that he forced Avitus to abdicate and appointed in his place another puppet Emperor, Marjorian. After Marjorian had failed to reconquer Africa from the Vandals Ricimer had him put to death. Had he not been a Goth Ricimer would of course have had himself proclaimed Emperor—as it was, he dared not go higher than the title Patrician. But after the death of Marjorian he made no new Emperor in the West. Leo, the Pope's namesake, became sole Emperor and Ricimer ruled Italy in his name.

Amid all this political whirlpool the western world could see but one fixed spot—the rock of Peter. It is not wonderful if papal authority grew as emperors and generals slew and were

slain, betrayed their people or were betrayed by them. Here
in Rome was a man of perfect integrity, boundless energy and
selfless devotion to God and man.

Leo must have been growing tired but he still preached, still
worked. In one of his sermons he rebukes superstitious practices
lingering on from heathen worship even among his flock; as
men mount the steps of the basilica they turn towards the rising
sun and bow their heads in its honour. In another sermon he
blames those who neglect the Christian celebration of the city's
deliverance. Clearly they were celebrating after another
fashion. Was it the "games", he asks, or the intercession of
the saints, that saved Rome? "Our liberation was not, as the
impious hold, due to the movements of the stars, but to the
unspeakable mercy of almighty God."

Leo asked for gratitude to God but never to himself. He has
been called a cold man, but surely he was only a very reserved
one. There is no trace in his letters of the emotionalism often
to be seen in the other Pope called the Great—Gregory I.
There are few allusions to individuals. But just occasionally
this reserve breaks, and in writing to a bishop who had wanted
to lay down his office Leo tells us a little of the spirit by which
his own life was inspired.

> I am amazed that your beloved self is so much upset . . .
> that you should say that the one thing you want is to be
> set free from the labours of the episcopate and would rather
> pass your life in silence and tranquillity than remain in the
> task entrusted to you . . .

The persecutions, foretold by St. Paul, he goes on, can come
from rebellious subordinates and slander, as well as from
torture and bodily suffering. And how shall thieves and robbers
be resisted if the watchman leaves his post! Leo entreats
him to remain and advises him in what spirit to carry on his
ministry.

> Sins should be hated, not men. The swollen must be
> reduced, the weak borne with, and what must needs be
> punished severely should be treated not in a spirit of revenge
> but of healing.

It is strange that we should know no details about Leo's last days. He died on November 10th, 461. Even the epitaph inscribed upon his grave has perished, but the words of this letter give us the spirit of his whole life and by them we can best remember him. He was the good watchman who would never desert his post from fear of thieves and robbers. He was the good physician who approaches a sick world in the spirit of healing.

"Feed my lambs", Christ said to Peter: "Feed my sheep." Leo believed that he too had received this mandate. His whole life was an ardent obedience.

XV: THE CREATIVE SPIRIT

A World Ends and a World Begins

UNDER the early emperors the population of the Empire
had grown steadily; some sixty million under Augustus,
eighty million under Marcus Aurelius. After that began
a fall which went on without interruption. To take a spectacular
figure, Rome itself had numbered about a million under the
early emperors; in the sixth century its population was about
fifty thousand. St. Benedict foretold that the city would not
perish under the barbarian blows but would wither and die.
As houses day by day decayed and fell, St. Gregory reminded
Romans of his words.

Rome was, of course, exceptionally hard hit by siege, famine
and pestilence, but all over the Empire some cities were
destroyed in war, others simply disappeared. The countryside
became more and more thinly inhabited. By the seventh
century Italy, the Alpine and Danubian provinces, Gaul,
Spain and Britain together had only some ten million inhabitants. This was after the absorption of barbarians in considerable numbers—although not the vast numbers implied in
contemporary descriptions. It is difficult to compare this
figure with the eighty million peak figure which was the total
of the whole Empire, but it is still almost incredibly small if we
look at a map and remember the large cities the area had
contained.

What was the reason for this strange phenomenon? There
were plagues—under Marcus Aurelius and Justinian. But
Constantinople, quickly repopulated, was the one city that grew
while the others were shrinking. Centuries later the Black
Death was similarly followed by a rapid recovery of population
throughout Europe. There were wars—but our modern world
wars have shown how fast the previous figures in population are

overtaken and surpassed. The increase since World War II has been spectacular.

Was imperial Rome dying for lack of the will to live?

Whatever the cause, this drop in population partly explains why the Empire fell apart before it could be built up into medieval Europe. The arts declined, and with them education and commerce, as the population supporting them disappeared. Books were no longer written in the numbers which had maintained an immense industry of copyists. Rivers and harbours were neglected and allowed to silt up because so few ships were entering them. Above all, the land went out of cultivation in a depopulated countryside.

This helped the emperors who, needing men for their armies, or fearing sword and fire if they refused to admit the barbarians peacefully into the Empire, required land for more and more *foederati*. At first a third of the land had been ceded, but in some provinces it came to be two-thirds. In an already well-cultivated, densely populated countryside this would have been impossible, but with so much derelict land, large numbers could be absorbed.

As the *foederati* consolidated their position and set up their own kingdoms within the Empire, their kings still kept the old structure intact. They ruled their own people by their own laws, but Romans they ruled by Roman Law, through Roman officials. And for a long time the kings ruled in the name of the Emperor. The boy Romulus has been called the last of the "phantom emperors" of the West. But the Roman Empire East and West was one entity: and when, near the end of the fifth century, Odoacer deposed Romulus and allowed no successor, he sent the imperial insignia to Constantinople.

The highest ambition of a "barbarian" king was to hold also a high position in the Roman army, and it was often refusal of such office by the Emperor, still more the giving of it to a rival, that produced rebellion. And rebellions grew more and more frequent, rivalries more and more fierce, the kingdoms more and more independent of the Imperial Government. By the fifth century the last days of the Empire in the West seemed to have come. There were Visigothic and Vandal kingdoms in France and Africa, Franks and Burgundians west of the Rhine, Huns devastating eastern and western provinces.

The western centre of government had been moved by Theo-dosius from Gaul to north Italy—more convenient for keeping in touch with the East, but ineffective for guardianship of the western frontiers.

Only the discovery by the invaders that the Empire could become, as Fustel de Coulanges has put it, "not an enemy but a career", saved it from total destruction. Athaulf the Visigoth, who had aspired to create and rule a new Empire, decided that his own people were too undisciplined—that the laws of Rome were needed. His glory would be to restore the Roman name with the Gothic strength.

So too thought Theodoric, Gothic ruler of Italy, and if the sixth century almost concluded the story of Rome's Decline and Fall it may, in another aspect, be looked at as a period of creation and new birth. For, as Christopher Dawson has so dramatically shown in his *Making of Europe*, the material for a new civilisation was to be found "in the obscure chaos of the barbarian world".

Barbarism is not the same thing as savagery; as we have seen in Ireland, a high tribal culture can exist without cities, without even reading and writing. It is the culture of Homer's Greece, not of Cicero's Rome, yet it is a culture. Some of the tribes now surging against or settled within the Empire were almost savages, but others had this culture in a greater or less degree and could through it be made amenable to the higher culture of Greece and Rome. From Greece had come "all that is most distinctive in western as opposed to oriental culture— our sciences and philosophy, our literature and art, our political thought and conceptions of law and of free political institu-tions". The Roman genius had in turn worked upon it, the Church had poured new light upon its possibilities. She more than any other force had created *Romania*, and now the con-ception of Romania must be enlarged to the inclusion of new barbarians whose own contribution would not prove negligible. There were present the three elements of the new world—the *imperium*, weakened, yet still powerful; the *gentes*, an unformed vigorous new life; the *ecclesia*, which proved, in fact, the creating power training the wild new life and saving what could be salvaged of the old. The Latin language was "an ark which carried the seeds of Hellenic culture through the deluge of barbarism", and, strange though it seemed, it was the dying West, not still triumphant Byzantium, from which the creative power chiefly emerged.

Paulinus of Nola speaks of a Christian missionary who is also a Roman when he says:

> ... *per te*
> *barbari discunt resonare Christum*
> *corde Romano placidamque casti*
> *vivere pacem*

"Through you the barbarians learn to utter Christ from a Roman heart and to live purely in tranquil peace."

In the earlier centuries of the Christian era the Eastern Fathers had been all-important. None in the West approached in influence the great Alexandrians—Clement, Origen and Athanasius—the Cappadocians—Basil and the two Gregories—Chrysostom of Antioch, Cyril and the rest. They had not only given to the West the great line of philosophical and theological ideas which Ambrose and Jerome continued and Augustine gloriously developed, but had also established the tradition whereby the Church's bishops became the social leaders, and rhetoric, which had become atrophied in the schools, "recovered", as Dawson puts it, "vital relation to social life".

But now East and West were widely separated by language, frequently the Church of Constantinople was in schism, at no time was it as near to Rome as were the races inhabiting Italy and Gaul, whose conversion and integration had become matter of vital importance for social and religious life. The Church in the East was captive—it was increasingly an instrument of imperial policy. Nor was the Byzantine habit of kidnapping popes likely to endear Constantinople to the Western peoples. The West suffered far more than the East not only from the barbarian inroads but from the imperial attempts at reconquest; the men from the East were foreigners, often hated more heartily than the barbarians themselves. In Africa the Roman armies under Belisarius were joyfully welcomed as liberators, because of the religious persecution of the Arian Vandals. But, after a few years of oppressive taxation, many would have welcomed the Vandals back. In

Italy, where Theodoric was well liked, it was hard to persuade the people that they owed any sort of allegiance to these Greeks who left famine and pestilence in their train.

The sixth century marks the hour of a really deep cleavage between East and West—briefly bridged in appearance by Justinian, widening in reality, as Constantinople shone in splendour and Rome decayed and starved. But while Constantinople was entering upon her last magnificent era both in Church and State, the West was putting forth a secret growth visible later in the world of Christendom.

Four great men were born as the fifth century drew towards its close: Justinian and Boethius, St. Benedict and Cassiodorus. Justinian was born in 483. Of the other three we do not know the exact birth date; probably not much after 480. Cassiodorus and Justinian both lived to a great age—Justinian until 565, Cassiodorus until 575. Benedict died earlier—exactly when we do not know. Boethius was executed by Theodoric in 524.

These men are the most important figures of the sixth century. All were determined on a line of action, all had a purpose, one has been called the Great. Yet perhaps he was the least of the four in real achievement, if human happiness and divine knowledge are the proper objects of men's lives and permanence a test of men's achievement.

1: Rebuilding the Ancient World

Justinian the Great

Justinian was forty-five when he became Emperor—yet he reigned for thirty-eight years. Nephew of Justin and given by him the elegant education proper to the Byzantine aristocracy, he had imbibed a special taste for theological argument. Amid the splendours of the imperial palace he led a frugal, even ascetic life. He drank no wine, ate little and that chiefly vegetables, could fast from all food for two consecutive days and needed almost no sleep. He loved to spend his evenings surrounded by theologians. He loved even better giving birth to imperial rescripts on theology, inspired sometimes by these conferences, issued as encyclicals to be accepted by the whole Church.

This extension of absolute rule to the spiritual sphere was not new; other emperors had attempted it but not so fully. And it is significant that one counterbalancing democratic element disappeared during this reign. The people were deprived of their voice in the election of bishops. Justinian's laws laid down that the local "notables", together with the clergy, should put forward three names, but that the final choice should rest either with the patriarch, the metropolitan or the bishops of the province. "In practice," comments Louis Bréhier, "the Emperor's will or that of his representative was all that counted."[1]

No previous emperor had carried Caesaropapism to quite such a high point. None perhaps would have justified it with such total confidence. Justinian had set himself two goals: restoration of the Empire to its pre-barbarian state and an end to the discord in the Church. The historian may see a solitary figure trying to hold back a tidal wave, the Christian may comment, " *Nisi Dominus . . .* "

Procopius, secretary of Belisarius and chronicler of the period, tells us that the Armenian ambassador said of Justinian, "The whole world does not contain him"—and his reign marks not only a check in the advance of Rome's foes, but a recovery of vast parts of the lost Empire. This was said in 539, and he had by that date laid the Armenians under tribute, contained the Persians and conquered his other Eastern enemies, subdued Africa and Sicily and almost subdued Italy. Before he died he had completely reconquered Italy, Corsica and Sardinia and partly won back Spain. The reconquest was undertaken as the reduction of revolting subjects, not the subduing of alien kingdoms. The barbarian kings were still not independent monarchs, but over-powerful and rebellious deputies. Yet they had grown so powerful and the battle line was so long and so divided that only a general of vast genius could have achieved what Belisarius did for Justinian. His steady loyalty and his monarch's ingratitude are alike astonishing.

Justinian also planned and saw through to accomplishment a vast work on the legal system of Rome—the famous Code completed in little over a year, and the Digest, in which it is computed that one hundred and six volumes were compressed

[1] Fliche and Martin, *Histoire de l'Eglise*, vol. iv, p. 538.

into five and a quarter. This took three years and the work was rounded off by the Institutions—a manual for students of the principles of Roman Law. The Code of Justinian not only lies at the base of the laws of most European states, it has also enormously affected the law of the Church. In the Byzantine Empire itself his work gave birth to the conception of the *Nomocanon*—a synthesis of ecclesiastical and civil law.

To Justinian was due a partly new conception of the Church's structure: that of the five patriarchates. The apostolic sees had always been held of high importance. Rome always placed first, Constantinople had at Chalcedon been intruded over Alexandria into second place. In Justinian's legal system these sees became patriarchates placed in hierarchical order. Rome was still first, the Pope being "the chief of priests"; next, as new Rome, came Constantinople (to which in the following century a disciple of St. Andrew would be attributed as founder, to manifest its apostolicity). Next came Alexandria, the patriarch of which continued to use the name Pope, then Antioch and finally Jerusalem. Between these patriarchs and the Emperor was established a system of exchange of synodal letters, the inscription on their church's diptychs of names of the living and the dead, and regular diplomatic representation of Pope and Patriarch at the Court of Constantinople. Much of this had existed before, but was by Justinian systematised and embodied in Church Law.

The reign of Justinian is famous also for the buildings that sprang up all over the Empire. Some of the most glorious are at Ravenna, but the Emperor sought out and brought to Constantinople Anthemius, whose work alone might have won the title given to the whole reign—"the golden age of Christian art". The word "golden" is especially appropriate to his Ravenna mosaics, with the deep glow that surrounds and seems even to underlie the other colours. But above all was the great church of Sancta Sophia in which mosaics and marbles, "like a meadow full of flowers in bloom", enhanced the marvellous harmony of its proportion. Sir John Mandeville, after all his travels, called it "the fairest church in all the world". Justinian cried out, "I have vanquished you, Solomon."

"The church," says Procopius, "is singularly full of light

and sunshine; you would declare that the place is not lighted
by the sun without, but the rays come from within itself, so
profuse is the light poured in . . . Not by human strength or
skill but by the favour of God this work was perfected; the
mind rises sublime to commune with God, feeling He cannot
be far off, but must delight to dwell in the place which He has
chosen . . . No eye ever wearied of it, in the church they rejoice
and afterwards they praise and magnify what they have seen."

The story of Justinian's wife, the Empress Theodora, is even
more extraordinary than that of Eutropius. Her father, a
bear-keeper in the amphitheatre of Constantinople, died when
she was no more than seven. She and her sisters made a living
from childhood by acting and miming, for which Theodora
showed special skill, winning much applause and laughter by
her comic sketches. Graceful, vivacious, even lovely, Theodora
earned her living in dubious ways in Constantinople and
presently left it with her protector of the moment. She fell into
poverty in Alexandria and made her way back to her birthplace, where, supported by some dream or omen that told her
she would become the wife of a great monarch, she changed
her way of living. She now earned a pittance by spinning wool
and lived a chaste life in a small house which she later turned
into a temple.

Theodora managed by luck or skill to attract the attention
of the patrician Justinian, who was already really reigning in
the name of his uncle. Justinian fell and remained passionately
in love with her. In the teeth of intense opposition from his
family he changed the law which forbade marriage between a
patrician and anyone who had been on the stage. After their
marriage and his uncle's death he insisted on treating her not
merely as his consort but as his equal colleague. "The Eastern
world", says Gibbon, "fell prostrate before the genius and
fortune of the daughter of Acacius. The prostitute who, in the
presence of innumerable spectators, had polluted the theatre
of Constantinople, was adored as a queen in the same city,
by grave magistrates, orthodox bishops, victorious generals
and captive monarchs."

Her power was stupendous. She could elevate the lowest
and abase the highest. She could judge, torture and condemn

to death. All these things she did, having, if we are to believe
the story which met with no contemporary contradiction,
secret prisons and torture chambers, kept constantly busy.
The patrician world she treated sometimes with a display of
haughty disdain, sometimes with the buffoonery of her old
profession. She seldom forgot a friend and never forgave an
enemy. And in all that he did Justinian kept her by his side
and lifted her with himself into the superhuman elevation that
the Byzantine monarchs had gradually been erecting for themselves. For Justinian's reign marked the culmination of the
change in imperial style from *imperator* to divine autocrat.
Surrounded by an atmosphere of mystery, he spoke as though
constantly inspired by God. Driven perpetually by an im-
perious ambition, he sought to rule the world as if himself
God, to reign, in overwhelming splendour, over an Empire
subdued by him, in a city created by him, that should surpass
all that the world had hitherto known.

But history has been forced to record the darker side of this
golden reign. The suffering caused by the military campaigns
was largely fruitless because too much was attempted. The
army could not guard frontiers so wide. Narses was a skilful
general, but a genius like Belisarius did not appear again, and
all Justinian had won was lost in the end. The Gothic kingdom
had brought, on the whole, peace and good government. Now
Italy, fought over repeatedly, was a prey to starvation and
pestilence. Rome was besieged and besieged again, was for
forty days totally deserted. The imperial officials imposed a
heavier taxation and enforced it more cruelly than the Gothic
monarchs.

Taxation was indeed the curse of this golden reign. Not in
the reconquered countries only but throughout the Empire
the Emperor's need for money created a reign of terror. Long
before Justinian the Empire had been overtaxed, but now new
heights were reached. Money was needed for the endless
campaigns, for buying off the Persians, for erecting the
magnificent buildings, for supporting the magnificent Court.
John the Cappadocian was a name of terror, torturing men for
their tribute, torturing his own subordinates, well supplied
with secret dungeons where they could be securely kept.

The most splendid city of this age of splendour was built on ruins. After the populace, in the Nika revolt, had burnt down most of old Byzantium, Justinian came forth holding a book of the Gospels and swearing to redress their wrongs. They retorted with shouts of anger and incredulity. For a while the Cappadocian was dismissed—but more lenient administration failed to gather in the taxes and he was reinstated. Only when Theodora, who hated him, managed to convince Justinian of his disloyalty, was he finally disgraced. Even those historians who admire Justinian as "a man of destiny", carrying out inexorably "the purposes of history" (whatever they may be), have confessed that he did so at the expense of "a sacrificed generation".[1] The splendour was dazzling but its foundations were human misery and despair.

RELIGIOUS DICTATOR

It was in the religious field that Justinian exerted his greatest personal efforts. Despite the edicts against it, there was still much paganism in the Empire. As an intellectual force it was weakening, and when Justinian closed the University of Athens there were few students there and probably a shortage of teachers. The spectacular sound of this act has given it undue importance; he had already violated men's consciences far more deeply. A few months after his accession an edict was promulgated commanding that all his pagan subjects with their wives and children should be instructed and baptised in the Christian religion. This was followed by another edict proclaiming death for any who should return to paganism or take part in clandestine worship.

John of Ephesus was a curious Monophysite monk, so zealous in preaching that he boasted of having converted some hundred thousand peasants in the mountains near Smyrna, and of having obtained their willing aid in the destruction of their sacred groves and temples. (As an evangelist he taught not Monophysite but Catholic doctrine.) Coming to Constantinople, John denounced to the authorities outstanding pagan citizens—grammarians, sophists, doctors; these men were condemned to be flogged—and to be taught the catechism. Some of them were mutilated and paraded naked on the back

[1] See Bury, *Later Roman Empire*, vol. i.

of a camel. Their books were publicly burnt. These affronts to
human dignity were not likely to recommend the religion
of Christ and were utterly contrary to the Church's teaching,
which says that no man may (or can) be constrained to believe
against his conscience.

Constantine had called himself Bishop of the Pagans.
Justinian acted as Bishop of the Jews. He showed more clemency
towards them than he did to pagans or heretics, but he forbade
those rabbis to teach who denied the Last Judgement and the
Resurrection, or who refused to accept the angels as part of
God's creation. They were to be expelled from the Jewish
community. He legislated for the advantage of the Diaspora
Jews by ordering that the Scriptures should be read in the
synagogues in Greek and Latin, since many congregations
did not understand Hebrew.

But it was Christians, heretical and orthodox, who received
the fullest attention of the theologian-emperor throughout
his reign. According to John of Ephesus he offered to convert
by argument some Manichees, among them senators and
women of noble birth, discovered at Constantinople; but failing
to convince them, he ordered them to be burnt. Going further
than his uncle Justin, he excluded heretics from civil and
military office, municipal dignities and the liberal professions.
They could not testify in court, make wills or inherit. Their
churches were to be shut; they could not baptise, ordain or
worship.

From all this legislation one heresy remained practically
immune—that of the Monophysites; the ultimate result of this
was that Justinian's final persecution was directed against
orthodox Catholics and supremely against the Pope. The
Empress Theodora, herself a Monophysite, protected a
monastery of five hundred monks in the palace of Hormisdas
and another beyond the Golden Horn, where John of Ephesus
would stay when in Constantinople. There they could live
freely, being forbidden only to wander through the town.
Outside Constantinople Theodora saw to it that Monophysite
bishops should acquire sees and ordain a clergy for the future.

Besides the natural weakness of a husband in love with a
strong-willed wife, Justinian was moved in all this by belief
in his own theological powers. Like Constantine, and with

more excuse, he was confident that he could bring about unity. For to the weight of his authority he could add the arguments of a trained intellect. Full of self-confidence he set to work to conciliate the Monophysites and thus bring them back into the unity of the Faith. Orthodox himself, he believed he could maintain Chalcedon while interpreting it for the Monophysites according to the mind of their idol St. Cyril of Alexandria. To do this he must make perfectly clear that the teaching of the Church was quite free from Nestorianism.

One problem Justinian had from which Constantine had been free—he really believed in the Papacy, had called the Pope first of all God's priests, had reunited Constantinople with Rome, had proclaimed that he honoured the Pope as a Father. At the head of his Code he had set the command of Gratian, Valentinian and Theodosius, that all the nations in the Empire must follow the religion given to the Romans by the Apostle Peter.

The first action taken against the Pope looked on the face of it purely political. Most reluctantly the great Belisarius, when Rome was under siege in March 537, ordered Pope Silverius before him and accused him of plotting to hand Rome over to the Goths. Silverius was stripped of his priestly vestments and the Roman clergy were commanded to depose him. He was sent into exile and Vigilius, former ambassador in Constantinople, was chosen in his place. But, according to both Procopius and the *Liber Pontificalis*, the whole affair was engineered by Theodora as a revenge for the Pope's refusal to confirm the re-election of the Monophysite Anthimus to the see of Constantinople.

It may be that Justinian believed the Pope *had* been plotting, but he proved later his own ingenuity in distinguishing the office from the man, proclaiming papal authority while maltreating a pope.

There was no political excuse in the case of Vigilius; he had merely hesitated to sign an edict of Justinian's condemning what came to be known as the Three Chapters. The *kephalia*, or chapters, were made up of selections from the works of three dead bishops solemnly anathematised by Justinian; Theodore of Mopsuestia, the master of Nestorius, Theodoret of Cyr, his fellow-student, and Ibas of Edessa.

The last two had been condemned at the Latrocinium and rehabilitated at Chalcedon. Justinian's edict is lost, its exact date unknown. It marks the culminating point of a usurpation of spiritual authority which yet the Emperor was determined to mask by gaining the Pope's assent. Vigilius, seized by soldiers, was taken to Sicily and left there ten months, brought to Constantinople and magnificently received. But when he still hesitated to obey the Emperor he was torn by beard and feet from an altar to which he clung, so violently that the altar supports broke and he was almost crushed to death; he was imprisoned in the palace where he had been lodged, with servants who had been ordered to insult him. Meanwhile, forged letters were sent to Italy in his name by Justinian.

Unfortunately Vigilius did not merely hesitate; he also vacillated; and it is not difficult to see why. The Council of Chalcedon had found fault with the writings of Theodoret and Ibas even while it rehabilitated them personally. There were dangerous elements in their works; if he could condemn these, yet save Chalcedon, then perhaps, as Justinian claimed, the Church could win back these Monophysites after whom he yearned. It is easy to imagine the persuasive quality of the long talks with Justinian and Theodora along these lines. But when Vigilius embodied his own cautious criticisms in a *judicatum*, he discovered that the Emperor would be content with nothing but a full condemnation of the Three Chapters. In like manner, when the Council of Constantinople was called, Justinian put forth a public statement making it perfectly clear that all the assembled bishops were to do was to give their assent to the judgement already passed by him.

Vigilius would not attend the council, which affirmed Chalcedon and condemned not only the Three Chapters, but also the famous anathemas of St. Cyril, accusing him of Apollinarianism. Cyril had himself tacitly dropped the anathemas; the Council of Chalcedon had censured the *writings* of Theodoret and Ibas though defending the men. But, although later Vigilius agreed to confirm this as the fifth General Council, it was emphatically an Emperor's council. Justinian had prepared it verbally by the anathemas on the Three Chapters and his earlier treatise against Origen —whose thinking he attacked as akin to paganism, Manicheism

and Arianism. It had assembled in his own city, so that few
Westerners could attend; he held over it threats of prison or
exile. Of the Roman clergy present two were imprisoned,
one banished. The *Liber Pontificalis* has Vigilius sent to the
mines, but he seems in fact to have remained, a sick man, in
Constantinople. After six months' hesitation he agreed to
confirm the council and a year later started for Rome, but
died on the way.

THE EFFECT ON THE EAST

To us of the West, Constantinople appears an eastern city,
but in Egyptian or Palestinian eyes it was almost west, and vast
lands stretching eastward had been involved in Justinian's
persecutions and compromises. No good can come from persecution—at any rate to the persecutor—but certainly no good
came either of the compromises whereby the Emperor had
striven to placate the Monophysites.

The basic doctrine of Christianity is the Incarnation, and this
had come to the world from the East. But from the East had
also come Gnosticism, Manicheism and other heresies which
shrink from the thought of God incarnate. Monophysitism
was a partly concealed form of this same shrinking—absorbing
the humanity in the Godhead to its virtual disappearance.
The Iconoclasts, who were soon to rock the Church, held the
same basic fear of matter: the same tendency to see God as
infinitely distant, unknowable, unapproachable by man. We
see something of the same feeling even in orthodox Eastern
mystics, such as the exquisite poet Ephrem of Syria. "Search
thou out the sea," he says, "but search not out the Lord of the
Sea." He loved the Faith as a hidden mystery but attacked
those who try "to see the air, to handle the light". But "we
have handled", says St. John the Evangelist, and the Light
Himself told St. Thomas to handle Him, told us all to eat Him
that we might have life.

St. Ephrem was fully orthodox, but medieval mysticism
suffered not a little from that other great Eastern—Dionysius
the Monophysite (called the Areopagite). He wrote much of
God's remoteness from man, of His total unknowableness,
though Christ had said, "Have I been so long a time with you

and have you not known me? Philip, he that seeth me seeth the Father."

The Monophysite heresy was more insidious than Arianism but just as dangerous. Equally it destroyed man's redemption, equally it lowered man's dignity. The lands that accepted it could more easily become a prey to the Moslem invasion, for Mahomet was the prophet of a lonely and distant God.

JUSTINIAN'S LAST YEARS

It was now the year 553 and Vigilius had been absent from Rome since 545. During that period the great plague had ravaged the Empire. Justinian caught it but recovered. In Constantinople so many died that there was none to bury them; the market places were full of corpses, commerce stopped and the rich city starved.

In 548 Theodora died. Hers had been the stronger character of the two. The picture of her as a sort of vampire, drawn from the *Secret History* attributed to Procopius, is almost certainly false. She showed greatness when, on the occasion of the Nika revolt, she successfully opposed the flight of Emperor and Court. "It is impossible for man", she said, "once he has come into the world, not to die; but for one who has reigned it is intolerable to be an exile." Her purple robe, being addressed as Queen, meant, she admitted, everything to her, but she had loyalty and probably love for her husband. She was often kind to other women; she also gratified her hates as an empress can.

Neither plague nor bereavement stopped Justinian's efforts to be reconciled to the Monophysites; indeed he probably felt the more eager to succeed in tribute to her memory. But his council brought profound disillusionment. While annoying many Catholics, it failed to gain the Monophysites. He seemed to lose hope, no longer sought to press on to further military victories, even neglected the maxim of Decius to keep the army satisfied. The Roman historian Agathias tells how the soldiers were kept waiting for their pay "and when the debt was paid at last, persons skilled in the rascally science of arithmetic demanded back from the soldiers what had been given them".

Meanwhile Justinian sat long into the night with books of theology before him. Was he studying, brooding, thinking of his dead wife or of his own future? For he believed in God and almost certainly in judgement and in hell. Yet his brooding issued in one of the strangest of all heresies—for he accepted the theory called phantasist, that the unity of Christ's nature made a special miracle of His will necessary for the sufferings of His passion to be real. This belief, started by Julian of Halicarnassus, was widespread in Egypt, but when Justinian put forth a dogmatic edict declaring it orthodox, a revolt of some magnitude began to stir among the bishops of the whole world. Justinian deposed the Patriarch of Constantinople and intruded a successor in his see, but he had reached the limit of his own long strange life, and in November 565 he died at the age of eighty-two.

The terrible picture drawn in the *Secret History* haunts the reader, but the mere facts of this long reign have enough in them of misery to weight the imagination. Whether Procopius wrote it or not, what this book supremely gives is the atmosphere surrounding Justinian's last years, and the deep bitterness left by his reign in the minds of the men he ruled.

"This book of pain and horror," says Bury, "leaves upon the mind the impression that the enlightened spirit of Justinian, his notable projects, his high thoughts, lived in the shadow of some malignant presence; that cowering by the throne of the Emperor, lurking in the gallery of the palace where he walked in meditation at night, ever attending his steps, moved some inhuman horror, some unutterable 'Dweller by the Threshold', through whose fatal power the destinies of himself and Theodora, Belisarius and [his wife] Antonina, John the Cappadocian and many other victims, were entangled in an inextricable mesh of hates and lust and bloodshed."[1]

2: Creating a New World

When we turn from New Rome to Old, there is a painful contrast in "the very superficial truth" of the two great cities. Byzantium might suffer plagues, famine, arson, but it had wealth and strength enough to rise from its ashes in renewed beauty. It was not dominated by an alien people. Its ruler,

[1] *Later Roman Empire*, vol. i, pp. 355-6.

even when most cruel, had taken pride in the city, once his dwelling, now his monument. But the renewed devastations of Rome brought her lower and lower; the great men of the time had to work in the dark hoping against hope for a better future.

We do not see the first growth of a plant as it springs from the root, yet plants grow among ruins, and growth had begun of a new life, not artificially stimulated by imperial patronage, but spontaneous, cut off sometimes but ever springing anew. Buildings were crumbling but men were still creative.

CASSIODORUS THE CIVIL SERVANT

The extraordinary conditions of this final stage of the Western Empire, this decisive moment in the Church's history, are wonderfully mirrored in the life of Cassiodorus, one of the last great men of Romania. His activities begin before those of Justinian and extend beyond the death of St. Benedict. Long as he lived, he often appears to have lived even longer, for his father too held office under the great barbarians who dominated Italy from the last third of the fifth century, and they are sometimes confused.

Neither Ricimer nor Odoacer claimed to be more than a soldier in the service of the Empire, but Odoacer in 477 forced the Roman Senate to send to Constantinople a letter asking that he be made a senator and stating that there was no further need for an Emperor in the West. Odoacer should be named Vice-gerent of the Emperor of the East.

Zeno did not dare refuse but it is interesting to note that the papal correspondence of the period entirely ignores Odoacer and treats Zeno in remote Constantinople as the sole legitimate monarch. Zeno himself was getting anxious at Odoacer's increasing strength and finally asked Theodoric, a leader of one of the tribes of Ostrogothic *foederati* settled in Pannonia, to attack him. Nothing was hastening the break-up of the Empire more than this imperial habit of employing barbarians against one another. Often akin in blood, totally uninterested in Rome, whole armies would change sides either for money or because the opposing leader struck them as handsomer or more warlike. Slaughter and destruction made countrysides barren, the people were again displaced to make room for the families of the new invaders.

When Theodoric marched into Italy it was not merely the invasion of an armed force, it was the migration of a nation. The practice of *hospitalitas* was again invoked to justify the settling of this nation on Italian soil with a diminishing native population and many thousands of untilled acres. Obviously it was to the interest of all that the settlement should be effected as peacefully as possible, that orderly government should continue, above all that there should be men in office looking after their interests. And so Cassiodorus the father, and later Cassiodorus the son, passed, apparently with no sense of disloyalty, from serving one Gothic ruler to serving the man who had slain him. Their loyalty was to Rome.

Even Theodoric never dared call himself King of Italy. He was king of his own subjects and like Odoacer he ruled them by their own laws. His Roman subjects were governed by the Roman laws, and the Roman officials at the Gothic court kept the old titles. Cassiodorus the father became in 503 Pretorian Prefect, and he appointed his son Flavius Magnus Aurelius Cassiodorus Senator (Senator was a name, not a title), *Consiliarius*, or assessor of his Court. The games and circuses of ancient Rome went on. The gifts of corn were continued, the monuments were preserved, new buildings erected, agriculture revived, marshes were drained, water supplies ensured throughout the new kingdom. Theodoric really was a great man and it is probable that the panegyric pronounced by Cassiodorus Senator, which gained him the important office of Quaestor, was perfectly genuine.

Cassiodorus had now the duties of revising, phrasing and collating the Emperor's laws, replying to petitions, giving audience to ambassadors and answering the letters they carried. He wrote, it has been said, with the pen of a Cicero dipped in barbarian ink. His letters give a vivid picture of the period, but they are strangely involved and he can never let pass the opportunity of using an illustration. The Venetians are water-fowl building their nests on the bosom of the waves. A delay in the corn supplies reminds him of the south wind, the echnesis or sucking fish, the shells of the Indian sea, the torpedo—a fish by the touch of which "a deadly chill is struck into the right hand of him who attacks it". His correspondent must have lost the thread long before the object of the letter was reached. "The echnesis is corruption trading on delays . . . the torpedo fraudulent pretence . . . let Your Greatness, whom it especially concerns to look after such men, bring them by a speedy rebuke to a better mind. Else the famine which we fear will be imputed . . . to official negligence whose true child it will manifestly appear."

Cassiodorus was now one of the first ten men in the country; we shall never know how much of his success Theodoric owed to his minister. "It was the policy of Theodoric," says Gibbon, "to disguise the reign of a barbarian"; but he sighs at the thought that "the union of the Goths and Romans might have fixed for ages the transient happiness of Italy; and the first of nations, a new people of free subjects and enlightened soldiers, might have gradually arisen from the mutual admiration of their respective virtues."

This was the ardent desire and aim of Cassiodorus. He wrote a History of the Goths. He served Theodoric faithfully. As Consul he later helped to allay any suspicions the Roman Senate might feel of the Gothic ruler's attitude, carrying out punctiliously the pretended consultations with them as to peace and war, communicating every nomination to them, appealing skilfully to their loyalty. And it was surely in part the triumph of Cassiodorus that Theodoric the Arian gave perfect freedom to his Catholic subjects. The contrast with Vandal Africa is total, and almost the only blot on Theodoric's reign came near its end. "The life of Theodoric," says Gibbon, "was too long, since he lived to condemn the virtue of Boethius and Symmachus."

BOETHIUS

Boethius must have appeared, even more than Cassiodorus, a man on whom Fortune consistently smiled. For he had risen swiftly in the political world, being Consul in 510, and seeing his two sons become joint consuls probably about 522. This was the culminating point of his career. Only two years later came his fall. It remained for Philosophy to tell him in his prison that his had been a "brittle felicity", that the jade had merely been up to her usual tricks.

The Emperor Justin, successor of Zeno and Anastasius, alarmed Theodoric by healing the religious breach between Rome and Constantinople. Roman clerics were now frequently visiting the Eastern capital. Theodoric suspected the senators Albinus and Boethius, of conspiring with the Emperor against him.

Boethius has been called the last of the Romans and it seems that he was still, in imagination, living in a free world. He has also been called the first of the scholastics. He was too much a philosopher to be a wary statesman. Perhaps success had come too easily; he belonged, after all, to one of the great Roman families; his father had been Consul before himself and his sons. Courageously he undertook the defence of Albinus—and found himself involved in the charge of conspiracy and thrown into prison, far from his home, his friends, his books. The active intellect of Boethius had found much food outside the life of politics; interested in mathematics and astrology, he had written a text book on music, founded on various Greek authorities, used at Oxford and Cambridge down to modern times. He had dreamed of working out a reconciliation between the thought of Plato and of Aristotle. He had written five theological treatises, from one of which Aquinas drew the famous definition of a person—"a complete individual substance of a rational nature". This treatise, against Nestorius and Eutyches, is of especial brilliance and the tragedy of so richly theological a mind lost to the world so early is present as one reads. He was probably no more than forty-seven when he died.

"Contact," says Romano Guardini, "means meeting with a historical figure which is unmistakably itself yet remains something universally valid. History cannot show many such figures, which by their very unrepeatable singularity lead straight to the essential things." Guardini was writing of Socrates, and this contact does seem to come quite specially where the great man with whom we make it has the chance to look death in the face unafraid and to reflect on life as he looks. Boethius in prison, discoursing with Philosophy, is no less revealing than Socrates in his home awaiting the hemlock in the company of his friends, or Thomas More in the Tower consoling his daughter for the death he must soon suffer.

All three had lived fully and richly, all three had held life precious, yet all three had chosen public disgrace and death rather than betrayal of their own conscience.

We must, Socrates had said, embark "as on a raft" upon the best of human doctrines to "risk the voyage of life, unless a stronger vessel, some divine word, could be found on which we might take our journey more safely and more securely". Boethius and More alike had that divine word, yet it is curious that his *Consolation of Philosophy* written in prison, a key book for the Middle Ages, was also hailed as a "golden volume" by Gibbon, who felt it to be totally free of what he deemed the superstitions of revealed religion!

Boethius is in fact a supreme example of the Catholic philosopher to whom the best in the past meant more than it had ever meant before. There is no attempt to evade the hurts of life, as he writes of his own fate. The Senate who, standing as free men, might well have changed the purpose of Theodoric, had unanimously voted Boethius guilty of treason and of magic practices. The blow may have been as heavy for the patriot, witnessing the degradation of his countrymen, as for the husband and father about to die. No wonder that Philosophy has first to say, "Let us wipe a little his eyes dimmed with the cloud of mortal things."

Then gradually he moves, alternating the effort of the mind with the relief of verse, into a meditation where the philosophy that consoles him is indeed religion.

> And who either conserves goodness or expels evils, but God the Ruler and Governor of men's minds? Who beholding from His high turret of providence sees what is fitting for everyone, and applies that which He knows to be most fitting . . . Wherefore God's wise disposition spares the man whom adversity might make worse . . . others are vexed with hardships that they may strengthen the powers of their mind with the use and exercise of patience. . . .
>
> For it is only a divine strength to which even evil things are good, when, by using them in due sort, it draws some good effect out of them. For a certain order embraces all things . . . It is impossible for any man either to comprehend by his wit or to explicate in speech all the frame of God's work.

The minds of men must needs be more free when they keep themselves in the contemplation of God, less when they come to their bodies, less still when they are bound with earthly fetters. . . .

But reason belongs only to mankind as understanding of things divine. . . . Wherefore let us be lifted up as much as we can to the height of the highest mind; for there reason shall see that which she cannot behold in herself. . . .

Life as we know it

hath not yet attained tomorrow and hath lost yesterday. And you live no more in this deep life than in that movable and transitory moment.

Eternity therefore is the perfect and changeless possession in its totality of an endless life.

Into that eternal present Boethius now entered by a cruel death. One of his minor consolations had been the thought of the prosperity of his wife's father Symmachus. But Symmachus mourned too openly, and on suspicion of an attempt to avenge his son-in-law, he too was executed the following year.

This great blot on the otherwise noble reign of Theodoric tormented the king's conscience. Procopius relates a story told by his doctor. The year after the death of Symmachus Theodoric saw one day in a large fish brought to his table the face and eyes of the aged senator with bitterly revengeful looks and teeth ready to tear him. Going straight to his room, he shivered beneath a pile of bedding and told his doctor how bitterly he repented the murder of Boethius and Symmachus.

A few days later Theodoric was dead from a violent attack of dysentery. It was the end of a time of great achievement and greater hopes. Cassiodorus, who had retired after the execution of Boethius, returned to serve Theodoric's daughter, a thoroughly Romanised woman, and her young son, a determinedly barbarian Goth. But the boy's death and the feuds that followed encouraged Justinian to send Belisarius into Italy and in or near 537, thirteen years after the death of Boethius, Cassiodorus (who had become Pretorian Prefect) retired for good. His dream of a Roman-Gothic state was shattered, and he had begun to turn his thoughts to the next world and to the light shed by it on the dark scenes of human conflict. Instead of writing letters about corn he now wrote a book about the soul.

CASSIODORUS THE MONK

Was Cassiodorus a Benedictine? Many medievals thought so, while some moderns have claimed that his influence on the Order was so great and changed it so much from St. Benedict's original idea that the later learned Benedictines ought in fact to be called Cassiodorians. The Rule of the Master, far longer than St. Benedict's, has been found in a manuscript almost certainly written at his monastery of Vivarium: was Cassiodorus the Master? If so, it is almost certain that this Rule is based on St. Benedict's and that Cassiodorian monasticism was at least the child of Benedictine. But if, as later research has suggested, the monks of Cassiodorus were just zealous copyists, this Rule may stem from Gaul, possibly from Lerins.[1]

Cardinal Schuster, in his Life of St. Benedict, notes that Cassiodorus speaks with enthusiasm of two monks. One he names—Dionysius, called Exiguus from his small stature, to whom we owe the division of years into B.C. and A.D.; one he leaves anonymous, but describes as "visited by divine omnipotence", made known to us "by divine inspiration"—and in him we must surely see St. Benedict. The Cardinal notes some striking parallels between the thought of Cassiodorus and the Rule of St. Benedict—and it would certainly seem probable that Cassiodorus, embarking in old age on his great project, would have sought counsel from an already experienced monk, the founder of many monasteries. Theories change so rapidly, whether based on new discoveries or on fresh arguments, that the next book to appear may well support the old tradition of Cassiodorus the Benedictine.

A double monastery was built on his ancestral estate: the higher one in the "pleasant recesses" of Mount Castellum was for solitaries, the other was called Vivarium because of the fish ponds made by Cassiodorus, fed from the river Pellena, on whose borders he also built baths for the use of the sick. He was

---

[1] For a brief and very clear account of this see Dom Cuthbert Smith, O.S.B., " The Problem of the Rule of the Master" in the *Buckfast Abbey Chronicle*, Summer, 1957, vol. 27, no. 2.

proud of his baths and ponds, of his self-feeding lamps, of his sundials for summer use and reliable water-clocks for winter and night time. There were treatises in the library on "the keeping of bees, doves and fish" and also on "gardens and cattle and other matters". "When these things are prepared for strangers and sick people they become heavenly, however earthly they may seem."

But for Cassiodorus the intellect was primary. We must always be listening for God's word, spoken in the past not only through prophet and psalmist but in all great literature, now spoken uniquely in Christ. He was haunted by the horror of destruction going on around him, he wanted to salvage all he could of human and divine learning, and in his little book called *An Introduction to Divine and Human Reading* we learn something of how he set about it.

Cassiodorus tells us that "the schools were swarming with students because of a great longing for secular letters" and "worldly wisdom". He had therefore begged Pope Agapetus to collect subscriptions and open a Christian school in Rome. Owing to "the struggles that seethed and raged excessively in the Italian realm" this had proved impossible. He will try, therefore, to supply the place of a teacher with books through which the "unbroken line of the divine Scriptures and the compendious knowledge of secular letters might, with the Lord's beneficence, be united."

He has sent, he says, for various books, but if a monk comes across any of them before these copies arrive, "let him strive zealously to transcribe". The library of the monastery must be built up "through the Lord's aid and your toil". Much has already been achieved. He himself is old but if death should come "with my sins forgiven—and I beg you to pray that it will", he still hopes that his object will be attained.

"Read unremittingly", he urges his monks: "Bring yourself to this task again and again; for the mother of understanding is constant and eager contemplation." He tells them how to copy, to punctuate, to correct—but oh how cautiously!— manuscripts that may be faulty. "Let frequent conversation", he says, "be sought with elders of extraordinary accomplishments . . . since they zealously relate to us what they have been able to learn in their long lives." He surely was of this band.

still full of "eager desire", never "sluggish", always "zealous" in learning and accomplishing, as he begs his monks to be.

He is enthusiastic about those things that "can be known by the mind alone". Sciences are "studies free from the snares of opinion . . . because they necessarily keep their own rules." They will in a well-constituted mind "lead us with the Lord's help to glorious theoretical contemplation." About music he is especially glowing. It is "diffused through all the acts of our life" as long as that life is one of virtue and in accord with God's will; when we sin music leaves us. "The sky and the earth and everything accomplished in them by the supernal stewardship are not without the science of music." Pythagoras has shown us a world made through music, music permeates religion, "the ten-stringed instrument of the Decalogue, the reverberations of the harp, timbrels, the melody of the organ, the sound of cymbals", above all the Psalms.

That he would still do work of high significance must have seemed unlikely when Cassiodorus laid aside the toils of office. Yet so it was. Cassiodorus the prefect is forgotten but the scholar, maker of scholarly tradition, will always be remembered. He has earned, says De Labriolle, "the undying gratitude of Western civilisation."

THE CHRISTIAN SCHOOL BEGINS

Universal literacy was impossible before the invention of printing, but an ideal of human values need not depend on literacy alone and could be at the basis of education. The Greeks had "an admirable technique for producing a perfectly developed type of human being". But men were not, in their eyes, valuable simply because they were men. This particular democratic idea was taught by Christianity alone. Man is valuable because he is an immortal spirit, created by God in His own image, redeemed by the blood of Christ. Therefore God's revelation was not merely for a chosen few but for all. A Christian education meant the imparting of that message.

"Christianity was an intellectual religion, but it was a religion for the masses, and the humblest of the faithful, however elementary their intellectual development, received something equivalent to what the culture of antiquity had haughtily reserved for a philosophical élite—a doctrine about being and life, an inner life and spiritual direction."[1]

As we reach the Lombard invasion of Italy, which Marrou has called the watershed lying between classical and Christian education, we meet three men who had received both a classical education and a higher Christian formation, who had passed from Caesar's service to the direct service of God. It is interesting to see how they reacted in the twilight of the classical, the dawn of the Christian, school.

Cassiodorus, as we have already seen, cared immensely for the Classics but he wanted primarily advanced Christian culture for the making of thinkers and philosophers, based on classical forms. He wanted, too, to preserve the classical heritage, and saw to it that his monks should bear their part in doing so.

Ennodius of Arles, his contemporary, later Bishop of Pavia, has left a description of a school at Milan which, like that in Rome, lasted on till the middle of the sixth century. Here the boys learnt Latin, Greek, grammar and rhetoric. They declaimed on the old classical subjects. Ennodius himself was a lawyer and helped boys in his charge with their declamations, but as soon as he was ordained a deacon he solemnly broke with pagan learning and wrote concerning a nephew who was thinking of the priesthood, "I should be ashamed to give any secular instruction to a man of the Church."

The spirit of Tertullian and of Jerome—in his bad middle manner—lived on still. Strife lasted into the Middle Ages, between these two opposing views, held even more absolutely in a changed world.

St. Gregory was more vehement than Ennodius; he had, as Marrou points out, come at the very lowest point of decadence in the classical tradition and had not received in any fullness what he later despised. But these three were all full of eagerness about that new thing which in the end was to salvage so much of the old—a Christian education.

The Romans attached great value to education and as the state schools went out of existence there were only two ways of getting it for their children: private tutors or monasteries. Some of the barbarians also realised the importance of at least learning to read and write; Theodoric had his daughter educated

---

[1] Marrou, *Education in Antiquity*, p. 339.

after the Roman fashion, members of the bureaucracy must read and write if they were to manage the states of their illiterate lords.

Reading is reading, whether you read pagan classics or the Bible, writing is writing whether you copy lists of pagan gods or the psalms of David. But the content makes a difference and the new culture coming into being made the Bible central for the layman as well as for the monk. Christianity had created letters for the illiterate peoples she had converted, now the classical culture of the Roman world was dying and the Church began gradually to offer an alternative.

In unbarbarised Constantinople the classical school continued down to the fifteenth century, when Turks took over the succession to Goths and Vandals. But in the West it was slowly dying. Marrou is of opinion that the generation which followed Ausonius, i.e., that of the early fifth century, was the last in Gaul "to be familiar with the normal system of Roman education, with its three stages—*magister ludi*, grammarian, rhetor". In Africa and Italy the system lingered on for more than another century but it grew feebler with every generation.

Anyhow, the mass of new Christians cared little for letters, and the beginning of the Christian school was simply a practical means of fitting monks to carry out their vocation and of educating the clergy for the care of their own people and the conversion of the heathen. Although to a certain extent the Roman aristocracy and the children of barbarian chieftains managed to take advantage of them, the monastic schools were as exclusively meant for future monks in the West as in the East, where St. Basil had forbidden his monks to accept lay pupils. But as he allowed very young children to be accepted and educated in his monasteries and as those who had no vocation departed when they were old enough to decide, he did in fact educate quite a number of laymen. There is much in his rule concerning children in monasteries. The Rule of St. Benedict has also something to say about the reception of children and of how they are to be educated. He admitted young boys, but these were not committed to the religious life until their fifteenth year, when they could leave if they wished. The Irish monks, with their usual tendency to extreme measures, often had children brought to them at birth to be made into monks.

In the days when the old classical school existed, a Christian boy would be sent there to learn his letters while the Church gave him the holy learning of Gospels, psalter and liturgy. This happened, for instance, to St. Athanasius. But in the absence of other schools bishops tended, like St. Augustine, to make the bishop's residence a kind of monastery for the education of young aspirants to the priesthood. St. Gregory of Tours (*b.* 538) was brought to his great-uncle St. Nicetius, Bishop of Lyons, and by him was taught to read and write, and learnt the Psalms by heart. The episcopal school of the sixth century was a sort of choir school, the boys being taught to sing as well as to read. They were "lectors", which meant that they must be able to read aloud well and clearly. They had also to work at Scripture. St. Caesarius had a group of boys in his house and he would ordain no one a deacon who had not read the entire Bible four times.

"To secure", says Marrou, "a regular supply of candidates for the priesthood it was necessary for the bishop himself to give them a general education as well as their specialised theological training, and thus there came into existence the episcopal school, which was to develop into the medieval university of the future." This development was far away; for the moment these schools were severely practical and limited in their objective, "they were, so to speak, merely technical schools designed to produce monks and clerics".

With the birth of the presbyterial, which became the village school, the possibility arose of a wide literacy. Again, it *began* only for the clergy. The second Council of Vaison in 529 urged "all parish priests to gather some boys round them as lectors, so that they may give them a Christian upbringing, teach them the Psalms and the lessons of Scripture and the whole law of the Lord and so prepare worthy successors to themselves".

As of old, education started with the alphabet, but now it led straight on into the sacred text. The master would take a board and write out a psalm or other passage, which the child would read again and again till he had it by heart. The first aim was mastery of the Psalter, the basis of the Divine Office. The new Christian school was largely modelled on the rabbinical school of many centuries. The Word of God was its basis, and the teacher, despised in Roman civilisation, was treated with the religious respect due to a rabbi—a master of sacred knowledge. Lessons were to be asked for "with the deepest veneration and a humble prayer", for the teacher had more to give than mere learning.

Gradually the presbyterial school became accessible to others than clerics, but the word "clerk" would always remind men of its origin. It had to make its way through the barbaric contempt for all book-learning, through the blood and tears, the starvation and plague which accompanied the descent of the West into the Dark Ages. But as it spread it was helped by the remnants of the classical culture stored in the monasteries, by the bringing of books from Constantinople, where the old schools of antiquity still lived on, by the growing Christian culture of books written and translated. The Irish scholars, the Benedictine monks in Saxon lands, the interchange with Rome, all deepened and enriched the new intellectual world slowly created out of the barbarian hordes. Old classical elements would reappear; Goth and Celt and Lombard and Saxon would make their special contribution to a new synthesis at the heart of which was the Word of God uttered in the Christian liturgy.

Did Cassiodorus to some degree anticipate this development? Abbot Chapman has pointed out that he told his two abbots Chalcedonius and Gerontius to create among the labourers and their families on the monastery estates something very like the Benedictine oblates of a later period. These *coloni* are to be treated as *confratres*. "Let a second order of monasticity [*conversationis*] be imposed upon them; let them frequently assemble at the holy monasteries; and let them blush to be yours, if they are not recognised to be of your own institute."[1]

Frequent attendances at the monastery almost certainly meant some initiation into the liturgy. What more it meant we cannot tell, but a man as ardent for things of the mind as was Cassiodorus would surely not have left the mind of any man untilled. He speaks in moving words of himself and his fellow labourers as men "who sincerely long to enter heaven through intellectual exertions". He prays for the vision of God that can only come hereafter, but he seeks also to prepare for it as far as may be here below, by contemplating "with very great dread

[1] Quoted by Abbot Chapman, *St. Benedict and the Sixth Century*, p. 159, footnote.

and wonder" the Holy Trinity, Christ the King, and all those mysteries that are "the delight of Christians".

In these labours and contemplations he continued until the age of ninety-five or more, almost spanning a century of destruction, yet himself steadily creative.

ST. BENEDICT AND HIS RULE

After studying the start of monasticism in the East and in Ireland, after reading the animated discussions concerning the Rule of the Master, one might wonder what there was left for Benedict to do. The answer to individual questions of dependence may never be answered by scholarship. The answer to the great question of creativeness has already been given by achievement. No one of his predecessors, mighty as many of them were, created the new world of monasticism which was Benedictine, the new world of Christendom of which monasticism was the brain and heart.

Abbot Chapman has conjectured that the Rule was commissioned by the Pope and designed for all the monks of the West. He traces its influence on the Code of Justinian. Cassiodorus, he thinks, certainly followed it. Twelve monasteries, each of twelve monks and an abbot, were established by Benedict at Subiaco as well as the famous Monte Cassino. Through Italy, all Europe and presently England it spread rapidly, often absorbing earlier forms of monasticism.

Apart from the Rule the only certain primitive knowledge we have of Benedict is in the *Dialogues* of St. Gregory the Great. The story in the *Dialogues* is full of miracles and marvels quite curiously unlike the sober, practical simplicity of the Rule. Yet both may have fully coexisted in the one man as did fighting, luxury and self-denying toil in the one world. It is true that stories of saints were by convention obliged to deal chiefly in the marvellous. But St. Gregory was not far removed in time from the man he wrote of; he had eye-witnesses to interrogate. Unless we think miracles intrinsically impossible, there seems no great difficulty in accepting Benedict's.

Some of the stories have in them less of the marvellous than of revelation of character and light on the ways of the age. That God should have answered the prayer of Scholastica so that a violent storm prevented her brother from leaving her ("What hast thou done, Sister?" said Benedict in dismay); that he should have foreseen the destruction of his monastery in such a period of destruction; that a man of his insight should refuse to be deceived when one of Totila's followers posed as the king himself—these things are like the "little miracles" that have happened to all of us, which could come in the mere course of nature yet which we feel impelled to receive as a special gift at God's hands.

But of course there is far more than this, and it is incredible that a man like St. Gregory, to whom in fact we owe a homily explaining the diminution of miracles in the "modern" world, should have set down the most startling stories without close examination. Surely here we face a whole attitude with which even Catholic scholars are apt to be infected, in reaction from the absurd degree of medieval credulity. If it is incredible that St. Benedict brought a heavy iron implement from the bottom of a lake to its surface, it becomes, I suppose, equally incredible that Our Lord should have called Peter to come to Him upon the waters of Genesareth. As Abbot Chapman points out, we have certain saints who were primarily known as wonder-workers and St. Benedict is one of them. Like St. Anthony, he visibly contended with the devil; like Gregory Thaumaturgus, he showed his power over the forces of nature. And like both these men his spiritual power was primary— "Ecce labora," Benedict said to the young monk to whom he had restored his scythe, "et noli contristari."

Roman and Goth came together into these monasteries of Benedict and were taught to labour and to rejoice in the face of grief and destruction.

Many studies have been made of the Rule of Saint Benedict. In Abbot Butler's "critico-practical" edition[1] the footnotes give many references to tacit quotations from previous rules and the writings of the Fathers. Yet the Rule remains profoundly original. Not only is it a Rule rather than a collection

---

[1] *Sancti Benedicti Regula Monasteriorum*, Friburgi, Brisgoviae, MCMXXVII. See also *The Rule of Saint Benedict* (in Latin and English) by Dom Oswald Hunter-Blair.

of precepts, but the emphasis of obedience is shifted from Abbot to Rule—the *magistra regula*, not simply the rule of the master but the rule which *is* master—from which none must lightly depart. The Rule is to bind the abbot in the nature of his commands. St. Benedict calls it "the least of rules which we have written for beginners". They may go beyond it in their reading, to Scripture, to the Fathers, to the Rule of "our holy father Basil"—but the Rule itself is "holy", is to be decisive: *magistra*. Emphasis is laid next on the services of the Psalms, prayers and reading from both Scripture and the Fathers. It was only gradually that the length of the reading became regulated: the abbot would give the signal to break off by the words "Tu autem Domine", the reader finishing, "Miserere nobis". Nothing is said by St. Basil about such readings: there are none of the prescriptions St. Benedict gives about breaking up the longer psalms, and which psalms are to be sung at which hours. Divine Office is here in its plenitude and it is the most important thing in the monastery. It is the *Opus Dei*. It is the chief life of the monk and all else is subservient to it.

It might be said that in making both Office and Rule so primary St. Benedict was creating a monastery, whereas St. Augustine and St. Basil were making monks who were to be largely their instruments for great external works. True, the Benedictine Rule proved marvellously adaptable in the conversion of countries and the creation of their civilisations. But a distinction in the beginning does seem to be that Augustine, Basil and other earlier founders (Martin of Tours, Caesarius of Arles) became bishops while their monastic rules were still fluid, and ran their monasteries into the current of their episcopal creativeness, while the Rule and the monastery were the direct instruments of Benedictine creativeness.

St. Benedict provided for a good many hours of private reading. Abbot Chapman holds that a reader of average pace would get through 150–180 volumes in a year. He does not speak of the work which was at Vivarium, and which became in the medieval Benedictine monasteries, so immensely important—the copying of manuscripts. Indeed, reading itself is placed below manual labour in the hours to be devoted to it. A part of this manual labour must have been copying, and writing boards and pens were, from the first, part of the monastery furniture. But St. Benedict certainly was not concerned, as was Cassiodorus, with literature as such—least of all with pagan classics.

Monastic life in the West took, however, a more definitely bookish form than—apart from St. Basil—it had taken in the East. Framed round the Divine Office, it called for a multiplication of psalters and books of Hours. It is possible for a man with a good memory—St. Anthony seems to have done it—to learn much of the Bible by listening to it in church. But the simplest way of learning a book is by reading it, and all the monks were obliged to be students of the Bible. This was the foundation of a Christian education and copying was called for if a monastery were to have an adequate supply of Bibles and other books to help in the understanding of Scripture, of doctrine, of the spiritual life. Cassian, St. Irenaeus, St. Basil, the commentaries of Origen and St. Jerome, St. Augustine's *City of God*, these and many others would keep copyists busy as they built up a monastic library. Even in the rule of St. Caesarius for women, it is laid down that they must all be educated, must read for two hours daily and must copy manuscripts. Then, too, the monks wrote history: Bede the Venerable and the Irish chroniclers followed in the steps of Jerome and Augustine in saving for us the records of their own age and much that had preceded it. Many of the great pagan classics have reached us by the same path, for as the cracks widened in Roman civilisation culture took refuge in the monasteries.

But stress on manual work in the Rule of St. Benedict was far wider in its implications and in its results. The monks often began their settlement in a new area by clearing a forest or reclaiming a swamp. After that there were gardens and farms to cultivate, animals to tend, grain must be ground into flour, bread baked, wool spun into yarn and woven into cloth. Bees were kept for honey—the sole method, in earlier days, of sweetening anything. Grapes were grown and wine made from them. A monastery was a city, with all its activities and dependencies, usually a self-supporting city.

"The monastery", said St. Benedict, "ought if possible to be so constituted that all things necessary such as water, a mill and a garden, and the various crafts may be contained within it;

so that there may be no need for the monks to go abroad, for this is by no means expedient for their souls." (Rule, ch. lxvi.)

Despite these words and the stability specially belonging to the Benedictine Rule, we find the founder toiling already at the work of conversion of the heathen which St. Gregory was to extend so widely. Here in the Italian countryside much paganism survived and St. Benedict strove mightily against it. His meeting with Totila has been the subject of many paintings—and the bitter answer God gave to his anguished prayers: that although the monks should live destruction would come upon their monastery. But he, like Gregory after him, lived in a world where destruction constantly overtook creation and man's hopes must be set high if he were to keep the energy to work and to be joyful.

Such going forth was not like that of the "gyrovagues", or the aimless migrations so common in the East. The monastery remained its centre; the work of conversion radiated from it whether the circle described was a wide one or a narrow.

Never at any stage did western monasticism present the same problems as eastern. When St. Benedict attacks the type of monk described as a gyrovague it is a matter of occasional individuals who cannot settle down in a monastery, not of disorganised crowds. All over Gaul, as we have seen, in Italy, Spain, Africa, above all in Ireland, were monasteries under various rules. The Council of Chalcedon, alarmed at the eastern developments, had laid down certain laws which included episcopal authority over all monasteries. Disputes and difficulties arose at times, and especially in Spain. St. Gregory, himself a monk, would later be inclined to grant more authority to monasteries, other popes and bishops to grant less, but the integration of the monastic life into the Church's structure proceeded far more smoothly and the monasteries of the West never became, as in the East, hotbeds of heresy or centres of conspiracy.

The city of Rome especially was ready for St. Benedict's form of monasticism for two reasons. It had been later than most of western Christianity in accepting monasticism as the ideal form of the ascetic life. More than anywhere else the earliest form of this life had persisted in what Jerome called "the church in the house". Many of the noblest Roman families converted to Christianity had established family churches, and they seemed for long to have achieved through them all that was needed.

Then, too, the old Roman tradition, long before the Christian era, had laid stress on the family. The *paterfamilias*, surrounded by his children and grandchildren, whose very slaves were part of his family, was the ideal. The Roman founders, Jerome and Paula in Bethlehem, Rufinus and Melania in Jerusalem, were nearer to this ideal than the great assemblies of the East, where we read of thousands of monks under a single abbot.

Even in the West, before St. Benedict, monasteries tended to grow too large for the abbot to be a father in the usual sense of the word. And this was, from the first, the special ideal of St. Benedict. No other founder had swiftly built twelve small monasteries rather than one large monastery, never had this relation between the father and his family been so essential to the spirit and the ideal, so tenderly carried out. The very emphasis on the Rule as binding the abbot and monks alike helped this relationship—for if there was hardship in obeying the Rule it fell on both alike; if the father must lay a burden on the son, the Rule was a limitation which gave liberties as well as commands.

THE NEW LIFE NURTURED BY BENEDICT

The sufferings of the sixth century were intense; looking back, historians have seen it as a "time of travail" from which a new world was to be born. The travail was long and the world, unlike a woman in labour, could see no new life in prospect. It was only aware of anguish and convinced that death was drawing near.

If one may hold the metaphor a little longer, the sixth century gave us St. Benedict as a midwife bringing the new life into the world, the Church cherishing and nourishing it, while Justinian, on whom the name Great was not implausibly bestowed, was striving to save the old world of Rome— striving by means more of death than of life. The achievement of his reign was gigantic—yet disregard of men as men defeated him in the end and undid much of his vast work.

The saints depend not on themselves but on God. "Whatever good work you begin to do," says the Rule of St. Benedict, "beg of Him with most earnest prayer to perfect it." The future was veiled for them as it is for all men, and often in these dark centuries they saw no future. But they knew that their abiding city was elsewhere, that the only thing certainly right in this world is to love God and to love man. They knew that "vain is the builder's toil if the house is not of the Lord's building". And God had His surprises for them.

"Gregory the First", says Newman, "did not understand his own act, when he converted the Anglo-Saxons; nor Ambrose when he put Theodosius to penance. The great Christian Fathers laid anew the foundations of the world, while they thought that its walls were tottering to the fall, and they already saw the fires of judgement through the chinks."

The Benedictine motto was "Peace", but the Rule was written and practised in the midst of constant warfare. St. Benedict spoke of his rule as for beginners, yet it has moulded multitudes of saints. And while at one end of the Empire the restless barbarians might watch in amazement the growth of these tranquil companies, at the other end was the more amazing spectacle of the splendour and luxury of the Byzantine court. How could the monks be so peaceful, the Court so frivolous, against the background of that seething world?

Newman sees in these monks the very essence of Virgilian poetry; they had in their lives not only all that Virgil had seen and so beautifully uttered of pastoral loveliness. Theirs was a "bringing back of those real, not fabulous, scenes of innocence and miracle" when God walked with Adam in the garden or angels visited the patriarchs. Newman longed for a Christian poet to bring out the full beauty of St. Benedict's mission with the same "ethereal fire" and "serene philosophy" as Virgil's own.

Newman did not need another Virgil as much as he fancied: the fire and the philosophy are both there when he is talking of the first Christian centuries. He never wrote the big book he had contemplated on the Church of the Fathers, but he wrote enough to give us those hints and insights which are the poet's chief gift. The sketch of the Church in third-century Africa, the fuller treatment of the school of Alexandria and of

Athanasius, the light thrown on doctrinal development, both
Christological and general, the vivid and crowded pictures of
the fifth and sixth centuries and especially of the Council of
Chalcedon—these are all, so to speak, wider than themselves.
Newman first sent me to the Fathers: after several years of
intensive study I returned to him for the better understanding
of what I had read. Newman resembled them; he is of their
stature, he looks at the Church, at history, as they did. Yet,
steeped in classical history, none could realise more fully than
he the tragedy of the decline and fall of Rome; at times his
voice has the tones of a Gibbon. But he knew how much
greater than Rome was the supernatural force ready to renew
the face of the earth, if men would but accept its fierce fire.
He realised the great things achieved by heathens, the miserable
failure of so many Christians, who carry, nevertheless, in their
feeble hands the Light that enlightens all men. And it was the
saints of the early centuries, in their allegiance to the Church
of their age, who brought him to the Church of today. "Be
my soul with the saints," he said, as he realised her continuing
identity.

Looking back, Newman could see what the saints could not
see—that they would in fact save situations humanly hopeless.
St. Augustine, St. Leo, St. Gregory all thought that, Rome
ending, the world would end with her. There was another
and a better world on which their hopes were set. Yet the
creative spirit working in them brought order from chaos, being
from nothingness, restoration out of destruction—not once but
again and again.

Christopher Dawson has developed the story of the making
of Europe out of the seething barbarian tribes, but none has
in one short page shown so well the mission of St. Benedict to
bring out of destruction a future that he himself hardly believed
in.

"He found the world, physical and social, in ruins, and his
mission was to restore it in the way, not of science, but of nature,
not as if setting about to do it by any set time or by any rare
specific, or by any series of strokes, but so quietly, patiently,
gradually, that often, till the work was done, it was not known
to be doing. It was a restoration, rather than a visitation,
correction or conversion. The new world which he helped to

create was a growth rather than a structure. Silent men were observed about the country, or discovered in the forest, digging, clearing and building; and other silent men, not seen, were sitting in the cold cloister, tiring their eyes, and keeping their attention on the stretch, while they painfully deciphered and copied and re-copied the manuscripts which they had saved. There was no one that 'contended or cried out' or drew attention to what was going on; but by degrees the woody swamp became a hermitage, a religious house, a farm, an abbey, a village, a seminary, a school of learning and a city. Roads and bridges connected it with other abbeys and cities, which had similarly grown up; and what the haughty Alaric or fierce Attila had broken to pieces, these patient meditative men had brought together and made to live again.

"And then, when they had in the course of many years gained their peaceful victories, perhaps some new invader came, and with fire and sword undid their slow and persevering toil in an hour. The Hun succeeded to the Goth, the Lombard to the Hun, the Tartar to the Lombard; the Saxon was reclaimed only that the Dane might take his place. Down in the dust lay the labour and civilisation of centuries—Churches, Colleges, Cloisters, Libraries,—and nothing was left to them but to begin all over again; but this they did without grudging, so promptly, cheerfully, and tranquilly, as if it were by some law of nature that the restoration came, and they were like the flowers and shrubs and fruit trees which they reared, and which, when ill-treated, do not take vengeance, or remember evil, but give forth fresh branches, leaves or blossoms, perhaps in greater profusion, and with richer quality, for the very reason that the old were broken off."[1]

With this glimpse of the future the collection may well end of key figures in the Church of the Fathers. For with the failure of Justinian we are plunged into the dark ages, while in another aspect Gregory is the first of the medieval popes.

[1] Newman, *Historical Sketches*, London, 1876, vol ii., pp. 410–411.

BIBLIOGRAPHY

AMAND, D., O.S.B., *Essai sur l'ascèse monastique de S. Basile*, Maredsous, 1949.

AMBROSE, St., *"On the Sacraments" and "On the Mysteries"*, trans. and ed. Thompson, B. D., and Strawley, J. H., London, 1950. *See also under* Dudden, F. H.; Labriolle, Pierre de; Paris, Pères Bénédictins de; Paulinus.

ANTIN, P., O.S.B., *Essai sur St. Jérôme*, Paris, 1947.

ANTIN, P., O.S.B., *Le Monachisme selon St. Jérôme*, Abbaye St. Wandrille, 1947.

APOSTOLIC FATHERS, in LIGHTFOOT, J.B., Bishop of Durham, *The Apostolic Fathers*, London, 1891.

1. *The Epistles of Clement of Rome.*
2. *The Epistles of Ignatius.*
3. *The Epistle of Polycarp.*
4. *The Martyrdom of Polycarp.*
5. *The "Didache".*
6. *The Epistle of Barnabas.*
7. *The "Shepherd" of Hermas.*
8. *The Epistle of Diognetus.*
9. *The Fragments of Papias.*
10. *The Reliques of the Elders Preserved in Irenaeus.*

ATHANASIUS, St., *Historical Tracts*, trans. and ed. anon., Oxford, 1843 (*A Library of the Fathers*).

1. *Encyclical Letter to all Bishops Everywhere.*
2. *Apology against the Arians.*
3. *Encyclical Letter to the Bishops of Egypt and Libya.*
4. *Apology to the Emperor Constantius.*
5. *Apology for his Flight.*
6. *Epistle to Serapion on the Death of Arius.*
7. *Epistle to the Monks.*
8. *History of the Arians.*
Appendix: *Letter of Alexander.*

ATHANASIUS, St., *The Life of St. Anthony*, trans. and ed. McLaughlin, J. B., O.S.B., London, 1924.

AUGUSTINE, St., *The City of God*, trans. Healey, John, ed. Tasker, R. V. G., London, 1945, 2 vols. (*The Everyman Library*).

AUGUSTINE, St., *The Confessions*, trans. Sheed, F. J., London, 1944.

AUGUSTINE, St., *S. Augustin: La Trinité*, trans. and ed. Mellet, M., O.P., and Camelot, T., O.P., Paris, 1955. *See also under* Bertrand, Louis; Dawson, Christopher; Gilson, Étienne; Marrou, H. I.

BALTHASAR, Hans Urs von, *La Théologie de l'histoire*, trans. Givord, R., Paris, 1955.

BARCLAY, William, *A New Testament Word-Book*, London, 1955.

BASIL, St., *The Ascetic Works of St. Basil*, trans. and ed. Lowther Clarke, W. K., London, 1925.

BASIL, St., *Collected Letters*, trans. and ed. Deferrari, Roy, London, 1926–34 (*Loeb Classical Library*), 4 vols.
See also under Amand, P.; Lowther Clarke, W. K.; Giet, Stanislas.

BATIFFOL, P., *L'Église naissante et le catholicisme*, Paris, 1909.

BATIFFOL, P., *La Paix constantinienne et le catholicisme*, 3rd ed., Paris, 1914.

BATIFFOL, P., *Saint Grégoire le Grand*, Paris, 1928.

BENEDICT, St., *The Rule of St. Benedict*, trans. and ed. Hunter-Blair, Abbot Oswald, O.S.B., 2nd ed., Fort Augustus, 1907.

BENEDICT, St., *Sancti Benedicti Regula Monasteriorum*, ed. Butler, Abbot Cuthbert, O.S.B., Freiburg-im-Breisgau, 1927.
See also under Chapman, John; McCann, Justin; Schuster, Ildephonse.

BERTRAND, Louis, *S. Augustin*, Paris, 1913.

BETTENSON, Henry (trans. and ed.), *The Early Christian Fathers*, Oxford, 1956.

BIDEZ, J., *La Vie de l'empereur Julien*, Paris, 1930.

BIELER, Ludwig, *The Life and Legend of St. Patrick: Problems of Modern Scholarship*, Dublin and London, 1949.

BOETHIUS, *The Theological Tractates and the "Consolation of Philosophy"*, trans. and ed. Stewart, H. F., and Rand, E. K., London, 1918 (*Loeb Classical Library*).

BOISSIER, G., *La fin du paganisme*, 2 vols., Paris, 1891.

BUDGE, E. A. T. Wallis (trans.), *The Paradise of the Fathers*, London, 1907, 2 vols.

BURY, J. B., *History of the Later Roman Empire from the Death of Theodosius I to the Death of Justinian*, London, 1923, 2 vols.

BURY, J. B., *The Invasion of Europe by the Barbarians*, London, 1928.

BURY, J. B., *The Life of St. Patrick and His Place in History*, London, 1905.

BUTLER, Abbot Cuthbert, O.S.B., *Benedictine Monachism*, 3rd ed., London, 1924.

CASSIODORUS, *An Introduction to Divine and Human Reading*, trans. and ed. Jones, Leslie Webber, New York, 1946.

CAVALLERA, F., *S. Jérôme*, Louvain, 1922, 2 vols.

CHAPMAN, Abbot John, O.S.B., *St. Benedict and the Sixth Century*, London, 1929.

CLEMENT OF ALEXANDRIA, *The Exhortation to the Greeks, The Rich Man's Salvation, and the fragment of an address entitled "To the Newly Baptized"*, trans. Butterworth, G. W., London, 1919 (*Loeb Classical Library*).

CLEMENT OF ALEXANDRIA, *Writings*, trans. Wilson, W., Edinburgh, 1867–9, 2 vols. (*Ante-Nicene Christian Library*).

CLEMENT OF ROME, St., *see under* Apostolic Fathers.

CONNELLY, Joseph, *Hymns of the Roman Liturgy*, London, 1957.

COULANGES, Fustel de, *La Cité antique*, Paris, 1930.

DANIÉLOU, J., *Origen*, trans. Mitchell, Walter, London, 1955.

DANIÉLOU, J., *Platonisme et théologie mystique: essai sur la doctrine spirituelle de S. Grégoire de Nysse*, Paris, 1944.

DAWSON, Christopher, *The Making of Europe*, London, 1932.

DAWSON, Christopher, *Religion and the Rise of Western Culture*, London, 1950.

DAWSON, Christopher, "St. Augustine and His Age", in Burns, T. F. (ed.), *A Monument to St. Augustine*, London, 1930.

DAWSON, Christopher, "Introduction", in Gibbon, Edward, *The Decline and Fall of the Roman Empire*, London, 1910 (*The Everyman Library*).

DIX, Gregory, O.S.B., *Jew and Greek*, London, 1953.

The Didache, see under Apostolic Fathers.

DUCHESNE, L., *The Early History of the Church*, London, 1911, 3 vols.

DUCHESNE, L., *L'Église au 6e siècle*, Paris, 1925.

DUDDEN, F. H., *Gregory the Great, His Place in History and Thought*, London, 1905, 2 vols.

DUDDEN, F. H., *The Life and Times of St. Ambrose*, Oxford, 1935.

ELIADE, Mircea, *Patterns in Comparative Religion*, trans. Sheed, Rosemary, London, 1958.

EPHREM THE SYRIAN, St., *Select Works*, trans. Morris, J. B., Oxford, 1847 (*A Library of the Fathers*).

EUSEBIUS, *The Ecclesiastical History*, trans. and ed. Lake, Kirsopp, London, 1926–32 (*Loeb Classical Library*).

FLEURY, Claude, *Ecclesiastical History*, trans. Newman, J. H., London, 1842–4, 3 vols.

FLICHE, A., and MARTIN, V., *Histoire de l'Église*, Paris, 1947–50.

Vol. II: Lebreton, J., and Zeiller, J., *De la fin du 2e siècle à la paix constantinienne*, 1948.

Vol. III: Bardy, G., Labriolle, P. de, and Palanque, J. R., *De la paix constantinienne à la mort de Théodose*, 1950.

Vol. IV: Bardy, G., Bréhier, Louis, Labriolle, P. de, and Plinval, G. de, *De la mort de Théodose à l'élection de Grégoire le Grand*, 1950.

FRAZER, Sir James George, *The Golden Bough*, abridged ed., London, 1954.

GIET, Stanislas, *Les Idées et l'action sociales de S. Basile*, Paris, 1941.

GILSON, Étienne, *Introduction à l'étude de S. Augustin*, 2nd ed., Paris, 1943.

GORE, Charles, *Leo the Great*, London, 1880.

GOUGAUD, Dom Louis, O.S.B., *Christianity in Celtic Lands*, trans. Joynt, M. London, 1932.

GRAVES, Robert, *Count Belisarius*, London, 1938.

GREGORY THE GREAT, Pope St., *The Dialogues of St. Gregory*, trans. P.W (1608), re-ed. Gardner, E. G., London, 1911.
See also under Dudden, F. H.; Batiffol, P.

GREGORY OF NAZIANZUS, St., *Grégoire de Nazianze: Discours funèbres*, trans. and ed. Boulenger, Fernand, Paris, 1908.

GREGORY OF NAZIANZUS, *Select Orations and Letters*, trans. and ed. Browne, C. G., and Swallow, J. E., Oxford, 1894 (*A Select Library of Nicene and Post-Nicene Fathers*).

GREGORY OF NYSSA, St., *Contemplation sur la vie de Moïse*, trans. and ed. Daniélou, J., Paris, 1941.

GREGORY OF NYSSA, St., *Encomium of St. Gregory, Bishop of Nyssa, on his Brother St. Basil*, trans. and ed. Stein, Sister James Aloysius, Washington, 1928.

GREGORY OF NYSSA, St., *The Life of St. Macrina*, trans. and ed. Lowther Clarke, W. K., London, 1916.

GREGORY THAUMATURGUS, St., *Address to Origen*, trans. and ed. Metcalfe, W., London and New York, 1920 (*Translations of Christian Literature, Series I, Greek Texts*).

HOLMES, W. G., *The Age of Justinian and Theodora*, London, 1905, 2 vols.

HUGHES, Philip, *A History of the Church*, London, vols. I and II, 1934–48.

IGNATIUS, St., *see under* Apostolic Fathers.

IRENAEUS, St., *Five Books against Heresies*, trans. Keble, John, London, 1872 (*A Library of the Fathers*).
See also under Apostolic Fathers.

JACQUIER, E., *Les Actes des Apôtres*, Paris, 1926.

JALLAND, Trevor, *The Life and Times of St. Leo the Great*, London, 1941.

JEROME, St., *Lettres choisies*, trans. and ed. Lagrange, F., Paris, 1921.

JEROME, St., *Select Letters of St. Jerome*, trans. Wright, F. A., London, 1933 (*Loeb Classical Library*).
See also under Antin, P., O.S.B.; Cavallera, F.

JÉRUSALEM, ÉCOLE BIBLIQUE DE (trans. and ed.), *La Sainte Bible, traduite en français sous la direction de l'École biblique de Jérusalem*, Paris, 1956.

JOHN CHRYSOSTOM, St., *On the Priesthood; Ascetic Treatises; Select Homilies and Letters; Homilies on the Statues*, trans. and ed. Schaff, Philip, New York, 1889 (*A Select Library of Nicene and Post-Nicene Fathers*).
See also under Palladius; Puech, Aimé.

JUNGMANN, J. A., S.J., *Public Worship*, trans. Howell, Clifford, S.J., London, 1957.

KENNEY, James F., *The Sources for the Early History of Ireland; an Introduction and Guide*, New York, 1929 (Vol. I: *Ecclesiastical*).

LABRIOLLE, Pierre de, *The Life and Times of St. Ambrose*, trans. Wilson, Herbert, London, 1918.

LABRIOLLE, Pierre de, *Histoire de la littérature latine chrétienne*, Paris, 1947.

LEBRETON, Jules, *Histoire du dogme de la Trinité*, Paris, 1928, Vol. II.

LEO THE GREAT, POPE, St., *The Letters and Sermons of Leo the Great*, trans. Feltoe, C. L., London, 1895 (*A Select Library of Nicene and Post-Nicene Fathers*).
See also under Gore, Charles; Jalland, Trevor.

LOWTHER CLARKE, W. K., *St. Basil the Great: A Study in Monasticism*, Cambridge, 1913.

McCANN, Justin, O.S.B., *St. Benedict*, London, 1937.

MacNEILL, Eoin, *St. Patrick, Apostle of Ireland*, London, 1934.

MARCUS AURELIUS ANTONINUS, *The Twelve Books*, trans. Long, George, London, 1890.

MARROU, H. I., *S. Augustin et la fin de la culture antique*, Paris, 1938.

MARROU, H. I., *A History of Education in Antiquity*, trans. Lamb, George, London, 1956.

MARTIN, V., *see under* Fliche, A.

MERSCH, Émile, S.J., *The Whole Christ*, trans. Kelly, John R., S.J., London, 1938.

MOHRMANN, Christine, *see under* Van de Meer, F.

MONCEAUX, P., *Histoire littéraire de l'Afrique chrétienne*, Paris, 1901–23, 7 vols.

NEWMAN, John Henry, Cardinal, *The Arians of the Fourth Century*, 4th ed., London, 1876.

NEWMAN, John Henry, Cardinal, *Callista: A Sketch of the Third Century*, London, 1876.

NEWMAN, John Henry, Cardinal, *The Church of the Fathers*, London, 1876 (*Historical Sketches*, Vol. II).

NEWMAN, John Henry, Cardinal, *Essay on the Development of Christian Doctrine*, new. ed., London, 1878.

O'RAHILLY, Thomas Francis, *The Two Patricks*, Dublin, 1942.

ORIGEN, *Origen on First Principles*, trans. and ed. Butterworth, G. W., London, 1936.
  See also under Daniélou, J.; Gregory Thaumaturgus, St.; Prat, F.

PAINE, Robert, *The Holy Fire; the Story of the Fathers of the Eastern Church*, New York, 1957.

PALLADIUS, *Dialogue Concerning the Life of Chrysostom*, ed. Moore, Herbert, London, 1921.

PALLADIUS, *The Lausiac History*, ed. Butler, Abbot Cuthbert, O.S.B., trans. Lowther Clarke, London, 1918.

PAPIAS, *see under* Apostolic Fathers.

PARIS, Pères Bénédictins de, *Vies des saints et des bienheureux*, Paris, 1956, vol. XII, Dec. 7th (*Life of St. Ambrose*).

The Passion of SS. Perpetua and Felicity, ed. and trans. Shewring, Walter, London, 1931.

PATER, Walter, *Marius the Epicurean*, London, 1918, 2 vols.

PATRICK, St., *Sancti Patricii, Iberorum Apostoli, Synodi, Canones, Opuscula, et Scriptorum quae Supersunt Fragmenta*, ed. Villanueva, Joachim Laurence, Dublin, 1835.

PATRICK, St., *Works*, ed. and trans. Bieler, Ludwig, London, 1953.

PATRICK, St., *Writings and Life*, trans. White, Newport J. D., London, 1920 (*Translations of Christian Literature, Series V, Lives of the Celtic Saints*).
  See also under Bieler, Ludwig; Bury, J. B.; MacNeill, Eoin; O'Rahilly, Thomas Francis; Stokes, Whitley; Todd, James Henthorn.

PAULINUS, *Vita Ambrosii*, in Migne (ed.), *Patrologia Latina*, Vol. XX, Paris, 1845.

POLYCARP, St.
  See under Apostolic Fathers.

PRAT, F., *Origène*, Paris, 1907.

PROCOPIUS, *Works*, trans. Dewing, H. B., London, 1914–40 (*Loeb Classical Library*), 7 vols.

PUECH, Aimé, *Histoire de la littérature grecque chrétienne*, Paris, 1928–30, 3 vols.

PUECH, Aimé, *St. John Chrysostom*, trans. Partridge, M., London, 1902.

RYAN, John, S.J., *Irish Monasticism: Origins and Early Development*, London and New York, 1931.

SCHUSTER, Ildephonse, Cardinal, O.S.B., *Saint Benedict and his Times*, trans. Roetger, Gregory J., O.S.B., London, 1953.

SMITH, Dom Cuthbert, O.S.B., "The Problem of the Rule of the Master", in *Buckfast Abbey Chronicle*, Vol. XXVII, no. 2, 1957.

STOKES, Whitley (trans. and ed.), *The Tripartite Life of St. Patrick*, London, 1887, 2 vols.

STRACHEY, Marjorie, *Saints and Sinners of the Fourth Century*, London, 1958.

TILLEMONT, Sébastien Lenain de, *Mémoires pour servir à l'histoire ecclésiastique des six premiers siècles*, Paris, 1701–12, 16 vols.

TIXERONT, J., *Histoire des dogmes dans l'antiquité chrétienne*, 6th ed., Paris, 1909.

TODD, James Henthorn, *St. Patrick, Apostle of Ireland*, Dublin, 1864.

VAN DER MEER, F. *Augustinus de Zielzorger*, Utrecht, 1949 (English translation in preparation).

VAN DER MEER, F., and MOHRMANN, Christine, *Atlas of the Early Christian World*, trans. Hedlund, Mary, and Rowley, H. H., London, 1958.

WADDELL, Helen, *The Desert Fathers*, London, 1936.

WADDELL, Helen, *The Wandering Scholars*, Penguin ed., Harmondsworth, 1954.

Also *passim* in:

WACE and PIERCY, *A Dictionary of Christian Biography and Literature*.

CROSS, *Oxford Dictionary of the Christian Church*.

CABROL and LECLERCQ, *Dictionnaire d'archéologie chrétienne et de liturgie*.

VACANT, *Dictionnaire de théologie catholique*.

The Catholic Encyclopædia.

INDEX

AETIUS, 302, 308, 311, 323, 324, 325
Agapetus, Pope, 351
Alaric, 191, 207, 228, 324, 365
Albina, 217, 221
Alexander, Bp. of Alexandria, 32, 82, 86, 87, 90, 150, 302
Alexandria, 27, 29–42, 52, 68, 82, 85, 89, 90–3, 95, 98–100, 102, 105, 108, 109, 110, 113, 118, 126, 129, 148, 149, 150, 152, 160, 236, 237, 249, 299, 300, 321, 322, 323, 334
Alexandria, Council of, 110–12, 145
Ambrose, St., vii, viii, 42, 104, 114, 125, 140, 160, 180–210, 211, 224, 233, 234, 238, 255, 259, 260–3, 266, 268, 282, 284, 297, 302, 303, 331, 363
Ammianus Marcellinus, 48
Anthimus, Bp. of Tyana, 150, 151, 153
Anthony, St., 34, 67–81, 82, 123, 132, 321, 358, 360
Anthusa, 158, 159
Antioch, 5, 6, 32, 42, 84, 85, 86, 92, 93, 100, 112, 113, 116, 119, 136, 144, 147, 150, 152, 153, 158–61, 163, 165–8, 177, 213–15, 249, 252, 299, 300, 321, 323, 334
Antoninus Pius, 10–12, 24, 25
Apollinaris of Laodicea, 146, 147, 234, 320
Aquinas, St. Thomas, ix, 55, 270, 279, 305, 347
Arbogast, 125, 205, 206, 207
Arcadius, 169, 171, 172, 173, 176
Arius, 42, 84, 85–7, 89–91, 93, 95, 96, 115, 150, 305
Arnobius, 251
Athanasius, St., vi, 8, 21, 41, 42, 68–70, 72, 74–8, 80, 82–114, 118, 119, 140, 144, 145, 147, 149, 150, 169, 187, 198, 199, 212, 216, 248, 276, 282, 285, 297, 298, 302, 309, 318, 321, 331, 355, 364
Athenagoras, 21, 24, 25

Athens, 127, 128, 129, 158, 236, 337
Attila, 307, 308, 323, 324, 325, 365
Augustine, St., vi, vii, ix, 39, 49, 61, 80, 91, 140, 158, 182, 184, 185, 188, 189, 191, 192, 198, 218, 223, 224, 227, 230, 235, 239, 256–77, 278, 283, 297, 303–7, 331, 355, 359, 360, 364
Auxentius, 197, 198, 200
Avitus, 325

BARCLAY, WILLIAM, 53
Barker, Sir Ernest, 273
Baronius, 32
Basil, St., ix, 42, 43, 80, 113, 114, 126–53, 154–9, 162, 166, 170, 184, 187, 192, 224, 227, 250, 268, 282, 283, 297, 303, 308, 331, 354, 359, 360
Basilides, 14, 33, 53, 54, 57
Batiffol, P., v
Bede, St., 285, 288, 360
Belisarius, 331, 333, 336, 339, 343, 349
Benedict, St., 34, 134, 239, 328, 332, 344, 350, 354, 357–65
Bethlehem, 214, 221–7, 228, 229, 230, 362
Bieler, L., 288 n., 290
Bithynia, 6, 10, 113
Blesilla, 217, 219, 220
Boethius, 81, 332, 346–9
Botheric, 202
Bury, J. B., 189, 190, 191, 275, 280, 286, 290, 293, 337 n., 343
Butler, Abbot, 109 n., 358
Butterworth, Dr., 43, 46 n.
Byzantium, *see* Constantinople

CAECILIANUS, 252, 253, 254
Caesarea, 32, 41, 135, 136, 138–41, 143, 147, 155, 160
Caesarius, 163–5
Caesarius, St., of Arles, 355, 359, 360
Calligonus, 196